Who's Who
IN THE GREEK WORLD

THE ROUTLEDGE WHO'S WHO SERIES

Accessible, authoritative and enlightening, these are the definitive
biographical guides to a diverse range of subjects drawn from literature
and the arts, history and politics, religion and mythology.

Who's Who
IN THE GREEK
WORLD

John Hazel

London and New York

First published 2000
by Routledge
11 New Fetter Lane, London EC4P 4EE

Simultaneously published in the USA and Canada
by Routledge
29 West 35th Street, New York, NY 10001

This edition first published 2002

Routledge is an imprint of the Taylor & Francis Group

Typeset in Sabon by Routledge
Printed and bound in Great Britain by TJ International Ltd, Padstow, Cornwall

British Library Cataloguing in Publication Data
A catalogue record for this book is available from the British Library

Library of Congress Cataloging in Publication Data
A catalogue record for this book has been requested

ISBN 0–415–26032–9

FOR LESLEY

Contents

Preface

I was originally asked by Routledge to revise John Warrington's *Classical Dictionary* in the Everyman series for inclusion in the Who's Who series, which was inaugurated nearly thirty years ago by Messrs Weidenfeld and Nicolson. *Who's Who in Classical Mythology* was one of the first titles in the series, in the writing of which I had the honour and pleasure of collaboration with Michael Grant. The title originally suggested for the present work, *Who's Who in the Classical World*, sufficed until it became apparent as the work was nearing its completion that it was far too long for a single volume in the series, so it was decided to divide the Greek and the Roman classical worlds into two books. Thus, this work is significantly different from Warrington's book, which fulfilled the role of a general dictionary and encyclopaedia, while the business of this book is biographical.

The book contains a wide range of entries on literary and historical figures from the Ancient World: starting from Homer and ending in Roman imperial times. The criterion I have adopted for literary and philosophical entries in the Roman period is the extent of their Greekness. Therefore, Plutarch, Plotinus, Lucian, Strabo and Galen are included in this volume. A small number of entries that straddle the two cultures will therefore perforce be repeated in the volume on the Romans which will follow this one. As regards historical figures, I have taken the year 100 BC as an approximate cut-off point between Hellenistic and Roman history in the eastern Mediterranean and western Asiatic contexts, though the last Macedonian queen of Egypt is included. Though there are a few entries that refer not to individuals, but to families and even nations, the main purpose of the book is to give an account of the lives and achievements of significant people of Greek language and culture.

Cross-referencing has been made easy by the printing of q.v. items in small capitals, with a figure in brackets where necessary to indicate which entry is in question. The spelling of Greek names adopted is conventional, the Latinised forms (with 'c' rather than 'k') being given. Brief bibliographies are appended to articles where suitable works exist.

I should like to acknowledge help received, each for a single entry, from John Muir, Dr Peter Jones and Professor Gregory Hutchinson. I should also like to acknowledge use made of the *Oxford Classical Dictionary* (3rd edn, 1998, Oxford: OUP) and *A Dictionary of Ancient History* (1994, Oxford: Blackwell), edited by Graham Speake, for establishing the factual basis of certain entries. The errors and deficiencies in the book are entirely my own.

John Hazel
1999

A

Achaeus (died 213 BC) A Seleucid general and rebel. In 223 he defeated Pergamon and won back the territory she had taken from the Syrian empire. In 220 he set himself up as independent from his king, ANTIOCHUS (3) III. He held out for a number of years until Antiochus penned him in Sardis and there besieged him for two years until he was finally betrayed and cruelly put to death.

Achilles Tatius (C2 AD) A novelist from Alexandria, the author of *Leucippe and Clitophon*, a novel in eight books told in the first person. The work was very popular in Egypt, and seven papyri have been found containing fragments of the novel. He may have written other works, including a biography of famous men and a book titled *On the Sphere*. According to the *Suda*, he later became a Christian and a bishop. See B.P. Reardon (ed.) (*c.*1989) *Collected Ancient Greek Novels*, Berkeley, CA; London: University of California Press.

Ada (ruled 350–341 BC and 334–an unknown date BC) A queen/satrap of Caria, a daughter of HECATOMNUS, who took the throne on the death of her sister ARTEMISIA (2). She shared power with her brother, IDRIEUS, to whom she was married (cf. MAUSOLUS and Artemisia) until his death in 344. Her brother, PIXODARUS, drove her from power in 341. She was reinstated by ALEXANDER (3) the Great in 334 when she 'adopted' him as her son.

Adea *see* Eurydice.

Adrastus (C6 BC) Son of GORDIUS, king of Phrygia, according to HERODOTUS (*Histories*, I. 33f.), who tells of his two accidental homicides: the first of his brother, which led to his exile at the court of CROESUS, king of Lydia; the second of Croesus' son, Atys, for which Adrastus killed himself.

Aeneas Tacticus (C4 BC) A writer on military matters. He is often identified with Aeneas of Stymphalus in Arcadia who was the general of the Arcadian Confederacy in 367. He wrote military treatises of which one, *Sieges*, has survived. Its chief interest lies in its assumption that the chief adversary of the defenders of a city is the enemy within, namely the political opposition.

Aenesidemus (C1 BC) A Sceptic philosopher, born at Cnossos in Crete, who taught at Alexandria. He aimed to restore the sceptical nature of the philosophy of the Academy which it had lost under ANTIOCHUS (15) of Ascalon. DIOGENES (5) LAËRTIUS and SEXTUS EMPIRICUS tell us much about his teaching, which was contained in a substantial body of writing.

Aeschines 1. of Sphettus (C4 BC) A friend of SOCRATES who was present at his death. He wrote court speeches of quality and taught rhetoric, but fell into poverty and found refuge at the court of Syracuse. He had to leave on the fall of DIONYSIUS (2) II in 356 and returned to Athens. He wrote Socratic dialogues (of which a few fragments remain), which were admired in antiquity for their authenticity in representing Socrates, as well as for their style.

2. (c.397–c.322 BC) An Athenian statesman and orator, as well as the chief opponent of DEMOSTHENES (2). He began his career as clerk to the politician Aristophon of Collytus and later to EUBULUS (1), then treasurer of the city and an influential democrat. His experience in the army and in politics had inclined him to conciliate PHILIP (1) II, king of Macedonia. In 347 he was a member of an embassy to persuade the Arcadians to join a common peace directed against Macedonia. He failed probably because of opposition from PHALAECUS, tyrant of Phocis, in Central Greece, who was not prepared to allow the alliance to occupy Thermopylae against Philip.

In 346 he was a member of the embassy, on which Demosthenes also served, of PHILOCRATES to Philip to try to rectify the situation. In 347/6, both men were members of the Athenian Council of State and became implacable political enemies. Though Demosthenes realised that an alliance must be made with Philip, Aeschines opposed his policy in favour of a common peace that was open to all Greek states. A further embassy went to Philip to secure his oath, but he refused to give it until he was ready to attack Phocis. He then seized Thermopylae and caused a crisis at Athens. In solving the crisis, Aeschines had some success in trying to reconcile the Athenians with military realities, but he was accused by Demosthenes of having been bribed by Philip. He rebutted the charge in his speech *Against Timarchus* (346/5), largely by attacking the morals of his opponent. Three years later, as the peace with Philip was becoming unpopular, Demosthenes tried to reverse the situation by once more prosecuting Aeschines, who saved himself with his speech *On the Embassy*. In 339, on an embassy to the Amphictionic Council at Delphi, Aeschines was guilty of serious misjudgement: by the violence of his speech to the allied assembly he precipitated action by Philip that ultimately led to his victory at Chaeronea. After the battle, Aeschines was again a member of an embassy to Philip, but thereafter withdrew from politics. He only emerged in 337 to attack Demosthenes. Ctesiphon proposed that Demosthenes be crowned in the theatre for his outstanding services to Athens. Aeschines prosecuted Ctesiphon (see *Against Ctesiphon*) for having acted unconstitutionally in so doing. The trial did not take place until 330 when Demosthenes defeated his adversary, delivering his famous speech *On the Crown*. Aeschines was soundly defeated, fined and retired to Rhodes to teach rhetoric.

Though Aeschines was outclassed by Demosthenes as an orator, he was no less patriotic. Nobody could then have saved Athens and Greece from the growth of Macedonian power. His surviving works are the aforementioned three speeches. See S. Hornblower, *The Greek World, 479–323 BC*, London: Methuen, 1983.

Aeschylus (525–456 BC) An Athenian composer of tragedies from Eleusis, of noble birth, the son of Euphorion. He fought at the battle of Marathon where his brother Cynegyrus died heroically, and perhaps at the battles of Salamis, Artemisium and Plataea in the Persian War. He began writing poetic drama in about 499 and won the first prize in 484 and at least twelve times after that. He wrote over eighty plays, of which only seven survive. The plays were composed and produced in groups of three or four, usually on a single narrative theme, such as that of the *Oresteia*, which is the only authentic ancient Greek trilogy to survive. Of his surviving plays, the *Persians*, on the theme of the effect of the defeat of Salamis on the Persian court, was produced in 472 and is unique among extant Greek tragedies in being concerned with a contemporary event and not with a myth. *Seven against Thebes*, produced in 467, is a tragedy concerned with the mythical attack on Thebes by seven champions to put Polynices on the throne; the *Oresteia*, together with the lost satyr play, *Proteus*, produced in 458, comprises a trilogy which tells the story of Agamemnon's return from the Trojan War; his murder by his wife, Clytaemestra, and her lover, Aegisthus; the vengeance that his son, Orestes, took on the lovers; and his subsequent persecution by the Furies. The *Suppliants* was a production of the 460s. It is the first part of a trilogy on the Danaids. *Prometheus Bound*, which tells of Prometheus' punishment at the hands of Zeus for giving fire to men, was one of his latest plays and has been considered by some, probably wrongly, to be by another hand.

Aeschylus made important innovations that brought tragedy to life, making him, in our eyes, its father. He introduced a second actor, reduced the part assigned to the chorus and was the first to delineate character. Though the choruses of his plays are long when compared with those of his successors SOPHOCLES and EURIPIDES, the magnificence of his language and the cosmic strength of his themes give his work a sublimity which is shown to have been appreciated in Athens both by the number of prizes he won and by the treatment he received in the satirical contest with Euripides in *Frogs*, a play of ARISTOPHANES (1).

He was accused before the ancient court of the Areopagus of having revealed the mysteries of Eleusis in one of his plays, but secured acquittal by claiming never to have been initiated into the mysteries. He went around 472 to Sicily to the court of the tyrant of Syracuse, HIERON (1) I, where he staged the *Persians* for Hieron and wrote a play in honour of the foundation of the city of Aetna. He died at Gela on a second visit to the island. The story of the tortoise dropped on his bald head by an eagle appears to be legend. He remained popular with the Athenians, winning prizes for his tragedies after his death, and was the subject of an Athenian decree that anybody wishing to produce one of his plays should be granted a chorus free of charge by the archon. See R.P. Winnington-Ingram (1983) *Studies in Aeschylus*, Cambridge: CUP; O.P. Taplin (1977) *The Stagecraft of Aeschylus*, Oxford: Clarendon Press; S. Ireland (1986) *Aeschylus*, Oxford: Clarendon Press for the Classical Association, Manville; T.G. Rosenmayer (c.1982) *The Art of Aeschylus*, Berkeley, CA: University of California Press.

Aesop (C6 BC) A Thracian slave who lived on the island of Samos and to whom is attributed the creation of the genre of fables – tales about animals which carry a moral. HERODOTUS, who also lived on Samos for a time and was familiar with its historical records, says (2. 134) that Aesop belonged to Iadmon of Samos and was the fellow slave of RHODOPIS. Whether Aesop wrote his tales down is doubtful, though the Greeks attributed the well-known collection of fables to him. Many myths, which defy the evidence we have, grew up about him. He was said to have been an envoy for King CROESUS of Lydia, and, according to ARISTOTLE (*Rhetoric*, 2. 20), conducted the public defence of an Athenian demagogue. According to Herodotus, an oracle told the people of Delphi that he was murdered as a scapegoat by their ancestors, and they called for somebody to come forward to claim compensation (which a grandson of Iadmon of Samos did). His prose fables were popular at Athens and, in his last days, Socrates told his friend CRITO (1) that on the instruction of his divine 'voice' he was putting them into verse. BABRIUS later turned them into Greek verse, and PHAEDRUS and AVIENUS into Latin verse. See B.E. Perry (1980) *Aesopica*, New York: Arno Press.

Aëtion (C4 BC) A painter, whose famous picture of the wedding of ALEXANDER (3) the Great and ROXANE is described by LUCIAN in his *Herodotus* or *Eëtion*.

Agasias 1. (*c.*100 BC) A sculptor of Ephesus in Asia Minor, son of Dositheus, who signed the Borghese warrior, which is now in the Louvre.

2. Another Ephesian sculptor of the same period as AGASIAS (1), son of Menophilus, some of whose signed work is on the island of Delos.

Agatharchides (C2 BC) A prolific writer on geography and history, born on Cnidus, who became guardian of a member of the Egyptian royal house around 116. Part of his *Red Sea* was preserved in the work of the ninth-century Byzantine scholar Photius.

Agatharchus (C5 BC) An Athenian painter, born on Samos. He was the first painter of stage scenery and wrote a treatise on the subject, which inspired the investigations of his contemporaries, ANAXAGORAS and DEMOCRITUS, into perspective, which Agatharchus was the first to use on a large scale. He was compelled by ALCIBIADES to paint his house.

Agathinus, Claudius (C1 AD) An eclectic philosopher from Sparta who was also a writer on medicine. He was a pupil of the Stoic pneumatist, Athenaeus of Attalia, and of the Stoic philosopher, L. Annaeus Cornutus. He followed the medical teachings of the Pneumatic school and wrote on the pulse and other matters. Our knowledge of him derives from references in GALEN and other authorities.

Agathocles 1. (361–289 BC) A tyrant of Syracuse, born in Himera. He had a fiery career: the son of a potter, he joined the Syracusan army, married the widow of his patron, Damas, and fought with distinction in wars against Acragas (Agrigento) and the Bruttii of southern Italy, but was exiled for a couple of spells for plotting against the oligarchic government of Syracuse. In 317 he returned with an army and overthrew the rulers whom, with the support of the lower class, he replaced. He conquered most of eastern Sicily, but when he attacked Acragas he was opposed by the Carthaginians, who defeated him at the battle of Licata in 311 and besieged him in Syracuse. He escaped from the city and carried the war into Africa, where in 310 he obtained help from OPHELLAS of Cyrene and nearly captured Carthage. Then he returned to Sicily, where the siege of Syracuse had come to an end, and defeated an attack from an alliance led by Acragas. A further venture into Africa failed, and he concentrated his attention on Sicily, much of which he ruled in peace for many years. He took the title of king in 304. He intervened in Italy and captured Corcyra, but failed to produce an heir. He pretended to restore the freedom of Syracuse, but bequeathed to her a period of anarchy after his death. He was an able and energetic tyrant about whom we have mainly hostile reports from the pen of his enemy, the historian TIMAEUS (2).

2. *See* LYSIMACHUS.

Agathon (*c.*448–401 BC) An Athenian tragic poet, the son of Tisamenus. He won his first victory for dramatic composition at the Lenaea in 416, as we learn from PLATO (1) in *Symposium*, which represents a feast in honour of that victory. In 411, he showed his political sympathies by congratulating the oligarch ANTIPHON on his defence speech when the latter was tried and condemned for his revolutionary activities. In the same year he was pilloried by ARISTOPHANES (1) in the comedy *Thesmophoriazusae* for his effeminacy. Around 407 he left Athens for the Macedonian court, where he remained until his death.

He showed originality in composing a tragedy, *Antheus*, which was not derived from any mythological source as nearly all previous tragedies had been. His style was influenced by the sophists GORGIAS and PRODICUS, and the few remaining fragments of his work display a pithy style (probably from their influence). On the other hand, Aristophanes' parody of his lyric poetry suggests a rich and voluptuous manner.

Ageladas or Hageladas (C6–5 BC) A sculptor from Argos as well as the reputed teacher of MYRON, PHIDIAS and POLYCLITUS. He produced a number of statues of victors at Olympia. His most famous work was the bronze statue of a striding Zeus at Ithome, which was commissioned by the Messenians settled at Naupactus, and a striding, boy-like Zeus for Aegeum.

Agesander (C1 BC) A Rhodian sculptor who was one of the creators of the Laocoön group.

Agesilaus II (445–359 BC) A Eurypontid king of Sparta, the son of ARCHIDAMUS (1) II. In 398, though lame, he succeeded his half-brother AGIS (1) II with the help of LYSANDER. In 396 he led an expedition to Asia Minor against the Persian satrap TISSAPHERNES, whom he routed. However, in 394 he was recalled to Sparta and had to lead his force back overland, meeting a confederacy of states opposed to Sparta at Coronea and defeating them. He was unwounded, but his victory was so costly that he had to give up Boeotia. In 390 he attempted to force a way through the Isthmus of Corinth, but was unsuccessful. He later permitted Spartan interventions against Mantinea, Phlius and Olynthus, in all of which pro-Spartan governments were installed, thus breaking

the terms of the Peace of ANTALCIDAS and incurring the hostility of Thebes (which he seized during peacetime in 382) and Athens, which ultimately led in 371 to a humiliating Spartan defeat at Leuctra. He tried to make the best of the ensuing period of crisis by organising the defence of Sparta when EPAMINONDAS invaded Laconia in 370 and 362. To replenish the Spartan treasury, he led mercenary expeditions to Asia Minor in 364 and Egypt in 361, and died at the age of 84 in Cyrenaica while on his way home. His younger brother was the admiral TELEUTIAS. His biography was written by his close friend XENOPHON (1).

Agis 1. II A Eurypontid king of Sparta, son of ARCHIDAMUS and half-brother of AGESILAUS II, who became king *c.*427. He led Spartan forces in their expeditions into Attica during the Archidamian War. In 418 he defeated Argos and subsequently won the decisive battle of Mantinea, which brought about the recovery of Sparta's influence in the Peloponnese and beyond. After the renewal of the Peloponnesian War with Athens, he was sent to occupy Decelea in Attica with a permanent garrison, and his absence and the removal of hostilities to Asia Minor reduced his influence at Sparta. He was involved with LYSANDER in the occupation of Athens in 404 and successfully invaded Elis. His son LEOTYCHIDAS being the natural son of ALCIBIADES, was ruled ineligible to succeed him.

2. III (died 331 BC) A Eurypontid king of Sparta who reigned from 338–331. While ALEXANDER (3) the Great was in Asia, Agis, with Persian support, led a revolt against the Macedonians and raised an army of 8,000 Greek mercenaries who had returned after the battle of Issus. He won over Crete and much of the Peloponnese, but Athens and Megalopolis refused to join him. He was killed by the forces of ANTIPATER (1) at the siege of Megalopolis, and Greek resistance to Alexander ceased.

3. IV (died 241 BC) A king of Sparta who reigned from *c*.243–241. He succeeded his father, Eudamas, as Eurypontid king and tried to solve Sparta's problems of debt and a falling population by radical means and a return to the constitution of LYCURGUS (2). There was civil strife leading to his Agiad colleague LEONIDAS (2) fleeing to Tegea. Agis' uncle, Agesilaus, at first supported him, but then turned on him while he was away in Aetolia, and Leonidas returned and took power. When Agis returned, the ephors put him, together with his mother and grandmother, to death. After his death, he was regarded as a martyr and gave inspiration to the next generation of Spartans.

Agoracritus (C5 BC) A sculptor born on Paros and a pupil of PHIDIAS. He is best-known for his colossal female statue (the head of which is in the British Museum). Pausanias writes that the statue was the loser in a competition for an Aphrodite, and that it was then bought by the people of Rhamnus as Nemesis. Other works of his are known, including a colossal *Mother of the Gods* for the Metroon at Athens.

Agyrrhius (*c*.400 BC) An Athenian democratic politician who introduced payment for attendance at the Assembly, namely one obol.

Alcaeus (born *c*.620 BC) A lyric poet from Mytilene in Lesbos who was contemporary with SAPPHO. Only the outline of his eventful life is known to us. His two brothers, Antimenidas and Cicis, together with PITTACUS, overthrew the tyrant of Mytilene, Melanchrus, but he was replaced in the tyranny by Myrsilus. As members of the aristocratic opposition to the tyrant, the family of Alcaeus went into exile. When Myrsilus was killed, Alcaeus expressed his joy in an ode. He was at first on friendly terms with Pittacus, who had been a supporter of Myrsilus, and the two fought together against the Athenians

at the battle of Sigeum. Alcaeus, however, disgraced himself in the battle by throwing his shield away and fleeing, as he tells in an ode. When peace was concluded, Pittacus was appointed dictator for ten years. Alcaeus could not accept this new tyranny and gave rein to his contempt for the tyrant in a number of poems, as a result of which he had to go into exile again. Alcaeus went to Egypt for a time and later to Thrace. Before giving up his tyranny in 580, Pittacus pardoned Alcaeus. The poet may be presumed to have returned to Lesbos, but we have no further information about him.

His poetry is known only from fragments. He wrote song lyrics, including drinking songs, political poems and hymns, with many allusions to myth, in the Aeolic dialect of his island with some epic forms and in a number of lyric metres, including the *Alcaic*, which is named after him. The Alexandrian scholars edited his work in ten volumes. His range was great, surpassed only by ARCHILOCHUS before classical times. He was a powerful user of invective and moralised without excess. His striking openings of poems, his strong descriptive powers, and his careful attention to changes of mood and form impressed and delighted the ancient critics. See D.L. Page (1979) *Sappho and Alcaeus*, Oxford: Clarendon Press and C.M. Bowra (1961) *Greek Lyric Poetry*, Oxford: Clarendon Press.

Alcamenes (C5 BC) A sculptor from Athens, said to be PHIDIAS' favourite pupil. No work of his can be regarded with certainty as extant. There are references to his works by PAUSANIAS (3), who attributes to him a figure of Procne from the Acropolis. Roman reproductions have allowed certain tentative identifications of his works, e.g. the *Aphrodite of the Gardens* and a *Hermes of the Gateway*. Pausanias' statement that he made the sculptures of the western pediment of the temple of Zeus at Olympia must on chronological grounds be mistaken.

Alcetas (C4 BC) A king of the Molossians of Epirus who, on being expelled from his kingdom, enlisted the aid of DIONYSIUS (1) I of Syracuse to regain his throne. He, in turn, assisted Dionysius in his colonising expeditions in the Adriatic. He also supported JASON (1) of Pherae against the Pharsalian Polydamas. In 375 he was induced by TIMOTHEUS (2) to join the Second Athenian Alliance and in 373 supported Timotheus when he was prosecuted.

Alcibiades (*c*.450–*c*.403 BC) An Athenian statesman and general, related to the ALCMAEONIDS, son of Clinias and Dinomache. After the death of his father in 447, he was brought up in the household of his kinsman PERICLES, then the leading statesman of Athens, who married his mother. His brilliance was recognised by SOCRATES, who saved his life at Potidaea in 432, and tried to influence him with his philosophy. He saved Socrates' life at the battle of Delium in 424. He married Hipparete, daughter of HIPPONICUS who was killed at Delium. In 420, after the death of CLEON, he became leader of the extreme democrats in opposition to NICIAS. He promoted the expedition to Sicily in 415 against the opposition of Nicias and was appointed with him and LAMACHUS as its commander. However, soon after the arrival of the expedition in Sicily, Alcibiades was recalled to Athens to stand trial on the charge of having been ringleader of a conspiracy that had been revealed by the mutilation of the herms. Alcibiades was suspected of plotting a change to the constitution and of impiety. He escaped from his escort at Thurii in Italy and went to Sparta, where he gave the Spartan government useful advice for the defeat of Athens, to send a general to direct Syracusan resistance to the Athenians, as well as to establish a permanent fort in Decelea north of Athens.

In 412 he tried to win over the Ionians to Sparta, but while he was away he lost the confidence of the Spartans (he had

begotten a son on the wife of King AGIS (1) II) and joined TISSAPHERNES, the Persian satrap of Asia Minor who nominally supported Sparta in the war. He then switched sides again and, after trying to bring Tissaphernes over to supporting Athens, he was elected general at Samos by the Athenian fleet, which he led in operations against the Spartans for the next four years, winning victories over MINDARUS at Cynossema, Abydos and Cyzicus and gaining Chalcedon and Byzantium. In 407 he returned to Athens and was received with popular acclaim. The people elected him supreme commander on land and sea. But, by now Sparta was receiving active support from CYRUS (2), and Alcibiades' ability to oppose them was limited. He was blamed for the defeat at Notium, which in fact had been caused by the imprudence of his subordinate, Antiochus, and was stripped of his command. He left Athens for his castle at Bisanthe in the Thracian Chersonese, and in 404, when Athens was finally defeated, he fled to PHARNABAZUS, Persian governor of Phrygia, who betrayed him to both his Spartan and Athenian enemies. See THUCYDIDES (2), *Histories*, VI, 15; W.M. Ellis (1989) *Alcibiades*, London: Routledge and D. Kagan (1987) *The Fall of the Athenian Empire*, Ithaca, NY; London: Cornell University Press.

Alcidamas (C4 BC) A rhetorician and sophist, born at Elaea in Aeolis, Asia Minor; he was a pupil of the sophist GORGIAS. His only surviving works are a treatise, titled *On Writers of Written Speeches* (also known as *On the Sophists*), in which he championed spontaneity in oratory as against the delivery of a carefully composed text, which was perhaps a dig at ISOCRATES who abandoned real speechmaking for pamphleteering; and *Odysseus*, a demonstration speech for pupils. Fragments of his *Museum* (or *Museum of Nature*) survive, but what it contained is disputed. Cicero admired his *Encomium on Death*, and we know of similar speeches on poverty and on the courtesan Naïs. His speech *For the Messenians* was remembered for a bold statement condemning slavery: 'God has set all men free, nature has made no man a slave'. He invented the notion of a poetic contest between HOMER and HESIOD.

Alcidas (C5 BC) A Spartan general and admiral in the Peloponnesian War. THUCYDIDES (2) is highly critical of his brutal attitude to prisoners and subject states, which damaged Sparta's reputation as a liberator. He commanded a force that attempted unsuccessfully to free Mytilene, which had revolted from Athens in 428, and killed a number of prisoners who were sympathetic to Sparta. He was also in command of a fleet in the same year at Corcyra, where there had been an uprising of oligarchs, and was supported by BRASIDAS. He was involved in the foundation of the Spartan colony of Heraclea in Trachis, which gradually withered through the hostility of its neighbours and the unpopularity of the Spartan governors among the settlers.

Alciphron (C2 AD) A writer of imaginary letters in Greek. His 118 letters purport to have been written by ordinary Athenians of the fourth century BC, such as fishermen, prostitutes and farmers, and are distinguished by the elegance of their style and language, which call the New Comedy to mind. See Loeb edition by E. Benner and F. Fobes (1949) Loeb Classical Library, Cambridge, MA: Harvard University Press.

Alcmaeon (C5 BC) A physician from Croton and a follower of Pythagoras. He wrote a treatise known to ARISTOTLE and explained health as being a condition of *isonomy* or a balance of conditions. He made a special study of the eye and conducted eye operations, and he taught that the brain was the seat of thought and emotions.

Alcmaeonids A powerful Athenian family claiming descent from Alcmaeon, son of the legendary Nestor. Its first notable member is Megacles, son of Alcmaeon, who as archon in 632 tricked and killed the followers of CYLON, which led *c.*596 to the expulsion of the family from Athens for sacrilege. They soon returned, and by favours performed for the king of Lydia they enriched themselves. Megacles married the daughter of CLEISTHENES (1), tyrant of Sicyon, and was father of the Athenian reformer CLEISTHENES (2). During the tyranny of PISISTRATUS at Athens, the family went into exile again, having fallen out with the tyrant even though he had been married to a daughter of Megacles. However, they had returned by 525 when Cleisthenes was archon. In 548 the family contracted to rebuild the temple of Apollo at Delphi, which was done so magnificently that it brought them popularity throughout Greece. PERICLES and ALCIBIADES were related to the family through their mothers.

Alcman (C7 BC) A lyric poet. There are two versions of his origin: one that he was a Spartan born in Messoa; the other, which has some support from fragment 16 of his poetry, that he was an Asiatic Greek from Sardis, originally a slave who gained freedom as a result of his talent. He wrote in a variety of metres in the Doric dialect, with added features from Aeolic, on subjects that range from the celebration of religious festivals at Sparta to hymns, gods and goddesses, Homeric material, night and sleep, food and natural creatures. His lyrics, which were later collected in six books, appear to have been composed to be sung by choruses of girls. There are exotic references to the Scyths, the Rhipaean mountains in northern Europe and the Issedones, which may have been derived from ARISTEAS (1) of Proconnesus.

Aleuadae A Thessalian family from Larissa claiming descent from Heracles and hence nobility. Starting from ALEUAS, they supplied Thessaly with military leaders, styled *tagos*. The tagos Thorax intrigued with the Persian king XERXES and collaborated with the Persians in the invasion of 480, which led to a temporary decline in the fortunes of the house. After the Persian War, the Aleuadae pursued a policy of friendship with Athens until 356 when PHILIP (1) II of Macedonia helped them against the sons of ALEXANDER (4) of Pherae, and married Philinna, who may have been an Aleuad. Their power was destroyed by Philip in 344 when he expelled Simos from Larissa.

Aleuas (C7 BC) A ruler of Larissa in Thessaly, head of the Heraclid clan, he was the first to establish himself as *tagos* of Thessaly with the power to raise an army of cavalry and light-armed infantry on feudal lines. He was thus able to assert the century-long domination of Thessaly over the other states of central and northern Greece. See ALEUADAE.

Alexander 1. I (reigned *c.*495–450 BC) A king of Macedonia and a son of AMYNTAS (1) I. He sided with the Persians in the invasion of XERXES in 480 and accompanied their march south, but helped the Greeks with advice to abandon the pass of Tempe and with information before the battle of Plataea. His support was rewarded by his admission as a Greek to the Olympic Games. He hellenized his court and issued the first Macedonian coinage. He invited the poet PINDAR to his court and claimed Greek descent. He cultivated the friendship of Athens.

2. II (reigned 369–368 BC) A king of Macedonia and son of AMYNTAS (2) II and EURYDICE. He intervened in Thessaly at the request of the ALEUADAE in their struggle with ALEXANDER (4) of Pherae. He was opposed by Thebes: PELOPIDAS ejected the garrison that Alexander had placed in Larissa, but later made an alliance with him. He was, however,

murdered by his brother-in-law, Ptolemy of Alorus, who succeeded him. He is credited with the creation of the 'foot-companions'. His brothers were Perdiccas III and PHILIP (1) II.

3. III the Great (356–323 BC) King of Macedonia and conqueror of the Persian empire. He was born in August 356 at Pella, the son of PHILIP (1) II and OLYMPIAS of Epirus. Philip appointed ARISTOTLE as his tutor in 342, and Alexander proved an able pupil. He quarrelled with his father over the succession, but distinguished himself in 338 at the battle of Chaeronea, where he led the cavalry that established Macedonian supremacy in Greece. When Philip was murdered in autumn 336, Alexander took the throne and destroyed his rivals, killing a half-brother and two cousins. There was much opposition to him from various quarters, including Athens, and Thebes stated its intention of ending the League of Corinth, which Philip had founded. Alexander marched southwards into Greece, turning the Thessalian blockade at the pass of Tempe, and was successful in quieting opposition, including that of Thebes and Athens, which he treated generously. In 335 he marched north to crush opposition in the Balkans and fought a brilliant campaign against the Thracians and the Triballi. He crossed the Danube and attacked the Getae, who fled, and made a treaty with the Celts. He then secured the western frontier of Macedonia in a campaign against the Illyrians. A rumour that he had been killed in this campaign and Athenian support for the move caused Thebes to rise against him, whereupon Alexander returned and attacked the city. He killed or enslaved most of the inhabitants and destroyed the city and its walls, sparing only the temples and the house of the poet PINDAR.

He then prepared to invade Asia. He organised his army of about 40,000 men – of whom barely a half were Macedonians and less than a quarter allied Greek contingents. He crossed the Hellespont in the early spring of 334 in order to free the Greek cities under Persian rule, and won his first victory over the Persian king, DARIUS (3) III, on the River Granicus in Mysia in May (see MEMNON). He advanced through western Asia Minor, setting up democracies in several places where there had been pro-Persian oligarchies. He disbanded his fleet and the following year assembled his army at Gordium in Phrygia, where he cut the famous Gordian knot. Having settled Persian attempts at a naval counter-attack in the Aegean and a plot instigated by Darius against his life, he marched southeast to Tarsus where he fell ill and was cured by a doctor suspected of treachery by his friend PARMENION. After reducing Cilicia, Alexander advanced against Darius' forces, which were in north-western Syria. He won his second great battle against Darius at Issus, near the Gulf of Iskenderun, despite the superior numbers and better position of the enemy. Though Darius himself escaped, his mother, wife and son fell into Alexander's hands. At this point, Alexander could have marched eastwards and attacked the lands near the Euphrates, but he preferred to clear the Mediterranean coastline of resistance and to defeat the Persian fleet on land. Therefore he went south and received the submission of most of the cities of Phoenicia, but had to besiege Tyre, which took him seven months and ended in the storming of the city and the enslavement of its people. Darius offered terms that included the transfer of Asia Minor to Alexander, but Alexander refused, showing his determination to conquer the whole empire. After this he went to Egypt, where he was welcomed as the people's deliverer from the Persian yoke. In early 331 he founded his new capital city of Alexandria and visited the shrine of Amun at Siwah in the Libyan desert. He was apt thereafter to claim to be the son of Zeus Ammon. In the spring he set out again to meet Darius, who still had a formidable army, including Greek mercenary infantry and excellent cavalry. On 1 October 331 the two armies met at Gaugamela near Mosul in Iraq on terrain which suited the Persians. Though he suffered considerable losses, Alexander won through clever tactics and determination, destroying Darius' huge army, and Darius fled to Media. The principal cities of the empire, Babylon, Susa, Persepolis and Ecbatana, surrendered to Alexander. Meanwhile in Greece, Sparta, which had never surrendered to Philip or Alexander, led a rebellion of states in the Peloponnese against the Macedonians, but was defeated by ANTIPATER (1) and forced to join the Greek League. Alexander pardoned all the rebels, except the ringleaders. He ended his campaign of vengeance by burning the ancient Persian capital, Persepolis, though this may have been an accident.

After Gaugamela, Darius had fled and been seized by BESSUS, satrap of Bactria. During 330 and 329, Alexander campaigned in the difficult, mountainous country to the north of his empire, from the Caspian Sea to the Hindu Kush. Using his Macedonian troops, he took no rest in summer or winter. When he reached Darius, after a forced march of eleven days, he found that Bessus had stabbed him and claimed his throne. Alexander had Bessus tried and, when condemned, put to death by his fellow countrymen. He proceeded to the conquest of Bactria and Sogdiana, which took him until spring 327 to accomplish. During this campaign, Alexander married ROXANE, daughter of the Sogdian king, Oxyartes, and sealed the reconciliation between himself and these northern peoples.

There was growing misunderstanding among the Macedonians over Alexander's attempts to win the support of the Persians and other oriental peoples. In 330 he had condemned PHILOTAS, the son of his right-hand man Parmenion, for treason in not revealing a plot, and Parmenion had himself been killed as a result, according to Macedonian custom. Alexander wore Persian dress on Persian occasions and encouraged his Persian subjects to prostrate themselves before him, which Greeks regarded as worship. However, he defended this practice to his Macedonian subjects and insisted that he was his old self among his soldiers and in Macedonian contexts. This was too subtle a distinction for the majority of his Macedonian followers to understand, and it led to bitterness and Alexander's killing of CLEITUS (1), who had saved his life at the Granicus. In spring 327, Alexander made his Macedonians prostrate themselves before him in the presence of his oriental 'kin'; but a Greek, Aristotle's nephew CALLISTHENES (1) of Olynthus, refused. Alexander never made this request again, but Callisthenes was later, according to one tradition, executed as having been involved in a plot led by HERMOLAUS, a Macedonian page who had been his pupil.

In the summer of 327, Alexander embarked on his invasion of India, which extended his borders to the River Indus. His army was much larger and more mixed in composition than that with which he had invaded Asia. There were now troops from all over the Persian empire, as well as Macedonians and men from the Balkans. He crossed the Hindu Kush and proceeded by the Khyber Pass to the River Indus. One of the local kings, TAXILES, had already offered submission and been confirmed in power. The Indian nations could not unite and presented Alexander with little opposition until he met PORUS and Abisares. He advanced to the River Hydaspes (Jhelum), where he found Porus facing him with a large army, including many elephants. By keeping his cavalry away from the elephants and by surprise tactics Alexander won a decisive victory over Porus, whom he captured after the battle and restored to a position of power under him. Here he founded the city of Bucephala in honour of his horse, Bucephalus, which had died there. He marched onwards into India, but at the

River Hyphasis (Sutlej) his men mutinied and refused to go further. They had heard reports of the might of the great Nanda kingdom of Magadha on the Ganges to the east and had reason to be afraid of this power. Alexander reluctantly returned to the Hydaspes and in 326, with a newly built fleet, sailed down the river to Pattala on the Indus Delta. On this journey, Alexander had to face much opposition from the native peoples, led by the Brahmans, which culminated in his war with the Malli in which Alexander was seriously wounded. The journey back to Persia (325) was to be a voyage of discovery. Alexander, with the bulk of the army, marched westwards towards Iran, while the fleet under NEARCHUS sailed along the coast and a section under CRATERUS (1) was sent on by an inland route. On this march, Alexander's men had to contend with the Gedrosian Desert in Baluchistan, where his guides lost their way. Eventually, he made contact again with Nearchus. Early in 324 he reached Susa, where he rested his troops and encouraged his Macedonians and Asiatics to mix by arranging for eighty of his officers to marry aristocratic Persian women and by himself taking Darius' eldest daughter, BARSINE (Parysatis), as his second wife. (Roxane's son, Heracles, had died in India.) In summer 324 he assembled his army at Opis in Mesopotamia, where he again tried to win the allegiance of the Persians by creating a mixed army, but offended the Macedonians, who mutinied because they had no sympathy with his aim of creating a partnership with the barbarians. He held a feast of reconciliation and allowed 10,000 Macedonians to return home under Craterus.

At the Olympic festival of July 324, Alexander announced the return of exiles to the Greek cities of the League, which he negotiated. The mercenaries were becoming ever more an anachronism in the new order he envisaged. ANTIPATER (1), his viceroy in Greece, was authorised to use force in applying this decision. He also asked the Greek states to pay him the honours due to a god, which many did. He spent the winter in Ecbatana, capital of Media, where his closest companion HEPHAESTION died. In 323 he marched to Babylon where he intended to collect his army and navy and plan his next campaign. Here he caught a serious fever and died on 13 June. He left no heir or successor (Roxane's second son, ALEXANDER (6), was as yet unborn and his surviving son, Heracles, was a bastard and unacknowledged), but on his deathbed he gave his ring to PERDICCAS (2). His body was buried in the city of Alexandria in Egypt, which he had founded but never revisited (see PTOLEMY 1).

Alexander, the pupil of Aristotle who admired Achilles and Heracles, appears to have had political and social ideas beyond his time which were mostly incomprehensible to his simple Macedonian soldiers. He almost certainly evolved a policy of uniting his great empire in a way in which racial distinctions would not determine precedence or the contribution which each could make. On the other hand, his deep-seated Hellenism led him to introduce Greek ways and Greek thought to a vast area to which they were new and in which they had a long-lasting effect. His premature death led ultimately to the collapse of his empire into half a dozen states (many of which eventually fell to Roman domination within the following 300 years), which were ruled by the generals of his army. There is a sense in which Rome was to be the true heir of Alexander. See ARRIAN's *Anabasis*, based largely on PTOLEMY (1) I's account and other favourable sources, and PLUTARCH's *Life of Alexander*. See also G.T. Griffith (ed.) (1966) *Alexander the Great*, Cambridge: Heffer; R. Lane Fox (1973) *Alexander the Great*, London: Allen Lane; R. Stoneman (1997) *Alexander the Great*, London: Routledge; A.B. Bosworth (1988) *Conquest and Empire*, Cambridge: CUP.

4. (ruled 369–358 BC) A tyrant of Pherae in Thessaly. He was a man of great energy and brutality who met with opposition from the other Thessalian cities which he tried to bully into submission. After the death of his uncle, the tyrant JASON, he seized power at Pherae and arrested PELOPIDAS, the Theban general, in 367 while the latter was on an embassy and held him until EPAMINONDAS forced him to release him. He was defeated at Cynoscephalae by Pelopidas in 364 and compelled to join the Theban alliance. He was murdered by his wife, or the sons of Jason, in 358.

5. (reigned 342–330 BC) A king of Epirus, brother of OLYMPIAS and uncle of ALEXANDER (3) the Great. PHILIP (1) II of Macedonia, his brother-in-law, gave him the kingdom of the Molossians of Epirus, expelling Arybbas, and marrying him to his daughter, Cleopatra, in 336. Alexander brought the rest of Epirus under his control in an alliance of which he was the leader. In 333 he crossed to Italy at the invitation of Tarentum and helped them in a war against the Lucanians, Bruttii and Messapii. He was highly successful and was soon in command of the whole of southern Italy. A war with the Samnites brought him to the edge of Roman territory. He made an alliance with Rome, which was then the strongest power in central Italy. However, his Greek allies in Italy let Alexander down and Tarentum deserted him. During further hostilities in Lucania, he was killed near Pandosia by a Lucanian deserter.

6. IV (323–*c*.311 BC) The posthumous son, who never held power, of ALEXANDER (3) the Great by ROXANE. Born in the year of his father's death, he was jointly declared king with PHILIP (2) ARRHIDAEUS, his feeble-minded uncle, but became a pawn in the machinations of Alexander's successors. He and his mother fell into the hands of CASSANDER, the great enemy of Alexander's house, at the siege of Pydna in 316. ANTIGONUS (1) the

One-eyed used Alexander IV's name in his attempt to restore the empire of Alexander. Consequently, Cassander, who had kept Alexander IV and his mother in confinement at Amphipolis, murdered them.

7. (*c*.290–245 BC) A son of CRATERUS (1) who succeeded his father as viceroy of Corinth and Euboea. Under the influence of PTOLEMY (1), he declared himself independent in 250. He had to fight Athens and Argos, after which ANTIGONUS (2) GONATAS of Macedonia accepted his usurpation. His kingdom was split by the battle of Chaeronea in the year of his death. His widow was the patroness of EUPHORION (2).

8. (reigned 272–240 BC) A king of Molossia in Epirus and son of PYRRHUS. He led an invasion of Macedonia during the Chremonidian War in conjunction with Athens (267), but was routed and driven from his kingdom by ANTIGONUS (2) GONATAS. He was subsequently restored *c*.260 with Aetolian help.

9. Aetolus (C3 BC) A poet and man of letters from Pleuron in Aetolia who *c*.285 was charged by PTOLEMY (2) II PHILADELPHUS of Egypt with the arrangement of the tragic works in the library at Alexandria. He later, *c*.276, moved to the court of ANTIGONUS (2) GONATAS in Macedonia. Only fragments of his poetry survive.

10. Balas (reigned 153–145 BC) An incompetent ruler of Syria who gained the throne by pretending to be the son of ANTIOCHUS (4) IV. He killed DEMETRIUS (6) I in battle with the help of the Jewish Maccabees. He had the support of Rome, Egypt and Pergamon, but was defeated and dethroned by DEMETRIUS (7) II with Egyptian help. He married Cleopatra Thea, eldest daughter of PTOLEMY (6) VI, but lost her to Demetrius.

11. Zebina (reigned 128–122 BC) A pretender to the throne of Syria who was set up in power by PTOLEMY (8) VIII of Egypt, but was defeated and killed by ANTIOCHUS (8) VIII GRYPUS in 122.

12. Jannaeus (reigned 103–76 BC) A king and high priest of the Jews, of the Hasmonean family, younger son of John HYRCANUS. He succeeded his brother, ARISTOBULUS (3), and advanced the monarchical aspect of his rule as shown by his coinage on which he placed Greek and Aramaic, as well as Hebrew, inscriptions. He expanded the Jewish state by conquering Galilee, Peraea, part of Ituraea, and a number of Greek cities across the Jordan and on the coast of Palestine. He had to face popular revolts and the anger of the Pharisees. On his death he was succeeded by his wife, Alexandra Salome, who reigned successfully until her death in 67. She recovered the favour of the Pharisees. Their sons were Hyrcanus II and Aristobulus.

13. of Abonuteichos (C2 AD) A Paphlagonian mystic attached to the worship of Asclepius. He was attacked by LUCIAN in his work *Alexander or the False Prophet*. He taught that Asclepius, the god of healing, had been reborn in the shape of a serpent called Glycon, and he built a temple in which he delivered oracles with a large tame serpent wearing a human head-mask. He excluded Epicureans and Christians from his rites, and made a large fortune by his prophecies, even establishing an office in Rome. Lucian attempted to investigate his frauds, but was nearly assassinated for his pains. Alexander gained a large following including an influential Roman named Rutilianus. After he died, aged 70, the cult survived him.

14. of Aphrodisias (C3 AD) A Peripatetic philosopher. He came to Athens in about AD 198 and became the foremost commentator on the works of ARISTOTLE and the head of the Lyceum. He dedicated his treatise *On Destiny* to the emperors Septimius Severus and Caracalla. Much of his work, including commentaries on

Aristotle's *Metaphysics*, I–V, *Topics, Prior Analytics*, I, *Meteorology* and *On Perception*, survives. There is a translation of *On Destiny* by A. Fitzgerald (1931), London: The Scholartis Press.

Alexandra Salome *see* Alexander (12).

Alexis (C4 BC) A comic poet from Thurii in southern Italy who was taken as a child to Athens, where he later acquired citizenship. He is said by the *Suda* to have written 245 comedies and won victories in the theatre of Dionysus at Athens. A considerable number of fragments of his plays survives, as well as around 130 titles. His work of the Middle Comedy marks a transition between the Old Comedy of ARISTOPHANES (1) and the New Comedy of MENANDER (1). He is said to have taught the latter playwright and also to have been his uncle. The fragments display much talent. He survived until around 275, and PLUTARCH tells a story of his dying while being crowned on the stage at the age of 106.

Alyattes (reigned *c*.610–560 BC) A king of Lydia in western Asia Minor and founder of the Lydian empire. His father, Sadyattes, bequeathed to him a war with Miletus, but he concluded a treaty of peace and alliance with Miletus in 604. He drove the Cimmerians out of Asia Minor, advanced his frontier to the River Halys, and in 585 fought a war with the Medes during a battle of which there took place the solar eclipse that THALES had predicted. He subdued the Carians and took a number of Greek cities. His tomb, which is still visible north of Sardis near Lake Gygaea, has a diameter of 260 metres and is topped by a huge phallus three metres thick.

Alypius (*c*.C3 AD) A Greek writer on music. His *Introduction to Music*, which is extant, is our best source of knowledge of the Greek musical scales.

Amasis 1. (reigned *c*.569–526 BC) A pharaoh of Egypt who championed the native Egyptians against APRIES, who relied extensively on foreign mercenaries from Ionia and Caria. He developed a pro-Hellenic policy and granted Greek traders rights and privileges at the port of Naucratis on the Nile Delta. He was an unconventional but successful ruler who made numerous alliances with the Lydians and various Greek states, including Samos under POLYCRATES, in fear of the Persians who overwhelmed Egypt a year after his death.

2. (C6 BC) An Athenian potter: the 'Amasis painter', whom he employed between 555–525, decorated amphoras, cups and other vessels. See STESICHORUS.

Ameipsias (C5 BC) An Athenian writer of Old Comedy and a contemporary of ARISTOPHANES (1), whom he defeated at the City Dionysia competition of 423 when the *Clouds* took third place, his *Connus* being second. In 414, at the same festival, his *Revellers* beat Aristophanes' *Birds*. His work has not survived, although we have seven titles.

Ammonius (C2 BC) A Greek literary critic, he was a pupil of ARISTARCHUS (3) of Samothrace. He wrote commentaries, which have not survived, on HOMER, PINDAR and ARISTOPHANES (1) – this last probably being a treatise on the individuals satirised in the plays of Aristophanes and other writers of Old Comedy.

Amyntas 1. I (reigned *c*.540–498 BC) A king of Macedonia who gave refuge to the Athenian tyrant HIPPIAS after his expulsion from Athens in 510.

2. II (reigned *c*.393–370 BC) A king of Macedonia. After a period of anarchy following the death of his cousin, ARCHELAUS, he became king and made alliances with whichever Greek state could offer him the strongest support. He was an astute diplomat and kept the Illyrians and

Dardanians to the north at bay. He was succeeded by his son, ALEXANDER (2) II, and PHILIP (1) II was his third son.

Anacharsis (C6 BC) A Scythian prince who travelled in Greece and on his return home was put to death for trying to introduce the Phrygian cult of the Great Mother to his homeland. Stories were told about him by HERODOTUS, who saw him as a philhellene, and by EPHORUS, for whom he appears to have been a type of 'noble savage'. He was used as a character by an unknown, later philosophic writer (see *The Letters of Anacharsis*) to convey the objections of Cynic philosophy to contemporary corruption. Cicero translated one of the letters into Latin (*Tusc.*, 5. 90) and the idea lay behind Montesquieu's *Lettres Persanes*.

Anacreon (*c.*570–485 BC) A lyric poet born at Teos. He left his native island *c.*545 when it was threatened by the Persians and went with his fellow Teans to found the colony of Abdera in Thrace. He was summoned at some time to Samos by the tyrant POLYCRATES (1), who wished him to teach his son music. He was with Polycrates in 522 when the message came luring the latter to his death. Anacreon was then brought by HIPPARCHUS (1), son of the tyrant PISISTRATUS, to Athens, where he stayed, making an excursion to Thessaly *c.*514. He was honoured at Athens, where he died, with a statue on the Acropolis. His poetry was edited by ARISTARCHUS (3) in six books. It includes hymns, love songs, convivial poems, epigrams, dedicatory verse and epitaphs, which were usually written in simple metres. His works display lively imagination and humour, and are often concerned with pleasure. The so-called *Anacreontea*, poems in imitation of his style, were written in the second century BC.

Anaxagoras (*c.*500–428 BC) A philosopher of the Ionian school, born at Clazomenae, son of Hegesibulus, he was the first philosopher to live at Athens, to which he moved probably at the time of the Persian invasion of 480. He stayed there for thirty years, becoming the friend and teacher of PERICLES and EURIPIDES. In about 450 he was put on trial by the Athenians for impiety and was only saved from death by the eloquence of his friend, the statesman Pericles. Consequently he went into exile from Athens to Lampsacus, where he lived until his death.

His philosophical system derived from a theory that an Intelligence (*nous*) governs the universe, which is itself made up of an infinite number of particles of various kinds, all contributing to the composition of every object. A fragment of his writing states: 'in everything there is a portion of everything save Intelligence'. It is this Intelligence that is the life-force in both animals and vegetables. He was influenced by the fall of a meteorite at Aegospotami in about 468, and studied astronomy, giving an explanation of eclipses. In the *Defence Speech of Socrates* (*Apology*) by PLATO (1), he is said to have been a materialist thinker and to have taught that the sun was a lump of rock and the moon a mass of earth. ARISTOTLE bears witness to the great popularity of Anaxagoras in antiquity. He wrote a book, *On Nature*, of which important fragments survive.

Anaxandridas II (reigned *c.*560–*c.*520 BC) A king of Sparta. His first wife was barren, so the ephors compelled him to take another wife, by whom he was father of CLEOMENES (1) I.

Anaxarchus (C4 BC) A philosopher, born at Abdera, of the school of DEMOCRITUS. He was admired by ALEXANDER (3) the Great, whom he accompanied to Asia. After Alexander's death, he was caught by his enemy, Nicocreon, king of Cyprus, who put him to death by pounding him in a stone mortar.

Anaxilas (ruled 494–476 BC) A tyrant of the Greek city of Rhegium on the straits of Messina. He seized from Syracuse the city of Zancle on the opposite side of the straits and settled there Greeks who were friendly to him, Samians at first and then Messenians, who renamed the place Messana (now Messina). He supported Carthage against Syracuse in 480 (see HAMILCAR), but later made an alliance with the Syracusan tyrant HIERON (1) I, to whom he gave his daughter in marriage. He won the mule-cart race at Olympia.

Anaximander (c.610–c.545 BC) A philosopher, born at Miletus, of the Ionian school. He wrote c.546 the first philosophic treatise in prose, *Nature*, which has not survived. He taught that the primary origin of all things is the Indeterminate, which he held to be eternal. He conceived of the universe as consisting of countless worlds, in strict symmetrical balance with each other and subject to the rule of law (*Dike*). He taught that the sun and moon travel in circles passing under the earth, and the earth (a flat disc) remains at the centre without falling owing to its equilibrium with regard to the extremities of the cosmic system. He was the first to speculate about the size and distance of the sun and the moon. He drew the first map of the inhabited world and held an evolutionary theory of the development of animals and men. He also introduced into Greece the gnomon, an instrument he used for astronomical observation.

Anaximenes (C6 BC) A philosopher of the Ionian school, born at Miletus, who flourished around 546. He may have been a pupil of ANAXIMANDER, whose views on cosmology he appears to have developed. He taught that air or vapour exists which continually nourishes a world which is constantly coming into and out of being in a cyclical way. He also taught that matter is all derived from this vapour, which becomes fire when rarefied, and, when condensed, water and earth and stone. This physical account of the origins of matter proved influential upon later thinkers.

Andocides 1. (C6 BC) An Athenian potter who signed nine vases that have survived. Some of his ware was painted by the 'Andocides Painter', a successor of EXECIAS, of whose work twelve pieces survive: all are red-figure and he is regarded as being the inventor of the technique.

2. (born c.440 BC) An Athenian politician and orator. He was of aristocratic Athenian ancestry and in 415 became involved in the episode of the mutilation of the statues of Hermes (herms) on the eve of the departure of the Sicilian expedition. This act was interpreted at Athens as not only impious, but also as treasonable and an attempt to derail the expedition. As a member of a political club, Andocides came under suspicion of being implicated in the plot, and was arrested and imprisoned. There was also a charge that the associates of Andocides had held a profane parody of the Mysteries of Demeter at Eleusis. To save his skin and gain immunity from prosecution, Andocides confessed and denounced others with an account that may have been mostly untrue. He was set free, but quickly fell victim to a decree proposed by Isotimides that barred from temples and the market-place any who, like Andocides, had confessed to being involved in impiety. He could no longer live in Athens and so became a merchant and traded successfully. After two unsuccessful attempts to regain his full citizenship, he eventually took advantage of the amnesty of 403 and returned home only to be prosecuted in 400/399. In his trial, he successfully defended himself with the still extant speech, *On the Mysteries*. He was sent as an ambassador to Sparta in 392/391 with others to negotiate peace and, on his return, argued before the Assembly in favour of the terms, but the Athenians rejected them and the embassy was prosecuted for treason. Andocides anticipated the verdict by going into voluntary exile, disappearing from history. Three of his speeches survive. He was not a professional speaker and broke many of the 'rules' of composition, but was nevertheless powerful and effective as an orator.

Andriscus (mid-C2 BC) A fuller (clothes cleaner) of Adramyttium near Pergamon who in 150 claimed to be Philip, the son of PERSEUS, last of the Macedonian kings. He looked for help from DEMETRIUS (6) I of Syria, who turned him over to the Romans. He escaped from Rome to Asia Minor where he was given some assistance by the wife of a prince of Pergamon. He led an army of Thracians into Macedonia, winning two victories and establishing himself as king in 149. He overran Thessaly and allied himself with Carthage, but in 148 he was defeated by Q. Caecilius Metellus and was subsequently put to death. Rome then turned Macedonia into a province.

Androcleidas *see* Ismenias.

Andromachus (C4 BC) A ruler of Tauromenium. See TIMAEUS and TIMOLEON.

Andronicus (C1 BC) A Peripatetic philosopher from Rhodes. He did much work on the text and ordering of ARISTOTLE's works, which had been brought to Rome by Sulla, and brought the Peripatetic School back to the study of Aristotle and THEOPHRASTUS. He was probably head of the Lyceum until 44.

Androtion (born *c.*410 BC) An Athenian politician and local historian who was a son of the oligarch Andron and a pupil of ISOCRATES. He held many official positions and was an ambassador to MAUSOLUS in 355. He was prosecuted by his enemies, who included DEMOSTHENES (2), and exiled in 346 for making an illegal proposal. He then lived in Megara where

he published *c.*342 a study of Athenian history to 346 in an eight-book work entitled *Atthis*, of which some sixty-eight fragments have survived. He worked hard to provide an accurate account, though he shows pro-Athenian bias. ARISTOTLE used his work as a source for his *Athenian Constitution*, and PHILOCHORUS used it for his own *Atthis*.

Anniceris (C3 BC) A philosopher from Cyrene. In his time the Cyrenaic school split into three factions, one of which he led. He stressed the importance of a habit of wise conduct in the training of a philosopher.

Antalcidas (C4 BC) A Spartan general and diplomat. In 393/2 he was sent to Sardis to convert Tiribazus, the Persian governor of Lydia, to a policy favouring Sparta as a better friend than Athens. In 388 he negotiated peace with the king, ARTAXERXES (2) II. In the same year he obtained Persian assistance against Athens and blockaded the Hellespont with the help of a Persian fleet, forcing Athens to accept the peace which bears his name and by which Persia took control of the whole of Asia Minor, while Athens kept only the islands of Imbros, Lemnos and Scyros. All other Greek cities were to be independent. After Sparta's defeat at Leuctra in 371, Antalcidas lost his influence with Artaxerxes and, because the king preferred the Theban PELOPIDAS in negotiations for peace *c.*367, he committed suicide.

Antenor (C6 BC) An Athenian sculptor. He made a famous group of Harmodius and ARISTOGITON, who killed HIPPARCHUS (1), the younger son of the tyrant PISISTRATUS, which was taken by the Persians from the Acropolis in 480 and restored to Athens in the fourth century to stand in the market-place. Two bases signed by him have been found on the Acropolis.

Anticlides (C3 BC) An Athenian historian, mythologist and antiquarian who wrote a history of ALEXANDER (3) the Great and produced romantic and rationalised interpretations of myths and legends.

Antigonus 1. I the One-eyed (382–301 BC) A Macedonian king of part of Asia Minor. He was the son of Philip of Elymiotis and one of ALEXANDER (3)'s generals. He was appointed governor of Phrygia in 333 when Alexander moved east. In 321 after Alexander's death, his friend ANTIPATER (1), regent for Alexander's son, appointed him commander of the army in Asia. After the death of Antipater in 319 and his campaigns against Alcetas and EUMENES (1), which led to the latter's death after a three-year struggle in 316, he aspired to rule the whole of Alexander's empire. Other former generals of Alexander, however, declared themselves independent rulers of the areas they controlled and formed a coalition against him, though POLYPERCHON passed on to him his title of regent. The war (from 315–311) did nothing to diminish his strength. However, SELEUCUS (1) seized the eastern half of the empire, including Babylon, and Antigonus took on his various rivals in a series of wars. After defeating PTOLEMY (1)'s fleet in 306, he assumed the title of king. His enemies, Ptolemy of Egypt, CASSANDER of Macedonia, Seleucus of Babylonia and beyond, and LYSIMACHUS of Thrace, all of whom later assumed royal titles, combined once more against him and defeated him in 301 at the battle of Ipsus in Phrygia. He himself fell in the battle at the age of 80. He was succeeded by his son, DEMETRIUS (2) THE BESIEGER, whose rashness in battle was partly responsible for his death. See R.A. Billows (1990) *Antigonus the One-eyed and the Creation of the Hellenistic State*, London: University of California Press.

2. II Gonatas (*c.*320–239 BC) A king of Macedonia, the son of DEMETRIUS (2) the Besieger and Phila, daughter of ANTIPATER (1), as well as grandson of ANTIGONUS (1). After 287 he was in charge of his father's European possessions and became titular king of Macedonia in 283 on his father's death, but the country itself was in the hands of LYSIMACHUS and subsequently PTOLEMY (16) CERAUNUS. He lost Thessaly and dissolved the Achaean League, but made peace with ANTIOCHUS (1) I, king of Syria. In 277 he seized Macedonia after defeating an invasion by the Galatians. In 275 PYRRHUS, king of Epirus, returned from his campaign in Italy and attacked and defeated Antigonus. However, in 272 Antigonus regained his throne after Pyrrhus had made a rash attack on Sparta, and overran the whole of Greece as far as the Isthmus.

Athens and Sparta, *c.*266, combined to attack him in the Chremonidian War in which Antigonus captured Athens. He declared war on Egypt, which had supported his previous enemies, and gained mastery over the Aegean Sea and its islands. He lost Corinth when its governor rebelled and failed to regain it in spite of several attempts. He made peace with Achaea and died in 239. He was an able general and a patron of learning and literature, as well as being interested in philosophy. He proved popular with the Macedonians and restored his country's integrity. The meaning of his nickname is unknown.

3. surnamed III Doson ('Going to give') (*c.*263–221 BC) A king of Macedonia, son of DEMETRIUS (4) the Fair of Cyrene who was a half-brother of ANTIGONUS (2) II and so a nephew of ANTIGONUS (2) II GONATUS. In 229, on the death of DEMETRIUS (2) II, he was left guardian of PHILIP (3), the heir to the throne, and married Demetrius' widow, Phthia. He had some military successes and recovered Thessaly, which he subsequently abandoned. When in 227 the army mutinied, he seized the throne of Macedonia. He campaigned in the region of the Aegean Sea and won some territory. However, CLEOMENES (2) III, king of Sparta, was menacing the Achaean Confederacy, which appealed to Antigonus. In 224, having received a promise from ARATUS (2) to give him the Acrocorinth, he led his army to the Isthmus. He won Arcadia and created an alliance under his control. In 222 he defeated the Spartans at Sellasia and seized their city. However, his luck then ran out: he had to defend Macedonia against the Illyrians, burst a blood-vessel while engaged in battle, and died. He was succeeded by Philip V, whom he had supplanted and adopted.

4. of Carystus (C3 BC) A writer and bronze-worker who spent time both at Athens – where he wrote *Lives of Philosophers* and was connected with the Academy – and at Pergamon at the court of king ATTALUS (1) I. His statues honoured the victory of Attalus over the Gauls. His biographies were well written and accurate, and he also published works of art history and a book of *Extraordinary Tales*. Some of his work survives.

Antimachus (born *c.*444 BC) A poet and critic from Colophon. He wrote an elegiac poem called *Lyde* to console himself over the loss of his mistress of that name, as well as a *Thebaid* and other poetry. He acquired such a reputation that PLATO (1) is said to have sent a friend, Heraclides, to collect his poems. Only fragments of his works survive. His edition of HOMER's epics anticipates the scholarship of the Alexandrian poets of a century or more later, as does the style of many of his poems, which the fragments show to have been innovative, learned and difficult.

Antiochus 1. I Soter ('Saviour') (324–261 BC) A Macedonian king of much of what had been the Persian empire. He was the son of SELEUCUS (1) I and his Bactrian wife, Apama. Before his father's death, he governed the eastern provinces of the kingdom as king jointly with his father, who gave him STRATONICE, his own second wife, in marriage. A story was put about that he was passionately in love with his stepmother. She bore him three children, ANTIOCHUS (2), Seleucus and Apame, who was later married to MAGAS of Cyrene. He succeeded his assassinated father in 281 and secured the western part of his kingdom by marching rapidly from Bactria to Syria, which was in a state of serious unrest. He made his peace with his father's assassin, PTOLEMY (16) CERAUNUS, and, after the latter fell, Antiochus made a treaty in 278 with ANTIGONUS (2) GONATAS, his brother-in-law, the next king of Macedonia, which brought lasting peace between the two states. He lost much territory in Asia Minor, partly to Egypt in two wars with the Ptolemaic kingdom, the first in 279 and the second from 274–271. But he defeated the invading Galatians (Gauls) in Asia Minor, probably in 273, and thus earned his surname. He lost much territory to EUMENES (2) I of Pergamon who revolted from Seleucid rule in 262. He fell fighting the Galatians in 261.

2. II Theos ('The God') (*c.*287–246 BC) A Seleucid king of Syria and lands to the east. He was the second son of ANTIOCHUS (1) I and STRATONICE (the first son, Seleucus, seems to have been executed for treason by his father). He became king on his father's death in 261. He allied himself with Macedonia against Egypt and regained much of the territory in Asia Minor that his father had lost to Pergamon (see ATTALUS I). On making peace with Egypt, however, he put his wife, LAODICE (1), away and took in her place BERENICE (2), the daughter of PTOLEMY (2) II PHILADELPHUS, who bore him a son. During his reign or the next, the satrap of Bactria, DIODOTUS (2), declared his province independent. After Antiochus' death in 246, Laodice led a rebellion which overthrew Berenice and her son, leading to their deaths. SELEUCUS (2), Laodice's son, succeeded Antiochus.

3. III the Great (*c.*242–187 BC) A king of Syria and lands to the east. He was the second son of SELEUCUS (2) II and succeeded his brother, SELEUCUS (3) III, in 223. The kingdom was then falling apart owing to secessions by a number of eastern nations, and Antiochus did much to restore it and give it manageable frontiers. He married LAODICE (2), daughter of MITHRIDATES (2) II of Pontus, thus allying himself with a powerful neighbour. He fought a war against Egypt to recover the occupied parts of Syria and Palestine, but was defeated at Raphia near Gaza in 217. He besieged the rebel ACHAEUS in Sardis from 215–213 and by defeating and killing him won back lost territory in Asia Minor. In 212 he embarked on an eastern campaign that lasted seven years. He regained much territory, taking Media from the rebellious governor, Molon, and recovering Seleuceia from him, but he could not subjugate Parthia or Bactria, with which he concluded treaties of peace giving him nominal suzerainty. However, he did acquire Armenia and led his forces into Afghanistan and northern Arabia, thereby earning his epithet 'The Great'. In 203/2 he made a secret treaty with PHILIP (3) V of Macedonia to share the overseas possessions of Egypt, and in 202–198 he conquered the parts of Syria and Palestine in Egyptian hands. He gave the JEWS a charter to guarantee their religious practices, including the levying of tax for the temple. He also created a state cult of himself as king and Laodice as his queen.

The hostility of the Roman Senate was aroused by the collaboration between Syria and Macedonia, especially when in 196 Antiochus invaded Europe to recover the Gallipoli Peninsula in Thrace, where he rebuilt the city of Lysimacheia, and met an embassy from Rome which had been sent to negotiate peace. After fruitless negotiations lasting three years, Antiochus invaded Greece and was defeated in 191 by the Romans at Thermopylae and compelled to abandon Europe. Hannibal,

an exile from Carthage, had taken refuge at the court of Syria *c.*195 and had tried to persuade Antiochus to invade Italy.

Hostilities were renewed, and in 190 Antiochus was defeated by Lucius Scipio and P. Scipio Africanus at Magnesia near Mt Sipylus in Asia Minor. A treaty was made in 188 at Apamea by which Antiochus gave up all his territory west of the Taurus range and paid 15,000 talents. He also lost Armenia, which rebelled and became a separate kingdom under ARTAXIAS (1) I. He had previously lost eastern lands to DEMETRIUS (8) of Bactria. Thus, Syria ceased to be a Mediterranean power. He was killed in Elymais (on the border of Persia) while trying to take treasure from a temple to meet the demands of the Romans. He was succeeded by his second son, SELEUCUS (4) IV.

4. IV Epiphanes ('The Glorious') (*c.*215–162 BC) A king of Syria, third son of ANTIOCHUS (3) III, he succeeded his elder brother, SELEUCUS (4) IV, in 175. He fought a successful war against Egypt (170–168) and was preparing to lay siege to Alexandria when Rome intervened and compelled him to retire. He concentrated his attention on Palestine, an important frontier province, which he attempted to hellenize. He installed a garrison in Jerusalem and dedicated the temple to Olympian Zeus but, in doing so, aroused the opposition of the JEWS, which led to the rising under Mattathias and his sons, the Maccabees, which came to a head after Antiochus' death. In 165 he defeated and captured ARTAXIAS (1) I, king of Armenia. He died in 164 after trying, like his father, to plunder a temple in Elymais and went mad. Some called him '*Epimanes*' ('mad') to parody the title, *Epiphanes*, which he had assumed.

5. V Eupator ('of a good father') (173–162 BC) A king of Syria, son and successor of ANTIOCHUS (4) IV, he was 9 years old at the time of his accession in 164. He reigned for two years through his regent, Lysias, and in 162 was dethroned and put to death in Antioch by DEMETRIUS (6) I when he came from Rome to claim the kingdom. During his reign, Jerusalem was restored to its former Jewish position according to the principles laid down by ANTIOCHUS (3) III.

6. VI Epiphanes ('The Glorious') (c.148–138 BC) A king of Syria, son of ALEXANDER (7) BALAS and Cleopatra Thea, daughter of PTOLEMY (6) VI. In fact, he did not really reign at all. He was nominated in 144 by the general DIODOTUS (3) TRYPHON as heir to the throne in opposition to DEMETRIUS (7) II. In 142 Diodotus deposed and succeeded him and in 138 killed him.

7. VII of Side (c.159–129 BC) A king of Syria. He was born in and brought up at Side in Pamphylia, the second son of DEMETRIUS (6) I and brother of DEMETRIUS (7) II, whom he succeeded after the usurpation of DIODOTUS (3) TRYPHON (see ANTIOCHUS 6). He attacked and defeated Diodotus in Antioch (138), reconquered Judaea briefly in 134, which had been an independent Jewish state, and in 130 took Babylon from the Parthians. In 129, however, he was defeated and killed in battle by the Parthians, which finally ended Seleucid pretensions in the East.

8. VIII Grypus (reigned 125–96 BC) A king of Syria. He was the younger son of DEMETRIUS (7) II and succeeded his brother, SELEUCUS V; however, his half-brother, ANTIOCHUS (9) IX, disputed the throne with him, and they fought until 122 when they agreed to divide the kingdom, the latter taking Phoenicia and Coele Syria and Grypus taking the remainder. He was assassinated in 96.

9. IX of Cyzicus (died 95 BC) A king of Syria who disputed the throne with his elder half-brother, ANTIOCHUS (8) VIII Grypus until 122, when they reached an agreement. After the death of Grypus, Antiochus of Cyzicus tried to seize his

brother's share of the kingdom, but had to face Grypus' son, SELEUCUS (6) VI, fighting against whom he was killed in 95.

10. X the Pious Son of ANTIOCHUS (8) VIII. In 95 he routed SELEUCUS (6) VI, who had killed his father, and then overwhelmed Seleucus' brother, ANTIOCHUS (11).

11. XI He was drowned in the River Orontes while fleeing from ANTIOCHUS (10) the Pious.

12. XII The younger brother of ANTIOCHUS (11) who called himself Dionysus, but is known to history as Antiochus. He claimed the throne, but was killed in battle against the Arabian king ARETAS (3) III.

13. XIII the Asiatic (reigned 69–65 BC) The last Seleucid king of Syria, he was a Roman puppet until Pompey deposed him and made Syria into a Roman province.

14. the Hawk (c.263–226 BC) A king of part of Asia Minor, the second son of ANTIOCHUS (2) II of Syria and LAODICE (1). He was made joint ruler by his elder brother, King SELEUCUS (2) II, but separated the Seleucid provinces in Asia Minor from the rest of the kingdom when Seleucus was at war (246–241). In the War of the Brothers, with the support of ARIARATHES (3) III of Cappadocia and MITHRIDATES (2) II of Pontus, he frustrated Seleucus' attempts to recover his lost provinces. He married a Bithynian princess and allied himself with the Gauls of Galatia, but met with opposition from ATTALUS (1) I of Pergamon who drove him from his possessions. He was killed in Thrace.

15. of Ascalon (died c.68 BC) A Greek philosopher and the founder of the 'Fifth Academy'. He was a pupil of PHILON (4) of Larissa whom he accompanied in 88 to Rome, where he got to know Lucius Lucullus. He changed his stance and reverted to the position of the Old Academy, returning to Athens, where he became head of the Academy in 79–78, during which time Cicero attended his lectures. His philosophy was eclectic and composed of Academic, Peripatetic and Stoic elements, and influenced Cicero's thought greatly.

16. of Syracuse (C5 BC) A historian whose *History of Sicily* (from mythical times to 442 BC) was used by THUCYDIDES (2) and whose *History of Italy* is quoted by the geographer STRABO. He wrote in the Ionic dialect.

Antipater 1. (397–319 BC) A Macedonian general and statesman who served PHILIP (1) II and ALEXANDER (3) the Great. In 346 and 338 he helped to negotiate peace treaties between Philip and Athens. He also supported Alexander's claim to the throne on Philip's death. Alexander left him to govern Macedonia and to supervise his interests in Europe while he was away in Asia. In 331, when AGIS (2) III of Sparta organised a rebellion against the Macedonians, Antipater won the aid of the Greek League, which Philip had founded, to help crush the Spartans at Megalopolis.

After Alexander's death in 323, the Greeks rose up against the Macedonians and besieged Antipater in Lamia in Thessaly (the Lamian War). He broke out, obtained reinforcements, and defeated the Greek coalition at Crannon. He imposed autocratic government on several Greek states, including Athens, where he caused the orator, DEMOSTHENES (2), to be condemned to death, which led to the latter's suicide. In 321 he joined other generals who opposed the regency of PERDICCAS (2). After the murder of Perdiccas, he was elected 'regent' by a conference of Macedonian generals and troops held in Syria at Triparadisus. He died after appointing POLYPERCHON as regent – a disastrous choice. His son was CASSANDER.

2. of Sidon (C2 BC) An epigrammatist, several of whose poems figure in the *Greek Anthology*, mingling conventional epitaphs with more important material, such as his poems on the Roman destruction of Corinth.

3. of Tarsus (C2 BC) A Stoic philosopher who succeeded DIOGENES (3) of Babylon as head of the Stoa at Athens and was himself the teacher of PANAETIUS. He committed suicide at an advanced age.

4. of Thessalonica (C1 BC) An epigrammatist and author of many poems in the *Greek Anthology*. He was a client of L. Calpurnius Piso.

5. of Tyre (died *c*.45 BC) A teacher of Stoic philosophy who introduced Cato of Utica to Stoicism.

Antiphanes (C4 BC) A writer of Middle Comedy of which, together with ALEXIS, he was the most distinguished representative. He produced his first play in 385 and won thirteen victories at the Athenian dramatic festivals. He wrote hundreds of plays of which we know the titles of 134. He was a native of Rhodes and died in Athens in 306. Many fragments of his plays have been preserved, showing him to have been extremely diverse in his subject matter.

Antiphilus of Byzantium (C1 AD) An epigrammatist; about fifty of whose poems are in the *Greek Anthology*, ranging from descriptions of accidents and paradoxes to poems about sailing and the sea.

Antiphon 1. (480–411 BC) An orator and thinker, the earliest of the ten 'Attic Orators'. He was born at Rhamnous and held strong oligarchic views. He wrote court speeches for others to deliver (he was the first to do this, and it became the normal Athenian practice) and gained a high reputation for them. He worked for foreign governments and important politicians. He was also a teacher and political thinker. THUCYDIDES (2), the historian, is said to have been his pupil, and he was almost certainly the author of treatises entitled *Concord* and *Truth*, fragments of which are preserved. In the latter he discussed the nature of justice and the relationship between nature and human convention. In 411 he was the brains behind the conspiracy against the democracy that led to the rule of the Four Hundred. He went to Sparta with an embassy to try to negotiate peace and oligarchic government in Athens, but failed, and the democracy was quickly restored. He did not flee like most of his colleagues, but remained to face trial. He spoke his finest speech in his own defence, and when the poet AGATHON congratulated him he said he would rather have pleased one man of taste than all the rabble. He was found guilty and put to death. His surviving speeches are partly rhetorical exercises, which were composed in three groups of four (*The Tetralogies*), in each of which there were two speeches for the prosecutor and two for the defence. We also possess three actual courtroom speeches, which all concern real cases of murder, *The Murder of Herodes*, *Against the Stepmother* and *The Chorus-Boy*. Only a fragment of his own defence speech survives. The greatness of Antiphon's achievement can be understood if it is remembered that there was no writing of prose in Attic Greek before his time: he had to break new ground in adapting the language, as well as establishing a style, and was influential on Thucydides and later Attic writers.

2. (C5 BC) An Athenian sophist and writer, contemporary with ANTIPHON (1), and probably the same man. He is reported to have been an opponent of SOCRATES and to have written about moral philosophy in a way that was critical of traditional ethical thinking. *Truth* and *Concord*, partly extant political treatises, are attributed to him. See ANTIPHON (1).

Antisthenes (*c*.445–*c*.360 BC) A philosopher and leader of a school which foreshadowed that of the Cynics. He was born in Athens, the son of an Athenian father of the same name and of a Thracian mother. After fighting in the Peloponnesian War at the age of 18, he became a hearer of SOCRATES and one of his most devoted followers. After the death of Socrates, he began to teach in the Cynosarges, a gymnasium at Athens for people of mixed ancestry. Here, though the chronology is difficult, DIOGENES (2) of Sinope may have become one of his pupils, and the name of the sect, Cynic, is derived from the latter's nickname, *kyon* ('dog'), or else from the name of the gymnasium where he taught. His philosophy was essentially moral and political. Like Socrates, he taught that virtue depends on knowledge and can, therefore, be taught; anybody who knows the meaning of the word 'virtue' must inevitably be virtuous; virtue consists of contempt of riches, adornment, honour and enjoyment; most pleasures are treacherous and not worth having; and the wise man is the best ruler. This doctrine had an influence on Stoicism. A few fragments of his Socratic dialogues survive.

Anyte (C3 BC) A poetess from Tegea in Arcadia. Her subject was nature and she wrote epitaphs for animals. Her lyric poems are lost, but eighteen of her epigrams, in the Doric dialect, are in the *Greek Anthology*.

Anytus (C5 BC) An Athenian politician. He was very rich and supported the democratic cause. He was elected general in 409 and bribed his way out of prosecution for the loss of Pylos. After the end of the Peloponnesian War, he aided THRASYBULUS in restoring democracy after the rule of the thirty tyrants. He was the leader of the three prosecutors of SOCRATES in his trial in 399, probably for genuinely patriotic reasons, believing that

Socrates had fostered the opponents of the democratic state.

Apama or Apame The name of the wife of SELEUCUS (1) I and of his granddaughter. See STRATONICE.

Apelles (C4 BC) A painter from Colophon, noted for the charm of his art, who worked under Ephorus of Ephesus, and later PAMPHILUS (1) of Sicyon. He became court painter to ALEXANDER (3) the Great. He made portraits of Alexander, his father PHILIP (1) II, and other courtiers. His most famous works were of Aphrodite rising from the sea, which was exhibited in Cos; Alexander portrayed as Zeus, with a thunderbolt, in Ephesus; an allegorical picture of Calumny, with attendant creatures; *Sacrifice*; and a self-portrait. He died in Cos while copying his Aphrodite.

Apellicon (C1 BC) A philosopher of the Peripatetic school in Athens. He was a native of Teos and had a valuable library, including many original works of ARISTOTLE and THEOPHRASTUS, which he had bought from the heirs of Neleus of Scepsis. He edited them badly. In 84 Sulla seized this library and took it to Rome.

Apion (C1 AD) A Greek scholar and commentator on HOMER, born in Alexandria and successor of THEON (1) as head of the Alexandrian school. He went to Rome during the principate of Gaius (Caligula) to complain about the Jews in Alexandria, and was opposed by the Jewish scholar Philo. He also wrote several books in the same vein, to which Josephus wrote a rejoinder (*Against Apion*). He later settled in Rome and taught rhetoric. He compiled a glossary of Homeric vocabulary, based on ARISTARCHUS (2), and used by HESYCHIUS.

Apollodorus 1. (C5 BC) An Athenian painter, known as *Skiagraphos* (the 'Shader'), from his invention of shading and colour gradation. Pliny the Elder says that

he 'opened the door of painting through which ZEUXIS entered'.

2. (C4 BC) An Athenian litigant and politician, as well as the son of the banker PASION. He quarrelled with his stepfather, PHORMION (2), and tried to prosecute him *c.*349 for embezzlement. His most famous case was his prosecution of the former prostitute Neaera for illegally claiming to be Athenian. This and other speeches were wrongly attributed to DEMOSTHENES (2), but were probably written by Apollodorus himself. In 348 he unsuccessfully proposed that the budget surplus be spent on military preparations rather than on entertainments for the people.

3. of Gela and 4. of Carystus Two Athenian poets of the New Comedy. The latter is better-known and was probably more successful. He wrote forty-seven plays and won five victories. He produced his first play around 285. His *Mother-in-Law* and *Claimant* were adapted in Latin by Terence (*Mother-in-Law* and *Phormio*). The Latin versions point to influence by MENANDER (1).

5. (early C3 BC) An Alexandrian pharmacologist who wrote treatises, used by NICANDER, on poisonous creatures and drugs.

6. (born *c.*180 BC) A writer on myth. He was a pupil of ARISTARCHUS (3) and left Alexandria for Pergamon and Rome in *c.*146. He was a fine scholar and left many works, the best-known of which is the *Bibliotheke* or *Library*, a collection of heroic myths. The surviving work under this title, however, derives from the first or second century AD. His theological work, *On the Gods*, survives.

Apollonius 1. of Rhodes (*c.*295–*c.*230 BC) A Greek epic poet and grammarian, born at Alexandria, but called 'the Rhodian' from his retirement to that island. He was a pupil of CALLIMACHUS (3), but later quarrelled bitterly with him over the stylistics of poetry. He taught rhetoric at

Rhodes with so much success that the Rhodians made him a citizen of their state. On the death of ZENODOTUS, he was appointed head of the library at Alexandria in which he remained until 247 when he was replaced by ERATOSTHENES. In this position he was the superior of Callimachus. He is said in the ancient *Life* to have publicly recited his *Argonautica* while still a youth, and to have had a poor reception, whereupon he revised the poem. The work deals with the story of Jason's quest for the golden fleece and of his love for Medea – the first treatment of the theme of love in epic poetry. In true Alexandrian style, Apollonius displays all his erudition in the poem, but it also has great literary quality. Apollonius wrote other shorter poems, epigrams and poems in honour of the foundation of a number of cities.

2. of Perge (*c*.265–190 BC) A mathematician and author of a work on *Conics*. One of the greatest mathematicians of antiquity, he was born at Perge in Pamphylia. He studied under EUCLID's pupils at Alexandria. He wrote his *Conics* in eight books for NAUCRATES, a geometer, but later revised it. He wrote many other works of which only one survives, *The Cutting-off of a Ratio*. He also made important discoveries in the field of theoretical astronomy.

3. (C1 BC) An Athenian sculptor and son of Nestor. He signed the Belvedere Torso in the Vatican and a cult statue of Capitoline Jupiter, dedicated in 69.

4. of Citium (C1 BC) A Greek physician and medical writer. A commentary he wrote on the Hippocratic treatise, *Joints*, is extant.

5. the Sophist (C1 AD) An Alexandrian grammarian who was the son of Archibius and pupil of APION. He wrote a Homeric dictionary, which survives in an abridged form together with a fragment of the original. His sources were ARISTARCHUS (3) and Apion's glossary.

6. of Tyana (C1 AD) A Greek philosopher from Cappadocia. He was a Neopythagorean who lived an ascetic life and went from place to place teaching. He laid claim to miraculous powers and pretended to be able to fly and to have foreknowledge of events, such as the death of the Emperor Domitian, for which he was tried but acquitted. He finally settled in Ephesus, where he opened a school, and according to Flavius PHILOSTRATUS died in AD 97. A few fragments of his writings survive. His *Life* by Philostratus is highly unreliable. Hierocles of Nicomedia compared his life with that of Jesus of Nazareth – to the detriment of the latter. Eusebius wrote a surviving reply.

7. Dyscolus (C2 AD) An Alexandrian grammarian and son of Mnesitheus. He worked in Alexandria and made a short visit to Rome. Four of his grammatical treatises survive – *The Pronoun, The Conjunction, The Adverb* and *Syntax* – and, though they are written in an obscure style in the everyday Greek of his time and with the asperity which lent him his nickname ('Bad-tempered'), they show a genuinely critical approach and an intention to make serious progress in the analysis of grammar based on rational principles. His influence, especially on Priscian, was profound. His son was HERODIAN.

8. of Tyre A fictional character, the hero of the romantic novel, *The History of Apollonius King of Tyre*, whose author is unknown. See B.P. Reardon (ed.) (*c*.1989) *Collected Ancient Greek Novels*, Berkeley, CA; London: University of California Press.

Apries (reigned 589–570 BC) A Pharaoh of Egypt whose use of Greek and Carian mercenary soldiers in his wars to extend his territory into Phoenicia and Cyrene (Libya), which were unsuccessful, caused the Egyptians to rebel against him. He was succeeded by AMASIS (1).

Araros (C4 BC) A poet of the Middle Comedy and the son of ARISTOPHANES (1). Besides producing revivals of two of his father's lost plays, he wrote six plays of his own, now lost, the first of which was produced in 375.

Aratus 1. (born c.315 BC) A Greek didactic poet from Soli in Cilicia and a pupil of Menecrates of Ephesus and ZENO, the Stoic philosopher, at Athens. In Athens he met King ANTIGONUS (2) GONATAS who c.277 invited him to the Macedonian court where he wrote a poem in honour of Antigonus' wedding. In his *Hymn to Pan* he celebrated Antigonus' victory over the Gauls. He also spent time at the court of Antigonus' brother-in-law, King ANTIOCHUS (1) I of Syria, but later returned to Macedonia. He died c.240. His major work was the *Phaenomena*, still extant, which is a verse treatise on astronomy and weather lore. He wrote it at the request of Antigonus, using the work of EUDOXUS of Cnidos as his source. The astronomy was suspect even in the time of its composition, and HIPPARCHUS (2) criticised it in a commentary. The poem was, however, widely admired. It was studied and translated by such diverse people as Cicero and Germanicus, and influenced Lucretius' poem *The Nature of Things* and Virgil's *Georgics*. He wrote much other poetry, now lost. See *Phaenomena*, trans. G.R. Mair (1955) in *Callimachus, Hymns, Epigrams*, Loeb Classical Library, Cambridge, MA: Harvard University Press.

2. of Sicyon (271–213 BC) A statesman and general from Sicyon. After his father Clemias was murdered in 264, he escaped to Argos where he was educated. At the age of 20 in 251 he overthrew the tyrant of Sicyon and brought the city into the Achaean Confederacy for defence against the Macedonian threat. He applied personally to PTOLEMY (2) II PHILADELPHUS of Egypt for economic support for his city, which he gained in the form of subsidies.

Aratus was chosen to head the confederacy in alternate years from 245, and in 243 he captured the Acrocorinth. In 241 he defeated the Aetolians at Pellene and brought them into the alliance, but was defeated by the Macedonians in 237. In 235 Megalopolis joined the confederacy, and Argos did the same in 229. After the death of DEMETRIUS (5) II of Macedonia in 229, Aratus assisted in the liberation of Athens. The Peloponnese was now liberated from Macedonian rule, but a new menace arose from Sparta. CLEOMENES (2) III defeated Aratus twice in 227, and Aratus felt constrained to appeal to Macedonia. ANTIGONUS (3) DOSON agreed in 224 to defend the confederacy in return for the Acrocorinth, and in 222 he and the confederacy defeated the Spartans decisively at Sellasia. Antigonus died shortly after the battle, and in 220 Aratus had to seek help from his successor, PHILIP (3) V, to resist the Aetolians. After the Peace of Naupactus in 217, Aratus found himself at odds with Philip over his opposition to Rome and proposal to seize Mount Ithome. He probably died from sickness rather than being poisoned on the orders of Philip, as rumour had it. The historian POLYBIUS used his memoirs as a source and regarded them as reliable.

Arcesilas 1. (reigned c.590–c.575 BC) The second king or tyrant of Cyrene in North Africa and a member of the family of the Battiads.

2. (reigned c.560–c.550 BC) The fourth Battiad king of Cyrene, known as 'the Cruel'. He alienated his brothers, who seceded to found the rival city of Barca. They formed an alliance with the native Libyans, who defeated Arcesilas. His brother Learchus murdered him.

3. (reigned c.530–c.519 BC) The sixth Battiad king of Cyrene. His powers were limited by the reforms of DEMONAX of Mantinea who had in the previous reign reformed the constitution of Cyrene and reduced the monarchy to the status of a figurehead. Arcesilas tried to recover his traditional power and was exiled. He recruited mercenary troops in Samos, then subject to POLYCRATES, and regained his kingdom. On the Persian invasion of Egypt in 525 he submitted to CAMBYSES and ruled as his subordinate. He was subsequently murdered in Barca.

4. (reigned *c*.463 to *c*.445 BC) The eighth and last Battiad king of Cyene. PINDAR wrote an ode in honour of his victory at Delphi in 462. He gave shelter to the Athenian survivors of the Egyptian expedition of 455. He was finally deposed and the monarchy overthrown by an uprising.

Arcesilaus (316–241 BC) A Greek philosopher born at Pitane in Aeolia. He first studied mathematics with AUTOLYCUS, with whom he went to Sardis where he was received by EUMENES I (2); he then went to Athens to study philosophy with THEOPHRASTUS. However, he became a close friend of CRANTOR and transferred his allegiance to the Academy. Around 266 he succeeded CRATES (3) as head of the Academy. He was a devoted scholar of PLATO (1), but introduced a note of scepticism into the school's approach to philosophical study and debate. He was regarded as the founder of the Middle Academy. He published nothing, but left a few poems: two epigrams are preserved. ERATOSTHENES was his pupil.

Archelaus 1. (C5 BC) An Athenian philosopher and a pupil of ANAXAGORAS. It is not clear what his views were, but he probably followed his teacher in the main, though he might have adopted some of the ideas of EMPEDOCLES. He is said to have been a teacher of SOCRATES during the latter's middle years.

2. (reigned *c*.413–399 BC) A king of Macedonia and an illegitimate son of PERDICCAS (1) II. He obtained the throne by assassinating his half-brother and other kinsmen. He reorganised the Macedonian army, improved training, and built good

roads and forts. He developed trade by adopting the Persian monetary standard and was a philhellene and particularly pro-Athenian in his policy, inviting artists such as ZEUXIS, EURIPIDES and AGATHON to his court, which he moved from Aegae to Pella to be more accessible to the sea and for better control of the frontier. He founded a theatrical festival at Dium. He captured Pydna in 410 with the help of THERAMENES and *c*.400 he intervened in Thessaly and made an alliance with Larissa. After his death, Macedonia suffered anarchy for ten years until the accession of AMYNTAS (2) II.

3. (C1 BC) A general from Cappadocia who served MITHRIDATES (6) VI, king of Pontus. He conquered Bithynia and central Greece in the First Mithridatic War between Rome and Pontus from 88–85 and was twice decisively defeated by Sulla, at Chaeronea and at Orchomenus in Boeotia. Mithridates commissioned him to negotiate peace with Rome, which he continued to do until 83. He deserted to Rome on the renewal of war and helped Lucullus in the Third Mithridatic War.

Archias (died 378 BC) A tyrant of Thebes who was imposed by Sparta. The Thebans hated him for his cruelty and plotted to kill him. The plot was nearly revealed to him at a banquet in a note that he received, but he postponed reading it and therefore died.

Archidamus The name of five Eurypontid kings of Sparta. The most important were these:

1. II (reigned *c*.476–427 BC) He distinguished himself by his response to the great earthquake at Sparta of 465, as well as in the subsequent Messenian War. He strove to prevent the outbreak of the Peloponnesian War with Athens in 432 (see Book 1 of THUCYDIDES' *History*). Having failed to do this, he led expeditions into Attica three times (431, 430 and 428) with some success. He also led the attack on Plataea in 429. He left two sons, AGIS II and AGESILAUS II.

2. III (reigned 361–338 BC) The son of Agesilaus II. Though he did not take part in the battle of Leuctra in 371, he led the army back and maintained Spartan integrity against her Arcadian neighbours in difficult times. He made an important contribution to Sparta's defence in 362 when she was attacked by the Theban general EPAMINONDAS. In 346 he supported Phocis in the Sacred War, but his attempt to seize Thermopylae was thwarted by the treacherous action of the Phocian PHALAECUS. He then took up a mercenary role in southern Italy and was killed in 338 at Manduria after intervening on behalf of Tarentum against the Lucanians. ISOCRATES wrote a 'speech' which Archidamus is imagined making in 366 to support Sparta's futile bid, favoured by his father, to reconquer Messenia.

Archigenes (C2 AD) A physician from Apamea in Syria and a pupil of AGATHINUS. He worked in Rome in the time of the Emperor Trajan. He had a theory of the pulse that GALEN borrowed, though in other respects they were at variance. He wrote much on medical subjects, but only fragments survive.

Archilochus (mid-C7 BC) An early poet from the mid-Aegean island of Paros who was the son of Telesicles and a slave woman. A poem of his refers to an eclipse of the sun, which is likely to be that of 6 April 648 BC. He took part in the colonisation of Thasos in the northern Aegean. On his return he quarrelled with Lycambes over marriage with his daughter, Neobule, who was at first promised and then refused, so he wrote an iambic lampoon against the family. He was a great innovator in metre and style. His subject matter ranges widely from poems of personal feeling to observation of life around him, fables and drinking songs.

His language is mostly Ionic Greek. There were many overtly sexual references in his poems, as well as personal attacks. A considerable amount of his work survives: *Epodes*, at least two of which are fables: the Roman poet, Horace, imitated the style if not the subject matter; *Elegiacs*, songs that are often of an epigrammatic style about personal experiences; *Iambic trimeters* mostly about his experiences of a personal nature, often bawdy or abusive, occasionally serious; and *Trochaic tetrameters* about more serious matters, such as accounts of battles and political appeals. He died fighting in a war against the Naxians. See A.P. Burnett (1983) *Three Archaic Poets*, London: Duckworth.

Archimedes (*c*.287–211 BC) A mathematician and inventor born in Syracuse, the son of an astronomer, Phidias. He was a close friend, if not a kinsman, of the Syracusan tyrant HIERON (2) II and his son, GELON. He may have visited Egypt. He corresponded with Alexandrian scholars such as ERATOSTHENES and CONON (2). He was popularly credited with the invention of the screw for raising water, artillery for the defence of the city against the Romans, and the principles of hydrostatics – as evidenced from the story commonly told of his bath: he had been consulted by the king as to the composition of a gold crown that the king had ordered, but suspected of being swindled by the substitution of silver for some of the gold. As Archimedes was stepping into a bath full of water, he noticed the overflow and realised that the problem could be solved by immersing the crown and equal weights of gold and silver, in turn, in water and measuring the difference in overflow. Having done this, he is said to have run through the streets of Syracuse shouting: '*heureka, heureka!*' ('I've got it!'). He was killed at the time of the fall of Syracuse by an angry Roman soldier against the order of his commander, M. Claudius Marcellus. While drawing a mathematical figure on a sandboard, Archimedes had failed to notice the man's arrival and rounded on him when he disturbed the sand. Marcellus gave him an honourable burial in the special tomb he had requested, depicting a cylinder circumscribing a sphere (he discovered the ratio of 3:2 between them). Cicero found the tomb in a neglected state when he was quaestor in Sicily. Cicero also reports that Archimedes made two spheres – a planetarium and a star globe – which were taken to Rome.

Archimedes wrote a wealth of books, some of which have survived. His interest in astronomy is shown by his reference to a theory of ARISTARCHUS (2) of a heliocentric universe, and by his citing the distances of the heavenly bodies in his work *The Sand-reckoner*. His work includes treatises on the sphere and cylinder, conoids and spheroids, spirals, centres of gravity of planes, and the area of a parabola. In the *Sand-reckoner* he demonstrates a numerical notation that easily encompasses enormously large numbers in words, based on a hundred million as we use ten; he describes a method of determining the areas and volumes of various figures by mechanical means; and offers a work on hydrostatics, which he invented from scratch. Eutocius wrote commentaries on some of his works. See T.L. Heath (1957) *The Works of Archimedes* New York: Dover; London: Constable and E.J. Dijksterhuis (1956) *Archimedes*, Copenhagen: E. Munksgaard.

Archippus (C5 BC) An Athenian comic poet of the Old Comedy. None of his work survives: we only have the titles of six of his plays. He won first prize in 415.

Archytas (C4 BC) A philosopher of the Pythagorean school and a mathematician. He lived in Tarentum and was a close friend of PLATO (1), who visited him in his home town. He laid the foundations of mechanics, distinguished harmonic from arithmetical and geometric progressions, solved the problem of duplicating the cube by using two half-cylinders, and contributed to the theories of proportion, music and acoustics. EUDOXUS (1) of Cnidos was his pupil. He re-created a school of Pythagorean philosophy and intervened to save Plato from detention in Syracuse. He is said to have drowned while crossing the Adriatic in 347.

Arctinus An epic poet who lived in Miletus and is said to have been the author of the lost *Aethiopis*, *Sack of Troy* and *Battle of Titans*.

Areus (reigned 309–265 BC) An Agiad king of Sparta who succeeded his grandfather Cleomenes II. At first he was under the regency of his uncle, CLEONYMUS. In 280 he held an unsuccessful war against Macedonia by invading Aetolia. In 272 he had to hurry back to Sparta from operations in Crete to repel an attack by PYRRHUS, king of Epirus. During the Chremonidean War, he failed to relieve the siege at Athens, being halted at the Isthmus by CRATERUS (2). He was killed in battle in 265 at Corinth.

Ariamnes

1. I (C5 BC) A satrap, or Persian governor, of Cappadocia.

2. II (reigned *c*.280–230 BC) The eldest son of ARIARATHES (2) II. He may have been responsible for winning the independence of the kingdom of Cappadocia from the Seleucids of Syria. He made his son, ARIARATHES (3) III, his co-ruler.

Ariarathes The name of several rulers of Cappadocia.

1. I (died 322 BC) The satrap of Cappadocia under DARIUS (2) II. He was born in 404. He resisted ALEXANDER (3) the Great's forces and after Alexander's death was captured and crucified by PERDICCAS (2) and replaced by EUMENES (1).

2. II (died *c*.280 BC) A nephew of ARIARATHES II. He lived in exile in Armenia

from 322–301 when he recovered the southern and central parts of his uncle's satrapy, but was subject to Seleucid suzerainty.

3. III (reigned *c*.250–*c*.220 BC) Joint ruler with his father, ARIAMNES (2) II, from around 250–230. He married into the Seleucid house, taking STRATONICE, daughter of ANTIOCHUS (2) II, as his wife. He proclaimed his independence from the Seleucid kingdom in about 250 and supported his brother-in-law, ANTIOCHUS (14) the Hawk, against his older brother-in-law, SELEUCUS (2) II, in the War of the Brothers (*c*. 239–236).

4. IV surnamed Eusebes ('The Pious') (reigned *c*.220–*c*.163 BC) Successor and son of ARIARATHES (3) III. He married Antiochis, daughter of ANTIOCHUS (3) III of Syria. After the latter lost the battle of Magnesia against the Romans in 190, Ariarathes deserted him for an alliance with Pergamon and Rome. He married his daughter, Stratonice, to EUMENES (3) II of Pergamon. He assisted Rome against the Gauls and PHARNACES (1), king of Pontus.

5. V surnamed Philopator ('loving his father') (reigned *c*.163–130 BC). Son of ARIARATHES (4) IV. He rejected, on Roman advice, a marriage alliance with Syria, for which DEMETRIUS (6) I expelled him from his kingdom and replaced him with a usurper. He appealed to Rome, which divided the kingdom between the two. Ariarathes then (*c*.157) recovered the lost portion with the help of ATTALUS (2) II of Pergamon. He sacked Priene to recover the treasure he considered had been stolen from him. He fell in battle while assisting the Romans against ARISTONICUS (2) of Pergamon.

6. VI (reigned 130–116 BC) Son of ARIATATHES (5) V. During his minority, his mother, Nysa, ruled harshly and the king of Pontus, MITHRIDATES (5) V, intervened and married him to his own daughter, Laodice. He was killed by GORDIUS, a

Cappadocian nobleman, who was in Mithridates' pay.

7. VII (died 101 BC) During his infancy his mother, Laodice, acted as regent. Cappadocia was invaded by the Bithynian king NICOMEDES (3) III, whereupon Laodice's brother, MITHRIDATES (6) VI of Pontus, also invaded the country. Laodice married Nicomedes, and Mithridates, claiming to be the protector of Ariarathes, placed him on the throne. However, Ariarathes objected to the presence of his father's assassin, Gordius, who was in league with Mithridates: the upshot was the murder of the king by Mithridates, his uncle, who replaced him with his own son, ARIARATHES IX.

8. VIII Younger brother of ARIATATHES (7) VII. The Cappadocian nobles rebelled against MITHRIDATES (6) VI and his son, and drove them out, choosing Ariarathes VIII as their king. Mithridates soon returned and expelled him. He died shortly afterwards – the last of his line.

9. IX (died 86 BC) A son of MITHRIDATES (6) VI of Pontus who was made king of Cappadocia by his father at the age of 8 in 101, with GORDIUS as regent. He was soon deposed by the Roman Senate, which allowed the Cappadocians to choose their own king. They chose Ariobarzanes I, whom Sulla installed in 95. Ariarathes was later restored after Tigranes of Armenia had removed his rival, but was once more deposed by the Romans in 89. He died fighting for his father in Thessaly. See ARIARATHES (7).

Ariobarzanes 1. of Pontus (C4 BC) A satrap of Pontus, son of Mithridates, whom he succeeded as satrap in 367. In the following year, he revolted from ARTAXERXES (2) II and founded the independent kingdom of Pontus. He received support from the Athenians, who were angry at the Peace of PELOPIDAS, and he and his sons were granted Athenian citizenship.

2. (reigned 266–*c*.250 BC) A king of Pontus, the son of MITHRIDATES (1) I, instrumental in winning Amastris for the kingdom.

Aristagoras (died *c*.496 BC) A ruler, under Persia, of Miletus and the son-in-law of the 'tyrant' HISTIAEUS whose place he took (*c*.505) when the latter was detained at the Persian court in Susa. He persuaded the Persians in 499 to attack Naxos, a rich and relatively democratic state, to restore the exiled nobles, and when this failed, acting on a secret message from Histiaeus, he raised the Ionian revolt, taking advantage of the general discontent with the Persian occupation. He restored the freedom of Miletus, and went to Greece to seek help. When the Spartans saw HECATAEUS (1)'s map of the world, they rebuffed him, wary of venturing so far from home, but the Athenians and Eretrians briefly gave support: Athens twenty ships and Eretria five. He also gained support in the Black Sea area and Cyprus. Though the Ionians took and burnt Sardis, the capital of the province of Lydia, the revolt, which had lasted for six years, eventually failed and the Persians won a decisive naval victory at Lade near Miletus in 494. Miletus was sacked and cleared of her inhabitants and Aristagoras took refuge at Myrcinus in Thrace, which had belonged to Histiaeus. He was killed by Thracians when they attacked Ennea Hodoi (Nine Ways). His actions precipitated the Persian invasions of Greece in 490 and 480.

Aristarchus 1. (C5 BC) A tragic poet from Tegea in Arcadia. He was contemporary with EURIPIDES and won two victories at the Athenian festivals. His *Achilles* was adapted by the Roman poet Ennius.

2. of Samos (*c*.310–*c*.230 BC) A mathematician and astronomer. He was a pupil of the Peripatetic philosopher STRATON of Lampsacus and worked at Alexandria. There is ample evidence that he proposed a heliocentric theory of the universe, which is vouched for by ARCHIMEDES in the *Sand-reckoner*, SEXTUS EMPIRICUS, and PLUTARCH, who also states that Aristarchus proposed the theory that the earth rotates on its own axis. Archimedes quotes Aristarchus as hypothesising: 'The fixed stars and the sun remain unmoved, and the earth revolves around the sun in a circle, the sun lying at the centre of the orbit'. However, this view was not adopted by any later ancient astronomer, except for SELEUCUS (7). It may have been suggested to Aristarchus by the work of HERACLIDES of Pontus. Aristarchus' only surviving work, *On the Sizes and Distances of the Sun and Moon*, is based, however, on a geocentric theory and for that reason is considered earlier. It is mathematically skilful, but erroneous because the method chosen to work out the distances is not ideal. He calculated the length of the year with great accuracy and invented a spherical hollow sundial. See T.L. Heath (1913) *Aristarchus of Samos*, Oxford: Clarendon Press and T.L. Heath (1932) *Greek Astronomy*, London; Toronto: J.M. Dent.

3. (*c*.217–145 BC) A Greek literary critic and grammarian from the island of Samothrace. He was a pupil of ARISTOPHANES (2) of Byzantium at Alexandria and founded there a grammatical and literary school, while acting as the tutor to the sons of king PTOLEMY (6) VI. He became head of the library at Alexandria (*c*.153) and in 145 on the death of his patron, the king, retired to Cyprus where he too died the same year. The school he founded at Alexandria lasted into the Roman imperial period and had distinguished pupils, including APOLLODORUS (5) and DIONYSIUS (4), the Thracian. He was a brilliant analyst of the works of HOMER, applying to them a 'scientific' method and a penetrating intellect. He produced critical editions not only of Homer, but also of HESIOD, PINDAR and other poets. He was more cautious and scrupulous than his predecessors in his treatment of the problems of the text of Homer, on which he had a conservative influence. ATHENAEUS reports that he was nicknamed 'the absolute scholar', and PANAETIUS called him 'the prophet' on account of his brilliance in critical thought. Not only did he publish commentaries and critical works on the poets, but also polemical writings aimed at rival scholars. He was admired by Cicero and Horace. Nothing of his work survives.

Aristeas 1. of Proconnesus HERODOTUS writes (*Histories*, 4.13) of Aristeas as a source of information about the lands to the north of the Scythians. He is said to have written a poem called *Tales of the Arimaspi*. Herodotus' account credits him with the power of ecstasis – the separation of body and soul. He claimed to have had the travels on which the poem was based during a seven-year disappearance. His actual existence is in some doubt.

2. (C3 BC) The supposed writer of a 'letter' professing to give an account of the translation of the Pentateuch into Greek during the reign of PTOLEMY (2) II Philadelphus.

Aristias *see* Pratinas.

Aristides 1. (C5 BC) An Athenian statesman, the son of Lysimachus and a cousin of CALLIAS (1). In 490 he was a general at the battle of Marathon, where he supported the plans of MILTIADES, which led to victory. He was archon the following year but was rejected by the Athenians as their leader in the forthcoming Persian War, being ostracised and banished in 482. He was, however, recalled two years later in a general amnesty to join the war effort and distinguished himself at the battle of Salamis in 480 where he led a party of hoplites which landed on the island of Psyttalea and dislodged the Persian garrison. However, HERODOTUS'

account seems to imply that he was still in exile at the time of Salamis. He was elected general for three years and led the Athenian army at the battle of Plataea in 479. After the Persian withdrawal, he helped THEMISTOCLES dupe the Spartans so as to bring about the rebuilding of the city walls of Athens, which had been destroyed by the Persians. In 478 and 477 he was responsible for the Athenian naval effort, which led to the liberation of the Asiatic Greeks and the islanders of the Aegean from Persian rule, as well as to frustrating the tyrannical ambitions of the Spartan general PAUSANIAS (1). He and his colleague, CIMON, son of Miltiades, then led the liberated Greeks into the setting up of the Delian Confederacy, and he was commissioned to write its constitution and fix the quotas of ships and money that each state was to contribute to the League's treasury at Delos. He died *c.*460, apparently in poverty, and the state had to support his daughters, which is strange as he had earlier been rich enough to be eligible for the archonship. He was known in his own lifetime as 'the Just'. This quality did not always endear him to his fellow citizens, as the anecdote about the illiterate who asked Aristides to write his own name on the ballot of banishment suggests: 'I am tired of constantly hearing him called "the Just" ' was the explanation he gave him; Aristides did as he was asked.

2. (C4 BC) A painter from Thebes. He was a pupil of Euxinidas and teacher of Euphranor. He was said to be the first to represent the soul, affections and emotions. He is thought to have painted the baby creeping to its dying mother's breast. He was probably the father of Nicomachus and grandfather of ARISTIDES (3).

3. (C4 BC) A Greek painter, who was possibly a grandson of ARISTIDES (2). His works, according to Pliny the Elder, included *Battle of Greeks and Persians* and a portrait of EPICURUS' pupil, LEONTION.

4. (*c*.100 BC) A writer from Miletus and the author or editor of six books of erotic *Milesian Tales*. These stories were often obscene and often contained an element of magic or horror. They were, however, distinct from the Greek novel. Some of the stories were preserved in later writers, e.g. *The Widow of Ephesus* in Petronius and some of the tales in Apuleius' *Metamorphoses*.

5. Aelius (C2 AD) A writer and public speaker from Mysia who studied Greek literature under Alexander of Cotiaeon, the teacher of the Roman emperor Marcus Aurelius. He also studied at Athens, perhaps under Herodes Atticus. On his visit to Rome, aged 26, he fell ill and went for a cure to the shrine of Asclepius at Pergamon. He lived the rest of his life at Smyrna, which was within easy reach of the shrine. His writings survive: the most interesting of which is his account, in *Sacred Teachings*, of his experiences in the healing shrine of Pergamon and his own religious perspective. His other works are speeches, encomiums of gods, and essays. *The Art of Rhetoric* is wrongly attributed to Aristides. In AD 178 he addressed a memorial to Marcus Aurelius after the earthquake at Smyrna and persuaded him to rebuild the city.

6. Quintilianus (C3? AD) A musical writer of whose life nothing is known. He wrote a treatise on music in three books, including a discussion of the use of music in education and medicine, and a metaphysical, perhaps Pythagorean, treatment of the relations between music, arithmetical relations, and the real world. It seems likely that DAMON (2), discussed in *Republic* 3 of PLATO (1), influenced his work.

Aristion (C1 BC) A tyrant of Athens who, as ambassador of the Democratic Party in 88, invited MITHRIDATES (6) VI of Pontus to invade Greece in a campaign of liberation from the Romans. He succeeded the anti-Roman Athenion as tyrant in 87. After Mithridates sent a force under ARCHELAUS (3), Sulla retaliated and besieged Athens. When the Acropolis fell in 86, Aristion was executed.

Aristippus 1. (C5 BC) A teacher of rhetoric and friend of SOCRATES. He was born *c*.435 at Cyrene in Africa and went in the last years of the century to Athens, where he became intimate with Socrates. He later became a courtier of DIONYSIUS (1) I, tyrant of Syracuse, a connection in which PLATO (1) was later involved. His daughter, Arete, was mother of ARISTIPPUS (2).

2. (C4 BC) A Greek philosopher and grandson of ARISTIPPUS (1) I. He founded a school of philosophy at Cyrene which taught that the pleasure of the moment is the only good and therefore the only goal worth pursuing. He also taught that the only reality in time is the present. He himself indulged in a life of luxury, and his doctrine anticipated some aspects of Epicureanism.

Aristobulus 1. (C4 BC) A Greek from Potidaea who travelled with ALEXANDER (3) the Great's army. He wrote a history of Alexander's life and campaigns, which ARRIAN used as a source to supplement PTOLEMY (1). He had a close knowledge of Alexander's life and campaigns, besides being well informed about the geography of his conquests.

2. of Paneas (C2? BC) An Alexandrian Jewish scholar who attempted to reconcile Hebrew religion and scripture with Greek philosophy. He wrote a commentary on the Pentateuch of which only small fragments survive in quotations in Clement, Anatolius and Eusebius.

3. (reigned 104–103 BC) A king and high priest of the Jews, as well as son of John HYRCANUS. He was the first of his family (the Hasmoneans) to assume the royal title. He was succeeded by his brother, ALEXANDER (11) Jannaeus.

Aristodemus 1. (C8 BC) An early king of Messenia. PAUSANIAS (3) records that he led his people to victory in the First Messenian War (*c*.735–715) with Sparta by offering in *c*.730 the sacrifice of his daughter to the gods of the Underworld, in response to the Delphic oracle, for the safety of his country. Eight years later he was elected king, and after desultory fighting for five years led his people to victory, but the next year (716) he killed himself on his daughter's grave. This account may be more fanciful than truthful, and mainly invented after the creation of the state of Messene in the fourth century.

2. (died *c*.492 BC) A statesman and general from Cumae in southern Italy. After winning a name by repelling the Etruscans from his city (*c*.524), he championed the commons against the nobles. In 505, in alliance with republican Rome, he defeated the Etruscans at Aricia near Rome and then seized power at Cumae as tyrant. After the battle of Lake Regillus, he gave refuge to King Tarquin the Proud of Rome.

Aristogiton (died 514 BC) An Athenian 'tyrant-slayer'. In 514 he and his kinsman, Harmodius, both members of the noble family of the Gephyraei, joined others in a plot to kill the tyrant HIPPIAS (1) at the Panathenaic festival. Their motives were almost certainly personal rather than political, but they nevertheless won fame as tyrannicides, even though the main aim of the plot failed. It was HIPPARCHUS(1), the tyrant's brother, who was killed, and Hippias' guards immediately slew Harmodius. Aristogiton was tortured and executed. After Hippias' expulsion four years later by the Spartans, their deed was recognised by the setting up of bronze statues and the composition of a quatrain by the poet SIMONIDES. A popular drink-

ing song hailed them as the creators of Athenian democracy and led the generality of Athenians to forget the facts of the expulsion of the tyranny. Both the historians HERODOTUS and THUCYDIDES (2), however, attempted to set the record straight. See M.W. Taylor (1981) *The Tyrant Slayers*, New York: Arno Press.

Aristomenes (C7 BC) Like ARISTODEMUS (1), he was a hero of Messenian resistance to Sparta. The story, probably mostly mythical, was that at the beginning of the Second Messenian War *c*.685, Aristomenes, son of Pyrrhus, was chosen as commander for his exploits in battle, and won a striking victory at Stenyclarus. Later, after the Messenians had been defeated in the third year of the War at the Great Trench, he resisted the Spartans for eleven years at Mount Hira, living off the land and robbing the Laconians. He was eventually captured with his men on a raiding expedition and they were all thrown into a ravine. All the men died, except him: he feigned death for three days and was then guided to safety by a fox. He returned to Hira, but was captured again and released by the help of a girl who later married his son. Eventually, in 668, Hira fell and Aristomenes went into exile in Rhodes, where he died. The story was told in an epic poem by RHIANOS. See PAUSANIAS (3), *Description of Greece*, Book 4.

Ariston 1. of Chios (C3 BC) A Stoic philosopher who founded his own school and led a movement back to the views of the Cynics. He held that the end of life is a matter of complete indifference.

2. of Ceos (C3 BC) A Peripatetic philosopher who probably succeeded LYCON as head of the Lyceum at Athens. From his writings, now lost, DIOGENES (5) LAËRTIUS derived biographical material, including the wills of Aristotle and other heads of the school. Like THEOPHRASTUS, he wrote on *Characters*. ERATOSTHENES was his pupil.

Aristonicus 1. (C3 BC) A Corinthian musician and a son of Nicosthenes. The people of Delphi gave him privileges for his composition of hymns. The tablet recording the award is datable to 222 and contains a hymn to Apollo.

2. (died 128 BC) A pretender to the throne of Pergamon. He was probably an illegitimate son of EUMENES (3) II of Pergamon and, after the death of ATTALUS (3) III in 133 and the bequest of the kingdom to Rome, led a rising against the Romans in favour of his own claim to the throne. He wished to establish a 'City of the Sun' in Asia Minor, and may also have supported a socialistic reorganisation of the state in favour of the poor and servile classes. He fought and won a battle against P. Licinius Crassus in 131, but was defeated the following year by the consul, M. Perperna, and executed at Rome. See IAMBULUS.

Aristophanes 1. (*c*.445–*c*.385 BC) The greatest Greek writer of comedies, the supreme master of the Old Comedy of the late fifth and early fourth centuries, and the son of Philippus. His sons were Philippus, ARAROS, and Nicostratus. His father may have owned property on Aegina, which was then in Athenian hands. He wrote his first comedy, *Banqueters*, in 427, but felt himself too young to produce it himself, the normal thing to do, and had it produced by CALLISTRATUS, who also produced the next two, *Babylonians* (for which the demagogue CLEON prosecuted him on the grounds of his having no legal right to his Athenian citizenship, and so made a life-long enemy of him) and *Acharnians*, which survives, and with which he won the first prize. Thereafter, he produced two of his own plays, handing yet others over to PHILONIDES, Callistratus, and his son, Araros, to produce. He wrote about fifty-four

plays of which eleven survive complete. He won three further first prizes.

Most of his plays are not comedies in the modern sense, but rather satirical stage-pieces in which the plots are often weak and the purpose is to create laughter out of the buffoonery of often recognisable characters from real life, and even, in *Frogs*, the god Dionysus. Consequently, they are of great historical interest, containing caricatures of the leading men of the day in all fields of life. He was against the continuation of the Peloponnesian War, which he ascribes to the influence of demagogues like Cleon. He was also opposed to the sophists, whom he regards as introducing pernicious ideas, and whom he ridicules in the *Clouds*, taking SOCRATES as their representative, with some reason. He also satirises in *Wasps* the Athenians' excessive fondness for litigation. The choral songs, however, are of great poetic beauty. In the parabasis, a choral song featuring in most of his plays, in which the members of the chorus address the audience directly, the poet is allowed to express his own views on a subject closely connected with the central theme of the play, and so we may assume that Aristophanes' own opinions are thus the basis of his satire.

His surviving plays are: *Acharnians* (receiving first prize in 425), against the Peloponnesian War and in which LAMACHUS was portrayed as a blustering warmonger; *Knights* (receiving first prize in 424), against Cleon in which the people replace him as leader with a sausage-seller; *Clouds* (423), satirising the sophists, which was a failure and was later revised; *Wasps* (422), against the fondness of old men for serving on juries; *Peace* (421), which celebrated the treaty of peace recently made with Sparta; *Birds* (414), in which a couple of Athenians desert their city for a new one, Cloudcuckooland, built by the birds in the sky; *Lysistrata* (411), in which the women of the Greek cities form a plot to withhold sexual relations from their husbands to make them agree to peace; *Thesmophoriazusae* (411), directed against the tragic playwright EURIPIDES; *Frogs* (receiving first prize in 405), in which Dionysus, god of the theatre, goes to Hades to fetch back Euripides from the dead, but, after a comic trial scene, brings back AESCHYLUS instead; *Assemblywomen* (392), in which women replace men in political life and make property common to all; and his second play to be entitled *Wealth* (388), (the first is lost). In this play the god of wealth is healed of blindness, which has unexpected consequences for mankind.

His plays fall into three chronologically distinct groups in which style and subject matter vary. There is a clear development in his approach from group to group. The earliest plays follow a strict structural pattern which must have been traditional and was also exemplified in the work of his rivals, CRATINUS and EUPOLIS. The *Birds* begins a middle period, in which there are changes in focus and treatment, leading to the last two plays, which display features of Middle Comedy: the political and topical references diminish greatly, the chorus becomes largely irrelevant to the action of the plot, and the parabasis disappears. In these developments, Aristophanes was the innovator. He was a master of poetic artistry and the Attic language. In particular, the beauty of his choruses is unsurpassed. See editions of his work by A.H. Sommerstein (ed.) (1980) *Aristophanes*, vol. 1: *Acharnians*, Warminster: Aris & Phillips, which contains general information. See also C.F. Russo, *Aristophanes*, trans. by Kevin Wren, London; New York: Routledge, 1994.

2. of Byzantium (*c*.257 BC–*c*.180 BC) An Alexandrian scholar of Greek literature. He studied in Alexandria under ZENODOTUS and CALLIMACHUS (3). He succeeded ERATOSTHENES *c*.194 as head of the Library of Alexandria. He made editions of the works of HOMER, HESIOD, ALCAEUS, ALCMAN, PINDAR, EURIPIDES and ARISTO-

PHANES (1). He also seems to have divided the writings of Plato into trilogies. He had a fine critical mind: he proposed that the real end of the *Odyssey* was at Book 23, 296, a point supported by many modern scholars. He introduced the use of symbols in a text to show passages of doubtful authenticity. Together with his junior, ARISTARCHUS (3), he was responsible for the establishment of the Alexandrian literary canon. He worked on the biographies of literary figures, and with this knowledge supplemented the work done by Callimachus. He was interested in the works of MENANDER (1) and wrote a treatise about his sources. He also had linguistic interests, writing on Greek grammar and accentuation (he first marked the tonic accent). He wrote books of proverbs both in prose and in verse. His only extant works are the 'arguments' he wrote of Greek plays; those for ARISTOPHANES (1), however, are of dubious authenticity.

Aristophon (*c*.435–*c*.335 BC) An Athenian politician who became active at the end of the Peloponnesian War. His period of importance, however, dates from the sixties of the fourth century. He favoured alliance with Thebes rather than Sparta and so came into conflict with CALLISTRATUS (2). He also opposed EUBULUS (1) over his financial management. He was prosecuted by HYPERIDES in 362. He successfully prosecuted TIMOTHEUS (2) for his failure in the Social War of 357. He opposed Athens' surrender of Amphipolis in the Peace of PHILOCRATES (346).

Aristotle (384–322 BC) In Greek, *Aristoteles*, one of the greatest Greek philosophers and men of science. He was born at Stagirus in Chalcidice, near Thessalonica, the son of Nicomachus who had been physician to King AMYNTAS (2) II of Macedonia, the father of PHILIP (1) II. He was by descent an Ionian Greek, for Stagirus (later Stagira) had been colonised from Chalcis in Euboea, where his mother, Phaestis, was born. As a result of his father's work, he probably spent part of his childhood at the court of Amyntas in Pella. At the age of 17 in 367, he was sent by his father to Athens and joined PLATO's school, the Academy, where he worked first as a student and later as a researcher and lecturer. He so distinguished himself that Plato nicknamed him 'the mind of the school'. He remained at the Academy as long as Plato was alive, and during that time his thought did not seriously diverge from that of Plato's. He may well have begun his research into zoology during this time. Nevertheless, long before Plato's death, he had lost sympathy with some Academic theories, as interpreted by other members of the school, notably SPEUSIPPUS, who was designated to succeed Plato as its head. Consequently, in 347, after Plato's death, feeling that in the Academy 'philosophy was being turned into mathematics', Aristotle left Athens with XENOCRATES and settled at Assos in the southern Troad in Mysia, where two former pupils of Plato, Erastus and Coriscus, were already living under the patronage of HERMIAS, who had himself been a student at the Academy and was now ruler of nearby Atarneus. Here, THEOPHRASTUS joined them and Aristotle opened a school. He and his followers remained there until 342 when Hermias was deposed and killed. Aristotle married his niece and adopted daughter, Pythias, and gave Hermias help in the negotiation of a treaty with Philip II. During their time under the protection of Hermias, Aristotle and Theophrastus spent much time at nearby Mytilene in Lesbos, Theophrastus' homeland, which afforded Aristotle the opportunity to do research into marine biology in the Lagoon of Pyrrha, as well as into other biological topics.

In 342 Philip II, who knew Aristotle from his father's time at the court of Macedonia, invited him to Pella to become tutor to ALEXANDER (3), in which post he remained for two years. He taught his pupil, then aged 14, the standard education of the time, HOMER's poems and the works of the tragedians. He also wrote for him two books that are now lost, *On Monarchy* and *Colonists*, which must have developed his own interest in politics. He retired to Stagirus in 340 when Alexander became regent for his father, and in 335, after Philip's death, he went back to Athens with the status of a metic, or resident alien, to be at the centre of philosophical activity. There, outside the city walls to the north-east, near a grove sacred to Apollo *Lykeios*, the Lyceum, he rented some buildings, which included a gymnasium and a covered walk (*peripatos*), from which the school took its name, Peripatetic. Here Aristotle wrote copiously and Alexander often sent him information and material that he thought would interest his former master and which must have been useful source material for study. Consequently, a great library grew, including manuscripts, maps and probably museum objects, which served as a prototype of all the great ancient libraries and which he and his colleagues used to prepare and illustrate their lectures. Aristotle organised the community that worked under him at the Lyceum with a set of rules and a symposium, which was held once a month for the discussion of topics of mutual interest. He also organised his students' research, for example the political studies that resulted in the accounts of the constitutions of 158 cities of the Greek world, of which only the *Athenian Constitution* survives. After the death of Pythias, Aristotle lived with Herpyllis by whom he had a son, Nicomachus.

On the death of Alexander the Great in 323, there occurred in Athens an outbreak of hostility towards Macedonia, and Aristotle, who had been on such close terms with Philip and Alexander, as well as being a friend of ANTIPATER (1) who, as the chief representative of Macedonia, was then hated at Athens, was threatened with a charge of impiety. Unlike SOCRATES in the same predicament, he fled to Chalcis, the mother city of Stagirus and his mother's native city, where he died within a year of what may have been cancer of the stomach or intestines. He was 62 at his death. His will, which reveals him as thoughtful and grateful towards his kin and those who had served him, was preserved by DIOGENES (5) LAËRTIUS.

An enormous *oeuvre* survives, but many works are lost, among which are his earliest works in dialogue form in the Platonic tradition. The most important of these were the *Protrepticus*, an exhortation to the philosophic life, which was used as a source by IAMBLICHUS for his work of the same name, and *On Philosophy*. Lost too are his collections of material for historical and scientific treatises, except for the *Constitution of Athens*, which was discovered on papyrus in Egypt in 1890, and a book entitled *Problems*, partly the work of his successors, on areas of difficulty in science. What survives consists of works on philosophy, politics, and scientific subjects. The genuine works are on logic and metaphysics: *Categories, On Interpretation, Prior Analytics, Posterior Analytics, Metaphysics, Topics, Sophistic Refutations*; on nature, including biology and psychology: *Physics, On the Sky, On Coming into Being and Passing Away, Meteorology, On the Soul; Parva Naturalia*, consisting of: *On Perception and Things Perceived, On Memory and Reminiscence, On Sleep, On Dreams, On Prediction by Dreams, On the Length and Shortness of Life, On Youth and Age, On Life and Death*, and *On Breathing*; on animal biology: *The History of Animals, On the Parts of Animals, The Movement of Animals, On the Gait of Animals, On the Reproduction of Animals*; on politics and ethics: *Eudemian Ethics, Nicomachean Ethics, Politics, Important Ethical Questions* (*Magna Moralia*), which however, are notes of his lectures written up by another, *Rhetoric*, and a substantial fragment of *Poetics*. Other works attributed to Aristotle are certainly spurious, and their real authorship can sometimes be conjectured.

Aristotle naturally left his works to the Lyceum on his death; but when his successor, Theophrastus, died, according to STRABO, he willed them to Neleus of Scepsis in Asia Minor, who kept them in a cellar to prevent the kings of Pergamon obtaining them. They were later sold to APELLICON, who edited them badly. But copies of many of the works had been made and were used in the Lyceum and even by EPICURUS and Alexandrian scholars. In 84, Sulla took Apellicon's collection to Rome where they were later edited by ANDRONICUS of Rhodes. Many works now lost existed at that time and some, including dialogues, were in a literary style which Cicero admired and described as a 'golden river'.

Aristotle always thought of himself as a follower of Plato, even though he rejected the theory of 'Ideas' and, in Ionian fashion, concentrated on the investigation of the tangible world. During his career, there was a clear development in his thinking which later scholars did not always take into account: it is vain to look for complete consistency throughout. The style of most of the works that have come down to us is difficult. It is not exactly lecture-note form, but it is compressed, elliptical, and in the nature of memoranda. These works are from his period as head of the Lyceum in Athens, but are otherwise undatable. His earlier lost works, from his more Platonist period, were often in dialogue form like many of Plato's writings. His methods were pursued by his successors, Theophrastus and STRATON (1) (though they criticised his reliance on the teleological explanations of natural processes), after which we must look to the heir of the Lyceum, the Museum at Alexandria, for the continuation of science in Aristotle's manner. See W.D. Ross (1923) *Aristotle*, London: Methuen and D.J. Allan (1952) *The Philosophy of Aristotle*, Oxford:

Oxford University Press. His work has been translated by J.A. Smith and W.D. Ross.

Aristoxenus (C4 BC) A Peripatetic philosopher and musician from Tarentum. He was trained in music by his father Spintharus and later by Lamprus of Erythrae. After living in Mantinea, while residing at Corinth, he met the exiled DIONYSIUS (2) II of Syracuse. He moved to Athens where he became a pupil of the Pythagorean, Xenophilus, and then of ARISTOTLE at the Lyceum. He was a prolific writer on many topics, but especially musical theory, and is said by the *Suda* to have written more than 450 books. Some of his work is extant: parts of his *Principles of Harmonics* and *Elements of Rhythm* survive. He wrote other works on music, as well as lives of philosophers and works on education. See CLEONIDES.

Arrian (AD *c*.86–160) The historian of ALEXANDER (3) the Great, Flavius Arrianus was born at Nicomedia in Bithynia. He was a friend and pupil of EPICTETUS (2), whose *Discourses* he preserved and published at Athens. In 124 he received the Roman citizenship from the Emperor Hadrian, in 133 he was appointed prefect of Cappadocia, and the following year he repulsed an invasion of the province by the Alans. He became consul in 146 under Antoninus Pius and died in the reign of Marcus Aurelius. His masterpiece is his *March Inland (Anabasis)*, the history of the expedition of Alexander. The title gives away the fact that it is modelled to some extent on the work of XENOPHON (1). His main source was PTOLEMY (1) I SOTER, supplemented by ARISTOBULUS (1). He wrote a supplement to it about India, called *Indica*. He wrote other works which are lost, including a *History of Parthia* and histories of Alexander's successors.

Arsaces (C3 BC) A leader of the Parni, a nation of the Caspian area, who *c*.250 rebelled against DIODOTUS (2), king/satrap of Bactria, and invaded Parthia, a province of the Seleucid empire, where they established a kingdom in 247, beating off attempts by SELEUCUS (2) II to overthrow them. Arsaces and his descendants expanded their rule to encompass much of the earlier Achaemenid Persian kingdom. He claimed descent from the Achaemenid family. The house he founded adopted many Persian ways, but were also recipient to the Greek methods of administration which were by now well established in their territory. They established their capital at Ctesiphon, the former Seleucid royal city. The Parthian kingdom was in many ways the successor of the former Persian empire, and proved a valuable buffer state between the Hellenistic and Roman powers on the one hand and the nomadic nations of central Asia on the other hand. The Arsacid dynasty was overthrown in AD 253 by the Sassanid dynasty of Persian kings.

Arses (reigned 338–336 BC) A king of Persia, officially known as Artaxerxes IV, who was the younger son and successor of ARTAXERXES (3) III. Like his father and brothers, he was poisoned by BAGOAS.

Arsinoë 1. (C4 BC) A former concubine of PHILIP (1) II, she married the Macedonian general Lagus by whom she was mother of PTOLEMY (1) I, king of Egypt, and ancestress of the Egyptian royal house, the Lagids.

2. II (*c*.316–270 BC) A queen of Egypt, the daughter of PTOLEMY (1) I and BERENICE (2) I of Egypt. She was married *c*.298 to LYSIMACHUS, king of Thrace, who appointed her ruler of much of north-west Anatolia. When he was killed in 281, she was briefly married to her half-brother, PTOLEMY (16) Ceraunos, who murdered her children by Lysimachus. In the same year she fled to Egypt and subsequently married her brother, PTOL-EMY (2) II, who had put away his former wife, ARSINOË (3) I, for plotting to kill him. During her reign of seven years or so, she exercised a great influence on her husband and country at a time of rapid expansion of the kingdom. She and her husband were deified as the *Theoi Adelphoi* ('brother-and-sister gods') by 272, and a region of Egypt, Fayum, was called Arsinoïtes after her. She bore children to Lysimachus, but not to her brother.

3. I (born *c*.300 BC) A queen of Egypt and the daughter of LYSIMACHUS and his first wife, Nicaea. She was married to PTOLEMY (2) II of Egypt *c*.289 and bore him his heir, PTOLEMY (3) III, Berenice, who married ANTIOCHUS (2) II of Syria, and Lysimachus. In 279 she was accused of plotting to kill her husband and banished to Coptus (she may have acted through jealousy of ARSINOË (2), whose return to Egypt *c*.280 must have threatened her position).

4. III (*c*.335–205 BC) A queen of Egypt and daughter of PTOLEMY (3) III and BERENICE (3) II. In 217 she was married to her brother, PTOLEMY (4) IV. A dozen years later she was murdered in a palace *coup*, shortly before her husband's own death. She is known from an autobiographical fragment of ERATOSTHENES to have been well educated and to have objected to her husband's behaviour. She bore him a son, PTOLEMY (5) V.

Artabanus 1. (C5 BC) A brother of DARIUS (1) I, king of Persia, and the trusted adviser of his son, XERXES.

2. The chief minister of XERXES. He killed his master, together with his son, Darius, in 464. When Xerxes' successor, ARTAXERXES (1) I, discovered the truth, he put Artabanus and his sons to death.

3. (C2 BC) A king of Parthia who *c*.127 succeeded his nephew, Phraates I, and,

after a brief reign, died fighting against invading Mongols.

Artabazus (*c*.387–325 BC) A Persian satrap of Phrygia, the son of PHARNABAZUS and Apame. He was appointed by his maternal grandfather, ARTAXERXES (2) II to succeed his father as satrap after the execution of his rebellious half-brother, Ariobarzanes, but rebelled (*c*.358) under ARTAXERXES (3) III with the help of Athens, and when the Athenians' resolve faltered, with the help of Pammenes the Theban. In 352, however, he gave up and fled to the court of PHILIP (1) II. In 345 his brother-in-law, MENTOR, arranged his return to Persia. He was with DARIUS (3) III at Gaugamela, but later went over to ALEXANDER (3) the Great, who made him satrap of Bactria. He relinquished this post in 327. PTOLEMY (1) I married his daughter, Apame (or Artacama).

Artaphernes 1. A brother of DARIUS (1) I of Persia and satrap of Lydia. He was principally responsible for defeating the Ionian revolt in 499. He was an enemy of HISTIAEUS of Miletus.

2. Son of ARTAPHERNES (1) and a commander of the Persian expeditionary force at Marathon in 490. He later led the Lydian and Mysian forces in XERXES' army of invasion in 480.

Artaxerxes 1. I (reigned 465–424 BC) A king of Persia, son of XERXES and Amestris, who succeeded to the throne after his father and brother were assassinated by ARTABANUS (2). On discovering the crime, he wiped out the murderer and his sons. He was nicknamed 'long-hand'. He put down rebellions in Bactria and Egypt, where Athens had been assisting the rebels and which held out until 454. He assented to the Peace of CALLIAS (1) with Athens of 449, which brought a period of peace and non-interference between Persia and Athens. He was generous to the JEWS, whom he allowed to recover their religious freedom under Ezra and Nehemiah (the latter had been his cup-bearer and was made governor of Judaea). He allowed his country's old Athenian enemy, THEMISTO-CLES, to reside peacefully in his empire as governor of Magnesia on the Maeander in Phrygia.

2. II (reigned 404–358 BC) A king of Persia, son of DARIUS (2) II and Parysatis, born c.436. He was nicknamed *Mnemon* because of his good memory. Originally named Arsaces, he succeeded his father in 404. His younger brother, CYRUS (2) tried to wrest the kingdom from him with Greek mercenary help in 401, but was killed at Cunaxa. In 399 Sparta intervened in Asia Minor and a long struggle took place, culminating in the Peace of ANTALCIDAS of 386. He tried to recover Egypt, but failed twice, in 383 and 374. He managed to suppress the Satraps' Revolt of 366–358 mainly because his enemies were not able to unite. His reign was a time of turbulence and disorder, but by his death he had established a measure of control.

3. III (reigned 358–338 BC) A king of Persia, as well as son and successor of ARTAXERXES (2) II. He was nicknamed 'Ochus' and obtained the throne by executing his three elder brothers. With the aid of his Greek general, MENTOR, and mercenary troops he succeeded in recovering Egypt and western Asia Minor. He allowed the eunuch, BAGOAS, to wield great power in the court and was poisoned, together with his elder sons, by Bagoas. He was succeeded by ARSES.

Artaxias or Artaxes (C2 BC) A king of Armenia, who had been a general in the army of ANTIOCHUS (3) III, and was the founder of the post-Seleucid kingdom of Armenia. After the battle of Magnesia in 189, with the support of the Armenians, he threw off Seleucid rule and established himself as king of Greater Armenia. Around 165 he was defeated and captured by ANTIOCHUS (4) IV.

Artemidorus (C2 BC) A writer on geography from Ephesus who travelled in the western Mediterranean area and Spain, and worked in Alexandria, producing eleven volumes on geography which are lost, but often quoted in surviving works. Besides his own researches, he used those of AGATHARCHIDES, the writers on ALEXANDER (3) the Great and MEGASTHENES. He was used as a source by STRABO.

Artemisia 1. (early C5 BC) A queen of Halicarnassus (now Bodrum). She acted as satrap for the Persian king, and her province extended to Cos, Nisyrus and Calymnos. In XERXES' invasion of Greece in 480, at the battle of Salamis, in her effort to escape the rams of the Greek ships, she rammed with her own ship and sank a Calyndian ship under her command. Xerxes, not understanding the situation, congratulated her. After the battle she persuaded Xerxes to flee and took some of his kinsmen back to Asia Minor.

2. (ruled 353–350 BC) A queen/satrap of Caria under loose Persian overlordship. She succeeded her husband and brother, MAUSOLUS, as sole ruler after ruling jointly with him. She commissioned the construction of the Mausoleum at Halicarnassus to be his tomb and memorial, but did not live to see it finished. She promoted the arts and ran a rhetorical competition in which THEOPOMPUS won the prize. She extended her province by the capture of Rhodes in 350, the year of her death. She was succeeded by her sister, ADA.

Asclepiades (early C3 BC) An epigrammatist from Samos who was also known as *Sicelidas*, 'the Sicilian'. He was the first and greatest Alexandrian writer of love epigrams and short convivial poems, and much of his verse survives in the *Greek Anthology*. Jointly with his friends, HEDYLUS and POSIDIPPUS (2), who wrote in similar vein, he published a collection called *Soros* ('The Heap'). He was attacked

by CALLIMACHUS (3), but won the friendship of THEOCRITUS. He gave his name to
the Asclepiad metres of prosody, which he
revived from ALCAEUS and SAPPHO.

Asclepiodotus (C1 BC) A Greek writer on
military tactics. His work, which is extant, is highly mathematical and is probably derived from POSIDONIUS.

Aspasia (C5 BC) The mistress or 'partner'
of PERICLES during the years of his political power. She was born in Miletus, the
daughter of Axiochus, and came to
Athens probably to pursue the career of a
courtesan. After Pericles and his wife
parted, around 440, she lived with him
and they had a son, illegitimate at first by
a decree proposed by Pericles himself
because of his mother's non-citizenship,
but later legitimised by decree after his
sons by his wife had died in the great
plague. He took his father's name and
later became a general. When Pericles
died in 429, she lived with Lysicles, a
cattle-dealer and politician who was killed
the following year. We do not know when
she died.

She was a woman of great intellect who
conversed with SOCRATES, as well as being
an accomplished teacher of public speaking. She acted as the hostess of Pericles'
household when he entertained his
friends, which roused indignation among
his enemies. The comic writer, HERMIPPUS
(1), prosecuted her in 431 for immorality
and impiety. Pericles, who was the real
object of the attack, defended her vigorously and won the case. See ARISTOPHANES'
Acharnians, 515f., PLATO's *Menexenus*
and PLUTARCH's *Life of Pericles*.

Astydamas 1. (C4 BC) An Athenian playwright, son of Morsimus who was AES-
CHYLUS' great nephew. He produced his
first play in 398. See also ASTYDAMAS (2).

2. (C4 BC) An Athenian playwright, son
of ASTYDAMAS (1), and famous for his
conceit. He may have been a pupil in

rhetoric of ISOCRATES before turning to
the career of his father. He (or his father)
won his first victory for drama in 372,
and he won further victories in the 340s.
The Athenians put up a statue to him in
the Theatre of Dionysus for his play
Parthenopaeus. He also wrote a *Hector*,
an *Alcmaeon*, *Achilles*, *Acamas* and *Antigone*. Only a few lines by either father or
son survive.

Athenaeus (late C2 AD) A writer from
Egypt who was born at Naucratis in the
Nile Delta and wrote only one known
work, the *Deipnosophistai* ('Scholars at
Dinner'), of which half (namely fifteen
books) survives. It appears to have been
completed after the death of the Roman
emperor Commodus in AD 192. It contains a wealth of quotations from all
branches of Greek literature, especially
Comedy; the guests at the symposium,
which is the dramatic scene of the work,
represent all manner of scientific and
literary specialisms, and are often ana-
chronistic or fictional. Athenaeus was a
great collector of interesting extracts, and
his quotations and other information
about classical writers are invaluable.
He lived first at Alexandria and moved
later to Rome. We do not know when
he died. See *Athenaeus*, trans. C.B. Gulick
(1927–41), 7 vols Loeb Classical Library,
Cambridge, MA: Harvard University
Press.

Athenagoras (C6 BC) A tyrant of Ephesus
while it was under Persian domination.

Athenodorus (late C5 BC) A sculptor who
made the statues of Zeus and Apollo,
which were dedicated by the Spartans at
Delphi in thanksgiving for their naval
victory at Aegospotami in 405.

Attalus The name of three kings of
Pergamon.

1. I Soter (269–197 BC) The founder of
the kingdom and the son of Attalus who

was a cousin of EUMENES (2) I. In 241 he succeeded his cousin as ruler and stopped the policy of conciliating his Galatian neighbours by payment of tribute. Consequently, he was faced with war against them. He defeated them thoroughly (c.231) for which he earned the title Soter, 'Saviour', and a monument which was surmounted with the well-known statue of the Dying Gaul. He also attacked ANTIOCHUS (14) the Hawk, who had seceded from the kingdom of his brother, SELEUCUS (2) II, and by 228 drove him out of Asia Minor, except Cilicia. However, he lost most of what he had acquired to the prowess of ACHAEUS, a general of ANTIOCHUS (3) III. He co-operated with Rome in her wars against the Macedonians, himself supporting the Aetolians who were trying to break away from PHILIP (3) V. In the Second Macedonian War of 201–197, he and the Rhodians joined forces with the Romans, who finally put an end to Philip's expansionist ambitions. He died just before the final victory of Cynoscephalae in 197.

Besides being an able general and diplomat, Attalus made his small kingdom an important power in Asia Minor and beyond. He was a great patron of the arts and philosophy. He was succeeded by his son, EUMENES (3) II.

2. II 'Philadelphus' (220–138 BC) The second son of ATTALUS (1) I who suc-

ceeded his brother, EUMENES II, in 159 as king of Pergamon. He was an able general and diplomat who outshone his brother to whom, however, he remained loyal. When he became king, he maintained the policy of supporting Rome, and caused trouble to Syria by his support of ALEXANDER (10) Balas as pretender to its throne in 150 BC. He won the support of Rome for his two wars against Bithynia. At Athens he beautified the market-place by building the Stoa which bears his name. He was nicknamed Philadelphus for his loyalty to Eumenes.

3. III (c.170–133 BC) The son of EUMENES (3) II and nephew of ATTALUS (2) II, he succeeded his uncle as king in 138. He only reigned for five years. By his will he bequeathed the kingdom to the Roman Senate, having no child of his own. His death led to the insurrection of ARISTONICUS (2).

Autolycus of Pitane (C4 BC) An astronomer and mathematician. Two of his works survive, *On the Moving Sphere* and *On Risings and Settings*. The former, the earliest extant Greek mathematical treatise, which deals with the poles and chief circles of the sphere, was used by EUCLID in his *Phaenomena*; the latter deals with the movements and periods of the stars.

B

Bacchiads The royal family of Corinth in the period before the tyranny of CYPSELUS (c.657). They claimed descent from Heracles and fostered the commercial, military and artistic prosperity of Corinth. There were 200 families related by blood to them who also bore the name, and who intermarried exclusively with each other. Cypselus and his followers drove the whole clan out of Corinth and they scattered as far as Illyria and Etruria.

Bacchylides (early C5 BC) A lyric poet who was born in Iulis on the island of Ceos. He was the son of Midylus and the nephew of SIMONIDES, whom he seems to have followed around, writing for the same patrons. We know some of his works from papyrus discoveries, namely fifteen odes, composed in honour of victors in the games, and six dithyrambs, which were written for performance at Athens in the dramatic festivals and may have been influenced by the development of tragedy. There are also fragments of hymns and other songs. Among the patrons of Bacchylides were ALEXANDER (1) I, king of Macedonia, and HIERON (1) I, tyrant of Syracuse. He appears to have been a rival to PINDAR at Hieron's court and to have incurred hostile references by Pindar in a couple of his odes, where he compares himself to an eagle and Bacchylides to a crow. Several of their compositions celebrate the same events. PLUTARCH states that he was exiled to the Peloponnese in later life, during which time he may have written an ode for the Spartans. He makes an interesting contrast to his contemporary, Pindar, with whom he shares an equal claim to being considered a brilliant poet and master of the lyric form and language, even though we have so much less of his work.

Bagoas (C4 BC) A eunuch minister of ARTAXERXES (3) III of Persia and his successor, ARSES, both of whom he poisoned. He tried to do the same to DARIUS (3) III, but was detected and killed by him.

Barsine 1. (C4 BC) A daughter of ARTABAZUS who married her uncle MENTOR of Rhodes, and, after his death, his younger brother MEMNON.

2. The elder daughter of DARIUS (3) III of Persia whom ALEXANDER (3) III the Great married in 324 BC. She was killed after his death to appease ROXANE.

Berenice 1. I (c.340–c.275 BC) A queen of Egypt, the daughter of Lagus, who was born in Macedonia c.340 and married Philippus, to whom she bore MAGAS, governor and later king of Cyrene, and Antigone, who married PYRRHUS of Epirus. She was a widow when she accompanied to Alexandria her aunt, Eurydice, who was to marry Berenice's half-brother, PTOLEMY (1) I, satrap and later king of Egypt. She eventually became her half-brother's mistress and then wife. She was immensely influential at his court and bore him ARSINOË (2) II and PTOLEMY (2) II Philadelphus.

2. (c.280–c.246 BC) surnamed Syra (The Syrian) because she married ANTIOCHUS (2) II. She was the daughter of PTOLEMY (2) II and ARSINOË (3) I. In 252, after the second Syrian War, she married Antiochus, who repudiated his wife, LAODICE (1), and disinherited her children. After Antiochus died in 246, Laodice attacked Berenice and her son, and put them to death to promote the succession of her own son SELEUCUS (2) II.

3. II (c.273–221 BC) A queen of Egypt, born in Cyrene, the daughter of MAGAS, king of Cyrene, and Apama, who was ANTIOCHUS (1) I's daughter. Though she was engaged to PTOLEMY (3) III, after her father's death in 253 her mother tried to marry her to the Macedonian, DEMETRIUS (4) the Fair, who had seized Cyrene for Macedonia. At this Berenice led an insurrection that succeeded and killed Demetrius. She married Ptolemy on his accession in 246 and bore him a son and heir. When her husband led an expeditionary force against Syria, she dedicated a lock of her hair to Aphrodite for his safe return. The poet CALLIMACHUS (3) wrote an elegy pretending that it had been received into the sky as a constellation, *Coma Berenices*. After the death of her husband in 221, her son recognised her as his co-regent, but shortly afterwards murdered her.

4. (died 55 BC) A daughter of PTOLEMY (12) XII the Piper, the eldest sister of the famous CLEOPATRA (5) VII, she was made queen in 58 when the people of Alexandria drove her father out. She married ARCHELAUS (4), but was put to death with her husband when Gabinius restored Ptolemy.

Berosus (early C3 BC) A priest of Bel at Babylon who wrote a history of Babylon in Greek in three books, which he dedicated to king ANTIOCHUS (1) I. Only fragments survive. The first book covered time down to the Flood, the second from then to 747, and the third to ALEXANDER (3) III the Great. Thus, much information about Babylonian history, as well as astronomy, was conveyed to the Greeks.

Bessus (C4 BC) A satrap of Bactria in central Asia in the Persian empire under DARIUS (3) III. After the battle of Gaugamela in 331, when Darius fled to the eastern provinces of his empire, his followers deposed him in favour of Bessus. In 330, as ALEXANDER (3) III the Great approached, Bessus had Darius stabbed to death. Bessus then fled to Bactria and proclaimed himself its king, but the next year two of his companions betrayed him to Alexander, who put him to death.

Bias (C6 BC) A politician of Priene in Ionia, the son of Teutamus, Bias was considered one of the SEVEN SAGES of Greece for his excellent advice to his fellow citizens to abandon their city at the time of the Persian conquest and migrate to Sardinia, which they failed to take.

Bion 1. of Borysthenes (c.325–c.255 BC) A teacher of philosophy of very humble origins in Olbia on the northern shore of the Black Sea. He was sold into slavery because of a fraud on the part of his father, but he received a good education from his master, a teacher of rhetoric, who set him free and made him his heir. Bion went to Athens where he studied under THEOPHRASTUS and in the Academy. He was influenced greatly by CRATES (2) and THEODORUS (1). He became a wandering lecturer in philosophy, frequenting the court of ANTIGONUS (2) II Gonatas and living on Rhodes. His teaching included Cynic and Cyrenaic elements, both the unconventionality of the former and the adaptable approach to life of the latter. He died at Chalcis in Euboea. Only fragments of his diatribes survive, but his influence on later satirists was considerable and his acid wit is alluded to by Horace (*Ep.*, II 2. 60). See R. Dudley (1937) *A History of Cynicism*, London: Methuen.

2. (*fl.* *c.*100 BC) A bucolic poet of the Hellenistic period who was born at Phlossa near Smyrna. He wrote erotic and sentimental poetry, in a simple language and style, of which only fragments survive. In spite of his traditional classification with THEOCRITUS, the pastoral element in his work is slight. The fine *Lament for Adonis* has also been attributed to him since the Renaissance on the evidence of the *Lament for Bion*, composed by a disciple, which suggests that he lived in Sicily. See also MOSCHUS.

Biton 1. *See* CLEOBIS.

2. A Hellenistic writer on technical subjects. He left a short surviving treatise on siege-engines and a lost work on optics.

Boethus 1. (C2 BC) A sculptor from Chalcedon. Three of his works are known, including a statue of ANTIOCHUS (4) IV on Delos and a bronze herm.

2. (C2 BC) A Hellenistic Stoic philosopher from Sidon. He studied under DIOGENES (3) of Babylon and applied principles of dualism to the Stoic beliefs, in psychology distinguishing between the rational and the irrational, in physics between the divine heavens and the rest which is profane, and the origin of the soul in fire and air. His interest in astronomy and weather is shown by his commentary on the works of ARATUS (1).

3. (late C1 BC) A Peripatetic philosopher from Sidon. He was a pupil of ANDRONICUS of Rhodes and may have headed the Lyceum after his death. He wrote commentaries on ARISTOTLE's works, now lost.

Bolus (C3 BC) A writer from Mendes in Egypt of whose work, *Sympathies and Antipathies*, fragments survive. His interest was in drugs, and one fragment shows the differentiation of natural and artificial materials used in their composition. His work was sometimes attributed to DEMOCRITUS. He also had an interest in the unexpected, and on that subject wrote a lost work, *Marvels*.

Brasidas (died 422 BC) A Spartan general of the Peloponnesian War and the son of Tellis. In 431, the first year of the War, he distinguished himself by the relief of Methone in Messenia. In 429 he commanded a ship in an engagement that was won by the Athenian admiral PHORMION (1), and in 428 he was a leader of an abortive attempt on the Piraeus. In 425 at Pylos he was captain of a ship, but sustained a wound and lost his shield to the enemy. In 424 he was raising troops near Corinth when he learnt of an Athenian attack on Megara, and by prompt action he saved Megara from Athenian occupation. Later in the summer, he was sent north with a small force of freed helots and other hoplites, and liberated many towns in Thessaly and beyond from Athenian rule, including Torone and Amphipolis. The whole Thracian coastal area was deserting Athens under Brasidas' determined pressure and moderate dealing. THUCYDIDES (2), the historian, who as general in charge of the nearest Athenian fleet failed to prevent the loss of Amphipolis, was exiled. After the armistice of 423, Brasidas continued his activities by supporting the rebellions of Scione and Mende. In 422 he won a brilliant victory over CLEON, who had been sent by Athens to recover Amphipolis, but himself received a fatal wound. He was buried at Amphipolis and was afterwards honoured there as a founder and hero. The deaths of Cleon and Brasidas brought the Archidamian War to an end. Thucydides ranks him above all other Spartan commanders (see his *History*, Books 2–5).

Bryaxis (died 312 BC) A sculptor and a member of the school of Scopas who adorned the Mausoleum of Halicarnassus. There is a signed base of an equestrian statue by him at Athens.

Brygus An Athenian potter who flourished around 500 BC. His best artist, the Brygus painter, is identified by nine red-figure vessels.

C

Calamis (early C5 BC) A sculptor, probably from Boeotia, who made fine statues of horses. PAUSANIAS (3) reports several of his masterpieces: a Zeus Ammon made for PINDAR and a Hermes for Tanagra. Pliny the Elder reports a colossal bronze Apollo for Apollonia on the Black Sea. LUCIAN admired a *Sosandra*, which may have been a model for statues of Aspasia of which Roman copies exist. Pausanias writes of a statue of Apollo the Protector from Evil, which stood in the Ceramicus at Athens.

Callias 1. (C5 BC) An Athenian statesman, the son of Hipponicus and a member of the Ceryces ('Heralds') family of hereditary torch-bearers at the Eleusinian mysteries. He was very rich and related to ARISTIDES (1). He married Elpinice, sister of CIMON. He fought as a very young man in the battle of Marathon in 490 and forty years later (*c.*448) negotiated the Peace of Callias in Cyprus with Persia, of which THEOPOMPUS (3) denied the existence. He may have been an ambassador to Sparta in 446 when the Thirty Years Peace was agreed. HERODOTUS reports that he went with a mission to the court of ARTAXERXES (1) I at Susa, but gives no date. He is said to have thrice won the chariot-race at the Olympic Games. He left a son, HIPPONICUS, who was a general in the Peloponnesian War.

2. (born *c.*450 BC) Grandson of CALLIAS (1). He was notorious as a spendthrift and a profligate for which ARISTOPHANES (1) ridiculed him in *Frogs* and *Birds*. The dramatic scene of PLATO (1)'s *Protagoras* and XENOPHON (1)'s *Symposium* are laid at his house. In 415 he prosecuted ANDOCIDES (1) for sacrilege. He was elected general (*c.*391) and with IPHICRATES led the Athenian light infantry near Corinth, which annihilated a Spartan brigade of hoplites. He took part in an embassy to Sparta (*c.*371) and successfully negotiated a peace treaty.

3. (mid-C5 BC) An Athenian writer of comedies who won first prize at the City Dionysia in 446.

4. An Athenian from the deme of Sphettus who (*c.*290 BC) was exiled from his native city and took refuge in Egypt. He returned to Athens under the auspices of PTOLEMY (1) I with mercenary troops from Egypt in 287 after the overthrow of DEMETRIUS (3) I the Besieger, and helped his brother PHAEDRUS (2) to resist a Macedonian siege. He was later honoured by the Athenians for his services. See T.L. Shear (1978), *Kallias of Sphettos and the Revolt of Athens in 286 BC*, Princeton, NJ: American School of Classical Studies at Athens.

Callicrates 1. (C5 BC) An Athenian architect who was responsible for the sanctuary of Victory (*Nike*) and the central wall of the Acropolis. He was associated with ICTINUS in the designing of the Parthenon.

2. (died *c*.148 BC) An Achaean statesman from Leontium in the northern Peloponnese. After the death of PHILOPOEMEN (182), he declared his absolute support for Rome, and, as general of the Achaean Confederacy a couple of years later, he recalled Spartan exiles and gave Sparta her local autonomy back. The Romans supported his rule after the close of the Third Macedonian War, despite his unpopularity with the Achaeans, until his death. POLYBIUS, whose father LYCORTAS Callicrates had opposed, was extremely hostile to him in his *History*.

Callicratidas A Spartan admiral who succeeded LYSANDER in 406 BC as commander of the fleet operating in the Aegean. He blockaded CONON at Mytilene, but after attacking a superior force off the Arginusae Islands was defeated by the Athenians and drowned.

Callimachus 1. The Athenian polemarch (general-in-chief) at the battle of Marathon in 490 BC. When MILTIADES, the exiled ruler of the Chersonese, advised him to meet the Persian expeditionary force in battle, he agreed, and played a heroic part in the action, in which he was killed. His bravery was commemorated in the Painted Porch in the Athenian marketplace and in two epigrams.

2. (late C5 BC) A sculptor who is said to have invented the Corinthian capital. PAUSANIAS (3) writes that he made a golden lampstand for the Erechtheion temple on the Acropolis and a seated statue of Hera for Plataea. Pliny the Elder considered that he spoilt his work by excess of detail. He was the first sculptor to use the running drill.

3. (*c*.305–*c*.240 BC) A poet and literary critic from Cyrene. He moved to Alexandria and became a schoolmaster in the

suburb of Eleusis. He was later appointed to a post of cataloguer in the library of the Museum, which he held from *c*.260 until his death. During this time, he made a *catalogue raisonné* of the library in 120 volumes. Among his pupils were ERATOSTHENES, ARISTOPHANES (2) of Byzantium, and APOLLONIUS (1) of Rhodes with the last of whom he quarrelled violently over the stylistics of poetry: his slogan was 'a big book, a big evil'. In response to Apollonius' epic, the *Argonautica*, he and his allies championed the smaller, well-wrought poem and treasured learning and allusive references in composition. He was extremely popular during and after his lifetime, as is shown by the vast number of papyri his works that have been discovered in Egypt. Many of his works are lost, though the extant *oeuvre* has increased considerably in the twentieth century because of papyrus finds.

His chief work was the *Causes* (*Aetia*), a series of poems in four books containing legends that explain the causes and origins of various rituals. This collection ended with a poem, *The Lock of Hair* (*Plokamos*), on the lost lock of Queen BERENICE (3) II, which Catullus translated into Latin, placed before the epilogue with its tribute to HESIOD as the forerunner of the Callimachean school. He also wrote a volume of iambic poetry, which seems to have had a satirical tone, and, like the *Causes*, must have influenced Roman satirists. Another development was that of the epyllion, or episode taken from epic and transformed into a miniature narrative, often with a single focus and rich description. Such was the *Hecale*, which was taken from the myth of Theseus. He also wrote *Hymns*, in style rather like the *Homeric Hymns*, and sixty-three *Epigrams*, which survived in anthologies. Nothing remains of his dramatic pieces, which are mentioned in the *Suda*. His prose writing was also extensive, including encyclopaedias on a wide variety of subjects, such as winds, nymphs, games, birds; commentaries; a study of the works of the philosopher DEMOCRITUS, and a chronological register of dramatic writers. He was a prolific writer on an immense variety of subjects and was very learned, though he did not allow this quality to destroy the life of his poems. He was greatly admired and a great influence upon later poets, such as MELEAGER and, in particular, the Romans, Catullus and the neoterics and Propertius and the elegists. See C.A. Trypanis' (1958) Loeb edition of his poems, Loeb Classical Library, Cambridge, MA: Harvard University Press; T.B.L. Webster (1964) *Hellenistic Poetry and Art*, London: Methuen; G.O. Hutchinson (1990) *Hellenistic Poetry*, Oxford: Clarendon Press.

Callinus (C7 BC) An elegiac poet from Ephesus of whose work some fragments have survived. The longest fragment is a rallying cry for the defence of the native land. He lived at a time when Asia Minor was invaded by Cimmerians and others from the north. He also mentions the fall of Magnesia to the Ephesians. His contemporary, the Spartan TYRTAEUS, may be compared with him.

Callippus (*c.*370–*c.*300 BC) An astronomer and mathematician from Cyzicus who migrated to Athens with Polemarchus, where he joined ARISTOTLE and worked to improve EUDOXUS' theory of concentric spheres to account for the movements of the heavenly bodies. He proposed two additional spheres each for the sun and the moon and one more for each for the planets. He also proposed a length of 365 and a quarter days for the year and consequently a cycle of 76 years, beginning in 330, to replace METON's cycle of 19 years.

Callisthenes 1. (*c.*360–327 BC) A historian of ALEXANDER (3) III the Great and a nephew of Aristotle. He was born at Olynthus and later accompanied Alexander on his campaign in Asia as the official historian. He wrote an account which

extolled Alexander as a champion of Greek culture, even describing him as a son of Zeus. However, he fell foul of Alexander over the issue of prostration, which he refused to perform, and was accused of complicity in the plot formed by the page HERMOLAUS. He was thrown into prison where he died. His works have not survived.

'Callisthenes' 2. A novel, *The Alexander Romance*, based imaginatively on the life of ALEXANDER (3) III the Great, was attributed to CALLISTHENES (1), but is certainly not his work. Its sources were material circulating after Alexander's death, including a history derived from the work of Clitarchus. It was written some time between AD 140–340, and, for all its mediocrity of style and structure, was highly successful, being translated into Latin and oriental languages. See B.P. Reardon (ed.) (*c.*1989) *Collected Ancient Greek Novels*, Berkeley, CA; London: University of California Press.

Callistratus 1. The producer of the three earliest of the plays of ARISTOPHANES (1).

2. (died 355 BC) An Athenian general and orator from Aphidna. He began his career by prosecuting the ambassadors who proposed peace with Sparta in 392. He was elected general in 378 and took the lead in creating the Second Athenian League: he organised its finances and drafted its constitution along lines that recognised the equality of its members, in contrast with the earlier Delian League of the fifth century. He opposed TIMOTHEUS (2) and in company with IPHICRATES prosecuted him unsuccessfully in 373. When Timotheus abandoned his naval command because of lack of funds and Iphicrates took over, he was among those who persuaded the Assembly to impose taxes on the rich to pursue the war against Sparta. He was a general in 372 when Athens took on Sparta and the League split, Thebes and JASON of Pherae going their own ways. Callistratus persuaded the Assembly to make peace with Sparta, and a conference was held at Sparta in 371 in which Persia also took part: the result was the King's Peace. After the battle of Leuctra, Thebes posed the chief threat, and in 369 Iphicrates was sent with a force to assist Sparta. Thebes, however, was victorious and Sparta's power was destroyed. In 366 Callistratus was impeached by Leodamas for treason and only saved himself by his rhetorical powers. He had a temporary recovery of influence and negotiated an alliance with Arcadia, but in 361 he was again impeached for having permitted an occupation of Oropus by the Thebans, which they refused to give up. He escaped to Macedonia and was condemned to death in his absence. After assisting King PERDICCAS (1) II to put his finances in order, he rashly returned to Athens in 355 and was put to death, despite sitting as a suppliant at the altar of the twelve gods.

3. (C2 BC) An Alexandrian grammarian and a pupil of ARISTOPHANES (2) of Byzantium. Like his master, he edited HOMER and wrote a miscellany, which ATHENAEUS quotes. He was hostile to ARISTARCHUS (3) for disloyalty to the teachings of their common master. A few fragments of his commentaries survive.

Cambyses (reigned 530–522 BC) A king of Persia, the son of CYRUS (1) the Great. In 525 he conquered Egypt with the help of POLYCRATES (1) of Samos and Greek mercenaries. He also marched on a fruitless expedition against Ethiopia and failed in an attempt to take the Oasis of Siwa, losing his army in the desert. In 522 a rebel magus, named Gaumata, impersonated his brother Smerdis, whom Cambyses had murdered in 525, and Cambyses died in Syria while returning from Egypt to suppress the rebellion. According to HERODOTUS (3.29ff.), he married two of his sisters and killed one of them. He is depicted by Herodotus as a cruel and irrational tyrant who revealed his murder of Smerdis to the Persians before dying of an accidental wound.

Candaules *see* Gyges.

Carcinus 1. (C5 BC) An Athenian tragic poet whom ARISTOPHANES (1) ridiculed in his *Peace* and *Wasps*. He may be the same person as the general mentioned by THUCYDIDES (2) in his *History*, 2. 23.

2. A grandson of CARCINUS (1) who was a tragic poet. He is said by the *Suda* to have written 160 plays and, according to an inscription, to have won eleven first prizes. ARISTOTLE makes several references to him and PLUTARCH praises his *Aerope*. He spent time at Syracuse at the court of the younger DIONYSIUS (2) II.

Carneades (214–129 BC) A philosopher from Cyrene who studied at the Academy in Athens under Hegesinus. He replaced his master as head of the Academy some time before 155, when the Athenians sent him on an embassy to Rome to protest against a fine imposed on Athens for trespassing on the territory of Oropus. His companions were the Stoic DIOGENES (3) of Babylon and the Peripatetic CRITOLAUS. In Rome he delivered two speeches on successive days: the first advocating the pursuit of justice and the second advocating unjust behaviour, which made a deep impression on the Romans. Cato the Elder had him expelled from the city. In 137 he resigned his post at the Academy and was succeeded by a namesake. Though he published nothing, his views long remained influential, and were handed down by his pupil, CLITOMACHUS.

He was regarded as the founder of the third or New Academy in place of the Middle Academy of ARCESILAUS. He took a yet more sceptical line than his predecessors, arguing that certainty is impossible and that we cannot distinguish between the true and the false in what our senses present to us. We have to weigh up the probability of truth or falsehood in making decisions on the 'persuasiveness' of the perceptions we receive. Cicero in his treatises on *Divination* and *The Nature of Gods* availed himself of many of Carneades' arguments against belief in gods, prophecies and fate.

Cassander (*c*.358–297 BC) A king of Macedonia and the son of ANTIPATER (1). In 324 he joined ALEXANDER (3) III the Great at Babylon. He is said to have been on bad terms with Alexander, and it is ironic that he should have ultimately emerged as his successor. In 319 his father, when dying, appointed POLYPERCHON to be his successor as regent and Cassander to be his deputy. Cassander soon drove Polyperchon out of Greece (see EURYDICE) and allied himself with PTOLEMY (1) I of Egypt. He fought against OLYMPIAS, the mother of Alexander who had murdered PHILIP (2) III Arrhidaeus and Eurydice (half-brother and sister-in-law of Alexander), and put her to death in 316. In the same year he got possession of ROXANE and ALEXANDER (6) IV at the siege of Pydna. In 311 a treaty with his allies, PTOLEMY (1) I, SELEUCUS (1) I and LYSIMACHUS, recognised him as regent during the minority of Alexander IV. The next year he murdered Alexander and his mother Roxane to prevent ANTIGONUS (1) I from using them to further his ambition of reuniting Alexander's empire under himself. Together with his allies, he finally defeated Antigonus at Ipsus in 301. He was then recognised as king of Macedonia and spent the last four years of his life in consolidating his monarchy. He was married to Thessalonice, a daughter of PHILIP (1) II, after whom he named the city that he founded. He also founded Cassandreia in Chalcidice and rebuilt Thebes, which Alexander had destroyed. He left sons who did not succeed him. In effect, his heir was his enemy DEMETRIUS (3) I the Besieger.

Castor of Rhodes (C1 BC) A historian who published parallel tables of historical and mythical events and personages from early Middle Eastern times down to his own, and was used as a source by Varro and Eusebius.

Cebes (C5/4 BC) A Theban friend of SOCRATES and an associate of SIMMIAS (1), previously a pupil of the Pythagorean philosopher PHILOLAUS. He figures in dialogues of PLATO (1), the *Phaedo* and the *Crito*, in the latter of which he shows willingness to help Socrates bribe his way out of prison. From the evidence of Plato's thirteenth letter, he was still alive in 366.

Cephisodotus (C4 BC) The name of the father and of the son of the sculptor PRAXITELES, who were also sculptors. Nothing is known for certain about the work of the elder, though he is said to have executed a number of statues for the city of Megalopolis, founded in 370. The younger Cephisodotus made sculptures of LYCURGUS (3), probably in 323 after his death, of MENANDER (1) in 291 after the latter's death, and which was placed in the Theatre of Dionysus, of statues for the altar of the precinct of Asclepius at Cos, of Anyte, of the *Entwining*, an erotic group in Pergamon, and of Leto, later placed on the Palatine at Rome.

Ceraunus *see* Ptolemy (16).

Cercidas of Megalopolis (*c*.290–*c*.220 BC) A Greek politician and poet, as well as an opponent of Lydiadas, tyrant of Megalopolis. When the latter fell from power in 235, Cercidas performed the service of lawgiver to his city. He became a friend of ARATUS (2) of Sicyon, the leader of the Achaean League, and acted as his envoy to ANTIGONUS (3) III Doson to ask for support against CLEOMENES (2) III of Sparta. He led a contingent of a thousand troops from his city in 222 at the ensuing battle of Sellasia. He achieved fame as a poet and Cynic philosopher: some fragments of his poetry (the *Meliambi*) survive, in which it is possible to see him as a social critic and satirist. He praises DIOGENES, the founder of the school, and shows the influence of BION (1) the Borysthenite. His posture as both jester and serious thinker may be derived from CRATES (2) of Thebes.

Cersobleptes (reigned 359–342 BC) The last independent king of the Thracian Odrysians. He was the son of COTYS and inherited a troubled kingdom after his father's murder, with two rival claimants to the throne to face as well as a war with Athens. The Euboean mercenary leader CHARIDEMUS, however, married his sister and became his adviser. Together they negotiated a treaty with the Athenian general CEPHISODOTUS which the Athenian Assembly refused to ratify. Athens took the part of Cersobleptes' rivals, and together in 358 they forced a division of the kingdom and the cession of the Chersonese to Athens. Cersobleptes repudiated this treaty in his turn, though the next year the Athenians, led by CHARES, enforced it. Cersobleptes now ruled a diminished kingdom in eastern Thrace. In 353 Chares recaptured Sestos and forced Cersobleptes into an alliance and giving up all the peninsula, except for Cardia. Then, with the help of Pammenes of Boeotia, Cersobleptes made an agreement with PHILIP (1) II of Macedonia and hoped to expel the Athenians from the Chersonese, but in vain. In 352, now allied with Athens, he was at war with his rival, Amadocus, and the cities of Perinthus and Byzantium. Philip intervened on their side when they were besieging Hera's Fort and forced Cersobleptes to capitulate. He gave Philip his son as a hostage. Athens remained the protector of Cersobleptes until 346 when Philip again attacked him, and Athens, on the proposal of DEMOSTHENES (2), abandoned him. He was finally subjugated by Philip, and his kingdom was annexed to Macedonia.

Chabrias (*c*.420–357 BC) An Athenian general and mercenary who served Athens as a general at least thirteen times, as well as hiring himself out to other states. In 388 he was allowed by the Athenian government to hire himself with a small amphibious force to EVAGORAS, king of Cyprus, for his war against Persia. In 378 he was one of the commanders sent to help Thebes against the Spartan king AGESILAUS II, and invented a successful method of defence against an advance by hoplites. In 376 he won a decisive naval victory over Sparta off Naxos, and after 370 he was engaged in the Peloponnese. In 366 he and CALLISTRATUS (2) were prosecuted by Leodamas for treason and had a narrow escape. Chabrias spent much time thereafter in service with the kings of Cyprus and Egypt against the Persians. Like Callistratus, he recovered power briefly before the battle of Mantinea in 362, but then in 361 went to Egypt where he served as a mercenary under Agesilaus. He again served his city in the Hellespontine area during the Social War, which broke out in 357, but was killed later in the year when he was commanding an Athenian fleet that was defeated by disaffected allies off Chios.

Chaeremon (mid-C4 BC) A writer of tragedies of whose works a few lines survive. ARISTOTLE calls his play, *The Centaur*, a 'rhapsody' and suggests that it was more appropriate for reading than for acting. Some lines from his *Oeneus* reveal his descriptive powers.

Chaerephon A friend of SOCRATES and a demesman of Sphettus. He consulted the Delphic Oracle about his friend and received the response that no man was wiser than Socrates. He was exiled by the THIRTY TYRANTS of Athens, but returned in 403. He died before Socrates' trial in 339. The *Apology of Socrates* by PLATO (1) reports that Socrates referred to him and the Delphic response in his trial.

Chares 1. (c.400–c.324 BC) An Athenian general who was notorious for his harsh treatment of Athens' allies. In 366 he was instructed by the Assembly to seize Corinth, an ally, and impose a democratic constitution, but he failed. He made (c.360) a disastrous intervention in Corcyra, which left the Athenian alliance as a result. In 357 he obtained sole command by denouncing his colleagues, IPHICRATES and TIMOTHEUS (2), to the Assembly. He then led an Athenian mercenary force by sea from Euboea to the Thracian Chersonese and so instigated the Social War between Athens and her allies. He blockaded Chios, but suffered a defeat in which CHABRIAS was killed. He then made war on Byzantium and other rebellious allies and remained in the Chersonese with sixty ships. In autumn 356 he was defeated at Embata in Chios. Athens was defeated, but tried to extricate herself from her difficulties by using Persia, and in 355 Chares hired the services of his mercenaries to ARTABAZUS and was thus able to pay them. He won a great victory over a Persian army (he called it the 'sister of Marathon'), but further Athenian attempts to check Persia were unsuccessful and Athens withdrew from Asia and brought the Social War to an end on unfavourable terms. In 352 Chares was again active in the northern Aegean and recovered Sestos with great cruelty to its inhabitants, defeating CERSOBLEPTES and forcing him out of the Chersonese, except for Cardia.

In 349, during the Sacred War against PHILIP (1) II, king of Macedonia, the Assembly sent Chares to Olynthus to the aid of the Chalcidian League with a fleet and mercenaries, but the situation deteriorated and in 348 Philip took Olynthus, which Athens could not reinforce. In 340 Philip renewed hostilities with Athens. Chares was ordered to relieve Byzantium, but the Byzantines did not trust him and rejected his help, allowing PHOCION to assist them instead. In November 339, Chares commanded an Athenian force of 10,000 mercenaries in Boeotia when Philip was threatening to invade the country. This force was destroyed in summer 338 when Philip seized Amphissa. Chares commanded Athenian infantry at the ensuing battle of Chaeronea, but kept away from Athens after the defeat. He was demanded as a hostage by ALEXANDER (3) III the Great in 335, but fled to Sigeum from where he continued resistance to Macedonian power, commanding a mercenary force at Mytilene in 333 under the pro-Persian MEMNON. He was with mercenaries at their headquarters in Taenarum (c.325), but was dead by 324.

2. (C4 BC) A writer from Mytilene in Lesbos. He served ALEXANDER (3) III the Great as his chamberlain and composed a massive and colourful account of Alexander's doings, which was used as a source by PLUTARCH. His work is lost apart from some extracts in ATHENAEUS.

3. (C3 BC) A Rhodian sculptor from Lindos and a pupil of LYSIPPUS. His principal work was the vast bronze statue of the sun god, Helios, 32 metres high, known as the *Colossus of Rhodes*, which was set up on a hill overlooking the city of Rhodes as a thanks offering in 304 for the deliverance of Rhodes from siege by the Macedonian king DEMETRIUS (3) I the Besieger. The statue, which was paid for by the sale of the siege equipment, collapsed in an earthquake about eighty years after its erection.

Charicles One of the THIRTY TYRANTS at Athens in 404 BC. ARISTOTLE reported him as the chief assailant of THERAMENES.

Charidemus (C4 BC) An Euboean mercenary leader who supported COTYS, king of the Odrysian Thracians, and his son CERSOBLEPTES, marrying a daughter of the former. He arranged a treaty under which Athens regained the Thracian Chersonese, for which he was awarded Athenian citizenship. He was active in the defence of Olynthus in 348 and formed a deep hostility to Macedonia. After the battle of Chaeronea in 338, he was appointed general to organise the defence of Athens, but was quickly replaced with PHOCION. In 335 ALEXANDER (3) III the Great made peace with Athens on condition that Charidemus was exiled. He went to Persia to offer his services, but in 333 King DARIUS (2) II killed him for his insolence.

Chariton (C1 AD) A novelist from Aphrodisias who was the author of the extant romantic novel, *Chaereas and Callirhoe*. He was secretary to a lawyer, Athenagoras, and was the first novelist in any European language whose work has survived complete.

The novel has a historical setting, though Chariton takes liberties with historical fact. It starts in Syracuse in the fourth century BC, though certain characters, such as HERMOCRATES, are drawn from the time of the Athenian expedition in the fifth century. During the course of the romance, both hero and heroine travel far, even to the court of the king of Persia. Chariton adopted a straightforward narrative style, without digressions, based on the style of the historian XENOPHON (1). See B.P. Reardon (ed.) (c.1989) *Collected Ancient Greek Novels*, Berkeley, CA; London: University of California Press.

Charmides A friend of SOCRATES and uncle of PLATO (1). He was the nephew of CRITIAS in whose house he was brought up. One of Plato's dialogues, in which he plays a prominent part, is named after him. XENOPHON (1) (*Mem.* 3.7) reports that Socrates encouraged him to enter politics. He was killed in 403 at the return of the democrats after supporting the regime of the THIRTY TYRANTS of which Critias was the leader.

Charon (C5 BC) A chronicler from Lampsacus whom later authors call the predecessor of HERODOTUS. According to the *Suda*, he was born in the reign of DARIUS

(1) I and wrote chronicles of Ethiopia, Persia, Greece and Crete, as well as of Lampsacus and Sparta, based on the magistracies, and a geographical work on the Atlantic Ocean. There are a few fragments from the Persian and Lampsacene chronicles, although some of the other titles may be false. The loss of his account of THEMISTOCLES' flight to Persia is regrettable.

Charondas (C6 BC) The lawgiver of Catana in Sicily. He legislated for other Chalcidian foundations in Italy and Sicily as well, including Rhegion. We know of him from ARISTOTLE's *Politics* and from DIODORUS (3) Siculus. However, the sources probably contain legendary material and contamination with later legislation.

Chilon (C6 BC) A Spartan ephor, the son of Damagetus, who held office in 556 and was responsible for enhancing the powers of the office so as to set the ephors on a level with the kings (Sparta had a dual monarchy, two kings reigning together). He is considered to have initiated the foreign policy that led to the establishment of the Peloponnesian League. He was regarded as one of the SEVEN SAGES of the Greeks as defined by PLATO (1) and was worshipped as a hero at Sparta.

Chionides (C5 BC) An Athenian comic poet and the first to receive a prize for a comedy, which he won at the City Dionysia festival in 487. The titles of two of his plays are known, *Heroes* and *Beggars*. According to ARISTOTLE (*Poetics*), he was, with Magnes, the earliest Attic comic writer.

Choerilus 1. (late C6 BC) An Athenian writer of tragedies who competed against AESCHYLUS and PRATINAS at the dramatic festivals. According to the *Suda*, he began writing in 523 and composed 150 plays, winning thirteen prizes. None of his plays is extant and only one title is known: the

Alope. He is said to have improved the masks and costumes used in tragic drama.

2. (C5 BC) A Greek epic poet from Samos. His chief work, of which fragments remain, was entitled *The Persian Wars* and included a catalogue of the nations that crossed with XERXES into Europe. The Spartan general LYSANDER befriended him in the hope of being sung in an epic, but in 404 he moved to Macedonia at the invitation of King ARCHELAUS (2).

3. (C4 BC) A Greek epic poet from Iasus in Caria who was paid by ALEXANDER (3) III the Great to accompany his expedition in 334 and celebrate his exploits in Persia. Horace ridiculed him in *Ep.*, 2. 1. 232–4 and in his *Art of Poetry* for his bad verse.

Chremonides (C3 BC) An Athenian politician and pupil of ZENO (2) of Citium. In about 267 he proposed a decree to join Athens to a Peloponnesian alliance led by the Spartan king AREUS and supported by PTOLEMY (2) II to oppose the Macedonians under ANTIGONUS (2) II Gonatas. The war, which was named after him and began in 266, was a disaster for Athens and ended in 263 with her surrender. Chremonides fled to Egypt where he was made admiral by Ptolemy and served in the Second Syrian War against ANTIOCHUS (2) II. He was defeated (*c.*258) by Agathostratus of Rhodes in a sea-battle off Ephesus which he survived by several years.

Chrysippus (*c.*280–207 BC) A Stoic philosopher, the son of Apollonius, from Soli in Cilicia. He studied at Athens at the Academy, where he attended lectures given by ARCESILAUS, but he came under the influence of CLEANTHES, head of the Stoa, who converted him to Stoicism. He succeeded Cleanthes in 232 and was responsible for saving Stoicism from disintegrating into factions. He wrote a large number of books, of which a few fragments survive, in which he expounded and restated the philosophy of ZENO (2)

and responded to attacks made on it by members of the Academy. In fact, he revised the basic tenets of the doctrine, especially in the technical aspects of logic, though it is difficult to identify his distinctive contribution because of the lack of written evidence. We have an incomplete catalogue of his works by DIOGENES (5) Laërtius in the *Lives of the Philosophers*.

Cimon (*c.*510–450 BC) An Athenian statesman and general, a member of the distinguished Philaid family, and the son of MILTIADES the victor of Marathon. His mother was a Thracian princess named Hegesipyle, daughter of King Olorus. He inherited great wealth and after his father's death in 489 he paid the colossal fine of fifty talents, which the Athenians had imposed on him for 'deceiving the people' at the siege of Paros. Like his father he was a passionate opponent of Persia and served as general many times against her in the 470s and 460s. He was a strong friend of Sparta.

He was sent on an embassy to Sparta after the Persian War in 479 and was the assistant of ARISTIDES (1) in winning over the Aegean islanders to supporting the new Delian League to protect its members against further Persian encroachment. In 476 he drove the Spartan general PAUSANIAS (1) out of Byzantium and subsequently captured Eion in Thrace from the Persians. A singular act was his seizure of the island of Scyros from the Dolopians and his settlement of Athenian colonists there. He found on the island a tomb containing bones, which he claimed were those of the mythical king of Athens, Theseus, and he brought them back for reburial in Athens. He now led the aristocratic opposition to THEMISTOCLES. Himself a Philaid married to an Alcmaeonid, Isodice, he had married his sister to the leading member of the Herald family, CALLIAS (1), and his chief rival, Aristides, was soon dead and gone. About 471, Themistocles was exiled from Athens by ostracism, and for a few years Cimon was Athens' most influential leader. His greatest success was the Eurymedon campaign *c.*467 in which he annihilated the Persian fleet on the south coast of Asia Minor. In 465 he founded a settlement of Athenian citizens at Nine Ways on the River Strymon in Thrace. He also liberated the Thracian Chersonese (Gallipoli Peninsula), which his father had ruled, and in 465 undertook the siege of the city of Thasos on the island of that name, which had defected from the Delian League. The settlement in Thrace was destroyed by the Athenian defeat at Drabescus, and the siege of Thasos lasted two years. After successfully completing it, Cimon returned to Athens in 463 to be prosecuted by PERICLES for abuse of power: it was claimed that he had taken a bribe from ALEXANDER (1) I, king of Macedonia, not to attack his kingdom. He was acquitted and the next year (462) took a force of some 4,000 Athenian heavy infantry to Messenia to assist the Spartans in the siege of Ithome after the rebellion that had followed the earthquake of 464. The Assembly authorised this intervention despite the opposition of the popular leader, EPHIALTES (2). The expedition proved a failure because the Athenian soldiers were more favourable to the cause of the Messenians than their masters and the Spartans sent them home. This reversal of Cimon's fortunes was sealed by his ten-year exile by ostracism in 461. In 458 he unsuccessfully appealed to Athens to be permitted to fight for his city in the First Peloponnesian War. There was a tradition that he was recalled on Pericles' proposal a year or two later.

After his return, Cimon was relatively inactive, though a focus of opposition to Pericles' democratic reforms. He was popular for his generosity and patriotism, and offered a less drastic approach to enforcing the loyalty of the empire than Pericles. In 451 he negotiated a five-year truce with Sparta and was appointed general in command of an expeditionary force against Persia in the eastern Mediterranean. He won a great naval victory, but died of a wound in Cyprus in the following winter. With him died the anti-Persian and pro-Spartan policy, and his political successor, THUCYDIDES (1), was unable to withstand the reputation and power of Pericles. He was protector (*proxenos*) of Spartan and Thessalian visitors to Athens, and named two of sons after these states, Lacedaemonius and Thessalus, besides one with the Ionian name Ulios. See THUCYDIDES (2), *History*, 1. 98–102; PLUTARCH, *Life of Cimon*; E. Badian (1992) *From Plataea to Potidaea*, Baltimore, MD; London: Johns Hopkins University Press; W.R. Connor (1968) *Theopompus and Fifth-Century Athens*, Washington, DC: Center for Hellenic Studies, distributed by Harvard University Press, Cambridge, MA.

Cineas (C3 BC) A Thessalian diplomat who served PYRRHUS, king of Epirus. After the battles of Heraclea and Asculum in southern Italy in 280 and 279, he was sent by Pyrrhus to Rome to negotiate peace. He offered terms that were rejected by the Senate at the instigation of Appius Claudius. He is said to have remarked that the Senate was an assembly of kings and that fighting Rome was like fighting a hydra.

Cleander (ruled 505–498 BC) A tyrant of Gela in Sicily whose father, Pantares, was an Olympic victor in 512. He enlarged the army, fortified the hills north of his city and laid the foundation for the conquests of his brother HIPPOCRATES (1).

Cleanthes (331–232 BC) A Stoic philosopher, born at Assos in Asia Minor, who was the son of Phanius. He lived for ninety-nine years and spent nineteen years as the pupil of ZENO (2) of Citium at Athens when Zeno was teaching in the Painted Colonnade (*Stoa Poikile*). In 263 he succeeded Zeno as head of the school, in which position he remained for the rest of his life. He added a strong religious dimension to the Stoicism of Zeno: he taught that the universe was alive and that its soul was god and that wrong thoughts were worse than wrong actions. He wrote a Hymn to Zeus, which is mostly extant, interpreting Stoic ideas with an emphasis on religion. He killed himself by refusing food.

Clearchus 1. (died 401 BC) A Spartan officer who commanded Spartan troops in the Hellespont area from 409. In 403 he refused to withdraw from Byzantium when ordered by the ephors and was driven out by the Spartans. He escaped to the court of the Persian pretender CYRUS (2), who was seeking to overthrow his brother, ARTAXERXES (2) II, and acted as Cyrus' agent in the recruiting of a largely Greek mercenary army known as the Ten Thousand. He commanded the Greek contingent at the battle of Cunaxa in 401 and, having disobeyed Cyrus' order to advance obliquely to the line, routed the opposing forces, but thus allowed the Persian cavalry to charge the native levies of Cyrus, who fled, and was himself killed. The Greek staff officers, including Clearchus, were later killed by the treachery of the Persian satrap TISSA-PHERNES at a conference.

2. (*c.*340–*c.*250 BC) A writer and philosopher from Soli in Cyprus. He was a pupil of ARISTOTLE and wrote commentaries on PLATO (1)'s *Republic*, as well as an encomium on Plato and other works which showed not only great learning but also an interest in the sensational. He was interested in riddles, proverbs, paradoxes, erotic material and zoology. He travelled widely, principally in the east, and visited Bactria. He wrote of the manner of life of various nations, with especial emphasis on the eastern peoples. Fragments of his writings are extant.

Cleidemus or Cleitodemus (*fl.* mid-C4 BC) A historian of Attica who concentrated on

the earlier period, though his work, in four books of which some twenty-five fragments remain, included an account of the Peloponnesian War.

Cleisthenes 1. (ruled *c.*600–570 BC) A tyrant of Sicyon who was a descendant of Orthagoras and, after displacing his brothers, ruled for thirty years. He was hostile to the Dorian Argives who had previously held sway in Sicyon: he fought a war with them after which he abolished the festival of Homeric recitations at Sicyon because of the glorification of the Argives in HOMER's epics. He wished to have the tomb of Adrastus, the mythical Argive hero who was greatly honoured among the Sicyonians, removed from his territory, but was forbidden by the Delphic Oracle to do so. He transferred the ceremonial chorus from being performed in honour of Adrastus to Dionysus, whose cult he founded there. HERODOTUS (*Histories*, 5. 68) claims that he changed the names of the traditional Doric tribes at Sicyon to rude ones, Pigmen, Swine-men and Ass-men, except for his own tribe, which he called the Rulers. Since the Delphic Oracle supported Argos, he participated in the First Sacred War in which he co-operated with the Athenians under SOLON to free Delphi from foreign interference, and captured Crisa, which commands the approach to Delphi by sea. He married off his daughter, Agariste, in Homeric style, entertaining her suitors for a year and eventually choosing as his son-in-law the Athenian Megacles of the ALCMAEONIDS whose father, Alcmaeon, had commanded the Athenians in the Sacred War.

2. (late C6 BC) An Athenian constitutional reformer, son of Megacles and grandson of CLEISTHENES (1) of Sicyon. Though his family, the ALCMAEONIDS, had been exiled by the Athenian tyrant PISIS-TRATUS, Cleisthenes was archon under Pisistratus' son HIPPIAS (1) in 525/4, but was sent into exile again *c.*514. When

Hippias was expelled by the Spartans under King CLEOMENES (1) I in 510, Cleisthenes returned and led one of the two rival aristocratic parties. He found the power-struggle to be going against him and, when his opponent ISAGORAS was elected archon for 508/7, he retaliated by taking the common people of Athens (who had previously supported the discredited tyrants) into partnership and by proposing radical constitutional changes, recognising the citizens' right to equality of treatment. The traditional four Ionic tribes were replaced for political purposes by ten new tribes and the whole of Attica was divided into thirty divisions, called *trittyes*, three to a tribe, with several demes in each. Thus, the territorial basis of the new tribes was spread throughout Attica. On this system a new council (*boule*) of five hundred was created with equal representation of the tribes (fifty from each tribe). The citizen roll was enlarged to include the poorer commoners by making citizenship depend henceforth on registration at the deme headquarters, and every man so registered could attend the Assembly. Deme membership would henceforth be hereditary. Cleisthenes may also have instituted ostracism, by which a vote could be held to send a citizen into exile. This had the effect of preventing faction by removing powerful party leaders when the people sensed that they were becoming too strong.

The aristocrats led by Isagoras resorted to force to block these reforms, and summoned back Cleomenes. The latter proclaimed the banishment of Cleisthenes and others for the curse incurred by the death of CYLON, and, after Cleisthenes had fled, Cleomenes arrived in Athens with a small force of troops. He banished the members of 700 families whom Isagoras had nominated as supporters of Cleisthenes, and tried to establish Isagoras as leader of an oligarchic government of 300 men. The council, whether the ancient Areopagus or the new council of Cleisthenes, called for resistance to the changes, and Cleomenes and Isagoras blockaded themselves in the Acropolis. After a couple of days, Cleomenes and Isagoras were allowed to leave Attica, but others were executed. The Athenians recalled Cleisthenes and his supporters and sent envoys to Persia for assistance. The Persians demanded submission, but Athens refused help on such terms. Cleisthenes' reform was left in place, but no more is heard of him, perhaps because of the Persian débâcle. He was, however, granted a tomb at public expense. His niece, Agariste, was the mother of PERICLES.

Though he is often regarded as the author of Athenian democracy, the ancient Athenians themselves were more impressed by the work of SOLON in this regard. See W.G. Forrest (1966) *The Emergence of Greek Democracy*, London: Weidenfeld & Nicolson; O. Murray (1980) *Early Greece*, London: Fontana.

Cleitarchus A historian of ALEXANDER (3) III the Great from Alexandria and son of DINON. Little is known of him and the dates of his life are uncertain, although he might have been a contemporary of PTOLEMY (2) II. He wrote a history, now lost, in at least twelve books. Some of his work sensationalised the events of Alexander's career and passed into the works of later historians, such as DIODORUS (3) and Curtius Rufus. His account seems to have been popular in the Roman imperial period and to have influenced the romantic novel.

Cleitus 1. (born *c*.380 BC) A Macedonian cavalry commander and son of Dropides. He saved the life of ALEXANDER (3) III the Great at the battle of the Granicus in 334, but was slain by the king in a drunken argument in 328 when he complained that Alexander was being compared impiously with the gods and ascribing too little credit for his successes to his Macedonians. When he reminded the king of the Granicus incident, Alexander killed him with his own hand. See Arrian, 4. 8.

2. (C4 BC) A Macedonian officer of ALEXANDER (3) III the Great. He was sent home in 324 with the veteran Macedonian soldiers and took part in the Lamian War when, as Macedonian admiral, he won two victories in 322 and closed the Dardanelles to the Greek alliance. ANTIPATER (1) made him satrap of Lydia in 321, but he was expelled by ANTIGONUS (1) I the One-eyed in 319. He became POLYPERCHON's admiral under orders to keep Antigonus out of Europe, but was defeated by NICANOR (1) of Stagira and killed soon afterwards in Thrace.

Cleobis and Biton Argive brothers who HERODOTUS (1. 31) relates were mentioned by SOLON in addressing CROESUS as being especially dutiful and consequently among the happiest of men: on a religious festival of Hera, when the oxen were late in arriving, they pulled their mother's cart nine kilometres to her temple, the Heraeum, and died that night as they slept in the temple, a fate which was the goddess' response to their mother's prayer to bless them. The statues which the Argives erected in their honour at Delphi have been found and are displayed there.

Cleobulus (C6 BC) A famous riddler of the sixth century BC from Lindus in Rhodes who was accounted one of the SEVEN SAGES of Greece. His daughter, Cleobulina, was also famous for riddles, and a comedy by CRATINUS was named after her.

Cleombrotus The name of three members of the Agiad royal family at Sparta. The first was a younger brother of LEONIDAS (1) I and acted briefly as regent for his nephew, Pleistarchus. The second was king of Sparta from 380–371 until he fell at the battle of Leuctra (See EPAMINONDAS). The third, who married into the family, was chosen king in 242 in place of LEONIDAS (2) II by the party of AGIS (3) IV. He reigned for two years before being banished to Tegea.

Cleomenes 1. I (reigned *c.*519–*c.*491 BC) An Agiad king of Sparta, the son of Anaxandridas. He intervened in Athenian politics on several occasions. He also aimed to expand and strengthen the Peloponnesian League, with which Sparta had surrounded herself. In 519 he brought about an alliance between Athens and Plataea in Boeotia, possibly to set Thebes, from which Plataea sought to be free, against Athens. In 510 he led a Spartan army to expel the tyrant HIPPIAS (1) from Athens, probably wishing to bring Athens into the League. In 508 he was summoned by the Athenian archon ISAGORAS and with a small force tried to prevent the constitutional reforms of CLEISTHENES (2), but was driven out. He tried again in 506, organising a large expeditionary force which he led to Eleusis without revealing that his aim was to restore Isagoras. When, however, he could no longer hide his purpose, he was deserted by the Corinthians and his colleague DEMARATUS. The Spartans were forced to withdraw. He refused, however, to allow Sparta to be involved in the Ionian revolt of 499. He led the army that defeated Argos at the battle of Sepeia in 494. When Aegina in 491 accepted the overlordship of the Persian king, DARIUS (1) I, Cleomenes went to Aegina, arrested the leaders of the state and turned them over to the Athenians who had complained of their treachery. But, because of continual friction with his colleague, he bribed the Delphic prophetess, Perialla, to declare Demaratus not to be Ariston's son and therefore ineligible to be king. Demaratus joined the Persians, but when the story of the intrigue became known Cleomenes fled to Thessaly. Then, having tried to stir up Arcadia against the Spartan alliance, he was invited back to Sparta. His family put him in the stocks, where he killed himself. He had a daughter, Gorgo, and was succeeded as king by his half-brother, LEONIDAS (1) I.

2. III (reigned 235–222 BC) An Agiad king of Sparta and the son of LEONIDAS (2) II. He married Agiatis the widow of the Eurypontid king, AGIS (3) IV, whose example inspired him to try to restore the ancient Spartan constitution. In 229 he took several parts of Arcadia from the Aetolians and ARATUS (2) of Sicyon. The next year he began a successful war with the Achaean Confederacy and, in the winter of 227/226, he seized power and claimed to restore the constitution of LYCURGUS (2), redistributing land and enrolling neighbouring Laconians and resident foreigners into Spartan citizenship, which had become depleted. He also removed and killed the ephors and cancelled debts. In 226 he captured the Arcadian city of Mantinea and won the battle of Hecatombaeon. After unsuccessful peace negotiations, Cleomenes took Argos in 225 and the next year attacked Corinth, but ANTIGONUS (3) III Doson of Macedonia, whom the Achaean Confederacy asked for help on the promise of giving him the Acrocorinth, intervened and Cleomenes had to retreat. Argos threw off Spartan rule and, though Cleomenes took Megalopolis in Arcadia in the winter of 223, he was decisively defeated by his united enemies at Sellasia in July 222 and fled from his kingdom to Egypt. After the death of his ally PTOLEMY (3) III, he was imprisoned by his son, but escaped and plotted to cause a rebellion in Alexandria. When he failed, he killed himself in late 220.

3. (died 322 BC) A Greek of Naucratis in Egypt whom ALEXANDER (3) III the Great appointed as one of his superintendents in Egypt. In 332 after his conquest, Alexander gave him a commission as financial manager of Egypt and governor of the eastern section, and instructed him to see to the building of his new capital of Alexandria. Cleomenes later made himself satrap of all Egypt without Alexander's consent and exploited his control of the export of grain to amass a fortune of 8,000 talents for himself. In 322 after Alexander's death, he was made deputy to PTOLEMY (1) I, who assumed the satrapy. However, he was later accused of grave offences by Ptolemy and put to death.

Cleon (died 422 BC) An Athenian politician and a rich man who inherited a tanning factory from his father. He started his career without office as an opponent of PERICLES in the Assembly at the outset of the Peloponnesian War. When Pericles died in 429, Cleon succeeded him in his role as demagogue or popular leader and for six years he led the war party. He took a tough line when Mytilene rebelled in 427, and persuaded the Assembly to impose the punishment of death on all her adult males, which the people repented of the next day. In 426 he prosecuted ARISTOPHANES (1) for his comedy, *Babylonians*, on the grounds that it was treasonable, but failed. Aristophanes, whom he accused of not having the right to Athenian citizenship, became his lifelong enemy. He went on viciously to attack Cleon by portraying him in the *Knights*. In 425, when DEMOSTHENES (1) by a bold plan and good luck had gained a foothold on Spartan territory at Pylos, Cleon prevented the success of negotiations for a favourable peace with Sparta and accused the generals of incompetence, going as far as to say he could himself capture the Spartan soldiers trapped on the island of Sphacteria. NICIAS (1) resigned his command in favour of Cleon, who was compelled by the people to undertake what he had boasted he could do. With Demosthenes' help he took the island and forced the Spartans on it to surrender.

He continued to promote the war with vigour. He supervised the collection of tribute from the allies of Athens and may have been responsible for an increase in the rates. He proposed an increase of 50 per cent in the pay of jurymen in the state courts. He also proposed in 423 the execution of the men of Scione, a city in

Pallene in Chalcidice, which had deserted Athens for BRASIDAS just after a year's truce had been negotiated. After the truce expired in 422, Cleon was elected general and led an expedition to recapture Amphipolis in Thrace, which THUCYDIDES (2) had lost. He recovered the cities of Torone and Galepsus, but was killed while reconnoitring outside Amphipolis. His death removed the greatest obstacle to peace, which was concluded within a year. See D. Kagan (1987) *The Archidamian War*, Ithaca, NY; London: Cornell University Press.

Cleonides (early C2 AD) An author on music theory. He wrote an extant *Introduction to Harmony*, which preserves much of ARISTOXENUS' theory. See also EUCLID.

Cleonymus (early C3 BC) A member of the Spartan Agiad royal family and the younger son of Cleomenes II. After his nephew AREUS became king in 309, he became his guardian, but aimed at kingship for himself. In 303 he led an army of mercenaries on expedition to Greater Greece (southern Italy), where he supported Tarentum against the Lucanians. He drove off the Lucanians, took Metapontum and seized Corcyra. Tarentum soon rose and expelled him, and he lost Corcyra. In 293 he assisted the Boeotians against DEMETRIUS (3) I the Besieger, without success, and in 279 he seized Troezene. He still claimed the Agiad kingship of Sparta and was expelled *c*.275. He joined King PYRRHUS of Epirus and helped him against Macedonia. In 272 they made a combined attack on Sparta and were defeated by Areus and ANTIGONUS (2) II Gonatas.

Cleopatra 1. A daughter of PHILIP (1) II of Macedonia and Olympias. In 336 she was married to ALEXANDER (8), king of Epirus. Philip was assassinated at the wedding.

2. I (*c*.215–176 BC) A queen of Ptolemaic Egypt, the daughter of King ANTIOCHUS (3) III and LAODICE (2), she married King PTOLEMY (5) V in 193. They had two sons and a daughter. When her husband died in 180, she ruled on behalf of her son PTOLEMY (6) VI until her death.

3. II (*c*.185–116 BC) A queen of Egypt, daughter of CLEOPATRA (2) I. She was married to her brother, PTOLEMY (6) VI (*c*.175). They and their brother, PTOLEMY (8) VIII, were co-rulers of Egypt from 171–164 during a war with ANTIOCHUS (4) IV of Syria in which Rome finally rescued Egypt. She became regent for her son PTOLEMY (7) VII in 145 on her husband's death, and married her other brother, Ptolemy VIII, in 144, whereupon he slew Ptolemy VII and made himself king. In 142 he took her younger daughter, his niece, CLEOPATRA (4) III, as wife without divorcing his sister, and made his new wife joint ruler. Cleopatra II led a rebellion against Ptolemy in 132 and she remained hostile to him until a public reconciliation was declared in 124. She had promised the throne of Egypt to her son-in-law, DEMETRIUS (5) II of Syria, but in 125 Ptolemy had him assassinated. After this she ruled jointly with her brother and daughter until 116 when Ptolemy died, leaving the kingdom to Cleopatra III. She herself died shortly after. Her son by Ptolemy had been murdered by him to promote the interests of his son by Cleopatra III.

4. III (died 101 BC) A queen of Egypt and daughter of Cleopatra (3) II. She was seduced by her uncle, PTOLEMY (8) VIII in 142 and married him, even though he was still married to her mother. He made her joint ruler and played his two wives off against each other. When Ptolemy died in 116, Cleopatra inherited the throne and installed her elder son, PTOLEMY (9) IX, though she preferred her second son. She led rebellions against Ptolemy IX in 110 and 108. In 107 she succeeded in banishing him to Cyprus and installing her second son PTOLEMY (10) X as king. She possibly died at his hands after having quarrelled continuously with him.

5. VII (69–30 BC) The most famous queen of Egypt and the daughter of PTOLEMY (12) XII the Piper. On his death in 51, as a result of his will, she became joint ruler with her younger brother, PTOLEMY (13) XIII. They supported Pompey in 49 in his war with Caesar and supplied him with ships and foodstuffs. In 48 Ptolemy's guardians, Pothinus and Achillas, expelled her, but Caesar came to Egypt in pursuit of Pompey, whom Ptolemy's men had murdered, and replaced Ptolemy with Cleopatra in the Alexandrian War. Ptolemy was killed in resisting Caesar, so Caesar made her other, younger brother, PTOLEMY (14), co-regent with her. Caesar left Egypt early in 47 with a garrison of three legions and in the summer Cleopatra bore him Caesarion, whose official name was Ptolemy Caesar. In 46 she joined Caesar in Rome and lived there in a villa, which he provided, until his death in 44 after which she returned to Egypt. She is said to have poisoned her brother, Ptolemy XIV, and made Caesarion joint ruler in his place. In 42 she attempted to help the Caesarians, but was foiled by Cassius Longinus who stole her troops. Marcus Antonius summoned her to Tarsus in 41 to account for her failure, and she persuaded him to kill her sister, Arsinoë. She invited him to Alexandria where he spent the winter. She later bore him twins. She did not see him again until 37 when he invited her to Antioch and they formed a permanent liaison. He recognised her twins and named them Alexander Helios and Cleopatra Selene. She bore him another son in 36, Ptolemy Philadelphus. In 35 she restored his financial losses after his Parthian campaign and he returned territories to Egypt that had been lost long before and some she had never held. As Octavian was irked by Antonius' treatment of his sister, Octavia, Antonius'

wife, he grew resentful of Cleopatra's power over Antonius and his propaganda painted her as a monster. In 32 he declared war on Egypt and Cleopatra. Antonius' forces were concentrated in Greece and Asia Minor, and Cleopatra sent them supplies. She moved her fleet to join his. After months of uncertainty, during which Antonius was deserted by most of his principal Roman supporters, the naval battle of Actium was fought off the coast of western Greece in which Antonius was defeated. There is no evidence for the story that Cleopatra began the rout by fleeing. The two with their most faithful supporters returned to Egypt, where Octavian pursued them. After Antonius' suicide, Cleopatra killed herself on 10 August 30 BC by applying asps to her body, fearing the threat of Octavian that he would parade her in his triumph. She was the last ancient ruler of independent Egypt. Octavian killed Caesarion, but spared Antonius' children by Cleopatra, whom Octavia took into her household. See R.D. Sullivan (1990) *Near Eastern Royalty and Rome*, Toronto; London: University of Toronto Press.

Cleophon 1. (late C5 BC) An Athenian political figure and the son of Cleippides who was himself elected general in 429. Cleophon, who followed the trade of lyremaker, became the principal demagogue, or popular leader, in 410 after the collapse of the oligarchic revolution and consistently opposed making peace with Sparta – even when things were at their blackest for Athens. As HYPERBOLUS had been assassinated in 411, he had a clear field to lead the extreme democrats. Like CLEON, he was a violent and intemperate speaker. He introduced the payment of a dole of two obols a day to the poor. He acted as treasurer until 406, and proved to be honest and efficient in the post. He spoke out against peace after the battles of Cyzicus in 410, Arginusae in 406, and Aegospotami in 405. After the collapse of democracy in 404, Cleophon was tried and executed by the oligarchic government of the THIRTY TYRANTS.

2. An Athenian tragic poet discussed by Aristotle in works including the *Poetics*.

Cleophrades (early C5 BC) An Athenian potter. The painter of a cup he signed, known as the 'Cleophrades Painter', was a prolific artist of great quality.

Clitomachus (*c*.187–109 BC) A Carthaginian philosopher originally named Hasdrubal. On migrating to Athens, aged 24, he changed his name and became a pupil of CARNEADES the Sceptic who founded the New Academy. In 140 he founded his own school of philosophy in the Palladium, a precinct in Athens. In 129 he returned to the Academy of which he became the head in 127. He left a large corpus of writings, none of which has survived. It was, however, influential in passing on the substance of Carneades' philosophical theories. He wrote *On Suspension of Judgement*, *On Philosophical Schools*, and a *Consolation* addressed to his fellow countrymen on the destruction of Carthage by the Romans in 146. He dedicated works to the Roman poet Lucilius and to L. Censorinus.

Colotes (*c*.310–*c*.260 BC) A philosophical writer from Lampsacus who studied under EPICURUS and supported the materialistic, atomist doctrine of the Epicurean school in argument with the Platonists, the sceptical ARCESILAUS, and the New Academy. He wrote treatises to demolish the arguments of several dialogues of PLATO (1), namely the *Lysis*, *Euthydemus*, *Gorgias*, and *Republic*. His attack on the premises of the myth of Er in *Republic* 10 is reported by Proclus. PLUTARCH wrote an attack (*Against Colotes*) on Colotes' proposition that sceptical suspension of belief is not a possible basis for life.

Conon 1. (*c*.450–392 BC) An Athenian admiral of noble family who was active at Naupactus in command of a fleet in 414. He served under the oligarchy in 411, and commanded fleets in the Aegean and the Hellespont from 407 until the battle of Aegospotami in 405, where he alone of the Athenian generals was vigilant, and from which he escaped with eight ships to Cyprus where he took refuge with the tyrant of Salamis, EVAGORAS. Ever anti-Spartan, he devised a policy of using Persian resources to revive the fortunes of Athens. To this end he encouraged PHARNABAZUS, the Persian satrap of Dascylium, to build up a fleet. He served under Pharnabazus as admiral in the naval battle of Cnidus in 394 when Sparta's fleet was destroyed. He then went back to Athens and supervised the rebuilding of the Long Walls between Athens and the Piraeus, thus restoring the independence of Athens. Conon was, however, arrested on a mission to Tiribazus, the satrap of Lydia in Sardis. A Spartan, ANTALCIDAS, had won the satrap's support and he had given money to aid Spartan naval recovery. However, King ARTAXERXES (2) II reversed this policy, but mistrusting Conon imprisoned him. However, he escaped once more to Cyprus where he died. He had won the gratitude of several Greek states, including his native city, for his restoration of democracy. His son was TIMOTHEUS (2).

2. (C3 BC) An astronomer from Samos who migrated to Alexandria, where he became court astronomer. In 245 he claimed to discover the lock of hair of BERENICE (3) II, wife of PTOLEMY (3) III, which she dedicated to Aphrodite for her husband's safe return from a war in Syria, as a new constellation, the *Coma Berenices*, between Leo, Virgo, and Boötes. He was a mathematician and a close friend of ARCHIMEDES. He wrote works, which do not survive, on conic sections and astronomy.

Corax (C5 BC) A rhetorician from Syracuse who was thought to be the first man to teach the subject of rhetoric. He is said to have divided the speech into three parts: introduction, discussion and conclusion, and to have taught his pupils how to handle these divisions. ARISTOTLE wrote of his craftsmanship, and he is known to have taught TISIAS, but there is no evidence of his writing anything.

Corinna A lyric poetess from Tanagra in Boeotia. The period of her lifetime is unknown and may fall in any period between the sixth and third centuries BC. She is known from substantial fragments of two poems found in a papyrus from Hermopolis in Egypt. The language, orthography, metre and subject matter argue for a later date, though she was thought in antiquity to be a contemporary of PINDAR. She wrote narrative poems for a circle of Boeotian women on mythological subjects in the Boeotian dialect, though she admitted other forms. She preferred Boeotian material, such as the *Seven against Thebes, Euonymie, Iolaus* and *The Return of Orestes*. The fragments are concerned with a contest between two Boeotian mountains, Helicon and Cithaeron, for the primacy in poetic inspiration and with the marriage of the daughters of the Boeotian River Asopus to gods. See MYRTIS.

Cotys A king of Thrace who in 360 BC captured Sestos and threatened to drive the Athenians from the Chersonese. He was, however, murdered in 359 and was succeeded by his son CERSOBLEPTES.

Crantor (died *c*.275 BC) A philosopher of the Academy from Soli in Cilicia. He started by moving to Athens and studying under XENOCRATES and became friendly with POLEMON (1), CRATES (3) and ARCESILAUS. He converted the last named from the Peripatetic school to the Academy and made him his heir. None of his works has survived, nor do they appear to have shown originality of thought. He wrote a commentary on the *Timaeus* of

PLATO (1), and a treatise *On Mourning*, which Cicero admired and imitated in his *Consolation* on the death of his daughter, Tullia.

Craterus 1. (*c*.370–321 BC) A Macedonian general of ALEXANDER (3) III the Great. He started quite humbly at the battle of the Granicus as the commander of a brigade and became the senior such commander in subsequent battles. He later replaced PARMENION, after the latter's death, as Alexander's right-hand man, often commanding an army in Alexander's place when the host was divided. He fought with distinction in Alexander's campaigns in Bactria and India. In 324 Alexander appointed him to lead the discharged veterans back to Macedonia and to take over the governorship of Macedonia and Greece from ANTIPATER (1). In fact, he co-operated with Antipater, his father-in-law, and upon Alexander's death the two worked together in opposing the Greeks in the Lamian War of 322. Craterus was killed in a battle against EUMENES (1) of Cardia, who was then ruler of Cappadocia.

2. (C3 BC) The son of CRATERUS (1), his mother was Phila, daughter of ANTIPATER (1). His younger half-brother, ANTIGONUS (2) II, appointed him to govern Corinth and the Peloponnese, later adding Attica and Boeotia. In 266 he stopped the advance of King AREUS of Sparta, who was trying to relieve Athens, at the Isthmus of Corinth.

Crates 1. (mid-C5 BC) An Athenian comic poet who won three victories for his plays, none of which has survived. One title is known, *Animals*, in which the animals refuse to be eaten by men. ARISTOTLE regarded him as the first to move comedy out of personal lampoon into more generalised and developed plots. He was also an actor.

2. (died 285 BC) A Cynic philosopher from Thebes. He was a pupil of DIOGENES

(2) of Sinope and one of the teachers of ZENO (2) of Citium, the founder of Stoicism. He married Hipparchia, whom he converted along with her brother, Metrocles, to his philosophy. They forswore property and lived a simple and exemplary life, though he caused scandal by having sex with his wife in public following Diogenes' teachings. He composed numerous poems of which useful fragments survive. He also reworked passages from the poetry of HOMER and SOLON in order to put across Cynic ideas in a lighthearted manner, rather than simply as parodies. See MENIPPUS (1) and OENOMAUS.

3. (died c.266 BC) An Athenian philosopher and head of the Academy, in which he succeeded POLEMON (1) and was succeeded by ARCESILAUS.

4. (C2 BC) A scholar, critic, and Stoic philosopher, the son of Timocrates, from Mallus in Cilicia. EUMENES (3) II, king of Pergamon, appointed him first head of the library he founded there, and c.168 sent him as an envoy to Rome, where he broke his leg in the Great Drain and, while he recovered, gave lectures which stimulated Roman interest in literature. He wrote a commentary on HOMER in which he maintained, out of Stoic dogmatism, that the epics were allegories of philosophical and scientific truths. He also wrote on HESIOD, EURIPIDES and ARISTOPHANES (1). He followed the Stoic interest in anomaly and rejected the Alexandrian classification, as found in the works of ARISTARCHUS (3) and ARISTOPHANES (2) of Byzantium, as being misguided. He constructed a sphere to represent the earth on which he drew a map of the continents. His work on the tides was refuted by SELEUCUS (7).

Cratinus (c.484–c.419 BC) An Athenian playwright of the Old Comedy. Only fragments of his works have survived, though he was greatly admired by ARISTOPHANES (1), who compared his style to a rushing torrent, and by Horace. He is said to have written twenty-one plays, constantly attacking PERICLES, and he won six first prizes at the City Dionysia dramatic festival and three at the Lenaea. The titles of plays of which we know the dates are *The Storm-tossed Women*, produced at the Lenaea in 426, *Satyrs*, produced at the Lenaea in 424, and *The Bottle*, a response to an attack made on him by Aristophanes in the *Knights*, exploiting his notorious drunkenness, which won the prize in 423, beating Aristophanes' *Clouds*. Less easily datable are *Archilochi*, written shortly after 450 as CIMON's death is reported as being recent; *Dionysus-Paris*, in which Dionysus took on the role of Paris in judging the three goddesses and stealing Helen, and which was an attack on Pericles for warmongering; *Thracian Women*, which partly touches on Pericles' escape from ostracism in 444; *Nemesis*; *Dionysuses*; *Cleobulinae*, named after the riddling daughter of CLEOBULUS; *Odysseuses*, about Odysseus and his crew, considered by the critic Platonius, in that it contained no political attack, to be Middle Comedy before its time; *Plutuses*; and *Chirons*. The use of plural forms of well-known personal names in titles of plays is also found in the works of his contemporary, TELECLIDES.

Cratippus 1. An Athenian historian who continued the *History* of THUCYDIDES (2) down to 394 BC. He appears to have been a contemporary of Thucydides and it is possible that he is to be identified with the writer (the so-called Oxyrhynchus Historian) of a *History of Greece* (*Hellenica*), two sections of which were found on papyrus. The fragments we possess show a mature and perceptive historian in the vein of Thucydides, without the speeches. See Bartoletti and Chambers (eds) (1993) *Hellenica Oxyrhynchia*, Stuttgart: Teubner; D. Kagan (1987) *The Fall of the Athenian Empire*, London: Cornell University Press.

2. (C1 BC) A philosopher of the Peripatetic school, a native of Mytilene and

contemporary of Cicero, who held him in high esteem. Cicero sent his son to Cratippus at Athens to study under him. He became head of the Lyceum in 44 in succession to ANDRONICUS of Rhodes.

Cratylus (C5 BC) An Athenian philosopher who followed the school of HERACLITUS and believed that nothing in the natural universe has any fixed position or constancy of composition. Even in old age, in despair of learning Nature's true names, he refused to name anything, preferring to point with his fingers. ARISTOTLE (*Metaphysics*) suggests that PLATO (1) was his disciple at some time in his youth and that he deduced from Cratylus' position the existence of a non-sensible universe (the theory of 'forms' or 'ideas') so as to allow for the reality of knowledge. Cratylus is a character in the Platonic dialogue of that name. He appears to have been somewhat younger than SOCRATES.

Creophylus An early epic poet from Samos who is said to have written *The Capture of Oechalia*.

Cresilas (mid-C5 BC) A Cretan sculptor from Cydonia who moved to Athens where he carved marble statues of PERICLES (copies of the head survive in several places, including the British Museum). Five signatures of his appear on statuary bases. A copy of his statue of a *Wounded Amazon*, for which he won a prize in competition at Ephesus with the greatest sculptors of his day, is in the Vatican. He also made a bronze of a wounded dying man, which is commemorated in several replicas.

Critias (*c*.460–403 BC) An Athenian oligarchic politician and playwright. He was of noble birth, being a member of the family of the mother of PLATO (1). He was a friend of SOCRATES and a pupil of GORGIAS in his youth and wrote poems and tragedies. He was imprisoned for having taken part in the mutilation of the

herms, but was released on the evidence of ANDOCIDES. He was not conspicuous in the revolution of 411 and afterwards worked for the recall of ALCIBIADES. When the latter again became unpopular, Critias was banished and went to Thessaly. He returned to Athens after the fall of the democracy in 404 and became one of the THIRTY TYRANTS, a committee set up by the Spartans to rule Athens. There is dispute as to exactly how extreme his attitude was in the persecution that followed. XENOPHON (1) in the *Hellenica* paints a picture of him as a cruel opportunist and the one who proposed the execution of THERAMENES, but ARISTOTLE, in his *Politics*, suggests that CHARICLES played that part. He was killed in spring 403 in the battle against THRASYBULUS (2). His memory was hateful to the democrats who subsequently attacked Socrates in 399 for his guilt by association with Critias. A fine writer, he wrote elegies and tragedies. Two titles of his plays, *Sisyphus* and *Pirithous*, as well as some fragments, survive. PLATO (1) made him a character in two of his dialogues, *Critias* and *Timaeus*.

Critius (worked *c*.480–460 BC) A sculptor who was probably Athenian. He worked with Nesiotes and in 477 they made a pair of bronzes of Harmodius and ARISTOGITON for the Acropolis to replace the pair made by ANTENOR, which had been stolen by the Persians. A marble copy of the group is now in the Naples Museum. On the strength of the style of this group, several other statues have been attributed to Critius, including the *Kouros* which is known as the 'Critius boy'. A total of six statue bases have been found on the Acropolis showing the names of Critius and Nesiotes.

Crito 1. A fifth-century Athenian who was a rich man and a devoted friend of SOCRATES. He attempted to intervene on Socrates' behalf at his trial in 399 BC and in his imprisonment. He also unsuccessfully tried to persuade Socrates to flee from jail before his execution. PLATO (1) gave his name to a dialogue.

2. A writer of the New Comedy. His *Ephesians* is dated to 183 BC, when it won second prize. He also wrote the *Aetolian* in 167 and the *Busybody*.

Critolaus (C2 BC) A Peripatetic philosopher from Phaselis and a head of the school. As an old man in 155, he accompanied the Athenian embassy of philosophers, the Academic CARNEADES and the Stoic DIOGENES (3) of Babylon, to Rome to protest against a fine imposed on Athens. We know little about his life or his writings.

Croesus (reigned 560–546 BC) The last king of Lydia before its conquest by the Persians in 546. He was born in 595, the son of ALYATTES of the Mermnad dynasty, and had to struggle with a half-brother to gain the succession. He became king in 560. He was proverbially rich and made offerings at Delphi to placate Greek opinion. However, he conquered the Greek cities of the Asia Minor coastline, starting with Ephesus, and subsequently ruled the whole of Asia Minor west of the River Halys (Kizil), except for Lycia and Cilicia. Croesus was alarmed by the Persian conquest of the Median empire in 549 and sought help from Egypt, Babylon and Greece. To forestall CYRUS (1), he invaded Cappadocia in 546 on the advice of the Delphic Oracle, fought an indecisive battle with Cyrus at Pteria, and retired to Sardis to seek reinforcements. Here Cyrus attacked him and caught him off his guard. He took Sardis and captured Croesus. The fate of Croesus is uncertain: HERODOTUS tells a tale that he was condemned by Cyrus to be burnt on a pyre, but was saved by the divine action of Apollo; BACCHYLIDES says that he had himself burnt to avoid capture by Cyrus. CTESIAS (preserved by the Byzantine scholar Photius) makes no mention of a pyre, but states that Croesus was appointed by Cyrus to rule a province of his empire in Media.

Ctesias (late C5 BC) A physician and historian who was born at Cnidus in Caria and became the private doctor of the Persian king ARTAXERXES (2) II, whom he accompanied in his campaign against his brother, CYRUS (2) the Younger, in 401. In 398 he was sent as an envoy to EVAGORAS and CONON (1). He wrote three works: *Persia*, a history of Persia in twenty-three books, a *Geography*, in three books, and *Indica*, an account of India. He wrote in opposition to HERODOTUS, an older contemporary, in the same Ionic dialect. His works were considered unreliable by the Greeks simply because they disagreed with Herodotus who was very highly regarded at Athens, and because Ctesias claimed to have had access to the royal Persian archives. None of his works has survived, but abridgements have been preserved in the works of the ninth-century patriarch of Constantinople, Photius, and others.

Ctesibius (C3 BC) An Alexandrian inventor, the son of a barber, who worked at the court of PTOLEMY (2) II and was a mechanical genius. Using pneumatic methods he invented a pump with a valve and plunger, a water-organ, an accurate water-clock, the first such, and a catapult for siege or battle. The treatise he wrote describing his inventions is lost and we have to rely on HERON, PHILON (3), and Vitruvius for accounts of them.

Cylon (C7 BC) An Athenian aristocrat who won an Olympic victory in 640 and, with the help of his father-in-law, THEAGENES (1), tyrant of Megara, tried to make himself tyrant in an Olympic year, perhaps 632. He seized the Acropolis with a small force of supporters, but failed to persuade the people and was besieged. He escaped and his supporters surrendered: they took sanctuary at an altar, but were killed with the compliance of the archon

Megacles the Alcmaeonid. This later led to the banishment of the ALCMAEONIDS.

Cypselus (C7 BC) A Corinthian tyrant, the son of Eëtion, a non-Dorian who claimed descent from the Lapiths, and of Labda, a woman of Doric race and of the ruling BACCHIADS. In about 657 he overthrew the Bacchiads and became tyrant with the support of the Delphic Oracle, which created prophecies about his childhood to the effect that he was marked out for rule and would displace the Bacchiads, and that men were sent to kill him. When they were near, his mother hid him in a chest from which he was named Cypselus ('chest'). The chest was afterwards on display in the temple of Hera at Olympia. His rule was mild enough for him to have needed no bodyguard, though HERODOTUS depicts him as harsh. However, he compares him favourably with his son PERIANDER. Corinth prospered greatly under Cypselus, as is evident from the vast export trade in pottery. He made rich gifts to the temples of Delphi and Olympia. He founded colonies on the route to the west, where Corinth already had powerful colonies with which she traded extensively. He died c.627 and was succeeded by Periander.

Cyrus 1. the Great (reigned 549–530 BC) The founder and first king of the Persian empire. He was the son of Cambyses and Mandane, and was a descendant of the legendary Achaemenes who gave his name to the Persian royal family. He may have been related to the Median king, Astyages. In 559, as head of the Persian clan of Pasargadae, he inherited the throne of Anshan. In 553 he revolted against his Median overlords and in 549 established his new kingdom, incorporating the Median empire under Persian rule. In 546 he conquered CROESUS' kingdom of Lydia. He went on to conquer the Babylonian empire in 538 and he extended his rule over almost the whole Iranian plateau. His rule was mild and he was sympathetic to the beliefs and customs of his subjects, allowing the JEWS to rebuild their temple to Yahweh in Jerusalem, and honouring the god Marduk at Babylon. He died in 530, probably in battle, on a campaign against the Massagetae east of the Caspian Sea. He was buried in the city of Pasargadae, which he had built, and was succeeded by his son, CAMBYSES. See J.M. Cook (1983) *The Persian Empire*, New York: Schocken Books.

2. (c.423–401 BC) A descendant of CYRUS (1) the Great and the second son of DARIUS (2) II and Parysatis. He was sent in 407 at the age of about 15 by his father to Asia Minor to be satrap of three provinces: Cappadocia, Phrygia and Lydia. He arrested some Athenian envoys he met on the way and held them for three years to keep his pro-Spartan policy secret. At Sardis he met and fell under the spell of the Spartan general LYSANDER, whom he assisted with money and enabled to outbid the Athenians for mercenary oarsmen. His father died in 404 and his elder brother, Arsaces, succeeded as ARTAXERXES (2) II. TISSAPHERNES, satrap of Caria, whom Cyrus had replaced as the leading Persian governor in Asia Minor, attempted to overthrow Cyrus by denouncing him to Artaxerxes as a traitor, but his mother pleaded successfully for Cyrus. However, on his return to his province he actively plotted to supplant his brother and persuaded the Spartan government to co-operate with him. He also collected a mercenary army ostensibly to attack the independent state of Pisidia. In spring 401, he led his army of 20,000 men, about half being Greek mercenaries, eastwards to the Euphrates at Thapsacus and thence downstream. Tissaphernes made haste to warn Artaxerxes of the danger, and the latter assembled a scratch army at Cunaxa about seventy kilometres north of Babylon. In the ensuing battle, though his Greek infantry performed well, Cyrus was killed. See XENOPHON (1), *Anabasis* and *Hellenica*.

D

Damastes (late C5 BC) A historical writer, little of whose work survives. A native of Sigeum in Asia Minor and a pupil of HELLANICUS, he wrote several treatises, including *Events in Greece*, a *Periplus* (description of the coastal regions of the Mediterranean), *Peoples and Cities*, *Poets and Sophists*, and *The Ancestors of Those Who Fought at Troy*.

Damocles (C4 BC) An obsequious courtier of the Syracusan DIONYSIUS (2) II, whom the latter invited to dinner after he had extravagantly praised the tyrant's happiness. Dionysius setaed him where he himself usually sat, but then pointed out the naked sword hung by a hair over Damocles' head, symbolising the price he had to pay for his apparent happiness. The source of the story is Cicero's *Tusculan Disputations*, 5. 61.

Damon 1. (early C4 BC) A Pythagorean of Syracuse who was renowned for his friendship with Phintias. The latter was condemned to death by the tyrant DIONYSIUS (1) I. To settle his affairs he obtained bail for which Damon stood surety. Phintias returned just in time for his execution, and Dionysius freed them both in admiration for their loyalty.

2. (mid-C5 BC) An Athenian writer on music who was a pupil of PRODICUS and Lamprocles, as well as the teacher of PERICLES. PLATO (1) greatly admired and wrote about him in the *Republic*. It seems likely that Plato's views on the moral effects of different scales were derived from Damon's work. Fragments of his work are published in H. Diels and W. Kranz (eds) (1952) *Die Fragmente der Vorsokratiker (Fragments of the Presocratics)*, Berlin: Weidmann.

Damophilus A painter who according to Pliny the Elder was one of the decorators of the temple of Ceres by the Circus Maximus at Rome dedicated in 493BC.

Damophon (C2 BC) A Greek sculptor from Messene who repaired the statue of Zeus at Olympia. Parts of a group, consisting of Demeter, Despoina, Artemis and the Titan Anytus, made by him, have been found at Lycosura in Arcadia. He made other statues for cities in the Peloponnese.

Darius 1. I (reigned 521–485 BC) A king of Persia, the son of Hystaspes, and a member of the Achaemenid family. He was one of a group of seven who in 521 overthrew a usurper to the Persian throne, Gaumata, a Magian who was impersonating Bardiya, the deceased brother of the former king, CAMBYSES. He was made king by his allies and had the task of putting down opposition in many places. He divided the kingdom into twenty provinces, named satrapies, which were governed by semi-autonomous hereditary rulers, many of whom were his kinsmen. They were overseen, however, by officers who were responsible to the king alone. The system continued almost intact until after the time of ALEXANDER (3) III the Great. He built palaces at Susa and at Persepolis, and invaded Scythia in 512 in a vain attempt to subdue the Scythians. When the Ionians on his western frontier rebelled in 499, he suppressed the rebellion by 494 in spite of Athenian intervention, which had led to the destruction of Sardis, capital of the Lydian satrapy. He sought revenge on Athens for which he prepared an invasion fleet. In 492 an expedition against Greece foundered near Mount Athos, and a further expedition in 490 was defeated at Marathon. Darius was determined to crush Athens, but was prevented by a rebellion in Egypt, and he died before he could attack Greece again. He was succeeded by his son XERXES.

2. II (reigned 423–404 BC) A king of Persia, surnamed Ochus, the son of ARTAXERXES (1) I. He obtained the throne on his father's death by removing his brother, Sogdianus. He married his half-sister, Parysatis, who had a powerful hold over him. As a result of her influence, he became unpopular and there was a series of rebellions against him by satraps in Lydia, Syria and Media. He lost Egypt in 410. In the west, however, he was successful in weakening Athens during the Peloponnesian War through the diplomacy of TISSAPHERNES, satrap of Sardis, who in 412 made an alliance with Sparta, and through the diplomacy of his son CYRUS (2) from 407, which led to the ultimate defeat of Athens. On his death in 404, he was succeeded by his elder son ARTAXERXES (2) II.

3. III (reigned 336–330 BC) A king of Persia, the last member of the Achaemenid house. Of a collateral branch of the royal family, he was raised to the throne by BAGOAS, a eunuch minister who had poisoned ARTAXERXES (3) III and ARSES.

He himself killed the poisoner, but in 334 had to confront the invasion of his empire by ALEXANDER (3) III the Great, by whom he was defeated at the Granicus in the Troad and in 333 at Issus in north-west Syria. He tried unsuccessfully to negotiate a frontier on the River Euphrates with Alexander. His final crushing defeat was in 331 at Gaugamela in Babylonia where he panicked and fled towards the northeast. He was captured in 330 by BESSUS, satrap of Bactria, with whom his followers replaced Darius, who was stabbed as Alexander's forces approached. Alexander granted Darius a royal funeral and burial at Persepolis. Bessus was caught, tried and punished by Alexander for his treachery.

Demades (mid-C4 BC) An Athenian orator and politician, born c.380, who in 349 opposed DEMOSTHENES (2)'s policy to suspend payments to the Theoric Fund and build up forces to resist PHILIP (1) II in Chalcidice. He was captured at the battle of Chaeronea in 338 when Philip crushed the Athenian and Theban armies, and became a steady supporter of Macedonia. He negotiated the Peace of Demades, which did much to restore Athens' fortunes. After Philip's death in 336, he was prosecuted by HYPERIDES but acquitted, and negotiated with ALEXANDER (3) III the Great in 335 after the sack of Thebes and saved his city and its anti-Macedonian politicians from the king's anger. Together with PHOCION, he ruled Athens during Alexander's campaigns in the east and saved the city from joining the war of AGIS (2) III against Macedonia in 331. He secured Athenian recognition of the deification of Alexander. He was accused of accepting a bribe from the venal Macedonian rebel HARPALUS, for which he was fined. After Alexander's death in 323, he was disenfranchised, but reinstated in 322 to save his city from ANTIPATER (1) who had defeated the Greek coalition at Crannon. He negotiated peace terms and proposed a decree of death for Demosthenes and Hyperides. In 319 he went on an embassy to Macedonia to persuade Antipater to remove his garrison from the Piraeus. There CASSANDER, Antipater's son, caught him intriguing with ANTIGONUS (1) I the One-eyed and had him killed. Though he won fame as an orator, his speeches have not survived.

Demaratus (reigned *c*.513–491 BC) A Eurypontid king of Sparta who opposed the policies of his Agiad colleague, CLEOMENES (1) I, particularly in his dealings with Athens in 508–6 and at Aegina in 491, when he tried to obstruct Cleomenes' arrest of the pro-Persian leaders. Cleomenes then bribed the priestess of Delphi, Perialla, to declare Demaratus illegitimate. He was deposed in favour of LEOTYCHIDAS II and fled to the court of DARIUS (2) II of Persia. He warned XERXES that the Spartans would resist his planned invasion of Greece, and accompanied his expedition to Greece in 480. He was rewarded for his services with the gift of the lands of four cities in Asia Minor, including Pergamon. He lived there for a long time and was possibly consulted by HERODOTUS in the writing of his *Histories*.

Demetrius 1. (late C5 BC) An Attic sculptor from the deme of Alopece. He made portrait statues in a realistic style of Lysimache, the priestess of Athena Polias, Simon, an Athenian cavalry commander, and the Corinthian general Pellichus.

2. of Phaleron (*c*.350–283 BC) An Athenian statesman and philosopher who was the son of Phanostratus. He was a pupil of ARISTOTLE and THEOPHRASTUS and a Peripatetic philosopher. He entered politics in 325 and held the elected post of general for several years. After narrowly escaping death for his pro-Macedonian sympathies in 318, he was appointed by CASSANDER as governor of Athens in 317 and held the position of lawmaker and

virtual tyrant until his expulsion in 307 by DEMETRIUS (3) I the Besieger. During two years of constitution making (317–315), he revised Athens' laws on the lines of Aristotelian philosophy with the advice of THEOPHRASTUS, curbing extravagance, establishing a board of *nomophylakes* (guardians of the law) and regulating the duties of those undertaking services to the city. In 307 he fled from Athens to Thebes and then to Egypt, where he became an adviser to PTOLEMY (1) I, whom he urged to found the Museum at Alexandria. He collected many volumes for the library. He fell out with the king over the promotion of his son, who became PTOLEMY (2) II, and in whose reign he died in disgrace. He was a prolific writer of a variety of popular material, including moral treatises, speeches, works of literary and philosophical content, letters, etc., of which nothing has survived.

3. I the Besieger (*Poliorketes*) (337–283 BC) A king of Macedonia, the son of ANTIGONUS (1) I the One-eyed. In 321 he married Phila, daughter of ANTIPATER (1). In 317 and 316 he fought for his father against EUMENES (1) of Cardia. He was heavily beaten in 312 at Gaza by PTOLEMY (1) I of Egypt. In 306 he gained revenge by wresting Cyprus from the Egyptians and destroying their fleet. In 307 he delivered Athens from the oligarchic rule of DEMETRIUS (2) of Phalerum and restored the democracy. In 305 he invested Rhodes for a year for its failure to assist Antigonus, but failed to take it, thus earning his nickname. In 304 he revived the Corinthian League and won himself a stable foothold in Greece. In 301 Antigonus and Demetrius were defeated at the battle of Ipsus by a coalition of SELEUCUS (1) I, Ptolemy I, CASSANDER and LYSIMACHUS, and Antigonus was killed. The rash behaviour of Demetrius in the battle was partly responsible for his father's death. Demetrius fled to Ephesus – his Asiatic empire lost. In 298 he married his daughter Stratonice to

Seleucus. By 297 Cassander was dead: he had killed ALEXANDER (6) IV and PHILIP (2) III Arridaeus. Demetrius, after causing the death of Cassander's son, Alexander V, had the best claim to the throne of Macedonia through his wife Phila. He secured the kingdom in 294 by gaining the support of the army, but was driven out again in 287 by a coalition of PYR-RHUS of Epirus, Ptolemy and Lysimachus. He was a tactless and arrogant man whom the Macedonians were no longer prepared to follow in his ambition to reconquer his Asiatic empire. He led a small mercenary army to Asia Minor where he sustained his independence for two years until Seleucus captured him in 285 in Cilicia. He was subjected to his son-in-law's enforced hospitality until he died of drink. He was succeeded by his son ANTIGONUS (2) II Gonatas, who had remained in Greece.

4. the Fair (died 253 BC) A son of DEME-TRIUS (3) I the Besieger. He was sent by his half-brother ANTIGONUS (2) II Gona-tas, king of Macedonia (c.255), to take Cyrene in north Africa from the Egyp-tians. Having succeeded in his mission, he was the victim of an insurrection led by BERENICE (3) II and killed. He left a son, ANTIGONUS (3) III Doson.

5. II (c.276–229 BC) A king of Macedo-nia and the son of ANTIGONUS (2) II Gonatas. He succeeded his father in 239. On his accession, he divorced his childless wife, Stratonice, daughter of ANTIOCHUS (1) I, and married Phthia, daughter of ALEXANDER (5), who bore him the future PHILIP (3) V. Now in alliance with Epirus, Demetrius became embroiled in a war with the Aetolian and Achaean confederacies as the former tried to annex Acarnania: the Demetrian War. He succeeded in defending Acarnania and was successful in Central Greece where he won Boeotia, Phocis and Opuntian Locris from the Aetolian League: his general Bithys de-feated ARATUS (2) of Sicyon, a leader of the Achaean League, in 237. He suffered

a setback, however, c.236 when a revolu-tion in Epirus removed Alexander's suc-cessor and a democracy was created which joined Demetrius' enemies. He formed an alliance with an Illyrian king, Agron, to protect Acarnania, but was defeated and killed while fighting the invading Dardani. He was succeeded by ANTIGONUS (3) III who supplanted his son Philip.

6. I (187–150 BC) A king of the Seleucid kingdom of Syria. Demetrius I, the first king not to be called Seleucus or Anti-ochus, was his father SELEUCUS (4) IV's second son. He was an energetic young man, some 25 years old when he seized power in 162. He had been a hostage in Rome, but had escaped with the aid of POLYBIUS. He made his way home and overthrew his cousin, ANTIOCHUS (5) V, who was an 11-year-old child. Demetrius' reign had an auspicious start as he put an end to a rebellion in the east by an insurgent general, Timarchus, and in 161 subdued the Jewish revolt of the Macca-bees. The Roman senate recognised his title to the throne in 160 (he took the title *Soter*, 'Saviour'). Trouble came to him from Asia Minor: he wished for political reasons to marry his sister to ARIARATHES (5) V, king of Cappadocia, but that monarch refused, and Demetrius sup-ported a pretender to his throne. Ariar-athes' friend and ally, King ATTALUS (2) II of Pergamon, then stepped in and sup-ported a pretender to the Seleucid throne, ALEXANDER (10) Balas, a man of obscure origin who claimed to be a son of ANTI-OCHUS (4) IV. Balas had the support not only of Pergamon and Cappadocia, but also of Rome, Egypt and the Jews. Deme-trius was killed in battle by Balas in 150.

7. II (c.161–125 BC) A king of Syria, eldest son of DEMETRIUS (6) I, he took refuge in Crete on his father's death in 150, where he had gained the support of the king of Egypt, PTOLEMY (6) VI, whose eldest daughter, Cleopatra Thea, he mar-ried. After ejecting ALEXANDER (10) Balas from the throne in 145, he was forced a year later to share his throne with the general, DIODOTUS (3) Tryphon, who had first promoted the claims of the baby son of Balas, but then in 142 deposed the child and himself took power in Palestine, where Demetrius was unpopular for his oppressive treatment of the Jews. In 140, however, in a campaign against the Parthians, Demetrius was captured and held prisoner by them for ten years. In 129, after a decisive victory over the Syrians, the Parthians released him and he regained his throne. Four years later, while undertaking an expedition against Egypt, he suffered the indignity of being replaced on his throne by yet another pretender, supported by PTOLEMY (8) VIII, ALEXANDER (11) Zebina. On his return to Syria, Demetrius, who had taken the title *Nicator* ('Conqueror'), was defeated near Damascus by Zebina, and fled to Tyre, where he was assassinated by Egyptian agents (his mother-in-law, Queen CLEOPATRA (3) II of Egypt, had offered him the throne of that country). He left two sons and was succeeded by the elder, SELEUCUS (5) V, who was murdered by his mother within a year.

8. I (*c*.230–*c*.170 BC) A king of Bactria and Sogdiana, the son of EUTHYDEMUS (2), he became king on the death of his father *c*.186. During his father's reign he enlarged the territory by annexing Arachosia and Drangiana (approximately Afghanistan) from the Seleucid kingdom of ANTIOCHUS (3) III; he founded the city of Demetrias in Arachosia to seal his conquests. It is disputed whether or not he invaded India and established for a time a joint Indo-Bactrian empire. It is possible that a later Demetrius of Bactria (DEMETRIUS (9) II) accomplished that feat and issued bilingual coinage. Around 170 Demetrius was attacked and killed by EUCRATIDES.

9. II (reigned *c*.145–140 BC) Probably a son of DEMETRIUS (8) I who briefly ruled

a slice of the Bactrian kingdom in the Oxus valley after the death of EUCRATIDES.

10. (died 214 BC) A ruler of Pharos, a small island state in the Adriatic (now Hvar in Dalmatia), who gained his power by betraying Corcyra to Rome in 229. At the battle of Sellasia in 222 he helped ANTIGONUS (3) III Doson of Macedonia against CLEOMENES (2) III of Sparta. In 220 he broke his treaty with Rome by jointly ravaging the Greek coast and Aegean islands with the Illyrian SCERDILAIDAS. Consequently, in 219 Rome expelled him from Pharos and he took refuge with PHILIP (3) V of Macedonia, whom he encouraged in his opposition to the Romans. He became involved in Macedonian intervention in Messenia and was killed at Messene. See Polybius, *History* 3. 19.

11. of Ixion (C2 BC) A writer on grammar who quarrelled with ARISTARCHUS (3) and migrated to Pergamon, where he challenged the principles on which Aristarchus' criticism was based.

12. the Laconian (C2 BC) An Epicurean philosopher who criticised CARNEADES for denying that proof is possible, and explained EPICURUS' teachings about the concept of time.

13. of Apamea (C2 BC) A physician and writer on medicine in the tradition of HEROPHILUS. He wrote two major works that survive: *Signs* and *Affections*, which both show his interest in many physical and mental diseases and especially in gynaecology. He had an independent approach and was prepared to contradict Herophilus. There exists a papyrus reference to him and he is also known from later writers on medicine. See H. von Staden, *From Andreas to Demosthenes Philalethes* (1995).

14. of Magnesia (C1 BC) A writer, friendly with the Roman banker Atticus, who wrote lost works: a treatise on *Concord* and on writers and towns with identical names.

15. of Tarsus (C1 BC) A grammarian whom PLUTARCH made a character in his work, *The Failure of Oracles*. Plutarch reports that he visited Britain from where he returned to Tarsus. Two Greek inscriptions in the York Museum may have been composed by him.

16. The author of an extant treatise in Greek, *On Style*, which was incorrectly ascribed to DEMETRIUS (2) of Phaleron, but must be dated to the first century BC or AD. The work has a Peripatetic character and may be the work of Demetrius (see DEMETRIUS 15) of Tarsus. See D.A. Russell (1981) *Criticism in Antiquity*, London: Duckworth.

Democedes (C6 BC) A doctor of medicine from Croton in southern Italy. He practised in Athens and Aegina and then worked in Samos under the tyrant POLYCRATES (1). When Samos was captured by the Persians in 522, he was sent to Susa, the capital of Persia, where he practised medicine successfully for the family of DARIUS (1) I. He returned to Italy and settled in Croton where he married a daughter of MILON the athlete. He again left his city because of a revolution and moved to Plataea in Boeotia.

Demochares (*c.*360–275 BC) An Athenian statesman and orator of the late fourth and early third centuries. He was a nephew of the orator DEMOSTHENES (2). In 322 he publicly protested against the surrender of Athenian politicians, who had opposed Macedonia, to ANTIPATER (1). Consequently, he was forced to leave Athens. He returned in 307 after the restoration of democracy by DEMETRIUS (3) I the Besieger, and fortified Athens and allied her with the Boeotians during the Four Years' War with CASSANDER from 307–304. He was exiled (*c.*303) for ridiculing a decree to honour Demetrius. He

returned (*c.*287) and recovered Eleusis from ANTIGONUS (2) II Gonatas of Macedonia. He was a leading political figure over the next decade and negotiated financial support for Athens from PTOLEMY (1) I and LYSIMACHUS. In 280 he secured a decree vindicating Demosthenes. He left more than twenty-one books of speeches and historical writing, which have not survived. See P. Green (1990) *Alexander to Actium*, Berkeley, CA; Los Angeles, CA: University of California Press.

Democritus (*c.*460–356 BC) A philosopher who developed the atomic theory of LEUCIPPUS. The son of a rich citizen of Abdera in Thrace, he was said to have travelled widely in Egypt and the rest of the Persian empire. As a philosopher, he learnt from Leucippus, ANAXAGORAS, and perhaps PROTAGORAS. PLATO (1) and ARISTOTLE were both influenced by his thinking, and the latter mentions his name often, whereas Plato wanted to burn all his books. Our best authority for him is DIOGENES (5) Laërtius who records seventy titles of his works. The subject matter consists of physics, ethics, mathematics, music, and technical material. None of his works survives except for small fragments. The contributions of Leucippus and Democritus to the atomic theory cannot now be disentangled: it was in any case a response to the Eleatic theory of the one-ness and motionlessness of the universe, which denied the existence of empty space. The atomists rescued the real world as we know it by postulating the existence of the void. According to their theory, the atoms, which constitute reality, are many, small, solid and indivisible, of the same material, but of different shapes and sizes, and by moving around in the void produce the various material objects, solid, liquid and gaseous, of the visible world. The atomists could not explain the cause of motion. They also postulated the existence of many other similar 'worlds'. There was a consequent theory of perception and of the soul, which was considered as perishable as the body, as it, too, was made of atoms. The theory is best-known to us from the writings of EPICURUS and Lucretius. The ethical aspect of Democritus' theory is somewhat unclear to us, but he had in antiquity the reputation of cheerfulness (the 'Laughing Philosopher') and may have preached moderation, participation in politics, and democracy. We know almost nothing about his mathematics. Aristotle respected him as a biologist. He lived to a great age, dying at about 104 years. Democritus was a seminal figure in the development of thought, but he suffered in that posterity preferred the theories of his rivals and his works perished. His greatest successor was Epicurus, who seems to have disdained him. See G.S. Kirk, J.E. Raven and M. Schofield (1982) *The Presocratic Philosophers*, Cambridge: CUP.

Demonax (C2 AD) A Cynic philosopher from Cyprus. His biography, attributed to his pupil LUCIAN exists. He inherited wealth, but renounced his inheritance. He was a pupil of EPICTETUS, DEMETRIUS (16), Timocrates of Heraclea and Agathobulus. He lived a simple life, partly in Athens, travelled much, and starved himself to death when nearly 100 years old.

Demophanes and Ecdelus (C3 BC) Two citizens of Megalopolis in Arcadia who became famous as the liberators of their own city in 251 from the tyrant Aristodemus, whose murder they encompassed, and at the same time liberators of Sicyon, whose tyrant they helped ARATUS (2) to overthrow. Previously they had lived in Athens and studied under ARCESILAUS at the Academy. They also gave Cyrene in Libya a constitution, perhaps at the request of DEMETRIUS (4) the Fair. They were the teachers of their fellow citizen PHILOPOEMEN.

Demosthenes 1. (*c*.460–413 BC) An Athenian general of the Peloponnesian War and the son of Alcisthenes. He was elected

general in the early part of the war and, after an unsuccessful invasion of Aetolia in 426, he won a resounding victory in Amphilochia, beating a combined force of Peloponnesians and Ambraciots at Olpae and annihilating the Ambraciot survivors at Aedomenes. He thus destroyed the enemies' influence in north-western Greece. In 425, after losing his post of general, he was sent with a fleet towards Corcyra with the permission of the people to harass the Spartans in any way he could. Seeing that Sparta's weakness was the hostility of the Messenians, he landed with a force of men and fortified Pylos, later capturing an important force of Spartan hoplites on the adjacent island of Sphacteria. This move might have ended the war on terms favourable to Athens, but CLEON opposed peace. In 424 he failed in an attempt to take Megara, though he captured Nisaea; and later in the year, in a three-pronged attack on Boeotia, he failed to land his force at Siphae as his plan had been betrayed. This was a factor that led to the Athenian defeat at Delium. He held no further command until 413 when he was sent with reinforcements to rescue NICIAS (1) at Syracuse. He failed to recapture the heights of Epipolae in a night attack and urged Nicias to withdraw from Sicily, which he refused to do. During the subsequent retreat of the Athenians, Demosthenes commanded the rearguard: he and his men were surrounded in an orchard and, after surrendering, were killed. Demosthenes may have been an associate of Cleon's, but it is hard to see strong political leanings in him: he leaves the impression of an able strategist and a loyal citizen.

2. (384–322 BC) An Athenian statesman and orator of the fourth century BC who was much admired for his rhetorical power. His father died when he was 7 years old and left him a fortune from his cutlery and sword-making business; but the trustees of the will, his father's

brothers and friend, Therippides, misman-
aged the estate and left him with only a
fraction of his inheritance when he came
of age. They negotiated with him for three
years while he studied rhetoric, probably
under ISAEUS and EUBULIDES, and prepared himself for litigation. Aged 21, he
prosecuted his trustees with the extant
speeches, *Against Aphobus* and *Against
Onetor*, but had to wait two more years
until he received what was left of his
inheritance. He proceeded to make his
living as a writer of court speeches and as
an assistant to prosecutors in public trials.
From 355, after the close of the Social
War in which Athens had failed to disci-
pline her allies, Demosthenes took an ever
greater part in politics, evidenced by both
his court speeches and his speeches to the
Athenian Assembly. He argued that
Athens should strive to maintain her
independence and her power, and consequently build up reserves for war. From
352, when PHILIP (1) II of Macedonia
attacked Thrace, Demosthenes' principal
motive was opposition to Philip and
Macedonian imperialism.

His first speeches with political overtones were written for Diodorus, *Against
Androtion* in 355 and *Against Timocrates*
in 353. He himself delivered *Against
Leptines* in 354. These three speeches all
seem to have been directed against the
policies of ARISTOPHON. In 354 he also
spoke in the same cause in the Assembly
with the speech *On the Navy Boards* (*On
the Symmories*). His first direct approach
to foreign policy is represented by his two
speeches of 352, *For the Megalopolitans*
(urging that Athens support the Arcadians, whose capital was the city of
Megalopolis, against Sparta) and *Against
Aristocrates*, in which Demosthenes argued against the proposal to honour
CHARIDEMUS for his work in regaining
the Thracian Chersonese by negotiating
with the Thracian prince, CERSOBLEPTES.
He showed himself unrealistic in his
appreciation of Athens' power in the
Thracian area, but his main motive was

to attack EUBULUS (1). At this time,
Demosthenes regarded Cersobleptes as a
greater danger than Philip – an illusion
that was shattered late in 352 when Philip
attacked the Thracians and threatened the
Chersonese.

From this time Demosthenes made his
crusade against the Macedonian menace
his chief preoccupation. He made a series
of three speeches: the *Philippics*, in which
he sought to stir the Athenians against the
northern threat; the *First Philippic*, delivered in the Assembly in early 351, which
advocated stronger action to help Amphipolis, but failed in its purpose; and *The
Liberty of the Rhodians*, which he delivered late in the year to plead for support
for the democratic party of Rhodes against
an oligarchic government maintained by
the Carian monarchy. In this last speech,
he was again unsuccessful because his
arguments were weak and the time for
such intervention was unpropitious. Philip
was preoccupied during these years in the
west, but in 349 he turned his attention
southwards and intervened in Thessaly
and established friendly relations with
Persia. Philip besieged the city of Olynthus,
and Demosthenes delivered three speeches
in succession, the *Olynthiac Speeches*,
urging that full support be given to
Olynthus and that the practice of handing
over financial surpluses to the Theoric
Fund, for entertaining the Athenian people in the theatre, should be suspended in
the emergency. As a result, three expeditionary forces were authorised but could
not be sent in time, and in summer 348
Olynthus was taken by Philip. Demosthenes came into conflict with the party of
Eubulus, who supported a disastrous intervention in Euboea, which failed and
cost Athens the loss of the island as well
as allowing Philip to move up to Thermopylae and threaten Boeotia. After this
failure, Demosthenes claimed, probably
without justification, that he alone had
been against the intervention in Euboea.

Athens was now isolated and enfeebled,
and it was clear both to Demosthenes and

his opponents that the only hope lay in making peace with Philip and in assisting in the ending of the Sacred War, which had been going on in Central Greece since 355. Demosthenes made a temporary alliance with his opponents, and in the autumn of 348 defended PHILOCRATES, a supporter of Eubulus, when he was prosecuted for illegally proposing that negotiations be undertaken with Philip. In the Athenian year 347/6, Demosthenes was a member of the council and served on the embassy to Philip, which Philocrates led to Pella in early 346, and which made the Peace of Philocrates on terms favourable to Athens. Demosthenes was president of the Assembly that debated the proposal of peace, and did not himself speak, thus acquiescing in the decision to accept it. He was a member of a second embassy to Pella in May to receive Philip's oath to the treaty. Philip swore the oath in July while assembling his forces to finish off the Sacred War against Phocis. Philip twice called on his new Athenian allies to send troops to assist in the attack on Phocis, but on Demosthenes' advice none was sent. He asserted that Philip would seize the Athenians as hostages. Philip took Phocis without Athenian help, but did not invade Attica, as Demosthenes had feared. Demosthenes spoke for conciliating Philip in the late summer after the Athenians had snubbed him over his presidency of the Pythian Games at Delphi. He delivered his speech *On the Peace* in late 346 in which he argued for respecting the treaty, though he attacked its main proponent, AESCHINES (2), by attempting to have him prosecuted by Timarchus when his conduct was scrutinised on departing from office. Aeschines, however, anticipated the attack by himself successfully prosecuting Timarchus, who early in 345 was disenfranchised for immorality.

In 344 Demosthenes was sent on a counter-productive embassy to Argos, Arcadia and Messene to oppose Philip's influence in the Peloponnese, which led to protests from Philip and a strengthen-

ing of his power in the states in question. He sent a proposal to Athens that the treaty be turned into a common peace. In reply, Demosthenes delivered his *Second Philippic* in which he denounced Philip as hostile and unworthy of negotiation. He asserted that Philip had been able to take Phocis by bribing the Athenian envoys. In 343 HYPERIDES successfully prosecuted Philip's supporter, Philocrates, and Demosthenes had Proxenus fined. Demosthenes also renewed the attack on Aeschines with his court speech *On the False Embassy*, in which he accused his opponent of corruption in his dealings on the embassies to Philip. Aeschines, even with the support of Eubulus and PHOCION, barely escaped the death penalty. In 342 Philip adopted a more aggressive policy towards Greece, his proposal of a common peace having failed through Athenian intransigence, provoked by HEGESIPPUS. Demosthenes was sent with Hegesippus on an embassy to states in the Peloponnese and elsewhere to seek allies and support against Philip. Many alliances were made, but Sparta was isolated and Thessaly offered no hope. Philip advanced through Thrace to threaten the Athenian supply of grain, which was shipped from the Crimea through the straits. A stand-off occurred between Diopeithes, the Athenian commander in the Chersonese, and the Macedonians over the city of Cardia. Demosthenes delivered two powerful speeches, *On the Chersonese* and his *Third Philippic* in which he accused Philip of aggression. In these speeches he openly declared himself ready for war with Philip, though the pretext for war was weak because Diopeithes was the obvious aggressor at Cardia. He also delivered a *Fourth Philippic*, the authenticity of which is now generally accepted, in which he successfully demanded that Athens ally herself with Persia to further war against Philip. Demosthenes was the clear leader of Athens and secured alliances with Byzantium and Abydus. Hyperides won alliances with Rhodes and

Chios. Diopeithes was reinforced. There were further Athenian successes at Megara and in Euboea. In March 340 at an assembly of Athens' allies a decision was taken to gather men and money for war, and Demosthenes was voted a gold crown for his efforts.

In the summer of 340, Philip replied to Athens' belligerence by attacking Perinthus and Byzantium. He then denounced Athens' breaches of the peace, but the Athenian Assembly replied by tearing up the treaty. Philip's siege of Byzantium failed because of vigorous Athenian assistance. Demosthenes used his own funds in the cause and was appointed Fleet Commissioner. In 339 he succeeded in persuading the people to divert surplus funds from the Theoric (entertainment) Fund for military use. In the same year, Philip was elected leader of the Amphictionic League's forces. As Thebes had expelled a Macedonian garrison from Nicaea near Thermopylae, Philip had a pretext to interfere in Boeotia, and late in the year he advanced to Elatea. Athens countered by forming an alliance with Thebes, which was greatly alarmed by Philip's presence in Boeotia. Various military and diplomatic manoeuvres took place during the first half of 338, but Demosthenes kept the Athenians firmly committed to war and was crowned at the festival of Dionysus in March. In summer Philip captured Amphissa and forced the allies back to Chaeronea, where a decisive battle took place, probably in August. Philip won a complete victory and Demosthenes left the field of battle before the end to organise resistance at Athens.

Though Aeschines accused him of fleeing from the battle, Demosthenes had secured the defence of Athens and went on a voyage to ensure the grain supply did not run out. He remained popular enough to be voted to deliver the funeral speech for the dead of the year of Chaeronea. The peace terms, which were negotiated by others with Philip, allowed the state to exist enfeebled and to become an ally of

Macedonia and a member of a new Greek League. In 337 Demosthenes was elected chief commissioner of the Theoric Fund, and he had the Piraeus strengthened. Ctesiphon proposed that Demosthenes be crowned with gold at the City Dionysia in 336, but was prosecuted by Aeschines for the illegality of the act. Athens sent a contingent, which was requested by Philip, to fight for him in Persia on the advice of Phocion but, after the assassination of Philip, Demosthenes saw an opportunity to assert Athens' independence. However, Philip's son, ALEXANDER (3) III the Great, quickly marched south and crushed the opposition. Demosthenes was appointed a member of a party that was sent to apologise to Alexander for the disaffection shown by Athens in the aftermath of Philip's death. However, he could not go through with it and turned back from his mission. Alexander forgave Athens, however, and went north to settle the Balkans. A rumour of Alexander's death prompted Demosthenes to negotiate a grant of 300 talents from DARIUS (3) III to arm Athens against the Macedonians, and he promoted the return of Theban exiles and the expulsion of the Macedonian garrison from Thebes. After Alexander's return and the destruction of Thebes, he demanded the surrender of Demosthenes for his subversion of Thebes, and only the intervention of Phocion saved Demosthenes' life. Demosthenes continued to place his hopes vainly in the victory of Persia to liberate Greece. In 330 Aeschines revived his attack on Demosthenes by prosecuting Ctesiphon for the proposal to crown Demosthenes. The latter replied in Ctesiphon's defence with his most famous speech, *On the Crown*, and Aeschines lost the case so decisively that he went into permanent exile.

Demosthenes played a prominent but ineffectual role in the affairs of Athens under Macedonian rule until the HARPALUS incident of 324, which was his downfall. In summer 324, at the Olympic Games, NICANOR (1) proclaimed the return of all exiles, a matter of concern to Athens, which had ousted the Samians in favour of Athenian settlers and feared the displacement of the settlers by the Samians. Moreover, there had been countless exiles among the mercenary forces of Alexander, some of whom were brought home by Harpalus. Demosthenes protested publicly at the decision on an embassy he led to Olympia. When Alexander, in the same year, asked the Greek states to accord him divine honours for the services he had performed in avenging them on Persia, Demosthenes ridiculed his claim. On the sudden arrival of Alexander's unstable friend Harpalus, seeking refuge in Athens with a large treasure after his maladministration of Alexander's finances, Demosthenes proposed putting the money in the Acropolis, but seems to have taken some of it himself, possibly for purposes of state. Demosthenes, along with eight others, including DEMADES, was accused by HYPERIDES before the Court of Areopagus of appropriating twenty talents and was fined fifty talents. Demosthenes fled first to Aegina and then to Calauria, an island off Troezen. After Alexander's death in the summer of 323, Demosthenes supported Hyperides' plans to resist the Macedonians, which led to the Lamian War. Demosthenes was recalled to Athens and his fine was paid by the state. However, ANTIPATER (1), after his victory at Crannon in 322, threatened to attack Athens unless the ringleaders of the opposition to Macedonia were handed over. Demosthenes fled once more to Calauria, where he killed himself by poison in the temple of Poseidon, thus anticipating the sentence of death passed by the Assembly on Demades' proposal to placate Antipater.

Demosthenes was a complex and ambiguous figure who was quite often prepared to compromise with what he disapproved of to keep himself at the head of affairs. He was a man of the democratic city-state, an institution that was doomed by the advent of powerful monarchies from the fringe of the Greek world. He is remembered for his powerful speeches, which were composed with a clarity of style that was unequalled by his rivals. Besides political speeches delivered in the Athenian Assembly and courtroom speeches on public issues, he wrote many private legal speeches which have survived concerning civil cases, such as inheritance, guardianship, insurance, trespass and quasi-criminal cases of fraud and assault. Some sixty speeches of his have been preserved. See R. Sealey (1993) *Demosthenes and His Time*, Oxford, OUP; L. Pearson (1960) *The Art of Demosthenes*, Philadelphia, PA: American Philological Association, Chico; G.L. Cawkwell (1978) *Philip of Macedon*, London: Faber & Faber; and N.G.L. Hammond and G.T. Griffith (eds) (1979) *A History of Macedonia*, Oxford: Clarendon Press.

Dercylidas A Spartan general and harmost of Abydos. In 411 he was sent by the Spartan government to take Abydos and Lampsacus, which controlled the narrowest point of the Hellespont, from Athens. Dercylidas held on to the former and became its harmost. In 407 the Persian satrap PHARNABAZUS engineered Dercylidas' disgrace by denouncing him to Lysander. Dercylidas recovered and late in 399 was appointed successor to THIBRON (1) as Spartan commander in Asia Minor, where he was ordered to attack the Persian satraps. However, he lacked naval support and though he attacked Pharnabazus' satrapy, ravaged the west coast as far as Bithynia and secured several cities in Aeolis, as well as much booty, his campaign in Asia Minor achieved little. He crossed to the Thracian Chersonese, which he fortified by building a wall across the neck of the peninsula. In 397 he was again ordered to attack Caria, this time with naval support, and Pharnabazus and TISSAPHERNES, the two satraps of western Asia, combined forces to resist him. Dercylidas forced the Persians to offer peace terms, which King ARTAXERXES (2) II, however, refused to honour. The

Spartans sent their new king AGESILAUS II, in 396 to take over the command. In 394, after the battle of Cnidus, Dercylidas was sent by Agesilaus from Amphipolis to the Hellespont, where he won over the inhabitants of Abydus and Sestus and successfully defended his position against THRASYBULUS (2) and a combined attack by CONON (1) and PHARNABAZUS. Dercylidas remained at the Hellespont until 389, but never married. He was nicknamed 'Sisyphus' because of his cunning.

Diadochi The successors of ALEXANDER (3) III the Great, the Macedonian generals who divided up Alexander's empire after his death and the collapse of the arrangements for his succession. The Diadochi consisted of: ANTIPATER (1), who after the death of PERDICCAS (1) II was elected regent for Alexander's son; Antipater's son, CASSANDER, who murdered Alexander's son; ANTIGONUS (1) I the One-eyed and his son, DEMETRIUS (3) I; PTOLEMY (1) I of Egypt; LYSIMACHUS; EUMENES (1) (who was a secretary rather than a general and not a Macedonian) and SELEUCUS (1) I.

Diagoras (late C5 BC) A poet from Melos who was condemned to death at Athens for atheism in 411, but fled to Pallene and later to Corinth. Surviving fragments do not bear out his reputed atheism.

Dicaearchus (active c.326–296 BC) A philosopher of the Peripatetic school from Messene who spent much of his life in Sparta. He was a pupil of ARISTOTLE and a friend of THEOPHRASTUS. Only fragments of his works survive, but he was extremely influential and admired by ERATOSTHENES, Cicero, Josephus and PLUTARCH. His works include philosophical treatises; a dialogue entitled *The Soul*, which concerns the mortality and material composition of the soul; and a treatise entitled *The Destruction of Human Beings*, which regards people as more responsible for their destruction than

nature; geographical work on cartography (and possibly a description of the world as then known); lives of philosophers, including PLATO (1); literary history concerning HOMER and the musical and poetic contests; statements of the plots of works by the great dramatists EURIPIDES and SOPHOCLES (1); a history of culture entitled *The Life of Greece*; a treatise on the constitutions of Athens, Sparta, Corinth and Pellene; as well as other dialogues and treatises.

Didymus (c.80–c.10 BC) A very learned Alexandrian scholar and a prolific writer on literature: he was known as 'bronzeguts' (*Chalkenteros*) because of his enormous industry and 'forget-book' (*Bibliolathas*) because of inconsistencies in his writings. He is said to have produced 4,000 titles, most of which have perished. His treatise on ARISTARCHUS (3)'s recensions of HOMER, in which he tried to reconstitute Aristarchus' lost work by comparing copies and examining Aristarchus' commentaries, exists in fragments. Many scholia or marginal notes on Greek poetry arose from his commentaries. His method was to compile commentaries from the critical works of his predecessors, including TRYPHON: he did not do original research.

Dinarchus (c.360–c.290 BC) An Athenian orator from Corinth, a metic who composed speeches for others to deliver and the last of the Attic orators. Three of his speeches survive, all of which are connected with the HARPALUS affair (one of the speeches is also written against DEMOSTHENES 2). After the death of Demosthenes, when his rivals were all dead or in exile, Dinarchus flourished. In 322 ANTIPATER (1) appointed Dinarchus as governor of Corinth on behalf of the Macedonian state. Dinarchus later returned to Athens where he lived in comfort with the support of his friend DEMETRIUS (2) of Phaleron. DIONYSIUS (7) of Halicarnassus wrote his biography.

Dinarchus left Athens on the restoration of democracy in 307 and retired to Chalcis, from which he returned through the offices of THEOPHRASTUS in 292. His host, Proxenus, stole a considerable sum of money from him, for which Dinarchus successfully prosecuted him. He was not an original or very coherent speaker, lacking a clear-cut style of his own. HERMOGENES (2) called him 'a second-rate (*krithinos* lit. 'barley') Demosthenes'.

Dinon (C3 BC) A historian from Colophon who wrote a lost romanticised history of the Persian empire. It was popular in later times and influenced PLUTARCH in his *Life of Artaxerxes*. Dinon was the father of CLEITARCHUS.

Dio Chrysostom (*c*.AD40–115) A Greek rhetorician and popular philosopher. He was born at Prusa in Bithynia and his real name was Dio (or Dion) Cocceianus. *Chrysostomos* ('Golden-mouth') was a nickname given to him for his eloquence. He went to Rome to teach rhetoric and was influenced by the Stoic philosopher Musonius Rufus. Dio Chrysostom fell foul of Domitian, who banished him, and he spent the next years acting as a teacher while wandering through Greece and the Balkans. Nerva rehabilitated him, although he continued on his travelling ministry of preaching Stoic–Cynic philosophy. He was a friend of Trajan and, after retiring to Bithynia, was prosecuted at Nicaea before Pliny the Younger for mishandling a building contract. Eighty speeches attributed to Dio survive, although two were written by his pupil, Favorinus. Dio modelled his style on those of PLATO (1) and XENOPHON (1) and avoided excessive archaism, writing in the atticist style which was fashionable in his day. The subject matter of his speeches is very varied, though the exposition of his philosophical beliefs is common. He touches on mythology, morality, literature and politics. Several of his speeches were delivered to the Assembly of Citizens at

Prusa. See C.P. Jones (1978) *The Roman World of Dio Chrysostom*, Cambridge, MA: Harvard University Press.

Diocles 1. (late C5 BC) A Syracusan who banished HERMOCRATES while the latter was assisting the Spartans in the Peloponnesian War. He reformed the Syracusan constitution in 412 along democratic lines.

2. (C4 BC) A physician from Carystus in Euboea who spent most of his life at Athens. He was also the first physician to write in Attic Greek. He was influenced by ARISTOTLE, his contemporary, in his terminology. Other influences on him were the Hippocratic writers of EMPEDOCLES from whom he took the doctrine of the four humours, of the *pneuma* and the import of the heart, and the Sicilian school of medicine to which his father Anthemus belonged. He wrote extensively on medical topics, but only fragments remain. A work on animal anatomy is reported by GALEN. He wrote a herbal of which THEOPHRASTUS made much use. Pliny the Elder regarded him as second only to HIPPOCRATES (2).

Diodorus 1. (C4 BC) Known as Cronus, a philosopher of the Megarian school from Iasos who followed the teachings of ZENO (1) of Elea. He taught ZENO (2) of Citium, PHILON (2) the dialectician, and ARCESILAUS. His skill earned him the nickname 'Dialectician'.

2. (C3 BC) A writer of comedies from Sinope two of whose plays were presented at Athens in 288. He acted at Delos in 284 and 280. He may have been related to DIPHILUS.

3. Siculus ('The Sicilian') (C1 BC) He was a historian from Agyrium in Sicily who lived until at least 21. He wrote a world history, which was entitled *Bibliotheke* ('Library'), in forty volumes, from the earliest times to 54. His historical method guaranteed unreliability as he epitomized a large number of varied sources un-critically. Some of his books are preserved in full (1–5, 11–20), the rest are fragmentary. He seems to have used a relatively accurate, independent chronological source and to have built his narrative into it. His source for books 11–16 was EPHORUS, while books 18–20, relying on HIERONYMUS (1), on the successors to ALEXANDER (3) III the Great, rise to something approaching the quality of their original. He also used HECATAEUS (2)'s accounts of Egypt and of the JEWS. He made extensive use of TIMAEUS (2) for Sicilian history. Despite his deficiencies, he is a valuable source of information, as we lack the sources he drew on.

4. (C1 BC) A mathematician and astronomer from Alexandria, whose main contribution to knowledge was a work entitled *Analemma* on the geometry of the plain sundial. Part of his work, on determining the meridian, survives in Latin and Arabic translations.

Diodotus 1. (C5 BC) An Athenian politician who opposed the proposal of CLEON in 427 to kill all the male citizens of Mytilene in Lesbos (who had rebelled) and enslave the rest. The resolution was repealed just in time to save them. Instead, Mytilene's walls were razed, its land forfeited and the ringleaders of the revolt were killed.

2. A satrap of Bactria-Sogdiana in the Seleucid kingdom who between 255–240 BC rebelled against ANTIOCHUS (2) II or his son, SELEUCUS (2) II, and founded an independent kingdom. His success caused ARSACES, leader of the Parni, to invade the neighbouring territory of Parthia and to establish (*c*.250) a new kingdom there. Diodotus was succeeded on his death (*c*.235) by his son of the same name who made an alliance with the Parthians, but was overthrown in 226 by EUTHYDEMUS (2).

3. Tryphon (C2 BC) A king of the Seleucid kingdom of Syria. As a general of the army, he promoted the claims of the infant son of ALEXANDER (10) Balas, but then in 142 deposed and killed the child and himself seized power in Palestine where DEMETRIUS (7) II was unpopular for his oppressive treatment of the JEWS. However, internal strife led in 143 to the establishment of Hasmonean rule, and in 138 Diodotus was attacked and defeated in Antioch by ANTIOCHUS (7) VII of Side. Diodotus committed suicide.

Diogenes 1. of Apollonia (mid-C5 BC) A philosopher from Apollonia in Thrace, the son of Apollothemis. He was of the Ionic tradition and revived the theory of ANAXIMENES that air ('ether') is the first principle of the universe. He claimed that air was divine, intelligent and the moving spirit of things and that it was constantly transformed by rarefaction and condensation. We know little of his life, except that he visited Athens. His views were satirised by ARISTOPHANES (1) in 423 in his comedy *Clouds*. Though he borrows ideas from ANAXAGORAS and LEUCIPPUS, his approach to philosophy is remote from their materialism. He wrote a book entitled *On Nature*, much of which survives in quotation by Simplicius, although his other works have not survived. He made a strong contribution to medical science and is the successor of EMPEDOCLES in the Pneumatic school of medicine and advanced theories concerning respiration, generation, and the blood. ARISTOTLE preserved his account of the veins in *History of Animals* (511b 30). See W.K.C. Guthrie (1962–78) *History of Greek Philosophy*, Cambridge: CUP, vol. 2; and J. Longrigg (1994) *Greek Rational Medicine*, London: Routledge.

2. the Cynic (*c*.400–*c*.323 BC) A celebrated philosopher, born at Sinope near the Black Sea, son of Hicesias, who was manager of the mint, Doigenes was one of the founders of the Cynic school of philosophy. He migrated to Athens some time after 362 after his father, a coin-maker, had been exiled from Sinope for debasing the currency. Chronology makes it doubtful that he studied under ANTIS-THENES, who was probably dead before Diogenes reached Athens, but he was strongly influenced by Antisthenes. Diogenes was distinguished by the simplicity and poverty of his way of life and his rejection of conventions that he regarded as unnatural. By practising asceticism (*askesis*) he believed that the body could be trained to make do with very little (the principle of self-sufficiency, *autarkeia*). He taught that virtue consists in the avoidance of pleasure and that happiness could be attained by satisfying natural needs in the simplest practical way. Because of his unconventionality and the supposed shamelessness of his behaviour, he came to be known at Athens as 'The Dog' (*kyon*) and the term stuck with his school of thought ('Cynic'). He used drastic practical demonstrations and caustic wit as his main aids to teaching those who would hear him. Little is known of his life, though many legends grew up around such an eccentric character, for instance, the legend of his meeting with ALEXANDER (3) III the Great in which Diogenes is said to have requested, on being offered assistance by the king, that he move out of his sunlight. Diogenes was quickly adopted as a character in fiction and satire. He seems to have spent his later years in Corinth where he may have been the tutor of the sons of one Xeniades.

He wrote dialogues and tragedies of which a few fragments have survived. Much that is attributed to him in ancient writings must be spurious. His greatest disciple was CRATES (2). Diogenes had a considerable influence on the development of the Stoic creed: Stoics liked to see a transmission of philosophic doctrine starting with SOCRATES and descending through Antisthenes, Diogenes and Crates, to ZENO (2) of Citium.

3. the Babylonian (*c*.240–152 BC) A Stoic philosopher of the second century from Seleuceia on the Tigris, and hence known as 'the Babylonian'. He was a pupil of CHRYSIPPUS at Athens and succeeded ZENO (3) of Tarsus as head of the Stoic school. He was a reformer in terms of the development of Stoic thinking and started the changes in detail and presentation that are usually associated with his pupil, PANAETIUS. He was a member, with CAR-NEADES and CRITOLAUS, of a deputation of philosophers to Rome in 156 to plead for mercy after an Athenian incursion into Oropus in Boeotia. While he was in Rome, he won converts to Stoicism. He wrote the following works which have not survived: *Prophecy*, *The Guiding Principle of the Soul*, *Nobility*, *Speech* and *Athena*.

4. (C2 AD) An Epicurean philosopher of Oenoanda in Asia Minor who was known from a now fragmentary but important inscription set up in a portico in which he set forth Epicurean doctrine. The inscription includes copies of EPICURUS' letters, of which one was addressed to his mother, and letters written by Diogenes himself, one a defence of old age.

5. Laërtius (early C3 AD) A writer of biography, of whose own life nothing is known, though his name suggests an origin at Laërte in Cilicia. He wrote about the lives and doctrines of various philosophers in ten extant books, entitled *Lives of the Philosophers*. The early chapters include non-Greek thinkers. Thereafter, he divides the Greeks into eastern and western branches and the last chapters consist of the minority of those who do not fit his classification. He was uncritical in his use of sources and compiled the work of earlier biographers and philosophical epitomisers. Despite switching erratically between sources, he was, however, careful enough to name them. There is much retailing of anecdote and each thinker is dealt with twice, first in summary and then in a more expansive form. Some of his accounts are of great value, such as that of Stoicism in Book 7 and the long citations of EPICURUS. He also preserved the wills of PLATO (1) and ARISTOTLE. He also quotes some of his own poetry.

Diogenianus 1. (C2? AD) An Epicurean philosopher whose attack on CHRYSIPPUS' doctrine of fate is quoted by Eusebius.

2. (C2 AD) A compiler of geographical and lexicographic material from Heraclea in Pontus. See PAMPHILUS (2).

Dion (c.408–354 BC) A tyrant of Syracuse, the son of Hipparinus, who became both the brother-in-law and the son-in-law of the tyrant DIONYSIUS (1) I, and a close friend of PLATO (1), whom he met while the latter visited the court of Dionysius in 387. When Dionysius died in 367, Dion, uncle to the new tyrant, DIONYSIUS (2) II, invited Plato back to train him in philosophy. Subsequently, however, there was a power-struggle and in 366 the historian PHILISTUS persuaded Dionysius to banish Dion (Dionysius kept Plato briefly at his court). Dion went to live in Athens and associated with the Academy. Meanwhile, Dionysius had confiscated Dion's property and forced his wife to remarry. In 357 he returned to Syracuse, which he took with a small force during Dionysius' absence in Italy. He was made ruler by popular acclaim, but rapidly became unpopular through his anti-democratic attitude and was replaced in power by his deputy, HERACLIDES (2), who had won an impressive naval victory over Dionysius' forces. Dion went into exile at Leontini from where he was recalled when Dionysius made a further attack. Dion succeeded in repelling the attack and then had his enemy, Heraclides, assassinated. He resumed power and embarked on a programme of Platonic reforms. He became increasingly unpopular again, however, and was murdered, an act that was organised by an Athenian, Callippus, who briefly ruled

Syracuse. Dion's attempt at a benevolent tyranny failed because of the defects of his character, his lack of popular support, and insufficient military power.

Dionysius 1. I (c.432–367 BC) A tyrant of Syracuse and son of Hermocritus. He started his career in a government office and supported his father-in-law, the statesman HERMOCRATES, in his attempt to return to Syracuse from exile in 408. He showed talent as a demagogue and in 405, after Syracusan failure to relieve the siege of Acragas by Carthage, he persuaded the assembly to elect a new board of generals, himself included. Within a year he had ousted and liquidated his colleagues, thus bringing the period of democracy at Syracuse to an end. He became a general with full power, a position to which he was thereafter regularly re-elected until his death, and married Hermocrates' daughter. He suffered a double setback in fighting the Carthaginians and a popular revolt, which he put down harshly. He fortified the Epipolae hills which overlook Syracuse, turned the island of Ortygia into his private fortress, manned by his mercenary troops, destroyed the city of Naxos, which had opposed Syracuse, hired large forces of mercenaries, planted his supporters in Catana and Leontini, and attacked the Carthaginians again – this time with success. He defeated the Carthaginians in two wars, the first from 397 to 395 when, after capturing Motya in western Sicily, he overcame, with Spartan help, a siege of Syracuse by Himilco (a plague is reported to have struck down much of the Carthaginian force); and in 392 by dictating terms favourable to Syracuse, he confined the Carthaganians to the north-west of Sicily. Dionysius next invaded Italy and in 388, together with Lucanian allies, he won the battle of the River Elleporus against a combined army of Greek states of Italy. In 387 he took the strategic city of Rhegium (Reggio). At this stage, he was the strongest ruler in Magna Graecia, the Greek-speaking area of southern Italy and Sicily. He formed an alliance with the Spartan colony of Taras (Taranto) and advanced his influence to the Adriatic, where he joined the Parians in colonising the islands of Issa and Pharos (Vis and Hvar in Croatia) and allied himself with the exiled ALCETAS, king of the Molossians in Epirus, whom he restored to his throne. He also raided Agylla in Etruria and took rich booty. He renewed the war with the Carthaginians in 382, but c.375 he was seriously defeated at Cronium and had to cede the territory west of the River Halycus. He made a further attack in 368, when he took Selinus, Eryx and Entella, and besieged Lilybaeum, but died after a reign of thirty-eight years. After the suicide of his first wife in 405, he bigamously married Aristomache and Doris (the latter bore him his heir).

Though the government of Syracuse formally proceeded as normal, it was in fact manipulated by Dionysius and his close family. The basis of his power was his fortress in Ortygia, as well as his army and fleet, which were manned by selected mercenaries. He was a subtle and clever manipulator who learnt how to control the people by disarming them and keeping them strictly supervised. He uprooted populations and brought about the loss of traditional loyalties within the cities of Sicily and southern Italy. He had a large armaments industry and developed the use of artillery, such as catapults and siege engines. He relied on warfare and piratical plundering to maintain the loyalty of his mercenary supporters. He was a successful soldier, but his campaigns against his principal enemy, Carthage, were on the whole a draw (although he did save the island from conquest by Carthage). He brought prosperity to Syracuse and probably became popular with most citizens as time passed. He had ambitions as a poet and wrote a tragedy, *The Ransoming of Hector*, which won a prize at the Athenian Lenaea festival in 367, although many people mocked his plays. He

bought heirlooms of AESCHYLUS and EURIPIDES, and had statues erected of himself as Dionysus, god of the theatre. He was succeeded by his son, DIONYSIUS (2) II. See B. Caven (1990) *Dionysius I, War-Lord of Sicily*, New Haven, Conn.; London: Yale University Press; M.I. Finley (1954) *Ancient Sicily*, New York: Viking Press; and L.J. Sanders (1987) *Dionysius I of Syracuse and Greek Tyranny*, London: Croom Helm.

2. II (ruled 367–357 BC and 346–343 BC) A tyrant of Syracuse, eldest son of DIONYSIUS (1) I, born c.397. He became tyrant on his father's death and brought the war with Carthage to a quick end by making a treaty on the same terms as his father had after Cronium. He ruled for ten years and at first came under the influence of PLATO (1) through the intervention of his uncle and brother-in-law, DION, then at the instigation of the historian PHILISTUS. He banished Dion, but kept Plato at his court for about a year. Dionysius was very different from his ruthless father – he was short-sighted, no fighter, and far more inclined to the arts and philosophy. However Plato's aim of making him the first philosopher king failed, partly because the courtiers wished to preserve their power. In 361 Plato returned briefly, but found that Dionysius was now subject to other influences and less receptive to his advice. In 357, when Dionysius was absent in Italy, Dion returned, sailing from Greece with a mercenary army, and took Syracuse, although he failed to secure Ortygia, to which Dionysius repaired. In 356 HERACLIDES (2), Dion's lieutenant, blockaded Ortygia and expelled the unpopular Dion from Syracuse. Dionysius then unleashed his Campanian mercenaries on the city, which they ransacked for two days before Dion returned and was elected sole general. In 355 he took Ortygia from Dionysius, who held on to Rhegium and Locri in Italy. In 346 Dionysius re-emerged to take Syracuse from Hipparinus which he ruled for two years until he was blockaded in Ortygia by a would-be tyrant, the Syracusan Hicetas, who had established himself at Leontini with Carthaginian support. On the arrival from Corinth of TIMOLEON, who defeated the forces of Hicetas at Adranum, Dionysius allied himself with Timoleon for a while and shared control of Catana, but in summer 343 he was deposed by Timoleon and sent into exile in Corinth, where he lived for many years and supported himself by teaching.

3. Chalcus (C5 BC) An Athenian poet, nicknamed Chalcus ('Brazen') because he was responsible for the introduction of bronze coins into Athens. Some of his poems (elegies written for singing at parties) survive. He joined the colonisation of Thurii in southern Italy in 443.

4. (c.330–c.250 BC) A Stoic writer from Heraclea near the Black Sea who was a pupil of ZENO (2) of Citium. He wrote not only on Stoic philosophy, but also poetry and drama. A tragedy of his is named *Parthenopaeus*. He renounced Stoicism in old age as a result of a painful illness and starved himself to death. He thus became known as 'Turncoat'.

5. Thrax (c.170 – c.90 BC) Known as Thrax 'the Thracian', he was the son of Teres (a Thracian name) and the author of the first Greek grammar. He lived first in Alexandria and was a pupil of ARISTARCHUS (3) of Samothrace and later moved to Rhodes, where he became a teacher of rhetoric. He lectured on Nestor's cup and his pupils donated silver for a replica to be made for him to use in the lectures. One complete work survives, *The Art of Grammar*, which deals with the rules of correct writing and punctuation, parts of speech and some morphology, although syntax is omitted. This short treatise had an immense influence on Latin and later grammatical writers.

6. Scytobrachion (c.250 BC) A writer of mythological romances from Alexandria.

His nickname, Scytobrachion ('Leatherarm'), comes from the assiduity of his written production. He is sometimes confused with a Dionysius of Mytilene or Miletus. Only fragments of his work survive.

7. of Halicarnassus (C1 BC) A historian and literary critic from Halicarnassus in south western Asia Minor. In about 30 BC he moved to Rome where he taught rhetoric and became a great enthusiast for all things Roman. Much of his work survives, and his *Roman Antiquities*, of whose twenty books we have the first ten, began publication in 7 BC. The work is basically historical and contains careful research, which makes it a valuable source despite its strong moralising slant. He is an important and seminal writer on literature with developed theories of his own. He wrote the following works which survive: *On the Arrangement of Words*, which is a unique and ancient discussion of the effects of word-order on the sound of language; *Commentaries on the Ancient Orators*, mainly about the Attic orators and displaying hostility to the Asianic as opposed to the Attic style; *On Thucydides*; *Letters to Ammaeus*, which is about DEMOSTHENES (2) and THUCYDIDES (2); a *Letter to Cn Pompeius* on PLATO (1); and fragments of a work on *Imitation*.

Diophantus 1. of Sphettus (mid-C4 BC) An Athenian politician who assisted EUBULUS (1) in pursuing his policy of moderation in dealings with foreign states while opposing the rise of PHILIP (1) II.

2. (Date unknown) A mathematician from Alexandria who is the first ancient mathematician to have embarked upon an algebraic notation. His writings were the starting point for Pierre de Fermat's work on the theory of numbers in the seventeenth century. His work was in the tradition of practical Babylonian mathematics, like that of HERON. Some of his work survives: six books and the preface out of thirteen books of his *Arithmetica*; a treatise on polygonal numbers; some propositions on the theory of numbers from a lost work, the *Porismata*, survive as quotations in the *Arithmetica*. Some of the more advanced algebraic notation may have been a Byzantine addition.

Dioscorides (late C3 BC) A poet whose work is known from forty of his epigrams that are in the *Greek Anthology*. He wrote love poems and eight epigrams on famous poets. He followed the tradition of CALLIMACHUS (3), ASCLEPIADES and LEONIDAS (2) II.

Diotima (C5 BC) A priestess at Mantinea in Arcadia whom PLATO (1) states in the *Drinking Party (Symposium)* to have been SOCRATES' teacher and who, in the same work, is quoted as the authority for Socrates' doctrine of love.

Diphilus (C4 BC) A playwright from Sinope who was a contemporary of MENANDER (1) and who, like Menander, was a prolific author of New Comedy. Diphilus spent most of his life at Athens where he won three first prizes at the Lenaea festival. He is said to have written a hundred plays, of which the titles of sixty are known. Some fragments have survived which show the lively nature of his humour. Several of Plautus' plays are derived from Diphilus' plays, including *Rudens*, *Casina*, *Asinaria*, the lost *Commorientes* and *Vidularia*. He may have been related to the comic playwright DIODORUS (2), who was, however, much younger. Diphilus died at Smyrna at about the turn of the century.

Diyllus (C3 BC) An Athenian historian who was the son of PHANODEMUS. He wrote a history of the world, now lost, in twenty-six books down to 297. DIODORUS (3) Siculus and PLUTARCH used his work as a source.

Dorieus (late C6 BC) A member of the Agiad royal family of Sparta who was the younger son of King ANAXANDRIDAS II and half-brother of CLEOMENES (1) I. Because of the lack of prospects at home, he led two colonies: the first (*c.*514) to Cinyps in Libya which was expelled by Carthaginians after three years, the second (*c.*510) to western Sicily where he and his followers were killed by the local Segestans and Carthaginians. On the way to western Sicily he helped Croton to subdue Sybaris.

Dosiadas (C3 BC) An Alexandrian poet whose poem, *The Altar*, is included in the *Greek Anthology*. The poem is named after its altar-like shape on the page and purports to be a dedication made by the Argonaut Jason.

Dositheus (C3 BC) An astronomer from Pelusium in Egypt, a pupil of CONON (2) and a friend of ARCHIMEDES who dedicated several of his books to him. His writings are lost.

Draco (C7 BC) An Athenian law-maker who is said to have published a code of laws in the archonship of Aristaechmus (*c.*620). ARISTOTLE states in his *Constitution of Athens* that it was the first written code of Athenian law, although ZALEUCUS had already made one for Locri. Traditionally it was considered extremely harsh as death was the penalty for almost all offences. SOLON is said to have repealed these laws, except for the relatively mild homicide law. In the later fifth century a fictitious account of the Draconian constitution was invented in which the hoplites were enfranchised, and it was publicised for political ends. Draco's homicide law is generally accepted as genuine.

Ducetius (died 440 BC) A leader of the Sicels, an indigenous nation then inhabiting central and eastern Sicily. He forged a union of Sicel peoples and at first (*c.*460) allied himself with democratic Syracuse and opposed the remnant of mercenary troops left after the death of HIERON (1) I. He later came into conflict with Syracuse and Acragas, which felt threatened by his organisation of the Sicels and the founding of cities for them, in particular, the founding of the capital, Menaenum, in 454, and Palice. He initially defeated the Greeks, but (c.450) was decisively beaten and had to sue as a suppliant for his life. The Syracusans sent him into exile to their mother city of Corinth. He returned in 446 and founded Kale Acte in Greek territory, but his aim of creating a strong federation of Sicels was no longer viable.

Duris 1. (early C5 BC) An Athenian potter and vase painter of red-figure ware, several of whose works survive.

2. (c.340–c.260 BC) A tyrant of Samos and a historian, the son of Scaeus and a pupil of THEOPHRASTUS. His reign was uneventful, but he was a prolific writer of sensationalised history, some of which has survived in quotations by other authors, such as DIODORUS (3), DIOGENES (5) Laërtius and ATHENAEUS. He wrote a *History of Samos* in two books, histories of Greece in twenty-three books, histories of Macedonia, and a *Life of Agathocles* in four books, which PLUTARCH used as a source. He also wrote anecdotal works on the arts.

E

Echecrates (C4 BC) A Pythagorean philosopher from Phlius in the Argolid. A pupil of ARCHYTAS of Tarentum and of Eurytus, he became a friend of PLATO (1) and ARISTOXENUS. He is a marginal character in Plato's *Phaedo*, in which PHAEDO is represented as giving Echecrates an account of SOCRATES' last day and his discourse on the nature of life and death.

Ecphantides An Athenian writer of Old Comedy who was roughly contemporary with CRATINUS. He won four first prizes at the City Dionysia festival, but very little of his work survives.

Ecphantus A Pythagorean philosopher of uncertain date from Syracuse. Fragments of his work show that he taught that the universe is a sphere and is composed of entities that are driven by 'Mind' and directed by 'Forethought'.

Empedocles (*c*.493–433 BC) A philosopher, statesman and mystic from Acragas (Agrigento) in Sicily. The son of Meton, he was born into a prominent family (his grandfather, Empedocles, won the horse-race at Olympia in 496) and came to support the democrats, assisting in the overthrow of the oligarchy at Acragas, where he subsequently declined the offer of kingship. Empedocles was later exiled and retired to the Peloponnese. He visited the colony of Thurii in southern Italy shortly after it was founded in 443. There were legends about him, including the story that he jumped into the crater of Etna to prove his divinity. He died at sixty, possibly in the Peloponnese.

He was greatly respected among the ancients for his learning, eloquence and medical knowledge. He wrote two poems in hexameters: the first, *Nature*, gives an account of his philosophy; and about 300 lines of another, far longer poem also survive. It was admired by Lucretius, who wrote in the same didactic tradition of poetry. Empedocles responded to PARMENIDES and the Eleatic school with a pluralistic theory of the universe. He accepted their view of the permanence of real being and postulated the existence of a universe that is a spherical unit in which there are four elements ('roots') of which all things are composed: Fire, Air, Water and Earth, eternally mixing and separating through two contrary forces, which he called Love and Strife. Thus 'mortal things' come into being and pass away. Hence, the various objects that meet our senses are produced by the combination in differing ratios of particles of the four eternal elements. He further postulated a cosmic cycle in which Love (which brings unlike things together) and Strife (which unites like things) predominate alternately. This theory was greatly elaborated and is imperfectly understood. However, the basic theory of matter was influential on the Atomists, and after ARISTOTLE had subjected it to his own critique it was adapted by the Peripatetics and ultimately, the Stoics. Both PLATO (1) and Aristotle were influenced by Empedocles' biological theories of pores and vision. The four-element theory lasted for two millennia as a basis for scientific thought.

Empedocles' other work, the *Purifications*, of which about 100 lines have survived, has a more religious purpose and is connected with Orphism (the widespread Greek mystery-cult based on the mythical life and descent into the Underworld of Orpheus). In the poem he shows a belief in the transmigration of souls, which is hard to reconcile with his otherwise materialistic theory of matter. We simply have not enough of his text to see how the two doctrines may have been reconciled. See G.S. Kirk, J.E. Raven and M. Schofield (1982) *The Presocratic Philosophers*, Cambridge: CUP; and W.K.C. Guthrie (1962–78) *History of Greek Philosophy*, Cambridge: CUP, vol. 2.

Epaminondas (died 362 BC) The greatest general of Thebes. He had an education in philosophy under Lysis. A supporter of Theban democracy and an opponent of Sparta's interventionist policy, he was involved in the revolt of Thebes from her pro-Spartan oligarchic rulers in December 379. He was associated with PELOPIDAS in the formation of the Sacred Band, an infantry unit of men whose loyalty and fighting skills gave Thebes the core of an excellent army. There was a story, which cannot be verified, that Epaminondas saved Pelopidas' life at the battle of Mantinea in 385. Epaminondas was involved in attempts to re-create the Boeotian League of states under Theban leadership and was elected to its council as one of the eleven Boeotarchs. At a peace conference in 371 between the leading powers of Greece, he represented Thebes and prevented the other Boeotian

cities taking the oath separately, and so being recognised as independent participants. He thus asserted Boeotian union under Theban leadership. The result was that AGESILAUS II, king of Sparta, and the Athenians refused to accept Boeotian participation in the treaty. Thebes was then threatened by a Spartan force under CLEOMBROTUS. Epaminondas was one of the generals who led out a smaller Boeotian army, including the Sacred Band, and crushed the superior Spartan force in the plain of Leuctra (a short distance from Thebes). Epaminondas persuaded his colleagues to adopt a strategy of frontal attack with a heavily reinforced left wing, which led to the rout of the Spartans, whose losses in the battle were so great that they disbanded the army sent to restore the position.

Epaminondas secured a policy of extending the League and forming alliances with neighbouring non-Boeotian states. He led an invasion of the Peloponnese at the invitation of the Arcadian League in the winter of 370/369 and began by reducing the Arcadian cities of Orchomenus and Heraea, which were in revolt from the League, after which he invaded the territory of Sparta and marched as far as Gytheum, the port of Sparta. He liberated Messenia from Spartan control and thus broke the economic basis of Spartan power. He organised the construction of a new capital for the area on Mount Ithome, naming it Messene. On his return home in spring 369, Epaminondas, who had illegally retained his post as Boeotarch beyond the year's end, was impeached along with Pelopidas, but acquitted. In 368 he again invaded the Peloponnese, breaking through the defences on the Isthmus, and enabled the foundation of Megalopolis to take place, which led to the surrounding of Sparta by a ring of powerful enemies. Thus, Epaminondas became famous and led a state which was recognised as the champion of freedom and democracy in the face of a brutal Sparta and an Athens which was tainted by association. Several leagues of states were set up in Greece, inspired by the Boeotians, and Epaminondas took a part in their organisation. A huge defensive alliance came into existence in the Greek mainland under Theban leadership with headquarters at Delphi.

He won further renown in 367 when he forced ALEXANDER (4) of Pherae to give up Pelopidas, whom he illegally held as prisoner. In 366 as Boeotarch he led an army into Achaea in the northern Peloponnese and tried to win the states over to alliance with Thebes. However, interference with his more moderate arrangements by the Arcadian allies of Thebes, both there and at Sicyon, brought about the failure of his plans by enforcing the establishment of democracies. In 363 Epaminondas led a naval expedition to damage the interests of Athens. He sailed uncontested to Byzantium and by his presence encouraged other cities of the region to revolt from Athens, which was shaken by his initiative. On his return to Thebes, he protested against the punishment meted out to the people of Orchomenus for plotting against the democracy at Thebes. Shortly after, a split occurred in the Arcadian League, and early in 362 Epaminondas led the Boeotian army with allied contingents into Arcadia and attacked his enemies piecemeal before they could unite. In June he briefly assaulted Sparta and then moved speedily to Mantinea, where he engaged the enemy who were strongly placed. His troops were winning the day when he fell. So a great victory was lost: the opponents of the Thebans were relieved of its consequences and Greece once more lapsed into confusion. Epaminondas had been a brilliant general and was politically promising as a democrat and a moderate. The chief beneficiary of the lesson of his campaigns was PHILIP (1) II of Macedonia, who was at the time a hostage at Thebes. See J. Buckler (1980) *The Theban Hegemony*

371–362 BC, Cambridge, MA; London: Harvard University Press.

Ephialtes 1. A Trachinian from Malis, the son of Eurydemus, who for a bribe betrayed the Greeks in 480 by showing the invading Persian army the way around the passage of Thermopylae, which was blocked by the force of LEONIDAS (1) I. He took refuge in Thessaly, but was assassinated by a personal enemy after returning to Anticyra ten years later. The Spartans nevertheless honoured his killer, Athenades, as a hero.

2. (died 462 BC) An Athenian politician of the fifth century BC, the political heir of the discredited THEMISTOCLES. Ephialtes was a poor man, with a reputation for honesty, and deeply opposed to privilege. In 465 he led a naval force into the eastern Mediterranean. During his career, he and his associate PERICLES successfully prosecuted a number of members of the Areopagus – the ancient high court and council on which members of the nobility sat. He was an able speaker with a good knowledge of the constitution. In 463 he prosecuted the aristocratic CIMON on the grounds of receiving a bribe from ALEXANDER I, king of Macedonia, but failed to convict him. The next year he opposed CIMON's plan to take a force to assist the Spartans in the siege of Mount Ithome, where the Messenians were invested. Again, he failed, but he and Pericles took advantage of Cimon's absence in 462/1 to propose in the Assembly a reform of the constitution. The Areopagus was stripped of its powers, which, except for jurisdiction in homicide and certain sacrilege cases, were given to the Council of Five Hundred, who were appointed by lot from the Assembly. He thus enabled the people to be sovereign by putting into their hands the decision as to what was constitutionally legal. The Areopagus could no more interfere with the running of the Assembly. He was murdered shortly after this success by a Tanagran and was buried in the Ceramicus. His murder may have been instigated by those who had lost their privileges.

Ephippus (C4 BC) An Athenian writer of Middle Comedy of whose works a few fragments survive. Twelve titles are known to us and he won at least one prize.

Ephorus (*c*.405–*c*.330 BC) A historian from Cyme in Aeolis (Asia Minor), a contemporary of THEOPOMPUS (3) and, like him, a pupil of ISOCRATES. His major work was his *History* in thirty books from the mythical return of the descendants of Heracles to the siege of Perinthus in 340. His son, Demophilus, wrote the last book which dealt with the Fourth Sacred War (340–38). Ephorus was a serious and critical historian who compared his sources carefully. His work was accurate, though his understanding of warfare was thin. In this he is something of a contrast with his prolific contemporary Theopompus. The prime importance of his work lies in its use by DIODORUS (3) Siculus as the source for five extant books of his historical work, which says much about Ephorus' qualities as a historian (the influence of Isocrates is also clear). He was the first historian to divide his work into books, introducing them with prefaces. POLYBIUS states that he concerned himself with events outside the Greek world and included the Persian empire in the scope of his work. He was also interested in family histories, colonisation and the movements of people. Next to XENOPHON (1) he is the most important historian of his century, though we only know him at second hand. His work was also used as a source by Polybius, Strabo, Nicolaus and PLUTARCH. He also wrote a history of his native city, two books on discoveries and a treatise on diction. See G.L. Barber (1935) *The Historian Ephorus*, Cambridge: CUP.

Epicharmus (*c*.530–*c*.475 BC) A Sicilian writer of comedies who was possibly from Syracuse. Little is known of his work, except for the titles of his plays (of which we have thirty-seven). ARISTOTLE in the *Poetics* (1448a) states that Epicharmus was much earlier than Chionides and Magnes, the earliest Attic writers of comedy, in which case he must have already been writing in the sixth century. The fragments of his plays that survive show the plays as being predominantly burlesques on mythical themes and often concerned with Odysseus and Heracles. No lyrics have survived and our only evidence for a chorus in his plays is the plural names in some of their titles, but dialogue in a variety of metres is composed in the Sicilian Doric dialect. Many forged works were attributed to Epicharmus in antiquity on a variety of philosophical and other subjects. See L. Berk (1964) *Epicharmus*, Groningen: Wolters.

Epictetus 1. (late C6 BC) An Athenian potter and vase painter, a contemporary of the ANDOCIDES (1) painter. We have about 100 vases that he made, including thirty-nine vases that he signed as the painter and one that he signed as the potter. He was one of the first makers of red-figure ware and some of his vases show red-figure exteriors and black-figure insides.

2. (*c*.AD 55–*c*.AD 135) A Stoic philosopher from Hierapolis in Phrygia. In his boyhood he was a slave of the imperial freedman Epaphroditus, who let him attend the lectures of the Stoic teacher Musonius Rufus, and who later set him free. He became a teacher of philosophy himself and remained in Rome until the expulsion of philosophers by Domitian in 89, when he migrated to Epirus and settled at Nicopolis where he spent the rest of his life. He wrote nothing himself, but his pupil ARRIAN took down his lectures and published them in eight books, entitled *Discourses of Epictetus*, of which four survive. Arrian also published an extant résumé of his philosophy under the title *Encheiridion* (*Manual*), which was very popular and influenced the Emperor Marcus Aurelius. In fact, Epictetus' approach was very practical and simple, and he appealed to the common man much more than his Stoic predecessors had. He taught that man must not allow things beyond his reach to make him unhappy, but should seek freedom and happiness within the limits of his own will. He asserted that all men are brothers and considered that wrongdoers needed pity more than punishment. He taught that the universe was made by God and that Providence could never lead us astray.

Epicurus (341–270 BC) A philosopher, the son of Neocles who was an Athenian schoolteacher and a settler in Samos, where Epicurus was born, and his wife Chaerestrate. In his childhood, Epicurus was a pupil of the Platonist PAMPHILUS, and went to Athens in 323 to train for two years for military service as an ephebe (the poet MENANDER I served with him there). Either before or after his stay in Athens, Epicurus went to Teos to study philosophy under NAUSIPHANES, who taught him the atomic theory of DEMOCRITUS. Meanwhile, Epicurus' family had been expelled from Samos and had moved to Colophon, where Epicurus joined them and (*c.*312) formulated the philosophical ideas that inspired his life. In 309 he moved with his brothers to Mytilene, which was a Peripatetic stronghold. He was driven from Mytilene and went to Lampsacus, where he was more successful. In each place he taught philosophy and won adherents. In 306, with the financial support of his followers, he bought a house and a garden in Athens. The garden, which was a vegetable plot, not a pleasure-garden, became the meeting place of his disciples and the home of his school (known as the 'Garden'), where he also wrote abundantly. According to

DIOGENES (5) Laërtius, he wrote about 300 volumes. One of his main aims was to oppose the influence of the Academy and the 'astral gods' of PLATO (1). At Athens he may have known and influenced his contemporary, the Peripatetic STRATON (1) of Lampsacus, head of the Lyceum, who was equally hostile to the Platonists. Epicurus travelled little from Athens. He died in 270 and bequeathed his school (by a will that survives) to HERMARCHUS of Mytilene.

Epicurus' purpose was to show mankind that it is possible to live a life of undisturbed happiness (*ataraxia*), devoid of fear and worry, through right knowledge of the way the universe works: the main objects of fear, divine punishment and death, need not concern us, as the human 'soul' does not survive death and gods do not govern events, which are ruled by natural laws. According to his teaching, the universe and everything in it including ourselves and our 'souls' consist of atoms whose motion is governed by natural causes; nothing composed lasts for ever as the atoms move around, and their motion, temporary conjunction and ultimate dispersal explain the generation and dissolution of all objects including living things. On the other hand, the gods, who are perfect and eternal, live a happy existence untrammelled by the activities or sufferings of humanity. (This insistence on the existence of gods has puzzled many: its advantage was to avoid offending the piety of the average Greek of his day. Moreover it fits his opposition to the mechanical atomism of Democritus.) Much trouble can also be avoided by following the maxim 'live in secret', and keeping out of politics and public life: he taught that friendship rather than justice should be the cement that binds society together. His philosophy had three main branches, moral philosophy, physics and epistemology.

Though he wrote much, very little of Epicurus' writings has survived, mainly through the indifference of later ages or the active hostility of other creeds (principally Christianity). We have his will and three letters, which were written respectively to Herodotus (about nature), Pythocles (about meteorology) and Menoecus (about moral philosophy). He wrote many other letters whose recipients we know of and his evangelical epistolary fervour may be compared with that of Paul. There also exists a brief compendium of his teachings, in forty-four propositions, that was intended to be learnt by heart. Eighty-one similar sayings of his were discovered in the Vatican in 1888. Some fragments of his works have been discovered in Piso's library at Herculaneum. Our chief medium for understanding his philosophy is the Latin poem of Lucretius, *The Nature of Things*, which includes an encomium of Epicurus. It appears that Epicurus' principal work was entitled *On Nature*.

Epicurus was anxious to overcome the objections to atomism that ARISTOTLE had formulated and equally to avoid the rigid determinism of Democritus' theory. He postulated the existence of atoms that were indestructible and of the void in which the atoms move. Epicurus also postulated that atoms have the ability to join together to form the bodies that make up the universe, but their conjunction is always temporary and universes come into existence and disintegrate in indefinite series. He denied the Aristotelian proposition that there was a divine act of creation or 'first cause'. He also denied final causes or a divine purpose in the universe. He differed from Democritus in claiming that there is an element of randomness in the movement of the atoms. He argued that normally the atoms 'fall' under their own weight, but can change course by colliding with other atoms. However, Epicurus stated that there must be a slight swerve or deviation and on this he based his view that not everything is determined, but, especially in the behaviour of animate beings, there is a small but important part of their

behaviour that is not physically or biologically predetermined.

Epicurus' achievement was to add the moral dimension to the starkly physical theory of the earlier atomists so as to establish a pattern for the best way to live. The community of his followers and friends (including women and slaves) was intensely loyal to him and lived in a somewhat monastic way, simply and without self-indulgence, but with much cultivation of mental pursuits. The friendship generated by their communities was proverbial. However, their self-imposed privacy was a source of criticism in ancient times. In later times the Epicurean ideal was impugned and misrepresented, especially in the Middle Ages when 'epicure' undeservedly took on the connotation of gluttony. Karl Marx wrote his doctoral thesis on the relationship between Democritus and Epicurus. See N.W. De Witt (1954) *Epicurus and his Philosophy*, Minneapolis, Minn.: University of Minnesota Press; B. Farrington (1967) *The Faith of Epicurus*, London: Weidenfeld & Nicolson; E. Asmis (1984) *Epicurus' Scientific Method*, Ithaca, NY: Cornell University Press.

Epigenes (C6 BC) A poet from Sicyon said to be the first writer of tragedy. HERODOTUS (5.67) may have referred to his work when he wrote that CLEISTHENES (1), the tyrant of Sicyon, forbade choruses to be composed in honour of Adrastus and ordered that in future they be devoted to Dionysus.

Epimenides (C6 BC) A Cretan poet and prophet of legendary fame who was credited with the power of ecstasis (the separation of body and soul), like ARISTEAS (1) of Proconnesus. There was a story that he slept in a cave for fifty-seven years. PLATO (1) says that Epimenides visited Athens (*c*.500) and ARISTOTLE says that he purified Athens from the guilt of the murder of CYLON's supporters (*c*.632). Appropriately, he was the first to say that

Cretans were always liars (New Testament *Letter to Titus*, 1.12). He was believed to have written a *Theogony*, a *History of Crete* and other mystical works.

Epitadeus (early C4 BC) A Spartan ephor who passed a law authorising the ownership of property and its transfer from one party to another by either gift or will. The result was the creation of large privately held estates in Laconia.

Erasistratus (*c*.315–*c*.240 BC) A physician of the early third century BC from Iulis in Ceos who studied medicine in Athens and Cos and moved to Alexandria where he continued the anatomical research of HEROPHILUS and founded a school of medicine. More researcher than practitioner of medicine, he was influenced by the experimental methods of STRATON (1). He conducted vivisection on animals and perhaps on convicted criminals and made detailed descriptions of organs, giving an account of their physiological functions; for example, he formed an understanding of the function of the valves of the heart. He saw the importance of *pneuma* (breath) in the workings of the cardiovascular system for the maintenance of life. In his study of anatomy he recognised the difference between sensory and motor nerves, which were discovered by Herophilus. In dissections of cadavers he recognised changes in the body tissues due to disease and formed the view that the heart was the origin of veins and arteries. He worked on growth and digestion and explained disease as being caused by the excess of undigested food in the body. He denied that there were diseases special to women. He published a treatise on the human body entitled *General Principles*. He wrote other works, but none has survived except in fragments. He may have been for a time at the court of SELEUCUS (1) I and is reported to have advised the king (*c*.293) to transfer his wife, STRATONICE, to his son, ANTIOCHUS (1) I, on the grounds that he might become insane for love – a story that seems improbable on chronological grounds. Erasistratus may also have been connected with Samos.

Eratosthenes (*c*.276–*c*.194 BC) A writer on a variety of scientific and literary topics. He was born at Cyrene and studied under CALLIMACHUS (3) and Lysanias at Alexandria before living at Athens for several years where he studied philosophy under ARISTON (2) and ARCESILAUS. About 235 he was invited to Alexandria by PTOLEMY (3) III to become the tutor of his son, and in 247 he became head of the library in succession to APOLLONIUS (1) of Rhodes. His greatest work was on geography and he published a systematic treatise in three books entitled *Geographica*, in which he gave fairly accurate details of the measurement of the circumference of the earth and, less accurately, the sizes and distances of the sun and the moon. He also included physical and human geography and was used as a source by later geographers such as Strabo. He also wrote on literature, including a treatise entitled *On Old Comedy*, and on history, including a work on the chronology of political and literary events, in which he established a system of dating that was based on the Olympiads and made a list of the Olympic winners. His mathematical work was important. He dealt with definitions, musical principles and geometrical problems (*On Means* and *Doubling the Cube*). He composed a history of philosophy, works on moral philosophy, some poetry and brief 'epics' on *Hermes* and *The Death of Hesiod* (also named *Anterinys*). Only fragments of his writings survive. His contemporaries, perhaps out of jealousy, called him '*beta*', i.e. next in rank after the specialists in each field, and '*pentathlos*', i.e. 'all-rounder'.

Ergamenes (C3 BC) A hellenized king of Meroë in Sudan who was reported by DIODORUS (3) to have been a contemporary of PTOLEMY (2) II of Egypt.

Erinna (late C4 BC) A poetess from Telos, an island north-west of Rhodes, whose chief work is a poem entitled *The Distaff*, which is in the Doric dialect and of which fifty hexameter lines are preserved on papyrus. The poem was six times longer than the preserved lines and commemorated Baucis, who was a friend of the poetess. Three epigrams also survive in the *Greek Anthology*, two of which are epitaphs for Baucis' tomb. We learn from another poem in the *Greek Anthology* that she died at the age of 19.

Erucius (C1 BC) A poet from Cyzicus who composed fourteen of the epigrams in the *Greek Anthology*. One epigram quotes a line from Virgil's *Eclogues* and another shows an acquaintance with and hatred of PARTHENIUS.

Eubulides (C4 BC) A philosopher and logician from Miletus, contemporary with ARISTOTLE, who taught at Athens and succeeded EUCLIDES (1) as head of the Megarian school. He lampooned Aristotle and taught DEMOSTHENES (2) the art of speaking and argument. He was succeeded by STILPON.

Eubulus 1. (born *c*.405 BC) An Athenian statesman who became active in 354 when Athens was nearly bankrupt because of her long campaign to regain Amphipolis and the Chersonese and her defeat in the Social War. Eubulus was a commissioner of the Theoric Fund, which was established to provide money for the festivals. He proposed the law whereby any surplus money was transferred into the Theoric Fund. From that starting point, he became the general treasurer of Athens and prevented the Assembly from embarking on rash and costly military adventures. The result was to raise the prosperity of the state and gain the opportunity to engage on a programme of public works. Some small expeditions were undertaken, but large ventures were avoided. He advocated a common peace

among Greek states and the exclusion of PHILIP (1) II from Greek affairs. His allies at Athens were AESCHINES (2) and PHOCION. He supported the successful attempt to stop Philip's southward expansion at Thermopylae in 352 and the unsuccessful intervention to save Plutarchus, the tyrant of Eretria, in Euboea in 348. He tried to call a congress of Greek states in 347 to act against Philip, but failed to gain their support. He came under criticism for the conduct of his policy and his nephew Hegesileos was fined. DEMOSTHENES (2) accused him of weakness, but after the fall of Olynthus there was agreement that peace must be made with Philip. In 346 negotiations were conducted with Philip (see PHILOCRATES) and Eubulus supported the peace in the Assembly. After Philip's intervention in Phocis, Eubulus continued to support peace, despite Demosthenes' belligerence, and his influence steadily waned. He disappears from history after the battle of Chaeronea in 338.

2. (early C4 BC) A writer of Middle Comedy who wrote more than 100 plays of which we have the titles of fifty-eight. As several of his plays bear the same names as plays by EURIPIDES, it seems probable that he parodied or satirised tragedy. The fragments of his works show myth to have been a favourite subject of his. He won six victories at the Lenaean festival at Athens.

Euclid (Euclides) (born *c*.330 BC) A mathematician who was born in Alexandria and who taught mathematics there during the reign of PTOLEMY (1) I (306–283). We know little of his life, although his writings were very influential. Euclid's *Elements* is a mathematical textbook in thirteen books: the first six books are on plane geometry and owe a debt to HIPPOCRATES (3); books seven to nine are on the theory of numbers; book ten is on irrationals; and books eleven to thirteen are on solid geometry. *Elements* drew upon and superseded previous authorities and was used as a textbook until the beginning of the twentieth century. Its originality lies in its rational arrangement, and it still includes much of the original work of its author. Two books by other hands were later added to Euclid's manuscript. Euclid also wrote an elementary work called *Data*, containing ninety-five theorems. His other mathematical works are lost, but are known from commentaries, for example, by Pappus: *Fallacies*, *On Divisions*, *Corollaries*, *Conics* and *Surface loci*. He also wrote on astronomy (the extant *Phaenomena* and *The Moving Sphere*) and optics (although the extant works are spurious), and wrote a work on musical theory. The *Introduction to Harmony* and *Section of the Scale*, attributed to Euclid, are only partly his: the former was by CLEONIDES. See T.L. Heath (1913) *History of Greek Mathematics*, Oxford: Clarendon Press.

Euclides 1. (*c*.450–*c*.380 BC) A philosopher from Megara who was a close friend of SOCRATES and who was present at Socrates' death in 399. Euclides gave shelter and hospitality in Megara to PLATO (1) and other followers of Socrates. We know next to nothing of his teachings, except that he regarded the 'good' as having no opposite. He was in the habit of attacking his opponents' conclusions rather than their arguments, and thus the school of Megarians, which Euclides founded, earned the title 'Eristic' ('contentious'). He and his pupils were obsessed with the logical paradoxes with which the Stoics under ZENO (2) were later concerned. He was succeeded by EUBULIDES.

2. The Athenian eponymous archon for the year 403/2 BC when democracy was restored at Athens after the fall of the THIRTY TYRANTS. His year of office also marks Athens' adoption of the familiar Ionic alphabet in place of the old Attic alphabet.

3. *See* EUCLID.

Eucratides (C2 BC) The last effective Greek king of Bactria-Sogdiana, he was the son of Heliocles and Laodice. He waged a prolonged war to take over the kingdom of his predecessor, EUTHYDEMUS (3) (we do not know if they were related), whom he eventually defeated and killed (*c*.160). He gained a reputation for great military success and may have declared war on MENANDER (2), the Greek king of Punjab. He died in 145 – the victim of an assassination by one of his sons. He assumed the title of 'the Great' and left much fine coinage to commemorate his reign.

Eudemus (C4 BC) A philosopher from Rhodes and a friend of ARISTOTLE. Nothing is known of his life, although a fragment of a letter from him to THEOPHRASTUS, Aristotle's successor as head of the Peripatetic school, survives, in which he consulted the latter on a question concerning a point in Aristotle's *Physics*. Simplicius, who preserves many fragments of Eudemus' work on physics, reports that Damas wrote a biography of him which is now lost. Eudemus' work included histories of mathematics, astronomy and theology, as well as logic, rhetoric and zoology. Only his work on physics, which appears to be a revision of Aristotle's *Physics*, is known to us as a result of Simplicius' quotation of it. *Eudemian Ethics*, named after Eudemus, was not by him, but by Aristotle.

Eudorus (C1 BC) An eclectic philosopher from Alexandria. His works are lost: besides his *Distinction of Philosophic Argument*, he wrote commentaries on some of PLATO (1)'s works and on ARATUS (1)'s *Phaenomena* and a book *On the Nile*.

Eudoxus 1. (*c*.400–347 BC) A mathematician and astronomer from Cnidos. According to DIOGENES (5) Laërtius and others, he was a pupil of ARCHYTAS in

in 169. The war at first went badly for the Romans and they became suspicious of Eumenes' loyalty to them and transferred their support to Eumenes' brother, ATTALUS (2) II, who succeeded him. Eumenes' long reign saw the establishment of the famous library at Pergamon which was transferred by CLEOPATRA (5) VII to Alexandria. He also added many fine buildings to the city, including the great altar of Zeus.

Eupalinus (C6 BC) A civil engineer from Megara who bored a subterranean aqueduct under a hill on Samos for POLYCRATES (1).

Euphorion 1. (C5 BC) The son of the poet AESCHYLUS some of whose previously unperformed plays Euphorion is said to have presented at Athens and for which he won four first prizes. In 431 he defeated both SOPHOCLES (1) and EURIPIDES (*Medea*) with one of his father's plays.

2. (born *c*.275 BC) A poet and grammarian who was born at Chalcis in Euboea. He studied philosophy at Athens and made a fortune through a liaison with the widow of ALEXANDER (7) after his death in 245. He was then appointed chief librarian of Antioch in Syria by ANTIOCHUS (3) III the Great, in which post he spent the rest of his life. He wrote much verse and some prose, though very few fragments of either survive. His verse seems to have consisted mainly of epyllia, namely short epics, and we have three titles: *Hesiod*, *Mopsopia*, and *Chiliades*. *Mopsopia* was a collection of Attic tales, and *Chiliades* consisted of accounts of oracular responses that came true after a thousand years. His other poetry was based on myth and often very obscure. He plagiarised the works of his predecessors CALLIMACHUS (3) and APOLLONIUS (1). He had an influence on later Greek poets NICANDER, PARTHENIUS, and Nonnus, and on Catullus and his circle (whom Cicero mocked as 'singers of Euphorion') and the youthful Virgil.

Euphranor (mid-C4 BC) A sculptor and painter from the Isthmus of Corinth who worked at Athens. His work has not survived, except for a headless figure of Apollo Patroos from the Athenian agora. He was a pupil of ARISTIDES (2) and his work is known to us from Pliny the Elder. His paintings included a scene of the battle of Mantinea in 364, Theseus with Democracy and Demos (the People), and the Twelve Gods, all of which were painted for the Stoa of Zeus in the agora. Some of his sculpture was massive and included a priestess and portraits of PHILIP (1) II, ALEXANDER (3) III the Great and Paris in chariots. He wrote on colour and symmetry.

Euphron (ruled 368–365 BC) A tyrant of Sicyon, a popular ruler who came to power through a rising of the people against the aristocratic government. He was murdered at Thebes by exiled Sicyonians and honoured after his death as the 'second founder' of his city.

Euphronius (late C6 BC) An Athenian potter and vase painter. Five earlier vases are signed by him as painter and a dozen later ones as potter. He developed the dynamism of figures in movement in red-figure painting.

Eupolis (*c*.446–412 BC) An Athenian poet of the Old Comedy who wrote at least nineteen comedies of which many fragments survive. His first play was produced in 429 and he won at least four first prizes in both the Lenaea festival and the City Dionysia. He was a rival to ARISTOPHANES (1) and supported the war with Sparta, which Aristophanes opposed. He was greatly admired in antiquity and Horace ranks him with Aristophanes and CRATINUS. Titles of his plays include *The First of the Month*, produced at the Lenaea festival of 425; *Marikas*, which attacked the demagogue HYPERBOLUS, at the Lenaea festival of 421; *The Flatterers*, which ridiculed CALLIAS (2), produced at the City Dionysia in 421; *Autolycus*, produced in 420; *Cities*, produced *c*.420; and *Bathers*, *Captains* and *Commons*, of uncertain date. Eupolis was killed at sea.

Eupompus (C4 BC) A painter from Sicyon who founded a school of painting there. He advised his fellow townsman LYSIPPUS the sculptor to 'follow nature rather than any master'.

Euripides (*c*.484–406 BC) An Athenian writer of tragedies, born at Phlya in central Attica, the son of Mnesarchus and Cleito. Euripides came from a wealthy family of hereditary priests of Apollo Zosterius. He owned property on Salamis, where he sometimes wrote in a cave. He was a fine athlete in his youth, winning prizes at Athens and Eleusis. He was also a skilled painter and had a strong visual sense. He was highly educated, owning a large library, and was well acquainted with the leading philosophers of his day, such as PROTAGORAS (who first read aloud at Euripides' house an agnostic work he had written regarding the gods), ANAXAGORAS, SOCRATES and others, and so came to be associated in popular thinking with the sophists. He wrote, at the request of the archons, an epitaph for the men killed in the Sicilian expedition. He did not, however, get involved in politics, and references to him in the works of the comedians, especially ARISTOPHANES (1), suggest he was held in a certain notoriety because of his advanced or unconventional views. He married Melite, daughter of Mnesilochus.

He began his career as a playwright at the City Dionysia in 455, winning third place with three plays, including the *Pleiades*. He had little success with the Athenian theatre juries, winning first prize only four times in a long career. The views underlying his work were too advanced for many of his contemporaries and cut across traditional piety and family values. After his death, however, his popularity became great and his plays were generally preferred to those of his predecessors AESCHYLUS and SOPHOCLES. He has been portrayed, probably falsely, as a rationalist and a hater of women. In fact, women fascinated him, as is shown by his portrayal of them in several plays. He was deeply interested in the irrational side of the human psyche as witnessed by the theme of the *Bacchants*. It was not until 441 that he won a first prize, but we do not know for which play. The *Suda* states that he competed at the City Dionysia twenty-two times, which implies a production of sixty-six tragedies, and that he wrote ninety-two plays in all. A few of these plays were not originally put on at Athens, but had a first performance in Macedonia. We know of eighty titles, but only nineteen of his plays survive, including the early *Rhesus* and the comic satyr play *Cyclops*.

His plays show an original approach to the use of the traditional myths that had nearly always formed the basis of the plots of tragedies and which he continued to use, although with a different attitude from that of his predecessors. He seems to have felt it necessary to give the old stories new life by adopting a realistic stance or by giving them an unexpected twist. Aristophanes alludes to this innovation in *Frogs* (lines 959ff.) where he makes Euripides declare that he added a modern, everyday aspect to his stories. In his later plays the myths are sometimes little more than tales of intrigue and hence vehicles for entertainment.

Nineteen of Euripides' plays have survived: in order of composition, *Rhesus*, of unknown but early date, on a theme from HOMER's *Iliad*, Book 10 (its authenticity has been contested); *Alcestis*, performed with the lost *Cretan Women*, *Alcmaeon in Psophis* and *Telephus* in 438, won the second prize: it tells the story of Heracles' struggle to bring Queen Alcestis back from the dead after she had voluntarily died in place of her husband, Admetus; *Medea*, performed with the lost *Philoctetes*, *Dictys* and *Reapers* in 431, won the third prize: it tells of Jason's divorce from the foreign Medea so that he may marry the daughter of Creon, king of Corinth, and of Medea's vengeance and her murder of their children and the princess; *The Children of Heracles*, performed around 430, in which the children, after the death of Heracles, take refuge from the persecution of Eurystheus at the altar of Zeus in Athens, and to recover them Eurystheus makes war on Athens, is defeated and executed; *Hippolytus* (the title of two plays, one of which has survived) which is about the incestuous love of his stepmother Phaedra for Theseus' son, Hippolytus, her suicide before which she wrote a letter to Theseus falsely accusing him of raping her, and Theseus' vengeance upon his innocent son: Hippolytus won the first prize at its performance in 428; *Andromache*, performed around 426, the story of the life in slavery of Hector's widow, Andromache, threatened with death by Hermione, the wife of her owner, Neoptolemus, then protected by the aged Peleus, and finally becoming the wife of her husband's brother, Helenus; *Hecabe*, performed around 424, which combines the stories of Polyxena and the vengeance of Priam's widow, Hecabe, on Polymestor, a Thracian king, who has treacherously killed her son, Polydorus, whom Priam had put in his care at the beginning of the war; *The Suppliant Women*, performed around 422 on the aftermath of the siege of Thebes; *Heracles* or *The Madness of Heracles*, which tells of Heracles' slaughter of his children by his first wife, Megara, in a fit of madness sent by Hera, and the punishment consequently imposed on him, namely his famous 'labours', performed around 417; *Electra*, which is a version, contrasting with that of Sophocles, of the return of Orestes to avenge his father Agamemnon's death on his mother Clytaemestra, performed around 417;

Trojan Women, performed with the lost *Alexander*, *Palamedes* and (comic) *Sisyphus* in 415, perhaps Euripides' comment on the Athenians' slaughter of the men of Melos: the most poignant of his plays, presenting the suffering of the widowed women of Troy after their city had been sacked and their men killed; *Iphigenia among the Tauri*, performed around 414: Iphigenia, removed from Greece to the Crimea, the land of the Tauri, is a priestess of Artemis, but is bitter at her fate, and when her brother Orestes comes in search of the image of the goddess, she is persuaded to help him escape with the image; *Helen*, was performed along with the lost *Andromeda* around 412, about Menelaus' discovery of his wife, Helen, in Egypt on his way home from the Trojan War; *Orestes*, which was performed in 408; *Phoenician Women*, which deals with the war at Thebes between Oedipus' sons, Eteocles and Polynices, and their fatal single combat for the throne, is the longest of his plays, and was written around 410; *Ion*, a forerunner of the New Comedy, is about an illegitimate birth, deception, final recognition and reconciliation (performed around 410); *Bacchants* (*Bacchae*), deals with the arrival in Thebes of the new cult of the god Dionysus and the punishment of the king, Pentheus, for his failure to recognise the god's power, and was first performed in 405 after Euripides' death; *Iphigenia in Aulis*, which tells of Artemis' hindrance of the newly mustered Greek army from sailing to Troy, was performed in the same year; and *The Cyclops*, a comic 'satyr play' written late in his career. There are also fragments preserved on papyrus of some of the lost plays, notably of *Telephus*, *Cresphontes* and *Erechtheus*.

It is worth noting that of Euripides' surviving works, ten were a 'canon' which was preserved in a collection made c.AD 200 for school use, namely *Alcestis*, *Andromache*, *Bacchants*, *Hecabe*, *Hippolytus*, *Medea*, *Orestes*, *Phoenician Women*,

Rhesus and *Trojan Women*. The titles of the nine other plays are in the alphabetical sequence of the Greek alphabet from E–K, and it appears that a single volume from an Alexandrian edition has fortuitously come down to us. See T.B.L. Webster (1967) *The Tragedies of Euripides*, London: Methuen; S. Barlow (1986) *The Imagery of Euripides*, Bristol: Bristol Classical Press; J. Gregory (1991) *Euripides and the Instruction of the Athenians*, Ann Arbor, MI: University of Michigan Press; M.R. Halleran (1985) *Stagecraft in Euripides*, London: Croom Helm.

Eurybiades (early C5 BC) A Spartan admiral who was commander of the united Greek fleet in the campaigns of Artemisium and Salamis in 480. Sparta's contingent of ships was very small, sixteen at Salamis, but her military prestige accounts for his appointment. He disagreed with THEMISTOCLES over his plan to ensnare the Persian fleet at Salamis and to destroy the bridge of boats over the Hellespont.

Eurydice (died 317 BC) A Macedonian queen who was originally known as Adea. A granddaughter of PHILIP (1) II by his daughter, Cynane, Eurydice was married to Philip's son, her uncle, the feeble-minded PHILIP (2) III Arrhidaeus, in 322. In 317, relying on her popularity with the army, she deposed POLYPERCHON from the regency of Macedonia and made CASSANDER her chief minister. However, her attempt to disbar the child ALEXANDER (6) IV from the succession was defeated by OLYMPIAS, who murdered Philip and ordered Eurydice to kill herself.

Euthydemus 1. (C5 BC) A philosopher or sophist from Chios. He is a character in PLATO (1)'s dialogue of the same name: the accuracy of the portrayal is open to question.

2. (late C3 BC) A Hellenistic king of Bactria and Sogdiana who originated from Magnesia in Lydia. Having disposed of

his predecessor, DIODOTUS (2), in 226, Euthydemus turned his kingdom into a powerful state and added Aria and Margiana to it. He was recognised as king by ANTIOCHUS (3) III in 206 after a war in which Antiochus besieged his capital, Balkh, and tried to overthrow him. He was succeeded *c*.186 by his son DEMETRIUS (8) I.

3. Grandson of EUTHYDEMUS (2) and the son of DEMETRIUS (8) I of Bactria and Sogdiana. He was king from *c*.170–*c*.160 BC, and was defeated and killed by the rebel EUCRATIDES, who seized his throne. He issued the first nickel coinage.

Euthymides (late C6 BC) An Athenian vase painter of red-figure ware. Six vessels survive which bear his signature. He was a rival to EUPHRONIUS and one of his vases bears a text disparaging the other painter.

Evagoras (*c*.435–374 BC) A king of Salamis in Cyprus. Born into the royal family of Salamis, Evagoras was exiled as a young man, but regained the throne of Salamis in 411 with help from Soli in Cilicia and pursued a policy of Hellenizing Cyprus and supporting Athens: he received Athenian exiles at his court, including the admiral CONON (1). He was honoured by Athens for his help at the sea-battle of Cnidus in 394 when Conon overthrew Spartan sea power with Persian and Cypriot aid. However, *c*.391 hostilities broke out when Evagoras declared himself independent of Persia and made an alliance with Acoris of Egypt. He captured much of Cilicia and took Tyre. He received practical support from Athens (see CHABRIAS) and made an alliance with Caria. However, Athens withdrew her support when Evagoras declined to accept the Peace of ANTALCIDAS (386), and in 382 Persia moved against him in force, invaded Cyprus, and the following year won a naval victory over him at Citium. He negotiated successfully with the Persian commander, Orontes, and kept his kingdom. He was assassinated by a palace eunuch because of a personal grievance. He was succeeded as king by his son, Nicocles.

G

Galen (AD 129–c.199) A physician, anatomist and writer in Greek on medicine and philosophy. Galen was born at Pergamon in Asia Minor, the son of a rich, well-educated architect, Nicon, who gave him an excellent education in rhetoric, philosophy and mathematics. When Galen was 16, his father, under the influence of dreams, transferred him to the study of medicine in the precinct of the god Asclepius at Pergamon (which contained a facility for dream cures), and, after his father's death, he pursued his medical studies at Smyrna, Corinth and Alexandria. He returned to Pergamon in 157 to become doctor of the gladiatorial school, but finding this work distasteful he moved in 162 to Rome, where he quickly established a fine reputation and was in demand among the highest society. After four years, however, he had made enemies within his profession through his outspoken criticism, and withdrew to Pergamon, where he remained until 169 when the emperor, Marcus Aurelius, summoned him back to Rome, perhaps on account of the last illness of his co-emperor, Lucius Verus, to be court physician. He remained in this post during the reign of Marcus' son, Commodus, and the reign of Severus. He is generally said to have died in 199, but the date is uncertain and he may have survived well into the next century.

Galen, who was deeply religious and a monotheist, wrote copiously about both medicine and philosophy. He conducted practical experiments to prove his hypotheses, such as his work on the spinal cord, but once his theory was established he declined to conduct further experimentation. He drew on all four existing schools of medicine for ideas and created a body of medical knowledge and opinion that became universally accepted and remained authoritative for more than 1,500 years. In philosophy and for his account of creation he chiefly admired PLATO (1), and in medicine HIPPOCRATES (2) (in so far as the Hippocratic writings can be attributed to anybody), but was also greatly influenced by ARISTOTLE, and in anatomy and physiology by HEROPHILUS and ERASISTRATUS. His approach to medicine was teleological and he sought to discover the functions and purpose of the various organs of the body. Once this work had been done, there seemed to be no need for further research. In his early writings he concentrated on philosophy (these works are nearly all lost), but the medical treatises are driven by his religious and philosophical ideas. He refers to Christianity and Judaism among other 'philosophies' in his writings, tending to class them together and criticising their irrational nature. He knew LUCIAN, whom he considered to be a literary fraud. Many of his prolific medical writings survive and 350 authentic titles are known. About 100 works and fragments survive, and much of his material still needs editing. He made important discoveries in the fields of neurology and the cardiovascular system. He accepted the theory of the four humours and produced a synthesis of earlier discoveries regarding pharmacology and diet. Some of his works have come down to us in Arabic.

Galen's achievement in extending, fixing and codifying medical knowledge and in establishing an unchallenged body of scientific teaching and practice in the medical field was enormous, and it was not until the seventeenth century that his work was seriously questioned and revised. See G. Sarton (1954) *Galen of Pergamon*, Lawrence, KS: University of Kansas Press; G.W. Bowersock (1969) *Greek Sophists in the Roman Empire*, Oxford: Clarendon Press.

Gelon (C5 BC) A tyrant of Gela and Syracuse, the son of Deinomenes of Gela. In the 490s he was cavalry commander for HIPPOCRATES (1), tyrant of Gela. On the death of his master in 491 he became guardian of his sons, whom he dispossessed, taking the position of tyrant of Gela himself. In 485 he was behind a *coup* in Syracuse when the exiled aristocratic party sought his assistance to be reinstated and he transferred his seat of government to Syracuse. He greatly enlarged the city by transferring the populations of Camarina and Megara Hyblaea, which he conquered in the next two years, to his new capital. He also brought in some of the leading men of Gela, where he left his brother, HIERON (1) I, to act as his deputy. When the threat of the Persian invasion of Greece was imminent in 481, envoys from the leading Greek states came to Gelon to ask him for support, which he offered in concrete terms on condition of his holding the supreme command. The Greeks refused this, so he remained in Sicily to face the threat from Carthage which materialised at the same time as the Persian invasion of Greece. With the help of THERON, tyrant of

Acragas, he defeated the Carthaginian HAMILCAR's army at Himera, took a huge number of prisoners and exacted a large indemnity from Carthage with which he built temples in Syracuse and made rich offerings at Delphi. His mastery now extended to the whole of Sicily. However, he died two years later in 478 and was succeeded by his brother, Hieron. See Herodotus, *Histories*, 7. 157ff.; A.R. Burn. (1962) *Persia and the Greeks*, London: Arnold.

Geminus (C1 BC) A writer on mathematics, astronomy and geography. His elementary textbook, *Introduction to Astronomy*, is extant. We also know of a treatise on the classification of the mathematical sciences and the basic definitions and bodies of knowledge they contained, entitled *The Classification of Sciences*, which was quoted by later authorities, including Proclus and Simplicius. He also made an epitome of POSIDONIUS' *Meteorology*.

Glaucus 1. (early C6 BC) A metalworker from Chios who invented the process of welding iron and made an iron stand on which stood a silver bowl for ALYATTES, king of Lydia, mentioned by HERODOTUS, 1. 25.

2. (early C4 BC) A historian and critic of poetry and music from Rhegium. He wrote a work entitled *The Ancient Poets and Musicians*, of which fragments survive.

Glycon A sculptor of unknown date BC from Athens who was the maker of the Farnese Heracles in Naples which was found in the Baths of Caracalla at Rome.

Gorgias 1. (*c*.483–375 BC) A sophist or teacher of rhetoric from Leontini in Sicily. Quintilian states that he lived 109 years. Heir to the strong Sicilian tradition of court pleading, he first went to Athens in 427 on an embassy to seek help against

Syracuse and made a great stir with his speeches. He revolutionised the techniques of oratory and introduced a new interest in antithesis, rhythm and rhyme in speech-making and had a strong influence on ANTIPHON (1), THUCYDIDES (2) and ISOCRATES. PLATO (1), who wrote a dialogue named after Gorgias in which Gorgias is the principal speaker, shows respect for him, but wrote a parody of his style in the speech of AGATHON in the *Symposium*. We have examples of his rhetorical technique in the surviving works, the *Encomium of Helen* and *Defence of Palamedes*. There is also a substantial fragment of a *Funeral Oration*. He is credited with a philosophical dogma to the effect that nothing exists and if it did we could not know it. See G.A. Kennedy (1963) *The Art of Persuasion in Greece*, Princeton, NJ: Princeton University Press.

2. (mid-C1 BC) A teacher of rhetoric from Athens. He wrote four books on figures of speech which Rutilius Rufus abridged into an extant Latin version in one book. He appears to have favoured the Asianist style. See Cicero, *Ad Fam.*, 16. 21. 6.

Gryllus The name of both the father and the eldest son of XENOPHON (1). The son was killed at the battle of Mantinea in 362.

Gyges (C7 BC) An early king of Lydia. Previously a guardsman, Gyges took power *c.*687 by assassinating his predecessor, Candaules of Sardis, and marrying his widow, whose complicity in the crime is asserted by HERODOTUS (1. 8) in a fanciful tale. His policy was aggressive and he captured Colophon and attacked the Greek cities on the coast. He allied himself with Assyria to gain support against the Cimmerians. He made lavish offerings to Apollo's shrine at Delphi. He later deserted the Assyrians for Psammetichus, king of Egypt, whom he assisted in fighting his former allies. However, *c.*650 he was killed by the Cimmerians in a new invasion. He or one of his succesors was the first to issue genuine coinage in gold and electrum – an invention which was quickly adopted by the Greek states. He established the Mermnad dynasty and was succeeded by his son, Ardys.

Gylippus (late C5 BC) A Spartan general who was sent in 414 by the Spartan government to organise Syracusan resistance to the Athenian expedition. When he arrived, he found the Syracusans about to negotiate surrender and he stiffened the resolve of the Sicilians, winning the support of the native Sicels. Within a year he had annihilated the Athenian force and driven them into the interior of Sicily. He was unable to prevent the Syracusans from executing NICIAS (1) and DEMOSTHENES (1). In 405, after the defeat of Athens at Aegospotami, LYSANDER instructed him to convey booty and Persian money back to Sparta, but he stole 300 talents, was discovered, and fled into exile.

H

Hagesander (C1 BC–AD C1) A sculptor from Rhodes who was one of a group responsible for the carving of the Laocoön group in the Vatican museum. Other statuary groups by these sculptors, who include Athanodorus and Polydorus, were found at Sperlonga on the western Italian coast, and depict adventures of Odysseus.

Hamilcar (early C5 BC) A Carthaginian who was the son of HANNO and grandson of MAGO. HERODOTUS regarded him as king of Carthage (7. 165) and stated that his mother was a Syracusan Greek. When he was *sufet* (chief magistrate), he commanded a large army, which in 480 in alliance with Terillus, the deposed tyrant of Himera, and ANAXILAS of Rhegium landed in Sicily to overthrow GELON of Syracuse and THERON of Acragas. Hamilcar may have been in alliance with XERXES of Persia in a two-pronged attack on the Greeks. Herodotus believed that the battle he engaged at Himera, in which he was routed and killed, took place on the same day as the battle of Salamis.

Hanno (early C5 BC) A Carthaginian explorer of Africa and founder of settlements. He was sent out by the Carthaginian state (*c.*480) to explore the coast of West Africa and his exploits were recorded in a Greek *periplus,* or *voyage journal,* which it was claimed was a translation of his own account. He is said to have founded Mehedia, Mogador and Agadir, and to have reached Lixus on the River Draa south of Tangier. His further route, southwards along the west coast of Africa, is uncertain, although he may have got as far as Sierra Leone. He is claimed to have seen gorillas and sighted a mountain named the Gods' Chariot.

Harmodius *see* Aristogiton.

Harpalus (died 323 BC) A Macedonian nobleman contemporary with ALEXANDER (3) III the Great. Harpalus knew Alexander from childhood and, being a cripple, accompanied the king to Asia in a non-combatant role. He deserted his post after the battle of Issus in 333, but was reinstated in 331 and appointed treasurer with an office at Babylon. While Alexander was away on his expedition to India, Harpalus lived at Babylon in great ostentation and extravagance, and on the king's return fled with much money and a force of soldiers to Cilicia. In 324, Harpalus fled to Athens where, perhaps hoping to raise Athens in rebellion, he asked for refuge. DEMOSTHENES (2) at first opposed his admission, but when Harpalus had obtained entry without his troops he resorted to the bribery of Athenian officials, including Demosthenes and DEMADES. Later, however, Demosthenes saw the folly of opposing Alexander and proposed that Harpalus be detained and his money lodged in the Acropolis until Alexander should send an envoy to claim it. Harpalus, however, escaped, and half the money was found to have disappeared from the Acropolis, for which Demosthenes and Demades were subsequently tried. Harpalus meanwhile fled with his troops to Crete, where late in the year he was murdered by his subordinate, THIBRON (2). See A.B. Bosworth (1988) *Conquest and Empire*, Cambridge: CUP.

Hecataeus 1. (late C6 BC) An Ionian geographer and mythographer from Miletus, the son of Hegesander. Hecataeus made a map of the world based on ANAXIMANDER's map, which was probably the one used by ARISTAGORAS in his appeal to the Greeks for aid. Hecataeus wrote a systematic treatise on geography, *Guide to the Earth*, in two books, *Europe* and *Asia* (the latter including Africa). He used the method of following the coasts of the Mediterranean Sea and Black Sea, starting and ending at the Pillars of Heracles (Straits of Gibraltar), with digressions about various lands in the interior. We have more than 300 fragments of this work – many being short quotations from Stephanus of Byzantium. We do not know how much research he did himself. He also wrote *Genealogies*, or *Histories* (which then meant no more than 'enquiries'), on the ancestry of prominent families in terms of claims of mythical ancestors, and he traced many extant families, including his own, back to myth. He tried to show that rational, historical explanations could be found for the stories in the mythological tradition. Only forty fragments of this work survive (his preface shows a sceptical attitude to the Greek stories). HERODOTUS used his work as a source with caution, and was critical of him as a historian and mapmaker.

Hecataeus was also a member of the council at Miletus and spoke strongly against the proposal for the Ionian Revolt of 499. When the war was lost, he

recommended to Aristagoras that he build himself a fort as a base on the island of Leros to retake Miletus, but his advice was spurned. See L. Pearson (1960) *Early Ionian Historians*, Oxford: Clarendon Press.

2. (late C4 BC) A writer on Egypt from Abdera who was a pupil of the Sceptic philosopher PYRRHON of Elis. After visiting Thebes in Egypt in the reign of PTOLEMY (1) I, he wrote (*c*.300) a work entitled *Aegyptiaca* in which he described the history and institutions of the country in a very favourable light. He also added material on the JEWS – the first reference to them in Greek. This work was used as a source by DIODORUS (3) Siculus, who is the chief authority we have for Hecataeus' work. He also wrote the *Hyperboreans*, which is a fictional work about a population living in the far north of the world. Only fragments of his works survive.

Hecatomnus (early C4 BC) A Persian satrap, or governor, of Caria in southwestern Asia Minor and the son of Hyssaldomus. He came to power *c*.394 and commanded the Persian fleet in operations around Cyprus in 390. He was succeeded in 377 by his son, MAUSOLUS.

Hecaton (C2 BC) A Stoic philosopher from Rhodes who was a pupil of PANAETIUS and wrote on ethics. His works have not survived, though Cicero reproduced some of his arguments in his philosophical works.

Hedylus (early C3 BC) A writer of epigrams from Samos who lived in Alexandria. Twelve of his poems, which are mostly concerned with eating and drinking, appear in the *Greek Anthology* and ATHENAEUS' *Deipnosophistai*. Hedylus may have anthologised the poems of ASCLEPIADES (1) and POSIDIPPUS (2) with his own poems. See A.D.E. Cameron (1993) *Greek Anthology*, Oxford: Clarendon Press.

Hegemon (C5? BC) A parodist of comedy from Thasos. ARISTOTLE recognised him as the founder of Greek parody who, according to POLEMON (3), won prizes for his art at Athens. ATHENAEUS names him as a writer of the Old Comedy.

Hegesander (C2 BC) A writer from Delphi whose subject matter was the Hellenistic kings and their courts. He is known mainly from ATHENAEUS.

Hegesias 1. (C3 BC) A historian and rhetorician from Magnesia in Lydia. He wrote a *History of Alexander* of which fragments survive. As an orator he was ridiculed by Cicero and others as the founder of the florid 'Asianic' style.

2. (early C3 BC) A philosopher of the Cyrenaic school who taught at Alexandria. His doctrine, that happiness is unattainable by humanity and that all we can do is to avoid pain, caused many of his pupils to commit suicide and earned him the nickname *Peisithanatos*, 'death-persuader'. He so alarmed PTOLEMY (2) II with his teaching that the king exiled him from Alexandria.

Hegesippus (C4 BC) An Athenian orator and statesman, a contemporary and ally of DEMOSTHENES (2). He became active in politics *c.*355 when he proposed that Athens make an alliance with Phocis. He opposed the offer of PHILIP (1) II in 346 of the Peace of PHILOCRATES, despite its favourable terms, and led the opposition to Philip's proposal that it be extended into a universal or 'common' peace treaty in 344–3. Hegesippus was then sent on an embassy to Philip to seek the return of Amphipolis, which Athens had earlier renounced. However, Philip rebuffed his request and Hegesippus renewed his opposition to the 'common peace' in 342 and secured its rejection. His speech to the Assembly on the occasion of the debate is extant under the misleading title of *On Halonnesus*. The main thrust of the speech was to oppose Philip's offer of peace and to argue for a renewal of war. Hegesippus survived the battle of Chaeronea.

Hegetor An anatomist and doctor of uncertain date. Hegetor followed the tradition of HEROPHILUS, whose interest in anatomy he pursued. He wrote at least one medical work, *On Causes*, of which a substantial fragment survives. In it he criticises the Anatomists' tendency to jump to conclusions about the nature of one part of the body by analogy with another part. He was also interested in Herophilus' theory of the pulse.

Heliodorus 1. An Athenian writer on the monuments of the Acropolis. He published his work (*c.*150 BC) in fifteen books, which is known to us only from fragments.

2. An expert in poetic metre who worked on the metres of the comedies of ARISTOPHANES (1) *c.*AD 50, dividing the text into cola (metrical lines of verse).

3. (C3 or 4 AD) A novelist from Emesa in Phoenicia who wrote in Greek. He signed himself at the end of his book as the son of Theodosius and 'of the family of the Sun', suggesting devotion to the cult of Helios which was established at Emesa. We have no records of his life and his identification with a Christian bishop is unlikely. One novel of his has survived, namely *The Ethiopian Tale of Theagenes and Chariclea*, which is a romance concerning Chariclea, the daughter of Persinna, a queen of Ethiopia, who fell in love with a Greek nobleman, Theagenes, in Delphi where she lived as a refugee and outcast from her home after being exposed (as a baby) because her white skin incriminated her mother of adultery. With the help of an Ethiopian priest named Calasiris the pair eloped and, after many adventures, arrived in Ethiopia. Chariclea, after escaping from being sacrificed to the Moon, is eventually reconciled to her parents, the king and queen of Ethiopia, who marry her to Theagenes. The complex plot is expertly handled, and the novel begins intriguingly in the middle of the action, like HOMER's *Odyssey*. The novel is a text that is rich with literary devices and allusions and is stylistically brilliant. Its dramatic date is vague, but seems to be many centuries BC. It was very popular in later times in the Greek-speaking eastern Roman empire, especially at Constantinople, and was seen, quite without justification, as being in some way a Christian work. See G.N. Sandy (1982) *Heliodorus*, Boston, Mass.: Twayne; T. Hägg (1983) *The Novel in Antiquity*, London: Blackwell; translation by J.R. Morgan in B.P. Reardon (ed.) (*c*.1989) *Collected Ancient Greek Novels*, Berkeley, CA; London: University of California Press.

Hellanicus (480–*c*.395 BC) A writer on myth and history from Lesbos. His work is known to us from about 200 fragments, but he was clearly influential on later Greek historians. He was said to have been born at the time of the battle of Salamis, which accounts for his name meaning 'Greek victory'. He wrote five books which give rationalised and coherent versions of Greek myths, *Phoronis*, *Deucalionia*, *Atlantis*, *Asopis* and *Troica*, which were used as sources by DIONYSIUS (7) of Halicarnassus and APOLLODORUS (5). He also wrote a number of treatises on the ethnography of places in Greece, including Arcadia, Boeotia, Lesbos and Thessaly, and abroad, including Cyprus, Egypt and Persia. In his old age he lived in Athens and wrote the local history of Attica, naming it *Atthis*, which dealt with Athenian history to 404 in two books. He was interested in chronology and established a common chronology for Greek history by comparing lists of priests and priestesses, lists of archons, lists of victors in games, etc., though THUCYDIDES (2) was dissatisfied with its accuracy for the fifth century.

Hephaestion 1. (died 324 BC) A Macedonian general and close friend from childhood of ALEXANDER (3) III the Great, who called him 'my Patroclus' with reference to the *Iliad* (see HOMER). In 330, on the death of Philotas, he was appointed joint commander of the Companion cavalry with CLEITUS. He held several independent commands in the campaigns in Afghanistan and Pakistan. In 324 Alexander gave him the post of chiliarch (which is similar to a Persian vizier). In the same year, at the mass marriage of Macedonian men and Persian women at Susa, he married Drypetis, who was a daughter of DARIUS (3) III and Alexander's sister-in-law. But Hephaestion died suddenly in the autumn of 324 at Ecbatana from fever, causing Alexander in his grief to plan a funeral along Homeric lines, and though the pyre was of more normal dimensions Hephaestion's tomb was magnificent. He was not an outstanding general, but had a sympathy with Alexander's plans which endeared him to the king. See R. Lane Fox (1973) *Alexander the Great*, London: Allen Lane.

2. (C2 AD) A metrical expert from Alexandria who was probably also the tutor of the Roman emperor Verus. He wrote an influential work on poetic metre in forty-eight books, of which an abridgement of one book survives. His other, lost works are mentioned in the *Suda*. His main virtue is to have preserved fragments of lost poems, although his analysis of Greek tragic metre teaches us little that is new. However, he gives a good account of the colometry (analysis of line-lengths) of the comedies of ARISTOPHANES (1) (see HELIODORUS 2).

Heracles *see* **Alexander (3) III.**

Heraclides 1. Ponticus (C4 BC) A Greek philosopher of the Platonic school from Heraclea in Pontus on the Black Sea. He was of noble birth and rich enough to be able to go to Athens to join the Academy

and study there under its leader SPEUSIP-
PUS. For a time, in 361, he was the
temporary head of the Academy during
the third visit of PLATO (1) to Sicily. When
Speusippus died in 338, Heraclides failed
to be elected his successor, being narrowly
beaten by XENOCRATES. He had worked
in the Academy alongside ARISTOTLE
before the latter departed to the Lyceum.
He returned to Heraclea in 338 and lived
there at least until 322.

He wrote on a wide array of subjects,
and fragments of his works survive. Like
PLATO (1), he preferred to compose in
dialogue form. An incomplete list of the
titles of his works is preserved in the work
of DIOGENES (5) Laërtius' *Lives of the
Philosophers*, 5. 86ff. He appears to have
held an original theory on the nature of
the solar system: the Earth at the centre
of the system revolves on its own axis
once a day from west to east, the Sun
orbiting the earth annually from east to
west; and the two inner planets, Venus
and Mercury, orbit the Sun. He seems also
to have held the universe to be infinite
and the stars to be separate worlds. In
physics he held a theory, perhaps based on
Plato's *Timaeus*, that matter is composed
of elementary particles which, unlike
atoms, can divide or combine to form
new or different substances. He was also
interested in one of the main issues of the
age – eschatology – and used shamanistic
figures in his dialogues PYTHAGORAS (1)
and EMPEDOCLES, as well as Empedotimus and Abaris, whom he may have
invented. We possess fragments of an
account of Empedotimus' dream which
traces the origin of the soul to the Milky
Way and claims that it consists of light.
We have no real knowledge of his work
on ethics, metaphysics, music or poetry.
His style apparently had something of the
charm of Plato's, and appealed to Cicero
and PLUTARCH. See H. Gottschalk (1980)
Heraclides of Pontus, Oxford: Clarendon
Press.

2. (died 355 BC) A Syracusan democrat
who lent support to the exiled DION in his
attempt to take Syracuse in 357. He was
in charge of reinforcements and the following year followed Dion to Sicily,
where he won a spectacular naval victory
and blockaded DIONYSIUS (2) II on the
island of Ortygia. He then joined the
democrats with whom he drove Dion out
of Syracuse. But Dionysius escaped from
Ortygia and attacked Syracuse with a
force of mercenaries which ransacked the
city until Dion retook it. In 355 Dion
took Ortygia and had Heraclides murdered and was murdered himself shortly
thereafter.

3. (mid-C4 BC) A historian of Persia
from Cyme who wrote a work entitled
Persica (*History of Persia*) in five books.
ATHENAEUS included in his writings extracts from the work on the Persian royal
court. PLUTARCH used this as a source for
his *Life of Artaxerxes*.

4. Lembus (C2 BC) An Alexandrian
Greek scholar and writer, fragments of
whose works have come down to us. He
wrote abridgements of ARISTOTLE's
Constitutions of Greek Cities, of which
seventy-six fragments of slight value survive. He produced epitomes or abridgements of SATYRUS' *Lives* and SOTION's
Successions, which are biographies of
philosophers and were used by DIOGENES
(5) Laërtius for his own *Lives of the
Philosophers*, a history in thirty-seven
books, and possibly a life of ARCHIMEDES.
We do not know the subject of his
Lembeutic Statement.

5. (early C1 BC) A physician from Tarentum (Taranto in S. Italy). An empiricist,
he wrote fourteen works including treatises on therapy, diet and pharmacology.
GALEN made extensive use of his work
and praised his methods and skill. His
theory of the pulse is preserved in Galen.
About ninety fragments of his writings
survive. He had followed HEROPHILUS in

his early days and been a pupil of Mantias, but had transferred his allegiance to the empirical school of medicine, in which he excelled.

6. Ponticus (the Younger) (C1 AD) A Greek grammarian from Heraclea in Pontus. He was a pupil of the scholar DIDYMUS, and himself founded a school in Rome in the mid-first century. He wrote poetry which has not survived: ATHENAEUS mentions three books of obscure and erudite material in Sapphic hendecasyllables in the style of Lycophron.

Heraclitus (*c*.540–*c*.480 BC) A philosopher, of royal blood, from Ephesus in Asia Minor, the son of Bloson, who seems to have relinquished his position as king (which would have been merely titular) to his brother. Tradition holds that he wrote a book expounding his beliefs, which he deposited in the temple of Artemis at Ephesus. He was one of the first Greeks to write in prose and his style of writing seems such as he described the utterances of the Delphic Oracle, which 'neither says nor hides but points' (fragment 93). The surviving fragments indicate that, far from being a systematic account of a philosophical system, his book was made up of a series of cryptic aphorisms: hence he was known as 'the Obscure'.

He reacted against the established view that the reality of the world is a permanent single entity disguised by apparent but superficial change. His view was that everything is in a process of constant change and rearrangement, an eternal state of flux and conflict of opposites, which he colourfully expressed by saying that nobody ever steps in the same river twice and 'everything moves and nothing remains' (fragment 6). He reacted against ANAXIMANDER's doctrine that the elements are controlled by 'law' (*dike*) and responded that 'law' is rather a principle of disorder. He saw the universe as consisting of three elements, earth, water and

fire, which constantly change into each other, but always remain in the same proportions in the universe. He regarded fire as the supreme and life-giving element, and attributed to it some controlling power, or *logos* ('proportionality'), like that of law. His doctrine of the universe was that it is eternal and uncreated by gods or men, and that it consists of ever-living fire, which is 'kindled in measure and quenched in measure' (fragment 30). Regarding the human psyche or 'soul', he postulated that during life the *logos*, which was akin to fire, empowered the 'soul', but that in death it was overwhelmed by water. Thus, the dryness of the soul and its government by the fiery *logos* rendered a person wise and moderate.

Heraclitus was unsympathetic to some elements of Greek popular religion, especially the cult of Dionysus, and was strongly opposed to excess and intemperance. He was aristocratic in his political views and supported the rule of law. His originality was to have enquired into the nature of human discourse, especially in its use of opposites, and to have explained its logic. See G.S. Kirk, J.E. Raven and M. Schofield (1982) *The Presocratic Philosophers*, Cambridge: CUP; and M. Schofield and M.C. Nussbaum (1982) *Language and Logos*, Cambridge: CUP.

Herillus (early C3 BC) A Stoic philosopher from Carthage who studied philosophy at Athens under ZENO (2) of Citium, the founder of Stoic philosophy, and later set up his own school, which died out by *c*.200. He made knowledge rather than good conduct the primary goal of human life, and claimed that those whose main aim was virtue were failing to see the principal end, but rather aiming at a subordinate end.

Hermagoras (mid-C2 BC) A teacher and rhetorician from Temnos whose work was influential. We know the substance of his writings from later writers, such as Cicero,

Quintilian and HERMOGENES (2). His principal work was entitled *Invention*, and he brought the practice of debating on hypothetical subjects, often with a moral or philosophical purpose, into rhetorical education.

Hermarchus (early C3 BC) An Epicurean philosopher from Mytilene who became head of the Garden after the death of EPICURUS in 270, under whom he had studied. In his will Epicurus instructed his heirs to provide Hermarchus with funds to maintain the school at Athens. He also inherited Epicurus' library. Fragments of his works survive. Besides some letters, they were mostly attacks on other philosophers and their theories, PLATO (1), ARISTOTLE, EMPEDOCLES and the teachings of philosophy in general. Part of his teaching on the law of homicide and on natural rights is preserved in the writings of PORPHYRY. He was regarded by the Epicureans as an important authority.

Hermesianax (early C3 BC) A poet from Colophon who wrote love elegies, including a collection in three books under the general title *Leontion* ('little lion'), which was the name of his mistress. Book 3, of which a substantial fragment is preserved in ATHENAEUS' *Deipnosophistai*, contained fanciful tales of impossible love affairs between, for example, HOMER and Penelope, and SOCRATES and ASPASIA. He may also have written a poem entitled *Persian Tales*. His style and subject matter were typical of Hellenistic taste, showing interest in unhappy and grotesque love, aetiology and unusual linguistic forms. He was a friend and pupil of PHILETAS of Cos.

Hermias 1. (mid-C4 BC) A ruler of Atarneus (Assos) in Asia Minor and friend of ARISTOTLE. Though attacked by THEOPOMPUS (3) as a former barbarian slave who had murdered his master, he was vindicated through recognition as a true Greek at the Olympic Games. He studied

at the Academy of PLATO (1), though he never met Plato, and succeeded Eubulus as tyrant of Atarneus *c*.355 BC. He ruled with a gentler hand than his predecessor, and invited two Academic philosophers, Erastus and Coriscus, to share his power. Aristotle also joined them on his departure from the Academy in 346. Aristotle married Hermias' niece and adopted daughter, Pythias, and established a philosophical school at nearby Assos, being supported by a band of young men who had accompanied him there, namely XENOCRATES, CALLISTHENES and later THEOPHRASTUS. Hermias maintained himself in his principality, which was independent of the Persians, until 341. He had, with Aristotle's help, become an ally of PHILIP (1) II of Macedonia, and was in conference with MENTOR of Rhodes when the latter arrested him and sent him as a prisoner to the Persian court, where ARTAXERXES (3) III tortured him to find out Philip's plans and killed him when he remained silent. See G.L. Cawkwell (1978) *Philip of Macedon*, London: Faber & Faber; and Hammond and Griffith (eds) (1979) *History of Macedonia*, Oxford: Clarendon Press, vol. 2.

2. A poet of the third century BC from Curion in Cyprus who attacked the Stoic philosophers for hypocrisy.

Hermippus 1. (late C5 BC) An Athenian writer of the Old Comedy, brother of Myrtilus and a rival of ARISTOPHANES (1). He wrote forty plays, of which we have the titles of ten and about ninety fragments. He won five first prizes at dramatic festivals between 435–415. He followed the convention of satirising prominent political figures, such as CLEON and HYPERBOLUS. He also used mythological subject matter. According to PLUTARCH, Hermippus prosecuted ASPASIA, PERICLES' mistress. Pericles, the real object of the attack, successfully defended her.

2. (C3 BC) A biographer from Smyrna who wrote lives of poets, philosophers and lawmakers. He was an admirer of the poet CALLIMACHUS (3). He was used as a source by PLUTARCH and DIOGENES (5) Laërtius, who preserved some fragments of his works. He was happy to 'improve' history for the sake of sensational effects.

3. (C2 AD) A writer from Berytus in Lebanon who was born a slave and later became a pupil of PHILON (5) of Byblos. He wrote *Dream-interpretation*, *The Number Seven* and *Slaves Distinguished for Learning*.

Hermocrates (late C5 BC) A Syracusan general and statesman. In 424 at the peace conference of Gela he urged the native Sicilians to beware of Athenian meddling in Sicily. He became prominent in Syracusan politics and continued his campaign of opposition to Athens, organising resistance in 415 when the great expedition arrived. The following year he was elected general with special powers, but he had scant success. When the Spartan general GYLIPPUS arrived in 414, Hermocrates acted as his adviser and support until the Athenian expedition was completely defeated. In 412 he was appointed to command a Syracusan naval expedition to the Aegean but, after the battle of Cyzicus in 410, he was banished in his absence by the Syracusan assembly, led by the radical democrat DIOCLES. He went back to Sicily in 409, furnished with financial support by the Persian satrap PHARNABAZUS, and with an army of mercenaries attacked the Carthaginian sector of the island. In 407 he tried to negotiate his return to Syracuse, but was rebuffed and attacked the city with support from his party within it, including DIONYSIUS (1) I, perhaps intending to make himself tyrant, but was killed. He was admired by both THUCYDIDES (2) and XENOPHON (1). See B. Caven (1990) *Dionysius I*, New Haven, CT; London: Yale University Press.

Hermogenes 1. (early C2 BC) An architect from Priene or Alabanda in Caria. He built two temples, one to Dionysus on Teos and the other to Artemis Leucophryene at Magnesia on the Maeander. The Roman architect Vitruvius wrote of these temples and drew on them for his principles of proportion. His measurements of them, however, seem to have been inaccurate. He attributes to Hermogenes the rejection of the Doric order in favour of the Ionic order for temple design. Strabo admired the Magnesian temple. The strong Roman interest in his work influenced the architecture of the Augustan Age.

2. (C2 AD) A rhetorician and writer on style of the second century AD from Tarsus. He was considered to be an infant prodigy and was admired for his eloquence by the Roman emperor Marcus Aurelius. He produced a number of textbooks on the subject of style. Two extant works are genuinely his: *Issues*, which restates the doctrines of HERMAGORAS, and *Styles*. He used classical Greek orators, such as DEMOSTHENES (2), as his models. In *Styles* Hermogenes proposes seven distinct types of style: clarity, grandeur, rapidity, beauty, character, fidelity and effectiveness. This classification descends from DIONYSIUS (7) of Halicarnassus and from THEOPHRASTUS. It is similar to a scheme proposed in *The Art of Rhetoric*, which was wrongly attributed to the contemporary writer ARISTIDES (5). Other works attributed to Hermogenes are spurious: *Invention* and *The Method of Effective Speaking*. He was much studied in the Byzantine period.

Hermolaus A Macedonian youth and page of ALEXANDER (3) III the Great against whose life he formed a conspiracy in 328 and for which he was stoned to death. His teacher, CALLISTHENES, was later implicated and suffered for his supposed involvement.

Herodas or **Herondas** (mid-C3 BC) A poet, perhaps from Cos, where two of his dramatic poems are set. He wrote in the tradition of the mime, which consisted of short verse dialogues describing scenes from everyday life. The poems were composed in a special metre called iambic scazons or 'limping' iambics. He operated in Alexandria and may have moved in the circle of CALLIMACHUS (3). Like Callimachus, he claimed HIPPONAX as his model in this genre, and regarding subject matter owed something to the Doric mimes of SOPHRON of Syracuse. The text of his poems was only recovered in 1891 on the publication of a papyrus of the second century AD containing eight mimes and a short fragment of another mime. His works are realistic, sophisticated and subtle. The titles of the extant mimes are: *The Bawd*, *The Brothel-keeper* (a plaintiff's court speech in Cos), *The Schoolmaster*, *The Women Bearing Offerings* (set at the temple of Asclepius in Cos), *The Jealous Slave-owner*, *The Dildobuyer*, *The Shoemaker* and *The Dream*. Only a small fragment of *The End of the Fast* survives. The mimes were probably meant to be recited by a soloist with gestures and a minimal, somewhat stylised type of dramatic representation. See Loeb edition for text and translation by I.C. Cunningham (1993), Loeb Classical Library, Cambridge, MA: Harvard University Press; G.O. Hutchinson (1990) *Hellenistic Poetry*, Oxford: Clarendon Press; and G. Mastromarco (1984) *The Public of Herondas*, Amsterdam: J.C. Gieben.

Herodian (Aelius Herodianus) (late C2 AD) A grammarian from Alexandria and the son of APOLLONIUS (6). He was an expert on Greek accentuation on which he wrote treatises both for Homeric Greek and Attic Greek. Later, he included these in a larger work in twenty-one books entitled *General Accentuation*, covering the rules of accentuation (with numerous examples), vowel length, aspiration, enclitics, word junction, elision and the combination of words. His work, which only survives in epitomes, owed a debt to the work of ARISTARCHUS (3). One genuine work survives, *On Anomalies in Diction*. A dictionary, *Philetairos*, was formerly attributed to him. About thirty titles of other works are known and there are many quotations and some extracts. He repudiated some of his father's assertions based on analogy. He was the last and among the greatest of the original grammatical scholars in Greek.

Herodicus (C2 BC) A writer on various topics from Babylon. He was a pupil of CRATES (4) and wrote a treatise on the victims of comedy entitled *Those Attacked in Comedy*. His other works were *Against the Lover of Socrates* and a *Miscellany*.

Herodotus (484–c.425 BC) The historian of the Persian wars from Halicarnassus (now Bodrum) in Caria. His native city was Dorian but of Ionic culture, and he followed the convention of writing in the Ionic dialect which was well established as the language of research and philosophy. Halicarnassus was then under the Persian empire and its Greek inhabitants intermarried with the local Carian population. He was the son of Lyxes and Dryo, and was the nephew of an epic poet PANYASSIS with whom (c.465) Herodotus opposed the tyrannical rule of the Persian-appointed governor Lygdamis, for which he was banished and Panyassis killed. He moved to Samos where he lived on and off until 444 when he joined the Athenian colonisation of Thurii in southern Italy. He did not return to live in Halicarnassus after its liberation (c.450) by the Delian League. He probably travelled widely during those years and spent some time in Athens. Here he became a friend of the poet SOPHOCLES, and found much to interest him. He developed a strong admiration for the Athenians and is said to have read early drafts of his book to

Athenian audiences and, incredibly, to have been awarded the vast sum of ten talents by the Assembly to show appreciation of his work. To enable him to compose his *Histories*, literally 'enquiries' or 'researches', according to the standards of accuracy he had set himself, he travelled extensively and met and questioned as many authorities as he could, both actual participants in events and also their children and grandchildren. He appears to have been rich enough to finance his travels himself, although there is no evidence that he engaged in commerce. As he only knew Greek, he made use of interpreters in Egyptian and Persian contexts. He also used documents including many inscriptions found in Greek cities, but he relied mostly on oral evidence. He used the writings of previous historians critically, referring several times to his predecessor HECATAEUS (1), whose map of the world he regarded with suspicion. In his writing he was clear about the distinction between what he had seen and what he had only heard. He travelled extensively in Greece and Asia Minor. He went to Egypt where he followed the Nile as far as Elephantine Island near Aswan and also visited Cyrene in Libya. He toured the Black Sea area, including Scythia, and travelled to Babylon. He visited Phoenicia (now the Lebanon) and Gaza. Where he could, he was careful to question local people, especially priests and keepers of monuments. He got to know southern Italy and perhaps Sicily after his migration to Thurii, where he stayed until his death some time before 420 and where he did the bulk of his historical writing. His work was known in Athens by 425 when ARISTOPHANES (1) parodied it in his *Acharnians*: he may well have finished it by 430 as no event after that date is referred to in it.

The history that he wrote was conveniently divided after his death into nine books, which were named after the Muses. It is the first important European literary or historical work to be written in prose. His purpose, announced in his preface, was not only to give an account of the conflict between Greeks and Persians, but also to trace the origins and causes of the war and to set it in its geographic, sociological and ethnographic background. Consequently his book is filled with accounts of all sorts of outstanding deeds and interesting objects as he was keen to add biographical details. After a brief excursion at the beginning of Book 1 into mythical accounts of the origins of the quarrel between East and West, Herodotus takes the reign of CROESUS of Lydia as the starting point of his investigation. He traces the conquest of the Anatolian Greeks by Croesus, his acquaintance with SOLON of Athens, and his rash attack on the Persian empire. He deals with the Persian domination of the eastern Greeks and gives an account of the birth of the Persian state and its expansion down to the death of CYRUS (1) in 530. Book 2 is an account of the nature and history of Egypt, which was conquered by Cyrus' son CAMBYSES. In Book 3 he continues the history of Persia, including Cambyses' attempt to invade Ethiopia, the consequences of his death, the emergence of DARIUS (1) I and his reforms, the campaign against POLYCRATES (1) of Samos punctuates this account. Book 4 describes the unsuccessful Persian invasions of Thrace and Scythia and their expansion into Libya. Book 5 describes the Ionian Revolt and its failure, as well as the Athenian support for their Ionian kin. In Books 6–9 he describes the consequent Persian attempt to punish the Greeks and especially the Athenians for their intervention in Persian imperial affairs. Book 6 describes the Marathon campaign, Book 7 the accession of XERXES, his vast preparations and the expedition against Greece leading up to the battles at Artemisium and Thermopylae. Book 8 describes the Persian invasion of southern Greece, preparations for resistance, the battle of Salamis, Xerxes' departure and negotiations in the winter of 480/79. Book 9 rounds off the war with the final campaigns of Plataea and Mycale. Although the final narrative is continuous and chronologically sequential, at various places in the earlier books (and occasionally later) Herodotus provides a 'footnote' within the text to give information about particular cities or other matters that are to figure in what follows.

The style of Herodotus is very direct, personal and readable, gripping even, and without mannerisms. Besides the main narrative, which begins somewhat haphazardly but develops like a great river (a simile used of him by the Roman writers Cicero and Quintilian) into a smooth flow with the grandeur of a mighty epic poem, there are all sorts of digressions and insertions, especially in the earlier half of the work, which to some extent serve as footnotes to the main themes, but are regarded by their author as essential. He was keen to present his audience with great figures, such as men who profoundly influenced the flow of events: Solon, Croesus, Cyrus, Polycrates, CLEO-MENES (1) I, Xerxes, and THEMISTOCLES. He was deeply aware of the influence of the divine on human affairs and believed in the validity of oracles (though he dismissed those he believed to be false). Herodotus was however, above all open-minded and prepared to credit other people's sincerity of belief and the power of Asian and Egyptian as well as Greek religious experience. He was even-handed in his treatment of Greeks and foreigners, and gave barbarians credit for noble deeds where credit was due. He had a strong belief in the uncertainty of fate and the insecurity of human prosperity, and showed adherence to a principle of reciprocity in human affairs according to which people get their deserts and should expect to receive a kind of justice according to the fairness of their own acts towards others. He saw this principle working in human affairs as a cause of events rather than as a source of guilt. He

was always insistent on the importance of evidence and, when he was not sure of the evidence, he would say so and even cast doubt upon what he had been told while leaving it open to readers to judge for themselves. He did not try to make facts fit his own preconceived perception of history. Instead, he would give his opinions of evidence but stated quite openly the evidence he found difficult to accept. He was sometimes wrong – for instance, his disbelief that in the south of Africa the sun was in the north (4. 42) – but provided the evidence to rebut his view. The evidence provided by archaeology has often vindicated a point that Herodotus made, but which posterity otherwise could not accept. His written style is so easy and user-friendly that its success and beauty are too easily taken for granted, and the power of his descriptions of great actions and moving situations may be missed. He was prone to express warning comments on human affairs with brief general statements (gnomai), which do not cohere into a philosophy of history, but show his sense of order in events. From his work we gain an insight into Herodotus' sense of wonder and the awe which can make as great a man as Xerxes weep at the sight of his own forces as he reflects on the brevity of human life.

The greatest influence upon his style was that of HOMER. He seems to owe little to earlier historians and, though he knew and used Hecataeus' work, his style is much more accomplished than what we can tell of Hecataeus or the other early prose writers (logographoi), whose style, as appears from fragments, was simple and whose historical sense was primitive as they often uncritically mixed myth and history. Herodotus was not always appreciated as much as he deserved to be. THUCYDIDES (2) was his first adverse critic, suggesting that Herodotus was little more than a teller of tales – a romantic out to catch the attention of the casual reader. Nevertheless, Thucydides begins his introductory account from the point where Herodotus left off. Herodotus was also accused of deceit, notably by PLU-TARCH, who wrote an essay entitled *Herodotus' Spitefulness*. It was probably critical of him because Plutarch's own city of Thebes had a bad press at Herodotus' hands. More recent adverse critics over-play their hand: his epitaph 'Father of History' is more convincing, and fairer to him, than its perversion 'Father of Lies'.

See J. Gould (1989) *Herodotus*, London: Weidenfeld & Nicolson; D. Lateiner (1989) *The Historical Method of Herodotus*, Toronto; London: University of Toronto Press; W.K. Pritchett (1993) *The Liar School of Herodotos*, Amsterdam: J.C. Gieben; and Herodotus, *The Histories*, trans. Aubrey de Selincourt (1996), London: Penguin.

Heron or Hero (C1 AD) A mathematician and technologist from Alexandria. Nothing is known of his life. However, there are several books, most of which are genuine, bearing his name. He was known as 'The Engineer' (*Mechanikos*). His extant geometrical works are *Metrics*, on the measurement of surfaces and solids; *Definitions*; *Geometrics*; *Stereometrics* and *Measurements*. They are all on practical issues of measurement; the last three may be based more on his work than from his own pen. His extant works on mechanical devices are *Pneumatics*, a treatise on things that work by air, steam or water pressure; *The Production of Automata*, explaining the construction of 'miracle' working machines used in temples; *Mechanics*, surviving in an Arabic translation and which is mostly about the movement of weights and which offers the basis of statics and dynamics; *Optical Instruments*, which is about devices for measuring distances by sight at a distance; *Mirrors*, which survives in a Latin translation and is about the making of flat and curved mirrors; and *The Production of Artillery Pieces*.

Some lost works of Heron's are known to us, for instance a commentary on

EUCLID's *Elements*, partly preserved in an Arabic commentary; *The Weight-lifter*, which is about a machine for raising large weights by the use of gears and pulleys; *Waterclocks*; and *Hand-artillery*. Other works were compilations of his previously mentioned works on geometry. Heron's importance is primarily as a source of information about engineering and the mathematics of engineering in the ancient world. He used methods originating in Babylonia to solve the practical problems of applied mathematics, for instance, the formula for finding the area of a triangle, the solution of quadratic equations by arithmetic, and an approximation to irrational square roots and cube roots. In his works he combines utility with pleasure in the purpose of the inventions he describes, which include the siphon, the water-organ, pulley-systems, a lamp that regulates itself, and various mechanical toys. He drew on the work of predecessors such as CTESIBIUS. See A.G. Drachmann, *The Mechanical Technology of Greek and Roman Antiquity* (1963) and *Ktesibios, Philon and Heron* (1948).

Herophilus (born *c*.330) A physician from Chalcedon. After studying under PRAXA-GORAS of Cos, he went to Alexandria where he learnt much about anatomy from the dissection of cadavers and even from human vivisection, with the support of King PTOLEMY (2) II who allowed him to use convicted criminals. (Such experiments, even on corpses, were not done in Greece for religious reasons.) He was consequently able to discover the existence of the nerves and to distinguish sensory from motor nerves. He dissected and described the anatomy of the brain and eye, and believed the brain to be the seat of the mind. He assigned names to the anatomical features he found from the objects of everyday experience that they resembled. He wrote an account of the liver and identified the duodenum (which he named). He discovered the ovaries, which he considered analogous with the testicles. He also discovered the fallopian tubes and described the structure of the vascular system. He wrote a book entitled *On Pulses*, which distinguished arteries from veins and recognised that 'breath' is transported along the arteries by the blood. He also assigned significance to the various rhythms of the pulse beat, which he perceived in metrical terms like poetry. He acknowledged the importance of the pulse in the diagnosis of disease, and invented a special water-clock for measuring the rate of the pulse. He also wrote a book on *Midwifery* in which he sought to demystify the uterus, which was not understood and about which various superstitions persisted. He saw that women's bodies are essentially the same as men's apart from the difference of certain organs and that consequently women suffer from the same diseases as men. He discussed conditions peculiar to women, such as menstruation, in his *Reply to Common Opinions*. He also discussed the foetus and the length of pregnancy. He emphasized the importance of experiment no less than theory. He founded a school of medicine which lasted at least 200 years. Several of his books survive whole or in part. See H. von Staden (1989) *Herophilus*, Cambridge: CUP.

Hesiod (early C7 BC) A poet from Ascra in Boeotia who composed *c*.700. From his poems we learn that his father had emigrated from Cyme in Asia Minor, where he had been a sea-trader, to Ascra where he farmed. He had a brother, named Perses, with whom he quarrelled over his inheritance and whom he despised. Though roughly contemporary with HOMER, and though he wrote in epic metre, he is utterly different from Homer in other respects: his approach is didactic and he expounds rather than narrates. He claimed that the Muse called him while he was shepherding on the slopes of Helicon and told him to sing of the gods. He won a tripod as a prize for a song he sang at a

funeral at Chalcis in Euboea and was believed to have held a poetic contest with Homer, though this is likely to have been an invention of ALCIDAMAS. After he lost his lawsuit with his brother over his inheritance, he is said to have migrated west to Ozolian Locri and to have been killed in Oeneon in the precinct of Nemean Zeus by the local inhabitants. His body was later moved to Orchomenus in Boeotia on the orders of the Delphic Oracle.

The surviving poems attributed to him in ancient times are *Theogony* (*The Birth of the Gods*), *The Works and Days*, *The Shield* and *The Catalogue of Women*. Of these, *Theogony* is probably most authentic. In *Theogony*, after an introductory passage addressed to the Muse, Hesiod recounts the stories of the Titans and the first gods, including the displacement of the former by the latter. There are genealogies of divine powers and gods, many of them abstractions personified, and material on Prometheus and Tartarus. The marriages of the Olympian gods are described but a section on the loves of goddesses for men must be of much later date. Second in order of composition is the *Works and Days*, which is quite different: it contains a wealth of moral teachings to do with living a life of honest toil. He describes the work of agriculture and ends with a calendar of suitable days for performing rural or nautical undertakings. There is reference to myth: Prometheus and the story of Pandora and her jar of blessings. These are the only genuine works of Hesiod that have survived, and both show near-Eastern influences and ideas. The *Shield* is about Heracles, his birth and his battle with Cycnus. It contains a long description of Heracles' shield like that of Achilles in the *Iliad* of Homer (*Iliad*, 18. 478ff.). Its composition appears to date from the early sixth century BC. The *Catalogue* is a continuation of the genealogies of *Theogony*. Although in antiquity it was considered authentic, analysis of it now points to a date of 150 years later.

The poet's strong personality emerges from the two genuine works, a rather cantankerous peasant of deep piety, a misogynist and a pessimist, but an ally and friend of the working farmer. See R.C.M. Janko (1982) *Homer, Hesiod and the Hymns*, Cambridge: CUP; R. Lamberton (1988) *Hesiod*, New Haven, Conn.; London: Yale University Press.

Hesychius A lexicographer from Alexandria of unknown date, perhaps as late as the fifth century AD. An abridgement of his work has come down to us which, though greatly inferior to the original, is useful in certain respects, such as for dialect material and correct readings in literary, especially poetic, texts that have otherwise been lost through alteration.

Hicetas 1. (C5 BC) A philosopher and cosmologist of the Pythagorean school from Syracuse. Like his contemporary Pythagorean, PHILOLAUS, he taught that the Earth circles a central fire and that it rotates on its own axis.

2. (C4 BC) A tyrant of Leontini in Sicily. See TIMOLEON.

Hieron or Hiero 1. I (ruled 478–467 BC) A tyrant of Syracuse, the younger son of Deinomenes of Gela. When his brother GELON became ruler of Syracuse in 485 and transferred his seat of government to that city, he left Hieron in charge of Gela. Hieron fought in the battle of Himera against the Carthaginians in 480. Gelon died in 478 and Hieron succeeded him as tyrant of Syracuse, despite the claims of another brother, Polyzelus. From the start, he interfered in the affairs of the Italian Greeks, in 477 supporting Sybaris against her neighbour, Croton, and deterring his father-in-law, ANAXILAS of Rhegium, from attacking Locri. In 475 he subjugated the Ionians of eastern Sicily by destroying Naxos and resettling the

Ionian inhabitants of Naxos and Catane in Leontini. He refounded Catane as Aetna and repopulated it with Doric mercenaries: appointed his son Deinomenes its governor. In 474 he gave help to Cumae with a naval victory over the Etruscans, which ended their sea-power, and he founded a short-lived Syracusan colony on the island of Ischia. In 472 he was challenged by his ally Thrasydaeus, the ruler of Acragas (Agrigento), who wished to assert his leadership of Greek Sicily, but Hieron defeated and expelled him, and restored constitutional rule there. During his reign, Hieron welcomed poets, including AESCHYLUS and SIMONIDES, and philosophers to his court. He gave his patronage to PINDAR and BACCHYLIDES, and participated in the Olympic and Pythian Games, making lavish dedications at the sanctuaries. He died in Aetna in 467 and was buried there. He was succeeded as tyrant by his brother Thrasybulus, who was driven out a year later by a popular uprising of many Sicilian states, though Deinomenes retained Aetna. See M.I. Finley (1979) *Ancient Sicily*, London: Chatto & Windus.

2. II (C3 BC) A tyrant, and later king, of Syracuse. While a henchman of PYRRHUS king of Epirus, who controlled most of Sicily between 278–276, Hieron was elected general at Syracuse, of which he was a native, and reorganised the mercenary army of the city. Some time between 275–271 he used his position to seize power at Syracuse, and in 269 he led his army against the Mamertines of Messina, heavily defeating them, though the Carthaginians prevented him from taking Messina. He then took the title of 'king' of Syracuse, which he held for fifty-four years. In 265 he again fought the Mamertines and defeated them. In 264, in fear of the Mamertines' alliance with Rome, Hieron made an alliance with Carthage. In 263, however, he changed sides, agreed to pay Rome an indemnity and signed an alliance with Rome which guaranteed him security in his kingdom. For the rest of his life, until he died at the age of 92 in 215, he remained loyal to Rome and ruled peacefully within his own borders, which extended from Mt Etna to Noto in the south. In 248 the treaty with Rome was revised, giving Hieron the status of an equal with Rome. He prospered along with his kingdom and enjoyed friendly relations with a number of states beside Rome, including Egypt, Rhodes and Carthage. He escaped involvement in the First Punic War and the early years of the Second Punic War, and supplied Rome with grain and equipment during her crisis. He even helped to restore Carthage after the war (241) and co-existed with the Roman government in the rest of Sicily until his death. He married Philistis, the daughter of a Syracusan aristocrat named Leptines, and named his eldest son Gelon, though he made no serious claim to descent from his namesake HIERON (1) I. He made Gelon his co-ruler until his son's death. He established a fair fiscal system, which the Romans adopted after their annexation of Sicily. He built a fine palace on the island of Ortygia and beautified the city and his kingdom. He was a friend of ARCHIMEDES and was honoured by THEOCRITUS with an encomium. He was succeeded by his grandson, Hieronymus, who abandoned the alliance with Rome and was murdered soon thereafter. See M.I. Finley (1979) *Ancient Sicily*, London: Chatto & Windus.

Hieronymus 1. (364–260 BC) A soldier and historian from Cardia in the Thracian Chersonese. He was a follower of EUMENES (1) of Cardia and served him as an envoy when he was besieged at Nora in 319. ANTIGONUS (1) I the One-eyed, who was besieging Eumenes, formed a liking for Hieronymus and, after Eumenes' death at Gabiene, Antigonus became Hieronymus' patron and appointed him superintendent of the asphalt beds in the Dead Sea while he was in Syria in 312/1. Hieronymus fought at the battle of Ipsus

in 301 where Antigonus was killed, and DEMETRIUS (3) I appointed him harmost of Boeotia in 293. He ended his long life at the court of ANTIGONUS (2) II Gonatas in Macedonia. He died in 260 at the age of 104. He wrote an excellently researched and accurate history of the period he had lived through, from the death of Alexander in 323 to 272 (*The History of the Successors*), of which DIODORUS (3) Siculus made a digest, and of which some fragments have survived. His only strong prejudice was against Athens. His work was used as a source by ARRIAN, Diodorus Siculus, Justin and PLUTARCH. See J. Hornblower (1981) *Hieronymus of Cardia*, Oxford: Oxford University Press.

2. (C3 BC) A philosopher and literary historian from Rhodes. He spent most of his life at Athens: his patron was ANTIGONUS (2) II Gonatas. He began as a Peripatetic, but later founded an eclectic school of his own. We have the titles of some works: *The Poets*; *Historical Memorabilia*; *Miscellaneous Memorabilia*; *Isocrates*; *Correspondence*; *Symposium*; *Alcoholic Drink*; *Suspension of Judgement*; and a work on ethics. A few fragments of his works survive.

3. *See* HIERON (2) II.

Himilco 1. (early C5? BC) A Carthaginian navigator said to have sailed northwards from Cádiz for four months and explored the coastline as far as Brittany.

2. (died 395 BC) A Carthaginian general. As a result of an alliance between Carthage and Athens, he led an expedition against the Doric Greek cities of southern Sicily in 406 and sacked Acragas (Agrigento), Gela and Camarina. The next year he tried to take Syracuse, ruled by DIONYSIUS (1) I, but his army was ravaged by sickness and he made peace on terms favourable to Carthage which would have suzerainty over most of Greek Sicily. The war was renewed in 397 and Himilco returned as commander. He was unable to relieve Motya, an island fortress off the west coast, but in 396 he advanced along the north coast and took Messina. In 395 the Carthaginian admiral Mago defeated the Syracusans at sea off Catana and Himilco besieged the city. The troops of Dionysius came out and overwhelmed Himilco's army. Himilco sued for peace and withdrew his citizen soldiers from the island. On his return to Carthage he killed himself. See B. Caven (1990) *Dionysius I*, New Haven, Conn.; London: Yale University Press.

Hipparchus 1. (died 514 BC) An Athenian patron of arts and the younger son of the tyrant PISISTRATUS by his first wife. Closely associated with his brother, the tyrant HIPPIAS (1), he invited the poets SIMONIDES, ANACREON and LASUS to Athens and was involved in the contemporary interest in HOMER, probably introducing readings of the Homeric epics at the Panathenaic festivals. He is said to have planned the construction of the temple of Olympian Zeus at Athens. He was assassinated at the Panathenaic festival in 514 by Harmodius and ARISTOGITON, probably for personal reasons connected with a love affair. The murder caused Hippias to rule with much greater severity until he was overthrown four years later. See Thucydides, *History*, 6. 54ff.

2. (*c*.190–*c*.126 BC) An astronomer, mathematician and geographer from Nicaea who lived and worked in Rhodes. He was an original thinker, a practical scientist, and the inventor of trigonometry. He became closely acquainted with Babylonian astronomy and astronomical records (he may have spent time studying in Babylon). Though he did not accept the heliocentric theory of the solar system of ARISTARCHUS (2), his achievements place him in the front rank of ancient astronomers. One of his works survives in full, his *Commentary on the Phaenomena of Eudoxus and Aratus* in three books, in which he challenges the accuracy of their observations of the stars and constellations and offers a list of simultaneous risings and settings of stars. It has been possible to extract much information about his own stellar co-ordinates from it. His achievement in astronomy is mainly known to us from the *Mathematical Collection* (*Almagest*) of PTOLEMY (17).

He was above all a practical observer of the heavens and to establish his predictions made use of geometrical models and numerical parameters worked out from observation. He compiled a catalogue of more than 850 fixed stars, discovered the procession of the equinoxes, calculated the length of the mean tropic year to within six and a half minutes and worked out the length of the mean lunar month to within a second of the modern figure. He developed a theory of parallax and was thus able to predict accurately solar and lunar eclipses and estimate more accurately the sizes and distances of the Sun and the Moon (the latter's to a high degree of correctness). He used the Babylonian records he had acquired as well as instruments he had himself improved to assist him (he probably invented the plane astrolabe). His scientific honesty caused him to be sceptical of trying to formulate a theory of the planets because he felt the data were insufficient.

He was a fine mathematician who was interested in the application of mathematics to astronomy and geography, and his *Table of Chords within a Circle* was the equivalent of the sine-table in trigonometry. We know of his work on geography from STRABO. He wrote a work critical of ERATOSTHENES' *Geography*, showing up inconsistencies and errors of detail in the geographical data as well as mathematical mistakes. He also wrote on optics and mechanics (*Objects Depressed by Their Weight*, an astronomical calendar), and work on astrology. He produced a catalogue of his own work. His recorded observations span the period from 147–127.

Hippasus (C5 BC) A disciple of Pythagoras from Metapontum in Italy. He was a reformer of the earlier doctrine and c.450 founded a sect or branch named the *mathematikoi* which had a more scientific approach. ARISTOTLE attributed to Hippasus the belief in HERACLITUS' doctrine that the fundamental element of the universe is fire.

Hippias 1. (ruled 527–510 BC) An Athenian tyrant, the elder son of PISISTRATUS, whom he succeeded on his death. Initially, he ruled mildly and promoted leading aristocrats of all parties to the archonship, such as CLEISTHENES (2) in 525 and MILTIADES the following year. He probably encouraged his younger brother HIPPARCHUS (1) in his patronage of the arts and literature, and was behind the plans to build a huge temple to Olympian Zeus at Athens. The first Attic owl coinage probably dates from his reign. He reduced the tax on produce that his father had imposed from 10 to 5 per cent. After the murder of his brother by Harmodius and ARISTOGITON in 514 at the Panathenaic festival, Hippias' rule became harsher. The ALCMAEONIDS, including Cleisthenes, had been exiled in 514, and founded a fort on Attic territory at Leipsydrium from which they launched a campaign to remove Hippias, but failed. In 510, however, a Spartan expedition under CLEOMENES (1) I ejected him, and he fled with his family to Sigeum in the Troad and thence to the Persian court. He was a focus of disaffection with the new Athenian democracy and accompanied the Persian fleet to Marathon in 490. He died shortly thereafter.

2. (C5 BC) A sophist from Elis. Hippias was interested and well informed in a wide variety of subjects including rhetoric, literary style, poetry, music, grammar, mathematics and astronomy. He spent some time at Athens where he conversed with SOCRATES and inspired PLATO (1)'s dialogues the *Greater Hippias* and *Lesser Hippias*, which give a lively picture of him. He travelled widely in Greece to teach and practise oratory, and sometimes acted as a diplomat for Elis. He also wrote, but his works have not survived. We know of a *Trojan Story*, a *List of the Olympic Victors*, *The Names of Nations*, a *Collection* and an *Elegy on the Drowning of a Chorus of Messenian Boys*.

3. (late C3 BC) A geometer who studied curves and discovered the quadratrix, a regular curve that is not a circle. He has often been confused with HIPPIAS (2).

Hippocrates 1. (ruled 498–491 BC) A tyrant of Gela in Sicily. He succeeded his murdered brother Cleander in 498 with the support of GELON. He began his reign with an assault on Naxos, Zancle and Leontini, and had trouble at Zancle, the future Messina, which he quickly lost to some Samian refugees from Persian rule. In 492 he defeated Syracuse in a battle on the Helorus River and thus acquired Camarina from Syracuse and became its new founder. He was killed in battle with the Sicels at Hybla in 491, leaving the tyranny to his sons whom Gelon displaced.

2. (C5 BC) A physician and writer on medicine from Cos, roughly contemporary with SOCRATES (469–399), and known as the 'father of medicine'. However, his fame is as great as our ignorance about his life, teachings and writings. It became customary in antiquity for medical writers to publish their works under his name to lend them greater authority, and consequently there is nothing extant that can confidently be attributed to his pen. Thus there is a vast body of medical writings in Greek from a wide span of time which bears his name. Yet of the sixty works in the Hippocratic corpus, there is none we can positively identify as his because we do not have the knowledge of his style or achievement. It may be that he wrote nothing or that his own works are lost.

There exists an unreliable biography of Hippocrates, possibly by Soranus of Ephesus. Celsus transmits certain information about him, but it is PLATO (1) who offers some of the hardest evidence about his life and thought. In his youth Hippocrates lived in Cos where his father, an Asclepiad or supposed descendant of Asclepius, the god of medicine, trained him in medicine with the help of Herodicus of Selymbria, a gymnast. He then became a pupil of GORGIAS (1) of Leontini. He was the first person to separate medicine from philosophy, and taught medicine for a fee. Plato states in the *Phaedrus* (270c) that Hippocrates considered that the understanding of the nature of the body was dependent on an understanding of the nature of the whole. An anonymous papyrus (the 'London') containing medical material of the school of ARISTOTLE attributes to Hippocrates the belief that disease was related to a person's regimen or manner of life. Some sources say that he had children, including a son named Thessalus, and a son-in-law, Polybus, to whom writings are attributed. He is said to have died at Larissa *c.*380. Some fantastic and improbable anecdotes were also told about his life.

Ancient commentators provide further information about him which may have little basis in fact. GALEN saw him as a philosopher as well as a medical man, the head of a school of medicine based on Cos in competition with a school of Cnidus, and credits him with the theory of the four humours. HEROPHILUS and APOLLONIUS (8) of Citium also wrote about his work. See *Hippocratic Writings*, edited with an introduction by G.E.R. Lloyd and trans. J. Chadwick (*et al.*) (1950); W.D. Smith (1979) *The Hippocratic Tradition*, Ithaca, NY; London: Cornell University Press; and O. Temkin (1991) *Hippocrates in a World of Pagans and Christians*, Baltimore, MD: Johns Hopkins University Press.

3. (late C5 BC) A mathematician and astronomer from Chios. He did original work in geometry, foreshadowing some of EUCLID's work. Proclus states that he was the first person to write a book on the *Elements of Geometry*, covering substantially the same material as Euclid's first, third and sixth books. He was the first person to show that doubling the cube is equivalent to finding two mean proportionals between lines in a given ratio. He also solved the problem of squaring three of five lunes, which can be squared with a straight line and circle. ARISTOTLE states that he also developed a theory of comets.

Hippodamus (C5 BC) A town planner from Miletus. He was alive at a time of considerable expansion of Greek cities, partly caused by the destruction wreaked by the Persians on Athens and the cities of Asia Minor. He seems to have generally adopted the rectilinear plan of streets and to have been an expert in the choice of sites and in planning the layout of towns. Aristotle credits him with the invention of the grid pattern of streets and with the view that the ideal city should have 10,000 citizens. He also reports him to have held political theories and to have an effeminate appearance. He laid out the street plan of the Piraeus *c.*450 and went to the Athenian-led colony of Thurii in southern Italy in 443 where he was probably commissioned to plan the rectangular arrangement of the walls and streets. STRABO (14. 2. 9) attributed to him the planning of the city of Rhodes in 408. He may have had a hand in the planning of Priene, Olynthus and his native city of Miletus. It has been argued that he also designed standard residential houses. See J.B. Ward-Perkins (1974) *Cities of Ancient Greece and Italy*, New York: George Braziller.

Hippon or Hipponax (C5 BC) A philosopher from Samos. He lived much of his life in Athens and was interested in natural philosophy, taking a materialistic view. He thought that wetness is the basic principle – an argument stemming from the nature of semen and the brain, which he considered to be the abode of the soul. He was interested in the development of the body from the embryo to adulthood. He denied the existence of anything that cannot be perceived by the senses. The comic poet CRATINUS ridiculed him as an atheist and ARISTOTLE scorned him as a materialist.

Hipponax (late C6 BC) A poet and songwriter from Ephesus. He was expelled from Ephesus *c.*540 by the tyrant Athenagoras, and settled in Clazomenae where he lived in poverty. He turned to writing satirical verses of an uninhibited nature in a metre he invented, called the limping iambic or *scazon*, also known as the *choliambic* metre. Only fragments of his poetry remain, but we have enough to appreciate its robust style and the variety of its subject matter. We see him as a disreputable fellow, a brawler, drinker and womaniser, who expressed himself in vulgar, colloquial language and abused his enemies, using the weapon of epic parody – for example, on the glutton Eurymedontiades. His work was admired and imitated in the Hellenistic period. See M.L. West (1974) *Studies in Greek Elegy and Iambus*, Berlin; New York: de Gruyter.

Hipponicus (C5 BC) An Athenian general, son of CALLIAS (1) and father of CALLIAS (2). He was killed at the battle of Delium in 424. His daughter Hipparete married ALCIBIADES.

Histiaeus (ruled *c.*515–*c.*505 BC) A tyrant of Miletus under Persian dominion. Two years after he became ruler, he saved the Persian king DARIUS (1) I when he crossed the Danube to attack the Scythians: other Greek tyrants led by MILTIADES left to guard the bridge on which the Persians relied for retreat, and proposed its destruction. Histiaeus was rewarded with land in Thrace at Myrcinus (near the later settlement of Amphipolis). But he later

(*c.*505) fell under suspicion and was summoned by Darius to Susa where he was kept in honourable exile and consulted by the king on Greek and Ionian affairs. Meanwhile, his son-in-law, ARISTAGORAS, ruled Miletus. He sent a secret message to Aristagoras authorising the Ionian revolt of 499 against Persian rule. After the capture and destruction of the provincial capital of Sardis in 498, he asked the king to allow him to return to Ionia to negotiate the end of the rebellion. Darius agreed to his departure, but when Histiaeus returned he again fell foul of the local Persian governor, ARTAPHERNES (1). He dared not return to Susa, but made his way to Myrcinus. Absent from the battle of Lade in 494, he became a pirate, using Byzantium as his base and attacking various places in the islands and along the Asiatic coastline. In 493 he was caught in Mysia by Artaphernes' general Harpagus and impaled. See A.R. Burn (1962) *Persia and the Greeks*, London: Arnold.

Homer (C8? BC) The greatest and earliest Greek poet. However, 'Homer' is little more than a name to us apart from the traditional attribution of the two great epic poems inherited by the Greeks from times well before the classical period, the *Iliad* and the *Odyssey*. Greeks of the classical period had no idea when or where 'Homer' lived and composed his poems, but few doubted that they were the work of a single individual. Different authorities dated him to any time between the end of the Trojan War and 500 years after it. Since classical times, however, there has been a lively debate on the authorship of the two epic poems. Certain Alexandrian scholars were already prepared to question the unity of their authorship, assigning the two poems to different authors: they were known as the *chorizontes* ('dividers'). Modern scholarship since the eighteenth century (F.A. Wolf, *Prolegomena*, 1795) has re-opened the question and until the mid-twentieth century there were many 'analysts' who argued for multiple, layered composition by numerous bards at widely different times. This approach was encouraged by the growth of the study of comparative philology and the recognition of the variety of linguistic strands in the poems. The whole debate was known as the 'Homeric question'. More recently there has been a return to the belief that each poem is very largely if not entirely a unit of composition, and most scholars are now happy to attribute each work by and large to a single author, many indeed attributing both to the same poet. There are several reasons for this reversal: the recognition of the carefully constructed plots of the poems, each clearly the fruit of a single talent, the unity of character and the consistency of the social, economic and technological setting of events, and the effects of recent archaeological discovery and the results of research arising from it. However, there are, notwithstanding these common features, some significant contrasts between the worlds of the *Iliad* and the *Odyssey*, especially in the way the gods are presented and in the less archaic quality of the language of the *Odyssey*, and many modern scholars are prepared to accept that they may have been the work of two different people, or at any rate were composed at significantly different times.

The tradition about Homer is that he was a blind bard like his character Demodocus in the *Odyssey*. Seven cities claimed him, but only the claims of the Ionian cities of Chios and Smyrna, supported respectively by SEMONIDES and PINDAR, carry much weight. His being an Ionian by birth is supported by the language of the epics, which is predominantly of the Ionic dialect with an overlay of Aeolic forms (the Aeolic settlers of Lesbos and the Mysian coast were near neighbours of the Ionians). The currently favoured date of the composition of the poems is *c.*750 BC for the *Iliad* and *c.*725 BC for the *Odyssey*. The eighth century was the age of Greek colonisation

and the poems show an interest in the geography of the north-east, towards the Black Sea, and the west, towards Sicily and Italy. It was also the time when literacy was returning to the Greek world and it may be thanks to that fact that the poems were preserved for posterity even though they show much evidence of the techniques of oral composition and transmission, which accounts for the occasional inconsistencies in the poems ('Homer nodding'). Whether the poems were written down much before the time of PISISTRATUS is uncertain, though some modern scholars consider that they were actually composed in writing. While he was tyrant of Athens, Pisistratus *c.*540 BC had the poems definitively written down, preserved and recited regularly at the Panathenaic festivals.

The *Iliad*, alternatively entitled *The Anger of Achilles*, a poem of nearly 16,000 hexameter lines, is the story of a few days' action towards the end of the Trojan War while the Greek army commanded by Agamemnon was encamped in the plain between the sea and the walls of Troy. The poem was divided into twenty-four books, which fit the episodes of the plot very neatly, but are not usually considered to have been arranged by the author. The work is a unified dramatic whole: only Book 10 appears to be an interpolation introduced at a later time. The final book returns to the great issues that were raised by the first book. The action of the central books, 11–18, lasts a single day; that of 2–22 covers just four days, and the time-span of the whole action from start to finish is only a little over a month. But the poem points both backwards across the whole ten-year war and forwards to the future where there looms the foreboding of the death of Achilles and the destruction of Troy.

The *Odyssey* presents a contrast. Though it is in many ways a sequel to the *Iliad*, it is shorter, consisting of about 12,000 lines, and is set in a very different world. Geographically, it ranges over a vast area, including much of the Mediterranean and different parts of Greece (though the poet is ignorant of western Greek geography), besides venturing into entirely unknown territory, such as Calypso's island of Ogygia and the Land of the Dead. The construction of its plot, with a long flashback to the wanderings of the hero, is subtle and clever. The *Odyssey* fills in the gap in our knowledge of events since the end of the *Iliad* so that there is reference to things that happened in the interval before Odysseus set off from Troy for home. The *Odyssey* was also divided into twenty-four books, which, according to their subject matter, fall into groups of four. Many consider the quality of the last book and part of Book 23 to be inferior and unlikely to be Homer's work. This section tells the end of the story: the suitors' souls' arrival in the Underworld, the meeting of Odysseus with his father, Laërtes, and the final confrontation of Odysseus and his friends with the families of the dead suitors.

The time-scale of the *Odyssey*'s narrative is much greater than that of the *Iliad*, and its geographical scope far wider, but in many ways the techniques of composition of the two poems have much in common: the manner of suggesting action, but postponing it until later; abruptness of transition from episode to episode; the rapid build-up to a crisis and the reduction in tension after the crisis has passed; the delineating of character through what people say and do rather than by description, except for the briefest use of 'stock' epithets; the use of repeated formulae to punctuate action and provide direction to the narrative; and the use of extended, elaborate similes which relieve tension by removing the audience from the scene of action. No other early poet whose works have survived followed these techniques uniformly or produced work with the atmosphere of the two Homeric epics – a consideration which leads to the conclusion that the same man composed them both, though perhaps at a certain interval of time.

As a result of his fame, other works of a later date were subsequently wrongly attributed to Homer. Although composed in the same hexametric metre as the two great epics, they are considerably shorter, and one, the *Battle of Frogs and Mice*, offers a parody of the style of the *Iliad*. There are also thirty-three *Homeric Hymns*, which are addressed to various gods and goddesses, and the remains of the *Epic Cycle*, which are verse accounts of the mythical Theban and Trojan wars. Virtually nothing remains of the former, but from the latter we have summaries of the *Cypria*, *Aethiopis*, *Little Iliad*, *Sack of Troy*, *Returns of the Heroes* and the *Telegony*, which were mostly preserved by Proclus. We can glimpse in this remnant of the epic cycle a body of traditional material which had existed long before Homer's time and had doubtless been used by countless bards before him. After his time, it was still drawn on by the rhapsodes, or public performers, who continued to use the material long after the disappearance of oral composition. For prose translations of Homer, see J.M. Hammond's (1987) *Iliad*, Harmondsworth: Penguin and E.V. Rieu's (1991) *Odyssey*, London: Penguin, 2nd edn; for a verse translation, see *The Iliad and Odyssey of Homer*, trans. by R. Lattimore (1990) 2nd edn, Chicago; London: Encyclopaedia Britannica. For other works on Homer, see D.L. Page (1959) *History and the Homeric Iliad*, Berkeley, CA: University of California Press; G.S. Kirk (1962) *The Songs of Homer*, Cambridge: CUP; M. Parry (1987) *The Making of Homeric Verse*, Oxford: OUP; M.I. Finley (1954) *The World of Odysseus*, New York: Viking Press; J. Griffin (1983) *Homer on Life and Death*, Oxford: Clarendon Press; M.W. Edwards (1987) *Homer, Poet of the Iliad*, Baltimore, MD; London: Johns Hopkins University Press; I. de Jong (ed.) (1998) *Homer: Critical Assessments*, New York: Routledge.

Homeridae A guild of men, literally 'HOMER's children', who lived on the island of Chios and devoted themselves to the study and celebration of Homer's works. The rhapsodes, trained reciters of Homeric and other narrative verse, considered that the Homeridae had special authority in questions concerning Homer.

Hyperbolus (died 411 BC) An Athenian democratic politician, the son of Antiphanes. We cannot trust jibes by writers of comedies who pilloried him as being of foreign or slave origin. He replaced CLEON after his death in 422 as the leading demagogue and moved some sensible decrees in the Assembly. In 417 or one of the following years he attempted to have one of his aristocratic opponents, NICIAS (1) or ALCIBIADES, banished by a vote of ostracism, but the move backfired and Hyperbolus was himself banished. The procedure was thus brought into disrepute and never used again. He spent his exile in Samos, where he was murdered by the local oligarchs during the revolution of 411. See W.R. Connor (1984) *New Politicians of Fifth Century Athens*, Indianapolis, IN: Hackett Pub. Co.

Hyperides (389–322 BC) An Athenian politician and orator, the son of Glaucippus. He studied rhetoric under ISOCRATES and began his career by writing court speeches for clients. He prosecuted ARISTOPHON in 362 and subsequently attacked other prominent politicians. In 346 he came out in support of DEMOSTHENES (2) in opposition to Macedonian expansion and in 343 successfully prosecuted PHILOCRATES who had proposed negotiation with PHILIP (1) II and was forced into exile by Hyperides' action. After the Athenian defeat at Chaeronea in 338, he took the lead in organising resistance to Macedonia, and even proposed freeing slaves and giving citizenship to resident aliens to make up the enormous losses in manpower. He prosecuted DEMADES who

had become a supporter of the Macedonian cause and proposed a decree honouring Demosthenes. In 335 he urged his fellow citizens to reject ALEXANDER (3) III the Great's demand that Demosthenes and other opponents of Macedonia should be handed over. However, in 324 he was one of ten prosecutors of Demosthenes and Demades for their conduct in the affair of the money that HARPALUS had deposited at the Acropolis, some of which they were accused of misappropriating. In the same year Hyperides strongly supported his friend LEOSTHENES who, after Alexander's death, persuaded the Athenians to take part in a war against the Macedonians under ANTIPATER (1). After the death of Leosthenes and the collapse of the siege of Lamia, Hyperides was chosen to make the memorial speech (late in 322) for the Athenians killed in the Lamian War. Subsequently, in 322, after the defeat at Crannon, Demosthenes and Hyperides fled Athens in fear for their lives and were condemned to death in their absence. Hyperides was easily caught and put to death. Antipater is said to have cut out his tongue before killing him to punish him for his tirades against himself and the Macedonians.

None of Hyperides' seventy-seven speeches survived until, in the nineteenth century, papyrus copies of some of them were discovered and published. Unfortunately, his speech *Against Demosthenes* is fragmentary and far from complete. His style owed much to LYSIAS and the writers of Comedy. The critic 'LONGINUS', remarked on his wit, elegance, taste and tact. He appears to have had a light touch in handling serious matters. See S. Hornblower (1983) *The Greek World, 479–323 BC*, London: Methuen.

Hyrcanus, Johanan (John) (ruled 135–104 BC) A ruler and high priest of Judaea. Hyrcanus was the third son of the Hasmonean Simon Maccabaeus. After military exploits as a general against the Syrians, he succeeded his murdered father in 135, and held office until his death. After initial opposition from the Seleucid king of Syria, ANTIOCHUS (7) VII, who besieged Jerusalem, Hyrcanus made peace with him as well as an alliance against the Parthians. He renewed Hasmonean treaties with Rome. He annexed Samaria and Idumaea to the Jewish state and forcibly converted his Idumaean subjects to Judaism. His elder son, ARISTOBULUS (3) I, succeeded him briefly and was then succeeded by his younger son, ALEXANDER (12) Jannaeus. The increasing Hellenism of these reigns caused dissension among the Jewish people, especially the Pharisees. See also JEWS. See Davies and Finkelstein (eds) (1989) *The Cambridge History of Judaism*, Cambridge: CUP, vol. 2; R.D. Sullivan (1990) *Near-Eastern Royalty and Rome, 100–30 BC*, Toronto; London: University of Toronto Press.

I

Iamblichus 1. (C2 AD) A novelist, the author of *The Babylonian Tale* or *The Tale of Sinonis and Rhodanes*, short fragments of which have survived; a summary written by the ninth-century Byzantine scholar Photius is preserved in his *Bibliotheke* ('Library'). According to a marginal note in the summary, Iamblichus was a Syrian who had learnt the Babylonian language from a prisoner of that nationality who was captured in Trajan's time, though this may be a fiction designed to lend credibility to his story. He also claimed to have undertaken the learning of Greek in which he wrote his novel. It was a highly erotic and sensational fiction, and Photius comments on its skilful use of language and attractive characters. The material and its treatment are typical of ancient novels. See B.P. Reardon (ed.) (*c*.1989) *Collected Ancient Greek Novels*, Berkeley, CA; London: University of California Press.

2. (AD *c*.250–325) A Neoplatonist philosopher from Chalcis in south-western Syria. He was a pupil of PORPHYRY at Rome and later founded his own school in Syria, perhaps at Apamea. He was credited by later Neoplatonists with having systematised their philosophy and created a curriculum of study. However, he debased PLOTINUS' philosophical doctrine with oriental and Egyptian magic and ritual. Several of his works are extant: the first four books of *The Life of Pythagoras*, a compendium of earlier writings about Pythagorean theories; *An Exhortation to Philosophy*, possibly containing material from the lost *Protrepticus* of Aristotle; *General Mathematical Science*; *Nicomachus' Introduction to Arithmetic*; *The Theological Principles of Arithmetic* (the authorship of the last three is disputed); and *The Mysteries*, an attempt to reconcile magic and oriental religion with Platonic philosophy, which was attributed to him by Proclus in a work no longer extant. Fragments of other works also survive: *On the Soul*, *On the Gods*, letters and commentaries on PLATO (1) and ARISTOTLE, which were used as sources by later Greek Neoplatonists. See J. Finamore (1985) *Iamblichus and the Theory of the Vehicle of the Soul*, Chico, CA: Scholars Press; and D. O'Meara (1990) *Pythagoras Revived*, Oxford: OUP.

Iambulus A Hellenistic writer of unknown date: his name is Syrian. DIODORUS (3) Siculus preserves a summary of his fictional account of his fabulous journey to a Utopian island far away to the south of Arabia where he remains for seven years before being expelled and returning home via India. His work has echoes of HOMER's *Odyssey*, HERODOTUS and EUHEMERUS, and is a precursor of LUCIAN, but lacks any romantic element. In the Island of the Sun the people live happily for 150 years and then lie down and die. Men hold wives and children in common, worship stars and make their eldest citizen their ruler. See also ARISTONICUS (2).

Ibycus (C6 BC) A lyric poet, the son of Phytius of Rhegium (Reggio) in southern Italy. His dates are uncertain, and at the outside his active life spans the years 564–533. It was said that he might have become tyrant of Rhegium, but declined and left home for the court of POLYCRATES (1) at Samos – hence the saying: 'more foolish than Ibycus'. There he wrote poetry, which was later collected into seven books, mainly on personal, erotic and sensual themes, but including works of a more public nature, such as encomia, in the ancient dialect, resembling Doric, which is usual in choral lyric. He wrote an ode alluding to the beauty of Polycrates, perhaps a son of the tyrant. He wrote in a variety of metres and started, perhaps while still in Rhegium, by composing elaborate choral odes narrating myths in the style of STESICHORUS. Some considerable fragments of his work have survived and illustrate his powers of description and his use of original imagery. He shows a talent for describing nature and for expressing the pathos of love. There was a story that he was murdered in a wood near Corinth by robbers. Before dying, he called on a flock of passing cranes to avenge him. Later, at the Isthmian Games, one of the robbers gave himself away by exclaiming as a flock of cranes passed by, 'look, the witnesses of Ibycus'. He was buried at Rhegium. See C.M. Bowra (1961) *Greek Lyric Poetry*, Oxford: Clarendon Press; and D.A. Campbell (1967) *Greek Lyric Poetry*, London: Macmillan.

Ictinus (C5 BC) An architect, contemporary with PERICLES. His name, which means 'kite', may be a nickname and may indicate that he was not Athenian. In partnership with CALLICRATES (1) and under the general supervision of the sculptor PHIDIAS he drew up the plans for the Parthenon, which was begun in 447. He later published an account of his work in collaboration with Carpion; however, it has not survived. The structure and plan of the Parthenon show that its designers were expert and imaginative mathematicians: for example, the ratio $2^2:3^2$ is used in the proportions of the various parts of the building. He also designed the temple of Apollo at Bassae in Arcadia, probably before his work on the Parthenon, though the building was finished later. He had a hand, along with other architects, in the Telesterion or Great Hall at Eleusis where the mysteries of Demeter and Persephone were performed. See R. Carpenter (1970) *The Architects of the Parthenon*, Harmondsworth: Penguin.

Idomeneus A writer and philosopher of the late fourth and early third centuries BC from Lampsacus. He followed the Peripatetic school, though he was a friend of EPICURUS, who settled for a time at Lampsacus. He wrote biographies of the associates of SOCRATES of which some fragments have survived. He also wrote *On Demagogues*, which is on Athenian politicians, fragments of which PLUTARCH and ATHENAEUS preserved, and a lost *History of Samothrace*.

Idrieus (ruled 351–344 BC) A Carian governor of Caria in south-western Asia Minor under the Persians. He was the son of HECATOMNUS and younger brother of MAUSOLUS. He married his sister, ADA, who shared his power. He gave assistance in 350 to the Athenian mercenaries under PHOCION in Cyprus, where they put down a rebellion against ARTAXERXES (3) III, king of Persia.

Ion (c.490–421 BC) A writer from Chios of plays, poems and prose. He lived in Athens from c.466. In his *Peace*, produced in 421, ARISTOPHANES (1) paid tribute to him after his recent death. Very little that he wrote survives. He won at least one first prize at Athens for tragedy and another for dithyrambic poetry. ATHENAEUS says that he thanked the Athenians by giving every citizen a gift of Chian wine. Though eleven titles of his plays are known, the only fragments are of a satyr play, the *Omphale*. He also wrote drinking songs, hymns and poems in praise of individuals. He wrote a prose work of philosophy, *Triagmos*, which displays the influence of Pythagoras and postulates a threefold principle in everything. He wrote a *History of the Foundation of Chios* and *Memoirs*, in which he records his meetings with great contemporaries, CIMON, AESCHYLUS and SOPHOCLES (1). Substantial fragments of this highly original work survive, including a description of his conversation with Sophocles at a party in Chios. He also refers to SOCRATES and PERICLES – he compares the latter unfavourably with Cimon.

Iophon (C5/4 BC) An Athenian tragic poet, the son of the poet SOPHOCLES (1). Though none of his work survives, and he was accused of receiving help in his work from his father, he won first prize for a play in 435 and was second to EURIPIDES in 428. In *Frogs* of 405 ARISTOPHANES (1) suggests that Iophon was the best surviving poet. Iophon was said to have accused his aged father of senility to gain control of his property, but Sophocles turned the tables by reading out to the court his newly composed play, *Oedipus at Colonus*.

Iphicrates (*c*.415–353 BC) An Athenian general who was a professional soldier and the son of a shoemaker. He improved the equipment of the peltasts, or lightly armed infantrymen, by lengthening their javelins and arming them additionally with short swords rather than daggers. Thus in 390 he met a brigade (*mora*) of Spartan hoplites at Lechaeum on the Isthmus of Corinth with his mercenary peltast force and routed them, killing 250

men and dissuading AGESILAUS II thereby from trying to force a way through the Isthmus. He was then sent to the Hellespont, where in 389 he eliminated the Spartan admiral Anaxibius. After the Peace of ANTALCIDAS in 386, he served the Thracian king COTYS and married a daughter of his. In 373 he moved his operations to Egypt, where he supported an unsuccessful Persian invasion. After quarrelling with the Persian commander PHARNABAZUS, he returned to Athens and was sent with a fleet to Corcyra to relieve the island, which was occupied by a Spartan force. He was so successful that Sparta negotiated peace in 371, and he was awarded honours that were contested and for which he spoke vigorously. In 369 he was sent at CALLISTRATUS' proposal to help Sparta but, after failing to prevent EPAMINONDAS from invading the Peloponnese, he was appointed commander in the northern Aegean, where he supported a usurper, Ptolemy, as king of Macedonia. He then spent three years, 367–365, in an attempt to recover Amphipolis for Athens. He was later replaced by TIMOTHEUS (2) and retired to Thrace. In Athens' war with her allies in 356, Iphicrates and his son Menestheus were implicated in the failure at Embata, where he refused to engage the enemy and was prosecuted by CHARES, his colleague, but was acquitted after making a powerful defence speech, which is now lost. His career, however, was over. See J.G.P. Best (1969) *Thracian Peltasts*, Groningen: Wolters-Noordhoff.

Isaeus (C4 BC) An Athenian writer of court speeches, the son of Diagoras. Isaeus was born *c*.420, possibly in Chalcis in Euboea. As a resident alien, he was influenced by the speeches of LYSIAS and studied under ISOCRATES, himself being later a teacher of DEMOSTHENES (2). He wrote a treatise on speech-making which has not survived. We know nothing of his life or views, as all the speeches he wrote were for other people to deliver in court in pleading their own cases. All eleven genuine surviving speeches are about inheritance cases and were written between *c*.389–*c*.344. A twelfth speech of doubtful authenticity, in a long quotation by DIO-NYSIUS (7) of Halicarnassus, is of the latter date. Some fifty titles of genuine speeches were known in antiquity. Dionysius also wrote a sympathetic critique of Isaeus' style, pointing out, nevertheless, his divergence from the lucidity of Lysias in that he often seemed more concerned with convoluting the argument with insinuations and appeals to the emotions than with the plain exposition of a case found in the earlier writer. See G.A. Kennedy (1963) *The Art of Persuasion in Greece*, Princeton, NJ: Princeton University Press.

Isagoras (archon 508 BC) An Athenian aristocratic political leader, he may have been a member of the aristocratic Philaid family. During his year of office he was involved in a power struggle with CLEISTHENES (2), each leading one of the two aristocratic factions in the state. Isagoras appears to have represented those who wished to restore the old pre-Pisistratid form of government. Cleisthenes, however, by making a partnership with the common people, outflanked him and brought in a new, radically reformed constitution. Isagoras appealed to his friend, the Spartan king CLEOMENES (1) I, who intervened probably without the authority of the Spartan state and led a small force of Spartans into Attica, calling upon the Athenians to drive out the curse of the ALCMAEONIDS, a family of whom Cleisthenes was a member. Cleisthenes fled and Isagoras banished members of 700 households and attempted to abolish the council and replace it with a narrow oligarchy of 300 members. But there was a popular uprising led by the council against the Spartans and, after being besieged in the Acropolis, Cleomenes negotiated a safe-conduct for himself as well as permission for Isagoras to withdraw (some other oligarchs were executed).

Ismenias (died 382 BC) A Theban politician who, with his colleague Androcleidas, supported the Athenian democrat THRASYBULUS (2) in late 404 in his seizure of a fort at Phyle and subsequent invasion of Attica. This marked a departure from Thebes' traditional friendship with Sparta. These two fomented further trouble with Sparta in 395 when they provoked a war between Locris and Phocis, bringing the Boeotian League in on the side of Locris, and when ordered by the Spartans to submit to arbitration refused, and ravaged Phocis. This led to Spartan defeats and the Corinthian War. After the Peace of ANTALCIDAS in 386, the oligarchs were restored and their leaders, Leontiadas and Archias, induced the Spartan Phoebidas in 382 to seize the Theban stronghold, the Cadmea. He also arrested Ismenias, whose supporters, including PELOPIDAS, fled to Athens. Though Phoebidas' action was condemned at Sparta, Ismenias was tried for pro-Persian activities before a court of Sparta's allies, found guilty and executed.

Isocrates (436–338 BC) An Athenian writer of speeches and pamphlets. He studied under PRODICUS, GORGIAS, TISIAS and THERAMENES. He is said to have spoken up for Theramenes at his 'trial' by the THIRTY TYRANTS in 403. He was also acquainted with SOCRATES. His father Theodorus was a rich manufacturer who suffered financial ruin in the Peloponnesian War. Therefore Isocrates, who had earlier been a spendthrift, used his excellent rhetorical education to embark on the career of a commentator and pamphleteer, although he had neither the confidence nor the voice to speak in public himself. He began (*c*.400) by writing speeches for others to use in making pleas in court. However, feeling dissatisfied with his success as a speech writer, after a period (*c*.393–*c*.390) spent in Chios, where he became known as a teacher, he opened a flourishing and influential school of rhetoric in Athens. He published *Against the Sophists* to show the kind of education he offered, which was neither philosophical nor abstract in the manner of PLATO (1) (whose works he knew), nor the pseudo-science of the sophists. He had as many as a 100 students at one time, including some of the most important spirits of the next generation, men such as ANDROTION, EPHORUS, HYPERIDES, ISAEUS, LYCURGUS (3), THEOPOMPUS (3), TIMOTHEUS (2) and Isocrates of Apollonia. Isocrates, who charged his pupils ten *minae* for the course, became exceedingly rich from these fees, but had to pay heavy taxes to equip the fleet. In 353 he unsuccessfully defended himself against an *antidosis* or challenge over his ability to pay his assessment.

Between 390–380 he worked on his 'festival speech', the *Panegyric*, which was a reaction to the King's Peace of 386 and expounded the view that the Greeks should unite under the leadership of Athens and Sparta and drive the Persians out of the occupied Greek cities in Asia. He gave his support to the peace between Athens and Sparta, concluded in July 374 after Timotheus' naval victory over Sparta the previous year, which embodied Isocrates' desired dual hegemony. Timotheus had been Isocrates' most prominent pupil and he had even accompanied him on one of his campaigns and drafted his dispatches. Isocrates then wrote a series of open letters to prominent statesmen, AGESILAUS II of Sparta, DIONYSIUS (1) I of Syracuse, ALEXANDER (4) of Pherae and, perhaps, later ARCHIDAMUS (2) III of Sparta, asking them to lead an attack on Persia. He showed his hostility to the rise of Thebes when in 373 she seized Plataea, Athens' old ally, and he wrote a 'speech', *Of Plataea*, supposedly for delivery in the Assembly, to demand Athenian intervention. In 366 he published a 'speech' entitled *Archidamus* in which he imagined Agesilaus' heir, later Archidamus III,

making a youthful speech to the Spartan assembly in favour of recovering Messenia. His three speeches to Nicocles, king of Cyprus (one in commemoration of his father, EVAGORAS) also date from the period 372–365.

In 357 PHILIP (1) II seized and liberated Amphipolis, and Athens unsuccessfully fought the Social War against her allies. Athens was becoming bankrupt and Isocrates published two important 'speeches' in 355, *Peace* and *Areopagiticus*. In the former he protested against the war policy of the imperialist party and recommended that Athens join in a common peace of all Greek states rather than simply with her allies. He also urged the foundation of new Athenian colonies in Thrace. This proposal chimed well with the cautious policies of EUBULUS (1). The second publication, aimed at reforming democracy and perhaps owing something to the ideas of Theramenes, urged the Athenians to revert to an ancestral constitution under which the ancient council of the Areopagus would recover its powers of general supervision of public life. In writing it, Isocrates showed his concern about the likely prosecution of Timotheus and the rising influence of the baleful CHARES (1). In 353 he published the pamphlet *Antidosis* as his apology and a justification of his beliefs and educational methods.

The power of Philip was rapidly growing: he conquered Thessaly and seized Olynthus in 348, despite Athenian attempts to assist the besieged inhabitants. While the peace treaty between Athens and Philip, known as the Peace of PHILOCRATES, was being negotiated in 346, Isocrates composed his *Philip*, proposing to the king his leadership of a panhellenic confederacy and an expedition against Persia. He failed to understand Philip's need to protect his northern frontier, where he suffered a terrible wound, and wrote him a letter urging him to get on with the campaign against Persia. However, the letter was little different from the one he had sent to Agesilaus. But the idealistic plans he had nurtured were disappointed and Isocrates lowered his sights. In 342 he began his last important work, *Panathenaicus*, in which he compared the achievements of Athens and Sparta to the disadvantage of the latter. He was prevented by illness from completing and publishing this work until 339. However, he wrote a few personal letters, notably to ALEXANDER (3) III the Great and ANTIPATER (1). In 338 Philip destroyed the Athenian army at the battle of Chaeronea, and sent Antipater to negotiate peace. Isocrates met him and wrote a final appeal to Philip, in a third letter, to urge him to follow the proposals of *Philip*. In fact, a few years later, Alexander himself set about a similar programme. However, Isocrates, sick at heart at the apparent collapse of his hopes, died in autumn 338 at the age of 98, having, some believed, starved himself to death.

Isocrates made a great contribution to Greek education not only in its rhetorical aspect, but also in producing men of practical ability who could reason their way through the problems of leadership. He was, if nothing else, a conscious stylist. His tomb, which was surmounted with a high pillar carrying a siren, bore a bas-relief showing his teachers, including Gorgias. His style was exceedingly smooth and polished, and he strove to produce elaborately balanced sentences and to avoid harsh or repetitive sounds, elision and hiatus. Thus, he contrived a mechanical symmetry and predictability of expression which was inconsistent with vigour or freshness: the effect is a melodious monotony. Although he was not above plagiarising his own works, he took inordinate pains and time to compose his major writings. We have twenty-one of his speeches and nine letters, nearly all the certainly genuine works that he wrote. See G.A. Kennedy (1963) *The Art of Persuasion in Greece*, Princeton, NJ: Princeton University Press; G.L. Cawkwell in *Ancient Writers*, 1, edited by T.J. Luce (1982) New York: Scribner; and Y.L. Too (1995) *The Rhetoric of Identity in Isocrates*, Cambridge: CUP.

J

Jason (early C4 BC) A tyrant of the city of Pherae in Thessaly who was probably the son of LYCOPHRON (1). Jason was in the early 380s co-ruler with Polyalces. He pursued a policy of intervention in Euboea, and clashed with Sparta over Histiaea. He allied himself with Thebes and sent the Thebans supplies when the Spartans invaded their territory. In 374 Jason delivered an ultimatum to his only rival in Thessaly, Polydamas of Pharsalus, previously supported by the Spartans who now failed him. Jason was thus enabled to force Polydamas to agree to his election as *tagos*. He was briefly allied to Athens through his friendship with TIMOTHEUS (2), but preferred the friendship of Thebes. He formed close alliances with the Molossian king ALCETAS and, in 371, with AMYNTAS (2) II, king of Macedonia. In the winter of 373/2 he and Alcetas gave support to Timotheus when he was prosecuted at Athens for financial irregularity. He took no part in the battle of Leuctra in 371, but when the Thebans summoned him to help them destroy the Spartan survivors he instead persuaded them not to risk their gains in further warfare. He interfered, however, in Phocis and Locris, and captured the Spartan colony of Heraclea whose land he handed to Malis and Oeta. He imposed his rule on the Perrhaebi, whose territory lay on the boundary of Macedonia, and insisted on his hegemony over Macedonia and Epirus. In

370 he attended the Pythian Games at Delphi with his army, intending to preside over the event, but was assassinated there. Five of his assassins survived, but their motive for the deed was not satisfactorily explained. He may have intended to invade Persia, but his successors, his nephew ALEXANDER (4) and his sons, were unable to live up to his plans.

Jews The ancient Semitic nation who in classical times inhabited Judaea in the interior of Palestine. They were the most numerous survivors of the Israelites, being the descendants of the inhabitants of the southern kingdom after the split of Israel into two kingdoms in the time of Rehoboam. They were conquered by the Babylonians in 587 BC and their capital city, Jerusalem, was destroyed. Many Jews were at that time taken into captivity in Babylonia by the order of King Nebuchadnezzar II. This was the beginning of the *Diaspora* or 'scattering' of the nation. The Persians under CYRUS (1) overthrew the Babylonian empire in 539 and allowed the Jews to return to Judaea. They rebuilt the city in twenty-four years and constructed the Second Temple. Their land, known as Yehud, was ruled by a Persian governor, the highest Jewish official being the high priest. ALEXANDER (3) III the Great made a peaceful entry into Jerusalem in 332. After his death the country was ruled by the Ptolemies of

Egypt for 123 years. They too appointed governors and administered the country mildly. In 200 the Seleucid king, ANTIOCHUS (3) III, took Judaea from the Egyptians and his son, ANTIOCHUS (4) IV, was determined to reduce the influence of the Jewish religion. He installed a garrison in Jerusalem and dedicated the temple to Zeus. Jason, the brother of Menelaus, the Oniad high priest, seized the high-priesthood and co-operated in Antiochus' Hellenizing policy. This led to the rebellion in 167 of the Hasmonean priest Mattathias and his sons, the Maccabees ('hammers'), and the emergence of the Pharisees, a movement which Josephus compared to the Greek Stoics.

The Maccabees recaptured Jerusalem and reconsecrated the defiled temple in 164, but the struggle against hellenization continued. In 161 JUDAS MACCABAEUS made a treaty with the Roman Senate and, after he died in 160, his brother Jonathan led the opposition to the Seleucids. However, the usurper ALEXANDER (10) Balas appointed him high priest in 152 and governor of Judaea in 150. In 143 DIODOTUS (3) Tryphon killed Jonathan and, under his brother Simon, in 142 the Seleucid garrison was finally expelled from Jerusalem. Judaea flourished for the next eighty years, independent under the Hasmonean high priests except for a brief period, 135–134, when ANTIOCHUS (7) VII reasserted Seleucid rule. John HYRCANUS, son of Simon Maccabaeus, was high priest and ruler from

135–104. He made an accommodation with Antiochus VII and an alliance against Parthia, and expanded Judaea by taking Samaria and Idumaea. He forced the Idumaeans to adopt the Jewish religion.

His son, ARISTOBULUS (3) I, succeeded him, taking the title of king, but died a year later. ALEXANDER (12) Jannaeus, his younger son, then reigned until 76 and acquired new territories in Ituraea, Galilee, Peraea, Transjordan and along the Mediterranean coast. The king, however, became unpopular and was opposed by the Pharisees, and a civil war was imminent when Alexander died. His widow, Alexandra Salome, restored the situation and reigned peacefully until 69.

Judas Maccabaeus (died 160 BC) A Jewish revolutionary of the Hasmonean family and the son of Mattathias. He and his brothers led the revolt in 167 against the Seleucid attempt to take over the temple and citadel at Jerusalem and exclude the Jews from their holy place. With a band of loyal followers they drove out the 'pagan' cult, then fled into the desert, where they gained strength. When his father died in 166, Judas took command and gradually restored Jewish worship in the cities of Judaea. After recapturing Jerusalem and rededicating the temple in 164, he made an alliance with Rome. He continued a political struggle with the Jewish hellenizers and was killed in battle in 160. His brothers succeeded in driving out the hellenizers. See JEWS.

K

K For names with the initial 'K', see the equivalent entry under the initial 'C'.

L

Lachares An Athenian general who in 301 BC took part in the battle of Ipsus, in which ANTIGONUS (1) I was crushed, and used his mercenary troops first to prevent an attempt in 300 by his colleague, Charias, to make himself tyrant of Athens. Then, pleading that CASSANDER had so instructed him, he seized the tyranny for himself. He abolished compulsory military service for Athenian citizens and in 296, being otherwise unable to pay his men, he pillaged the Acropolis of its treasures, including the gold from the holy statue of Athena. His opponents seized the Piraeus and gained the help of DEMETRIUS (3) I the Besieger, and together they blockaded the city. He resisted strongly, but was starved into surrender in 295 and fled to Boeotia, using his stolen wealth to buy shelter. His fate is unknown.

Lacydes A head of the Academy of the mid-third century BC from Cyrene. He succeeded ARCESILAUS in 240 and held the headship until 223. He died in 205.

Lamachus (*c*.465–414 BC) An Athenian general in the Peloponnesian War who was first elected general in 435. Ten years later, ARISTOPHANES (1) satirised him in his comedy *The Acharnians* as a ranting soldier. In 424 he led an expedition to the Black Sea in which his moored ships were sunk by a flood and he had to escape by land through Bithynia. In 415 he was appointed by the Assembly to be one of the three generals in charge of the Sicilian expedition. His bold design to make an immediate surprise attack on Syracuse was rejected by NICIAS (1). He was responsible for the efficacy and speed of the blockade of Syracuse, but in 414 was killed in a skirmish after being cut off as he tried to aid some Athenians under pressure. His loss was a disaster as Nicias, a sick man, was left as sole commander until the arrival of DEMOSTHENES (1) the following year. After his death Aristophanes praised his bravery.

Laodice 1. (C3 BC) A member of the Seleucid royal family who was married to her cousin ANTIOCHUS (2) II, and bore him two sons and two daughters. In 252, after the Second Syrian War, Antiochus divorced Laodice and repudiated his children by her in favour of BERENICE (2), daughter of King PTOLEMY (2) II of Egypt, his ally, who bore him a son. On his death, Laodice, who had remained popular and lived in Antioch, seized power for her son, SELEUCUS (2) II, and organised resistance to an Egyptian invasion (the Third Syrian or Laodicean War, which lasted from 246–241). Antiochus named after her the city of Laodicea on the Lycus in Asia Minor which he founded.

2. (late C3 BC) A Seleucid queen, the daughter of MITHRIDATES (2) II of Pontus,

she was married to ANTIOCHUS (3) III in
221 at Zeugma (Seleuceia) on the Euphrates. She was, with her husband's
support and encouragement, charitable
on a royal scale as is shown by an
inscription from Iasus in Caria, where
she created a benefaction to provide
dowries for the daughters of poor citizens.
Her husband included her with himself in
the cult of the rulers. She had three
children, two of whom were kings of
Syria, SELEUCUS (4) IV and ANTIOCHUS
(4) IV, and a daughter, CLEOPATRA (2) I,
who married PTOLEMY (5) V, king of
Egypt. See also ARIARATHES (6) VI, ARIAR-
ATHES (7) VII and MITHRIDATES (5) V.

Lasus (C6 BC) A poet from Hermione, the
son of Charminus, born in the mid-sixth
century. He settled in Athens where his
patron was HIPPARCHUS (1), the second
son of the tyrant PISISTRATUS. There he
pioneered the art of the dithyramb and
established a competition in the composition of dithyrambs. He also composed
hymns and wrote the first musical treatise. He exposed Onomacritus' forgery of
an oracle to PISISTRATUS.

Leochares (C4 BC) An Athenian sculptor
mentioned as a young man in a letter of
PLATO (1) of 366 or after. He died c.310.
His energetic style contrasts with that of
his contemporaries, PRAXITELES, SCOPAS,
and LYSIPPUS. His surviving works include small bronze copies of his *Zeus the
Thunderer* and sculptures on the west side
of the Mausoleum of Halicarnassus showing a frieze of Amazons fighting, which is
now in the British Museum. He also
worked with Lysippus on a group showing a scene of ALEXANDER (3) III the Great
rescued from a lion by CRATERUS. Also
attributed to him are a royal Macedonian
group from the Philippeum at Olympia,
constructed in gold and ivory, including
both PHILIP (1) II and Alexander, and
which was dedicated after the battle of
Chaeronea; a statue of ISOCRATES, which
was dedicated by TIMOTHEUS (2); a statue

of Alexander on the Acropolis; a marble
Ganymede in the Vatican; the *Apollo
Belvedere* in the Vatican; and the *Demeter
of Cnidos*.

Leon 1. of Byzantium (died 339 BC) After
being educated in Athens at the Academy,
he led the resistance of the Byzantines to
PHILIP (1) II in 340 and, after support
from a fleet led by the Athenian CHARES
had been refused entry, he persuaded his
fellow citizens to admit the Athenian
PHOCION, who brought assistance. The
next year Byzantium made peace with
Philip, who sent the Byzantines a letter in
which he stated his refusal to pay a bribe
demanded by Leon for betraying the city,
and thus secured Leon's execution.

2. of Pella (late C4 BC) A Macedonian
writer who wrote an account of the
Egyptian gods asserting that they had
originally been mortal kings who had
made benevolent discoveries, such as agriculture. He dressed up his work in the
form of a fictitious letter from ALEXANDER
(3) III the Great to OLYMPIAS.

Leonidas 1. I (reigned c.489–480 BC) A
king of Sparta of the Agiad family, the son
of ANAXANDRIDAS II. Leonidas succeeded
his half-brother CLEOMENES (1) I after his
suicide (c.489) and married the latter's
daughter Gorgo, who bore him a son,
Pleistarchus. Leonidas' most notable exploit was his defence of the Pass of
Thermopylae. In 480, when the Persian
invasion of Greece was imminent and the
Persian advance through Thessaly was
reported, he chose an advance party of
300 selected Spartiates, all with living
heirs, and, even though the festival of
Carneia was in progress, which prevented
the departure of the main army, he led
them with some *perioikoi* (neighbouring
free Laconian allies) to Thermopylae,
picking up many other contingents as he
went, so that his force at the pass was
about 7,000 hoplites. An associated and
unsuccessful naval campaign took place

nearby in narrow seas off the cape of Artemisium. For two days Leonidas' force resisted the Persian onslaught, but then report came that the Persians had turned his flank after a path through the mountains had been betrayed by the Malian traitor, EPHIALTES (1). Leonidas managed to secure the safe departure of most of his army, but remained there with his Spartiates, some *perioikoi* and serfs, and 700 Thespian hoplites. The Theban contingent also remained under orders, but surrendered when the pressure became extreme. The rest of the army perished. Leonidas' body was decapitated and hung up on a stake. He was succeeded as king by his son.

2. II (died 235 BC) A king of Sparta of the Agiad house, the son of Cleonymus, he succeeded his great-nephew, Areus II, in 254. He opposed the constitutional reform in 243 of his colleague, AGIS (3) IV, and was deposed by him and succeeded by his son-in-law, Cleombrotus II. He lived for two years in Tegea in Arcadia. In 241 Agis was deposed while absent in Aetolia. Leonidas was restored and had him put to death.

3. of Tarentum (C3 BC) A poet who composed epigrams in the Doric dialect, about 100 of which are preserved in the *Garland* of MELEAGER. There are many epitaphs on simple working people, such as peasants, sailors and fishermen. Some poems, purporting to be autobiographical, claim he led a rough wandering life. The pose he adopts may be a convention that owes something to the Cynic philosophy (he wrote an epitaph for DIOGENES 2); on the other hand, he may have chosen this subject matter to meet the tastes of contemporary literary society. His work, which is highly sophisticated in diction and poetic technique, was much admired and imitated by later poets in Greek and Latin. See Alan Cameron (1993) *The Greek Anthology*, Oxford: Clarendon Press; and T.B.L.

Webster (1964) *Hellenistic Poetry and Art*, London: Methuen.

4. (or Leonides) of Alexandria (C1 AD) A poet who composed Greek epigrams of Callimachean wit and complexity at Rome. There are about thirty of these in the *Greek Anthology*. He had previously been an astrologer.

Leonnatus (C4 BC) A Macedonian noble related to ALEXANDER (3) III the Great through his paternal grandmother Eurydice, and a member of PHILIP (1) II's bodyguard. He went to Asia with Alexander and, after serving him as a diplomat, joined his bodyguard in 332, rising to generalship in 328 and an independent command in India in which he so distinguished himself that he was crowned by Alexander in 324 at Susa. After Alexander's death, he refused to obey an order of PERDICCAS (2) to join EUMENES (1) and help him conquer Cappadocia. In 323 Perdiccas appointed him satrap (governor) of part of Phrygia near the Hellespont and in spring 322 he took a contingent of troops to Greece to relieve ANTIPATER (1), who was besieged in Lamia. Leonnatus was killed in Thessaly in a battle outside Lamia by forces under the Athenian general Antiphilus.

Leontion (C4 BC) A female philosopher who wrote a lost polemic against THEOPHRASTUS which was admired for its style by Cicero.

Leosthenes (C4 BC) An Athenian general in the Lamian War of 323–322. He was elected general in charge of the defence of Athens in 324, having already gained military experience as a mercenary in Asia. He allied himself with the anti-Macedonian HYPERIDES and organised the repatriation of a large number of Alexander's mercenary troops, disbanded by the satraps, whom he encamped at Cape Taenarum in Laconia. Using these well-trained men and a host of Greeks from Athens and other cities, united in a Hellenic League he had negotiated, he marched north into Thessaly where he drove ANTIPATER (1) to take refuge in Lamia and besieged him there. He was killed during the siege in 322 and his death ended the opposition to the Macedonians. Hyperides spoke his funeral oration.

Leotychidas II (reigned *c.*491–469 BC) A king of Sparta of the Eurypontid house. His colleague, CLEOMENES (1) I, helped him to depose his cousin and rival, DEMARATUS, who fled to Persian territory. His assistance of Cleomenes in 491 at Aegina in response to Athens' complaint of Aeginetan medism gained hostages for Athens to secure Aegina's loyalty to the Greek cause. He was a successful commander in the Persian War, acting as admiral of the united Greek fleet in 479 and winning the decisive battle of Mycale on both land and sea. A year or two later he was involved in an expedition of the victorious Greek states to Thessaly to punish the cities that had joined Persia and took Pagasae, but could not capture Larissa. As a result of this, he was charged *c.*476 with accepting a bribe to spare the Thessalians and only escaped condemnation at Sparta by going into voluntary exile at Tegea where he remained until his death.

Leptines (C4 BC) An Athenian citizen whom DEMOSTHENES (2) prosecuted in 355 and who in 354 proposed the abolition of exemption from the duties of providing certain public services for military and cultural purposes. Demosthenes opposed him and his supporter Aristophon in a speech that survives (*Against Leptines*). Despite the statement of DIO CHRYSOSTOM, the proposal was probably passed.

Lesches (C7 BC) An epic poet from Lesbos to whom the composition of *Little Iliad* and *Sack of Troy* in the epic cycle were

attributed. These lost works included the stories of the suicide of Aias (Ajax), the enrolment of Neoptolemus, son of Achilles, after his father's death, the tricking of Philoctetes into coming to Troy, the Wooden Horse and Sinon's deception of the Trojans, the story of Laocoön, the fall of Troy and the departure of the Greek army. See also HOMER.

Leucippus (C5 BC) A philosopher from Miletus or Elea who was the inventor of the atomic theory of matter. He criticised and reacted to the theory of the unitary universe as postulated by PARMENIDES, and solved the problem of its conflict with seeming reality by postulating instead the existence of void and the multiplicity of spheres (namely the atoms) rather than the singularity of the universe in one sphere. According to THEOPHRASTUS he wrote two books which have not survived, *The Great World-System* and *Mind*. We know of his theories from the writings of others, such as DEMOCRITUS, ARISTOTLE and DIOGENES (5) Laërtius. EPICURUS, whether seriously or not, denied his existence. It is now impossible to disentangle his contribution to the theory from that of his pupil Democritus.

Libanius (AD 314–393) A teacher of rhetoric from Antioch in Syria who was of a rich and influential provincial family. Libanius was well educated at home and then at Athens, where he spent four years studying from 336. He then became a teacher of rhetoric at Constantinople, moving in 346 to Nicomedia. The Emperor Constantius II offered him a post as professor of rhetoric at Athens, which he declined, but in 354 he accepted an appointment to a chair of rhetoric at Antioch, where he lived until his death in 393. He had many distinguished pupils, including some Christians. Probable students of his were Basil of Caesarea, Gregory of Nazianzus, John Chrysostom, Theodore of Mopsuestia and the historian Ammianus Marcellinus. He became a friend of the Emperor Julian whom he probably met in Antioch. He remained a 'pagan' all his life in spite of which Theodosius I consulted him and gave him the honorary title of praetorian prefect.

He left a large extant *oeuvre*. Sixty-four speeches and more than 1,600 letters survive, as well as school exercises in rhetoric which he wrote for his pupils. From his writings much is to be learnt about the public and private life of his day, and educational and cultural matters are also richly treated. One of the speeches includes an autobiography composed nineteen years before his death and another is his funeral oration for the Emperor Julian, whose death was a great blow to him. He also wrote a speech in praise of Antioch. He wrote in a painstaking, even pedantic style. See J.H.W.G. Liebeschuetz (1972) *Antioch*, Oxford: Clarendon Press; and N.G. Wilson (1983) *Scholars of Byzantium*, London: Duckworth.

Lichas (died 411 BC) A Spartan noble and the son of ARCESILAUS. Steered by a foreign charioteer, his team won the four-horse chariot race at Olympia in 420 at a time when Spartans were banned from competing, and, consequently, when he crowned the victor, Lichas was given a beating by the umpires, which later became a pretext for Sparta to attack Elis. Lichas became notorious for allowing foreign visitors to attend the Spartan festival of Gymnopaedia. In 418 he negotiated a treaty of peace between Sparta and Argos, whose representative (*proxenos*) at Sparta he was. He led the rejection of a pact with Persia in winter 412 when a commission of eleven was sent to Miletus to advise Astyochus, the Spartan admiral, and so lost the Persians' offer to pay the Peloponnesian sailors. Lichas spoke out against Persian pretensions to all the territory it had ever held. A few months later, however, a further pact was agreed which accepted Persia's claims in Asia. Lichas died of sickness in Miletus.

'Longinus' A rhetorician, as well as the author of one of the most important works of ancient literary criticism, *On the Sublime*, of which about two-thirds survive. He can be dated to the first century AD, but we know nothing of him. Even his name is uncertain (the manuscript naming him as Dionysius or Longinus) and there is no evidence to identify the author with any known person. He wrote his treatise in response to a work of the same name by Caecilius of Caleacte which is not extant and which he considered an unsatisfactory account of sublimity in literature because it failed especially to explain the importance of its power to stir emotion. The book seems to have been unknown in ancient times and to have been preserved in a mutilated condition by a mere chance.

Sublimity was considered by ancient rhetoricians to be one of three styles of oratory (the other two are the dry, businesslike style and the moderate, pleasant style), but Longinus identifies it as the central element in the aesthetics of literature. He looks back to the great works of the past, including the poets as well as the orators, acknowledging also the power of the Hebrew book, *Genesis*. He sees the quality of sublimity as the result of special inspiration, perhaps of a supernatural nature, often found in certain passages of a literary work rather than in the whole, but susceptible to analysis and rational appreciation, and attainable by his contemporaries even though the great classical works of the past display it most readily. Longinus' work shows great originality, seriousness and a freshness of approach that distinguishes it from most other ancient works of criticism. It became known first through the paraphrase written by the French critic Boileau (1674), and was influential thereafter and passionately debated until late in the nineteenth century. It still commands deep respect. See D.A. Russell (1981) *Criticism in Antiquity*, London: Duckworth.

Longus The writer of a Greek novel, *The Pastoral Story of Daphnis and Chloe*, usually known simply as *Daphnis and Chloe*, about whom nothing is known. It has been conjectured that Longus was a native of Lesbos, where the novel is set, from details that seem to suggest personal knowledge of the island, though there are errors in his geographical knowledge. The literary fashions that he follows suggest a date in the late second or early third century AD. The story is romantic and rustic, yet playful and teasing, and seeks to fuse the well-established Greek tradition of the prose novel with the poetic tradition of the rural, pastoral scene as created by THEOCRITUS in the third century BC. The work, economically composed in four books, is prefaced by a description of a painting depicting a scene from country life, which the author claims is his inspiration for a didactic work written to enlighten the reader on aspects of life and love.

The novel, however, is essentially an entertainment. The bucolic idyll is adopted as the setting for the charm of its associations and the opportunity it gives for the gradual exposure of the reality of sexual love, with many of the standard elements of the ancient novel included, though less extensively than in many others: pirates, abduction, the threat of rivals, the intrusion of the town upon country simplicity and the eventual revelation that the lovers are really the children of very rich landowners and their marriage is quite attainable. The central theme of the story is the gradual awakening of love and the discovery of sex in a naïve and youthful couple. It is told with a certain distancing of the narrator from the characters and events he is describing, which lends charm to the tale. There is much play on the simple country religion of the pastoral folk, derived from the bucolic tradition: Pan and the Nymphs are the gods worshipped. Penetrating psychological analysis of motive pervades the book, characterisation is strong and the

story is enlivened by incidents like Daphnis' sexual initiation by an older woman and the warfare between Mytilene and Methymna. The novel rivals that of HELIODORUS (3). It was translated into French by Amyot in 1559 since when its popularity has been continual. Its influence on later literature, including Bernardin de St Pierre's *Paul et Virginie*, painters such as Corot, and Ravel, who composed a ballet on the theme, is clear. See R.L. Hunter (1983) *A Study of 'Daphnis and Chloe'*, Cambridge: CUP; T. Hägg (1983) *The Novel in Antiquity*, Oxford: Blackwell; G. Barber (1989) *Daphne and Chloe* and translation by C. Gill in B.P. Reardon (ed.) (c.1989) *Collected Ancient Greek Novels*, Berkeley, CA; London: University of California Press.

Lucian (C2 AD) A satirical prose writer in Greek from Samosata in Commagene on the Euphrates. Born *c.*117 in an Aramaic-speaking *milieu*, he was educated in Greek and received a sophistic training, perhaps in Antioch, where he practised for a time as a barrister, but changed his career to that of a sophistic rhetorician and lectured while travelling, going as far as Thrace, Italy and Gaul. He underwent a conversion to philosophy *c.*165, settled in Athens, and remained there for about twenty years, engaging in philosophy under the guidance of the Cynic philosopher DEMONAX, and writing profusely until he was appointed under the Roman emperor Commodus to a minor administrative post in Egypt where he died some time after 180. Our knowledge of his life is culled from his own writings, such as *The Dream*, which are not to be accounted reliable. He left a substantial prose *oeuvre*, about eighty genuine pieces, many in the form of dialogues, which were usually of a satirical nature. He was greatly influenced by the humorous writings of the Cynic philosopher MENIPPUS (1). He was also influenced by mime and the Old Comedy. He was acquainted with

GALEN, who regarded him as a literary fraud.

His best-known work is the imaginative fantasy *A True Story*, which is a humorous parody of fantastic tales such as those of HERODOTUS, in which he imagines himself on a voyage or journey of exploration which miraculously takes him off the planet to the Moon and later into the belly of a whale and to the underworld. It was the inspiration for works by Rabelais, Raspe (on Baron Münchhausen), Swift and Rostand (*Cyrano de Bergerac*). His Greek style is simple, clear and chatty, and his language classical Attic. Other works are the dialogues, superficially Platonic in tone, but really an original vehicle for satire and the questioning of received ideas, especially of religion, myth, philosophy, pedantry, and the like. He also wrote pamphlets in letter form, such as *Alexander* which was an attack on ALEXANDER (13) of Abunoteichos. In *Peregrinus* he attacks a religious maniac of that name. *Lovers of Lies* satirises superstition and *Statues* is an account of the major works of some of the great Greek sculptors. He discusses the nature and origin of his satirical production in *The Literary Prometheus*. *Demonax* is a description of his philosophy teacher. See G. Anderson (1976) *Lucian*, Leiden: E.J. Brill; J. Hall (1981) *Lucian's Satire*, New York: Arno Press; R.B. Branham (1989) *Unruly Eloquence*, Cambridge, MA: Harvard University Press; and C.P. Jones (1986) *Culture and Society in Lucian*, Cambridge, MA: Harvard University Press.

Lucius The supposed author of an extant picaresque novelette in Greek entitled *The Ass*, which survived with the works of LUCIAN, but is clearly not his work. The story, told in the first person, served Apuleius as the basis of his much longer and more serious novel, *The Metamorphoses*. See translation by J.P. Sullivan in B.P. Reardon (ed.) (*c*.1989) *Collected Ancient Greek Novels*, Berkeley, CA; London: University of California Press.

Lycon (*c*.300–*c*.226 BC) A Peripatetic philosopher from the Troas in Asia Minor, the son of Astyanax, he studied under STRATON (1) of Lampsacus and succeeded his teacher as head of the Peripatetic (Aristotelian) school of philosophers. He remained in the post for forty-four years, but was largely responsible for its decline. He was worldly and eloquent and preferred spending his time in pleasurable activities to teaching or research.

Lycophron 1. (died *c*.390 BC) A tyrant of Pherae in Thessaly who seized power *c*.406 and defeated his combined enemies, the aristocracies of the Thessalian towns, in 404. He made an alliance with Sparta and fought a further battle against Larissa in 395. The history of his reign is unclear owing to a lack of evidence. JASON appears to have been his son. See H.D. Westlake (1935) *Thessaly in the Fourth Century BC*, London: Methuen.

2. A tyrant of Pherae, probably the grandson of LYCOPHRON (1) and the son of JASON. He was one of the people who murdered ALEXANDER (4) in 359 BC. He became tyrant in 355. In alliance with ONOMARCHUS of Phocis, he was defeated by PHILIP (1) II, king of Macedonia, at the battle of the Crocus Field in 352. Expelled from Pherae, he joined the army of Phocis.

3. (born *c*.320 BC) A Hellenistic writer of tragedies from Chalcis in Euboea who emigrated to Alexandria *c*.284 where he obtained a post in the library as the curator of comic plays. He became a member of the literary group known as the Pleiad, and wrote tragedies and satyr plays: a few lines of his *Menedemus*, named after a friend, survive. A tragedy, titled *Cassandreis*, appears to have been based on recent events at the city of Cassandreia in Chalcidice. Little of his work survives.

4. (early C2 BC) The writer of an extant poem entitled *Alexandra*, whose real identity is unknown, but who may have adopted the name of LYCOPHRON (3) ironically to recall his combination of tragic composition and comic redaction. His work is datable from a reference to the victory of Flamininus over PHILIP (3) V at the battle of Cynoscephalae in 197 BC. The poem purports to be a prophecy uttered by Cassandra, daughter of Priam of Troy, and is both powerful and deeply obscure. It contains a prediction of the future power of Rome and runs to 1,474 iambic lines.

Lycortas (C2 BC) An Achaean statesman and soldier from Megalopolis. He was a friend of PHILOPOEMEN and supported his policy of a unified Peloponnese in the Achaean Confederacy with the enforced membership of Sparta, Messene and Elis. He held at different times both the post of *hipparch* ('master of the horse') and general, that is, leader of the confederacy. He fought in the war against NABIS, tyrant of Sparta, and appeared in 189 in Rome as ambassador of the confederacy to defend its policy against Sparta and Messene. After further negotiations with the Romans, he supported Philopoemen's attempt to coerce Sparta and Messene back into the confederacy in 182, and replaced him after his death as general, readmitting the seceding states to membership of the Achaean Confederacy. His policy, however, was attacked by CALLICRATES (2), who favoured a pro-Roman line, and he was unable to maintain Achaean neutrality in the Third Macedonian War. His son was the historian POLYBIUS.

Lycurgus 1. (C6 BC) The aristocratic leader of the 'Plain' faction at Athens and an opponent of PISISTRATUS. He was a member of the Eteobutad clan. His chief rival was Megacles, the ALCMAEONID leader of the 'Coast'.

2. A Spartan 'lawgiver' who may not be a historical person at all, and who is impossible to date. A tradition, which grew up in the sixth century and was known to HERODOTUS, claimed that he gave Sparta her constitution in the Great *Rhetra* (covenant) by which sound government was established. He is not credited by the poet TYRTAEUS with the creation of the *Rhetra*, and it seems likely that the Spartan system was the product of an evolutionary process. In any event, XENOPHON (1) attributed the constitution to him, and PLUTARCH wrote his 'life'.

3. (*c.*390–*c.*324 BC) An Athenian statesman and public speaker of noble ancestry who became influential after the battle of Chaeronea in 338, and organised and supervised the finances of Athens during the twelve years to 327. The authority by which he controlled finance is not clear, but it is clear that he improved the financial situation greatly and set in motion an ambitious building programme, including the reconstruction of the theatre of Dionysus in stone, the arsenal, and harbour and dock improvements. He also increased the size of the fleet. He had statues of the three tragic poets erected in the theatre and had official copies of their plays made. His policy, like that of his ally, DEMOSTHENES (2), was consistently anti-Macedonian, and he was one of the politicians whose surrender ALEXANDER (3) III the Great demanded in 335. He engaged in litigation and prosecuted Lysicles for his conduct as a general at Chaeronea, and in 331 arraigned Leocrates for treason on the grounds of his absence from Athens from 338–332 (his speech of prosecution is the only one still extant). He composed many other court speeches and had a reputation for his merciless attacks, though he was deficient as a stylist.

Lydiadas (died 227 BC) A tyrant of Megalopolis in Arcadia. In 251 he led an army against Sparta. He made himself tyrant *c.*243, but under pressure from the Achaean Confederacy resigned in 235, restoring democracy and bringing his city into the Confederacy. He was elected general (chief magistrate) several times and became a rival to ARATUS (2), alternating in the chief offices of the Confederacy with him. He was killed at the battle of Ladocea against CLEOMENES (2) III of Sparta in 227 when as cavalry commander he disobeyed Aratus' order and made a fatal charge.

Lygdamis (C6 BC) A tyrant of Naxos. An aristocrat, yet leader of the popular party, he seized power *c.*545 after being elected general and ruled until 524. He had lent support to PISISTRATUS in 546 when he seized the tyranny of Athens and loaned troops to help POLYCRATES (1) of Samos *c.*535 to take power in his island.

Lysander (died 395 BC) A Spartan of impoverished family who became the favourite and lover of AGESILAUS II, the younger son of King ARCHIDAMUS (1) II. An able soldier, he was given command of a fleet in 407 and defeated the Athenian navy at Notium with the result that ALCIBIADES was dismissed from his post as Athenian general. He courted the friendship of CYRUS (2), satrap of Phrygia, who lent him financial support. After the setbacks of 406, caused by CALLICRATIDAS' inefficiency, he was appointed in 405 as second in command of the navy (but effectively its admiral) and won the battle of Aegospotami in the Hellespont. He sailed towards Athens, establishing boards of ten men of oligarchic disposition (*decarchies*) under the control of Spartan harmosts in the cities he captured, and then conducted a blockade of Athens culminating in her surrender in 404. He established the rule of the THIRTY TYRANTS which was, however, short-lived as King PAUSANIAS (2) allowed the Athenians to restore democracy the next year. He was still, however, the most influential figure at Sparta and was behind his city's

support for Cyrus' claim to the throne of Persia in 401. He also helped his friend Agesilaus to become Eurypontid king on the death of AGIS (1) II in 398, and obtained for him command in a war against Persia in 396, but Agesilaus was jealous of Lysander's prestige and thwarted his efforts to restore the decarchies. He sent Lysander to the Hellespont where, with a Persian rebel named Spithridates, he made inroads on the satrapy of PHARNABAZUS. Lysander returned to Sparta in 395 and later in that year on the outbreak of the Corinthian War proceeded to Central Greece, raised troops from Phocis and Trachis, and attacked the Boeotians at Haliartus, but was caught and killed by a Theban force. His rashness had caused the failure of Spartan strategy and Pausanias ignominiously withdrew. Lysander was later accused of plotting to turn the Spartan monarchy into an elective office. See PLUTARCH'S *Life of Lysander.*

Lysias (*c.*459–*c.*380 BC) An Athenian orator whose father, Cephalus, was a metic from Syracuse and a friend of PERICLES. Traditionally said to be born in 459, he was probably considerably younger. After his father's death, he went with his brothers, Polemarchus and Euthydemus, to join the colony of Thurii in southern Italy where he studied rhetoric. The brothers were expelled from Thurii in 412 after the Sicilian expedition for their pro-Athenian stance and returned to Athens, where they established a successful shield-making business. In 404 they were persecuted by the THIRTY TYRANTS, who used their metic status and democratic sympathies as a pretext to confiscate their wealth. Polemarchus was killed, but Lysias escaped from prison to Megara where he assisted THRASYBULUS (2), a democratic leader. He was invited back to Athens on the restoration of the democracy in 403 and invested with citizenship, which was, however, cancelled almost at once on the grounds that

Thrasybulus' decree, granting the right to all foreigners who had helped restore the democracy, was illegal. He passed the rest of his life composing speeches for others to deliver as he was debarred from doing so as a metic. His earliest speech, if authentic, dates from 407. He delivered his *Against Eratosthenes* in 403 while a citizen to prosecute a former member of the Thirty Tyrants, the murderer of his brother Polemarchus. In 388 he published an influential political speech, the *Olympiac*, against the risk of civil strife. However, most of his works that have survived are court speeches, both public and private, which he wrote for litigants to deliver themselves. He is said to have composed more than 200 speeches: thirty-five survive complete or in part, though some may be spurious. He was a remarkably unaffected stylist, writing without adornment and expertly narrating events in a way that succeeded in convincing juries of their authenticity. He is mentioned as a character in works of PLATO (1), such as *Phaedrus* and the *Republic* (Book I). See K.J. Dover (1968) *Lysias and the Corpus*, Berkeley, CA: University of California Press; and E.J. Kennedy (1963) *The Art of Persuasion in Greece*, Princeton, NJ: Princeton University Press.

Lysimachus (*c.*355–282 BC) A Macedonian general and one of ALEXANDER (3) III the Great's successors. He rose in Alexander's service to become a royal bodyguard in 328. On his master's death in 323 he was appointed governor of Thrace, where he had to struggle with the reigning king, Seuthes. He ruled Thrace firmly and successfully, founding his capital of Lysimacheia at the entrance to the Thracian Chersonese in 309. He declared himself king in 306, without embroiling himself in the quarrels of his fellow successors until 302, when he joined a coalition to overthrow ANTIGONUS (1) Iand invaded Asia Minor where he employed delaying tactics until his ally, SELEUCUS (1) I, could arrive in force to

finish Antigonus off at Ipsus in 301. Thus Lysimachus extended his domain to the Taurus Range and enriched himself in Europe by consolidating his kingdom as far as the Danube and beyond. In 292, on an expedition beyond the Danube, he was captured by a Getic king, Dromichaetes, who released him on condition that he abandoned all territory north of the Danube. In 287 he made an alliance with PYRRHUS of Epirus in a war against DEMETRIUS (3) I of Macedonia, and in 285 he drove Pyrrhus out and occupied the whole of Macedonia and Thessaly. Thereafter, he became progressively more unpopular for his heavy taxes and arrogance towards the nobility, and in 283 he killed his son and heir, Agathocles, an excellent general who had rid his father's empire of any further trouble from Demetrius, to please his second wife, ARSINOË (2) II. The following year Seleucus invaded Asia Minor and defeated and killed Lysimachus at the battle of Corupedium. His kingdom broke up and Asia Minor became part of Seleucus' empire and the European section collapsed into anarchy. See H.S. Lund (1992) *Lysimachus*, London; New York: Routledge.

Lysippus (*c.*390–*c.*310 BC) A sculptor from Sicyon and the brother of LYSISTRATUS. He worked in bronze and concentrated on portraits. His style was revolutionary: he developed a technique of making bodies longer and heads smaller. He made the famous *Apoxyomenos* (a youth scraping oil off his body) appear to be rocking backwards and forwards with an arm outstretched into the onlooker's space (there is a copy of it in the Vatican). He was much in demand and made several portraits of ALEXANDER (3) III the Great which led to a new ideal in portraiture. The Farnese *Heracles* and the *Seated Heracles* are also attributed to him. He was active from *c.*370–315. He was a prolific artist and several copies of his works survive. He had three sons, who were also sculptors, as well as several pupils who formed his 'school' and continued to work well into the third century. His principal pupils were Chares of Lindos and Eutychides of Sicyon, and in the following generation Tisicrates of Sicyon and Xenocrates of Athens. Lysippus' son Euthycrates gained a fine reputation, especially for group sculptures.

Lysistratus (C4 BC) A sculptor from Sicyon and the brother of LYSIPPUS. Though less prolific than his more famous brother, he was quite as original: he introduced realism into portraiture by taking plaster moulds from the living faces of his subjects and correcting the wax casts he made from his moulds. He also appears to have taken casts from statues for teaching purposes and to make copies. His only known work is a portrait of Melanippe.

M

Maccabees *see* Jews.

Machon (mid-C3 BC) A comic playwright and writer of anecdotes, resident in Alexandria, where he is almost unique in having staged comedies. Two fragments of his comedies and his epitaph by DIOSCORIDES show that he was capable of pungent wit. Four hundred and sixty-two lines of his iambic verse telling scurrilous stories about well-known characters of low life were preserved by ATHENAEUS.

Magas (died *c.*255 BC) A king of Cyrene in north Africa and son of BERENICE (1) I. PTOLEMY (1) I, his stepfather, appointed him governor of Cyrene (*c.*308). After marrying a Seleucid princess, Apama, daughter of ANTIOCHUS (1) I, he declared himself king and independent of Egypt. He made up his quarrel with PTOLEMY (2) II by offering his daughter, BERENICE (2), to Ptolemy's son and heir, PTOLEMY (3) III.

Mago (died *c.*520 BC) A Carthaginian statesman of the second half of the sixth century BC. He reformed the army, changing it into a professional mercenary force led by Carthaginian officers. He consolidated Carthage's hold on Sardinia and founded a dynasty of rulers.

Manetho 1. (early C3 BC) An Egyptian priest from Heliopolis who wrote a history of Egypt (*Aegyptiaca*) in Greek in three books from earliest times until 323 BC which he dedicated to PTOLEMY (2) II. In it he divided his chronology into the thirty dynasties that are still recognised today. His work did not survive except for fragments that Jewish and Christian writers preserved. He made many mistakes and omissions, but was used as evidence for the chronology of the accounts of events given in the Hebrew scriptures.

2. 'Manetho' was the false name adopted by an astrological writer of the last century BC to whose work, entitled *Forecasts*, was added a range of other books of later date. The whole work, which survives in six books, is of little value. The author of Book 5 deliberately seeks to pass himself off as MANETHO (1).

Mausolus (ruled 377–353 BC) A ruler of Caria and Lycia who was nominally a satrap under Persian suzerainty, but who was effectively independent. He inherited his title from his father, HECATOMNUS, and formed friendly relations with the Persian government, though he extended his rule to parts of the Greek lands in Lydia and Ionia. In 357–355 he assisted Rhodes and other rebellious cities in their Social War with Athens, and in *c.*350 he annexed Rhodes, Chios and Cos. He moved his capital from Mylasa to Halicarnassus as his Aegean interests increased.

He briefly joined the Satraps' Revolt against King ARTAXERXES (2) II of Persia in 362, abandoning his allies when he foresaw failure. He ruled in partnership with his sister-consort, ARTEMISIA (2), who succeeded him. He planned and began to build an extravagant tomb for himself which Artemisia continued after his death. This Mausoleum became one of the wonders of the ancient world.

Megasthenes (*c*.350–*c*.290 BC) An Ionian historian and diplomat who travelled to the east of the empire of ALEXANDER (3) III the Great and lived at the court of Sibyrtius, satrap of Arachosia and Gedrosia (Sindh and Beluchistan), until 316. He entered the service of SELEUCUS (1) I who between 303, the date of a treaty, and 291 sent him on several embassies to India to the court of Chandragupta (see SANDRACOTTUS), king of the Maurya empire. Megasthenes used this opportunity to study the life of India, and wrote a study, along the lines of the work of HERODOTUS, of Indian history, geography, society, government, religion and mythology, entitled *Indica*. Though only fragments of this work have survived, we know it was highly influential and was used as a source by ARRIAN, DIODORUS (3), STRABO and Pliny the Elder. See J.W. Sedlar (1980) *India and the Greek World*, Totowa, NJ: Rowman & Littlefield; and T.S. Brown (1973) *The Greek Historians*, Lexington, MA: Heath.

Meidias (late C5 BC) An Athenian potter whose signed water-jug was painted by a hand whose work is recognisable elsewhere: the potter and the painter may be the same man.

Melanippides (C5 BC) A poet from Melos with the same name as his grandfather, also a dithyrambic poet, who won a prize at Athens in the Dionysia festival in 493. The grandson, whose work was admired by XENOPHON (1), developed the art of the dithyramb and abandoned the tradi-

tional strophe form by introducing lyric solos. We have parts of his *Danaids*, *Persephone* and *Marsyas*.

Melanthius 1. (C5 BC) An Athenian writer of tragedies and, if the same man, of an elegiac poem dedicated to CIMON. The tragedian was much mocked by the comic poets for his gluttony and effeminacy. ARISTOPHANES (1) parodies his *Medea* in the *Peace*.

2. (C4 BC) A painter from Sicyon, a pupil of PAMPHILUS (1), and his probable successor as head of a school of painters there. His fellow pupil APELLES acknowledged Melanthius' talent for composition. We know of one work, a painting of the charioteer Aristratus.

Meleager (C2–1 BC) A poet and philosopher from Gadara in Syria. He was brought up in Tyre, where he lived before retiring to Cos, where he died at an advanced age. He wrote in Greek in a number of genres; prose satires in the style of MENIPPUS (1), philosophical discourses written from a Cynic standpoint, and love poems in the short, epigrammatic mode. Only the last have survived. He published a volume of epigrams, both his own (some 134 poems) and those of about fifty poets of the previous two centuries, under the title of *The Garland*, which forms the basis of the *Greek Anthology* compiled in the tenth century at Constantinople. His surviving poetry is entirely erotic, both heterosexual and homosexual, and his style is rich as well as simple. He was influenced by CALLIMACHUS (3) and ASCLEPIADES (1) in style and subject matter. See Alan Cameron (1993) *The Greek Anthology*, Oxford: Clarendon Press; and T.B.L. Webster (1964) *Hellenistic Poetry and Art*, London: Methuen.

Meletus (C5 BC) An Athenian tragedian attacked for his dullness by ARISTOPHANES (1). He may have been the father of the

Meletus who prosecuted SOCRATES under the leadership of ANYTUS.

Melinno (C2? BC) A poetess who composed an extant ode in Greek in five stanzas in the Sapphic metre on the power of the Roman empire. She writes in the traditional dialect of choral lyric. John of Stobi, who quotes her poem, asserts that she was from Lesbos. Her date is disputed.

Melissus (C5 BC) A Samian admiral and philosopher. He was a follower of the Eleatic PARMENIDES and conceived the universe as an unchanging, infinite unity, without physical substance. He denied the existence of void or the possibility of motion. The fragments of his work which survive show that he upheld the Eleatic doctrine against the theories of ANAXAGORAS, DIOGENES (1) of Apollonia, EMPEDOCLES, and the atomists, LEUCIPPUS and DEMOCRITUS. He commanded the Samian fleet which defeated an Athenian fleet sent to blockade Samos in 441 BC.

Memnon (died 333 BC) A Rhodian general who opposed ALEXANDER (3) III the Great. He worked in co-operation with his elder brother MENTOR when together they were in the service of the Persian satrap of Phrygia, their brother-in-law, ARTABAZUS. In 362–360 they supported him when he joined a revolt of the satraps of Asia Minor against the Persian king ARTAXERXES (3) III, and c.353 Memnon accompanied Artabazus into exile in Macedonia. Mentor, meanwhile, won back Egypt for the king and (c.342) restored Artabazus and Memnon to Asia Minor, where, after Mentor's death, he succeeded him as commander of the Persian forces in Asia Minor. In 336 he led Persian resistance to a Macedonian invasion under PHILIP (1) II, and, before the battle of the Granicus in 334, proposed a scorched-earth policy, which the Persian generals rejected. The Persian king DARIUS (3) III, impressed by Memnon's strategic ideas,

appointed him commander-in-chief in 334. Memnon continued resistance behind Alexander's lines, fortifying Halicarnassus and building up a fleet in the Aegean with which he threatened Macedonia (Alexander having disbanded his own fleet). But Memnon was killed in 333 while besieging Mytilene in Lesbos. He had married BARSINE (1), Artabazus' daughter and Mentor's widow. See A.B. Bosworth (1993) *Conquest and Empire*, Cambridge: CUP.

Menaechmus (mid-C4 BC) A mathematician, a pupil of EUDOXUS and a friend of PLATO (1). He was the discoverer (in a primitive form) of the theory of conic sections, which he used to solve the problem of two mean proportionals. His work is lost, but is reported in a commentary on ARCHIMEDES by Eutocius.

Menander 1. (c.343–292 BC) The leading writer of New Comedy. An Athenian of good family, he is believed to have studied under the Peripatetic philosopher THEOPHRASTUS and the playwright ALEXIS, to whom he may have been related. He was a friend of DEMETRIUS (2) of Phaleron and the philosopher EPICURUS. He died at the age of about 50 while swimming in the Piraeus harbour.

Beginning c.323 he composed over 100 comedies of which we have substantial texts of four and fragments of varying lengths of several more. His plays were very popular in the centuries after his death, were translated and adapted by the Roman authors Plautus and Terence, and were copied in large numbers as is testified by their preservation on many tattered papyri in the rubbish-dumps of Egyptian cities such as Oxyrhynchus, the source of modern knowledge of them. The texts of his plays were all lost through neglect in the more puritanical times of the Byzantine empire. During his life he competed in the Athenian dramatic festivals with modest success, gaining eight victories. His plays were also produced in the growing number of theatres outside Athens. His subject matter and style are widely different from the Old Comedy of ARISTOPHANES (1), his plays being unpolitical entertainments without satirical purpose. Instead the interest is in the private world of the comedy of manners and the problems thrown up by the vagaries of contemporary Greek family life, though the situations created are usually far from normal. Love is always an ingredient in the plots and there is much common ground with the settings and treatment of several ancient Greek novels. He showed great talent in his use of the verse forms he inherited and his lines give the effect of everyday speech, heightened emotion being conveyed by subtle variations of pace in the versification. He was skilled at suggesting traits of character by the style of the speeches assigned to the different roles in his plays. There is considerable realism in the characters he presents, which come from all strata of society. Though the plays appear to present life as it is lived, Menander leaves the audience with the understanding that the most successful life is one directed by a spirit of tolerance and generosity.

Of Menander's comedies, *The Bad-tempered Man* (*Dyscolos*), which won the Lenaean competition in 317, is almost complete; *The Girl from Samos* is nearly all preserved; and we have half of *The Arbitration*, half of *The Shield* and nearly half of *The Rape of the Lock*. Substantial fragments are also preserved of *The Man from Sicyon* and *The Man Who Is Hated*, as well as shorter pieces from *The Double Deceiver*, *The Farmer*, *The Hero*, *The Cithara-player*, *The Carthaginian*, *The Girl Possessed by God*, *The Flatterer*, *The Ghost*, *The Women Drugged* and *The Girl from Perinthos*. There are also some 900 quotations from Menander in other ancient authors, ranging from a single word to several lines, but most lack a context. See R.L. Hunter (1985) *The New Comedy of Greece and Rome*, Cambridge: CUP; and S.M. Goldberg (1980) *The Making of Menander's Comedy*, London: Athlone.

2. (ruled *c*.155–130 BC) The greatest Greek king in India, known locally as Mininda, born at a village named Kalasi near Alasanda (Alexandria-in-the-Caucasus), and who was himself the son of a king. After conquering the Punjab, where he made Sagala his capital, he made an expedition across northern India and visited Patna, the capital of the Maurya empire, though he did not succeed in conquering this land as he appears to have been overtaken by wars on the north-west frontier with EUCRATIDES. When the latter was assassinated (*c*.145), Menander was able to consolidate his kingdom. He probably became a Buddhist. He married Agathoclea, a daughter of King Agathocles of the family of EUTHYDEMUS (1). Menander probably died while on campaign, though the Buddhists said he retired from power and handed his kingdom to his son. His ashes were divided between the many cities that aspired to keep them. His son, Straton, succeeded him and reigned under his mother's control. Menander issued a rich currency on which Greek and Indian motifs were combined, and he may have influenced the artistic development of statues of the Buddha and the construction of the stupas. He adopted the titles 'Saviour' and 'The Just'. See W.W. Tarn (1938) *The Greeks in Bactria and India*, Cambridge: CUP.

3. A historian of the kings of Phoenicia from Ephesus. He was used as a source by Josephus. His dates are unknown.

4. (C3 AD) A writer on rhetoric from Laodicea. He deals with a range of topics from hymns and encomia to the manner in which to make speeches appropriate to occasions, including addresses to Roman emperors. There are two such treatises extant which provide useful evidence for understanding some types of ancient literature, such as poems for weddings (*epithalamia*) and poems addressed to those leaving on a journey (*propemptica*).

Menedemus 1. (*c.*339–*c.*265 BC) A philosopher from Eretria in Euboea. While on military service in Megara he studied under STILPON, moved to Elis, where he studied in the school founded by PHAEDO, the friend of SOCRATES, became its head and moved it to Eretria. After a period of political activity, he was forced to take refuge in Macedonia at the court of ANTIGONUS (2) II Gonatas, where he died. No writings are extant.

2. (C3 BC) A Cynic philosopher from Asia Minor who studied under COLOTES and then under Echecles at Lampsacus. Colotes wrote a book attacking him.

Menelaus (late C1 AD) A mathematician and astronomer from Alexandria who made observations at Rome in 98 mentioned by PTOLEMY (17). PLUTARCH mentions him in his book about the Moon's face. Menelaus wrote an extant mathematical work in three books, transmitted through an Arabic translation, entitled *The Sphere*, on spherical geometry, which was probably mostly original. Lost works included a chord-table and an elementary geometry. See T.L. Heath (1921) *A History of Greek Mathematics*, Oxford: OUP.

Menestor (C5 BC) A botanist from southern Italy whose work is known through THEOPHRASTUS' refutation of his theories. A follower of PYTHAGORAS (1), he sought to distinguish between warm and cold plants according to the Pythagorean theory of the opposition of warmth and cold, thereby trying to explain the phenomenon of evergreen plants.

Menexenus (C5 BC) An Athenian friend of SOCRATES, mentioned in three dialogues of PLATO (1).

Menippus 1. (C3 BC) A satirist from Gadara in Syria. He was a Cynic philosopher and, according to a biographical note by DIOGENES (5) Laërtius, was a slave at Sinope who bought his freedom and settled in Thebes where he obtained citizenship and became a pupil of the Cynic Metrocles, brother-in-law of CRATES (2). He became a money-lender and made a fortune, which he lost, and committed suicide. This note is of dubious reliability, however, and he may well have lived his life in Gadara. His work has not survived apart from some 600 fragments, the brevity and damaged state of which makes intelligibility almost impossible, and it is tempting to imagine it as resembling that of his fellow Syrian, LUCIAN. We know that it consisted of a mixture of prose and verse in a wide variety of metres, and that the subject matter was dominated by social comment and humorously expressed popular philosophy. We know of the following titles of his works: *Necromancy* (*Nekyia*), imitating Crates' poetry, *Wills*, satirising the wills made by philosophers, *Letters Purporting to Be by the Gods*, *Arcesilaus*, *Diogenes for Sale*, recalling Lucian's *Philosophers for Sale*, and a *Symposium*. Several Greek and Latin authors were strongly influenced by Menippus so that the term 'Menippean satire' came into use to describe the genre of mixed prose and verse that he initiated. MELEAGER, OENOMAUS and Lucian, all from Syria, were influenced by his work and reputation. The Roman writers Varro (who wrote *Menippean Satires*), Horace (*Sat.*, 2.5), Seneca (in *The Pumpkinification of Claudius*) and Petronius (in parts of the *Satyrica*) all followed his lead to a greater or lesser degree. See J. Hall (1981) *Lucian's Satire*, New York: Arno Press; J.C. Relihan (1992) *Ancient Menippean Satire*, Baltimore, MD: Johns Hopkins University Press; and P. Dronke (1994) *Verse with Prose from Petronius to Dante*, Cambridge, MA; London: Harvard University Press.

2. (late C1 BC) A geographical writer who wrote a treatise describing the periphery of the Black Sea and the Mediterranean in three books giving place names and the distances between them. It was corrected and edited by Marcian. Part of Book I survives. See A. Diller (1952) *The Tradition of the Minor Greek Geographers*, New York: American Philological Association.

Meno (C4 BC) A pupil of ARISTOTLE who wrote a summary of the various doctrines of medicine known in his day, part of which is preserved in an anonymous papyrus in London which is a useful source of information on early Greek medicine.

Mentor (died *c*.340 BC) A military commander from Rhodes, and the elder brother of MEMNON. He married his niece, BARSINE (1), the daughter of his brother-in-law and ally, the Persian satrap ARTABAZUS. He assisted Artabazus in the revolt of the satraps in 362, and was granted land in the Troad as a reward for his service. After Artabazus fled to Macedonia in 353, Mentor went to Egypt where he became reconciled with ARTAXERXES (3) III, the Persian king, and after a long struggle completed the recovery of Egypt for him in 343. He was then promoted to be viceroy of Asia Minor and proceeded to crush the rebels there, bringing about the death of his neighbour, HERMIAS (1), the ruler of Atarneus. He was succeeded by his brother Memnon, who married his widow. See A.B. Bosworth (1988) *Conquest and Empire*, Cambridge: CUP.

Mesomedes (mid-C2 AD) A Cretan poet and freedman-courtier of the Roman emperor Hadrian. Fourteen of his poems on various subjects and in various metres survive (some are set to music).

Metiochus and Parthenope The hero and heroine of an anonymous Greek historical novel set in the court of POLYCRATES (1) of Samos and based somewhat inaccurately on events of the period. Its style resembles that of CHARITON. Three papyrus fragments survive and some reconstruction of the story has been made from a derived Persian romance. See B.P. Reardon (ed.) (*c*.1989) *Collected Ancient Greek Novels*, Berkeley, CA; London: University of California Press.

Meton (C5 BC) An Athenian astronomer who observed the summer solstice in 432 and in other years in collaboration with Euctemon, though his discovery was questioned by HIPPARCHUS (3) and PTOLEMY (17). He is said to have proposed a calendar with nineteen-year cycles to provide a reliable basis for the recording of astronomical data. His proposal was not adopted officially, nor have any of his writings survived. ARISTOPHANES (1) introduced him as a character in *Birds*, where he is presented as a comic town planner. He installed a mechanism for observing solstices on the Pnyx at Athens.

Metrodorus 1. (C4 BC) A philosopher from Chios and a pupil of the atomist philosopher, DEMOCRITUS. In his lost work *Nature* he combined the teachings of atomism with the Eleatic doctrine that nothing changes in the general universe. He also wrote a *History of Troy* and a work on weather (only fragments remain).

2. (*c*.331–278 BC) A disciple of EPICURUS from Lampsacus, regarded by his master as second only to himself. Epicurus mentioned him often in his books and corresponded with him. He dedicated two works to him and asked that Metrodorus should be remembered along with himself at the monthly festival. Metrodorus wrote copiously and fragments of his works exist. DIOGENES (5) Laërtius records a list of them.

3. (early C1 BC) A writer from Scepsis in Mysia and a friend of MITHRIDATES (6) VI of Pontus, who later killed him for deserting him to join King Tigranes II of Armenia. Cicero knew of him for his good memory, which Metrodorus himself wrote about. He may have also written books on geography, physical training, and a life of Tigranes.

Micon (C5 BC) An Athenian painter and sculptor who (*c*.470) decorated the temple of Theseus with paintings of Theseus and Minos and other works, and the Painted Portico (*Stoa Poikile*) in the agora (*c*.460) with a *Battle of the Amazons* and *Battle of Marathon*. In some of his work he is said to have collaborated with POLYGNOTUS. He also painted a scene of the Argonauts, the daughters of Pelias, and Butes in the temple of the Dioscuri, and made a sculpture of CALLIAS (1) at Olympia to celebrate his victory there in 472. His daughter, Timarete, was also a painter.

Midas (reigned 738–696 BC) A king of Phrygia mentioned by HERODOTUS as being the first non-Greek to make offerings at Delphi. He is said to have had a Greek wife, the daughter of Agamemnon, king of Cyme. He was overthrown by the Cimmerians and committed suicide.

Milon (late C6 BC) A wrestler from Croton in southern Italy. Many tales grew up about his fabulous strength: he is said to have won six victories in the wrestling contests of each of the Olympic and Pythian Games; to have carried a live heifer 100 metres and then slain it with one blow of his hand, and devoured all its flesh in the course of a day. His death is said to have come about because, in his old age, he tried his strength by forcing apart the two sides of a split tree trunk in which he got caught and, unable to extract himself, he was eaten by wild animals.

Miltiades (*c*.550–489 BC) An Athenian general and statesman, son of Cimon and a member of the Philaïd clan. He was

eponymous archon in 524/3. That year, however, his father, Cimon, after winning a third successive victory at Olympia, was assassinated on the secret orders of HIPPIAS (1), tyrant of Athens, who sent Miltiades to the Thracian Chersonese where his paternal uncle, also Miltiades, had founded a colony of Athenian settlers. Hippias then wished to re-establish control over the colony and sent Miltiades to succeed his brother, Stesagoras, as ruler. He married the daughter of Olorus, a Thracian king. The colony came under Persian dominion, and in 513 Miltiades assisted the Persian king DARIUS (1) I in his campaign against the Scythians and was left with other Greeks to defend the bridge over the Danube that Darius had left behind him. He later claimed that he had tried to persuade the others to destroy the bridge and prevent Darius' return, but HISTIAEUS, tyrant of Miletus, prevented such action. During a Scythian invasion, he had to leave the colony, but returned and supported the Ionian Revolt, which broke out in 499, and gained control of Lemnos. On the suppression of the revolt in 493 he fled to Athens where he was prosecuted for having acted as a tyrant in the Chersonese. He was acquitted and was elected to serve as one of the ten tribal generals in the Marathon campaign in 490. He was subject, however, to the leadership of the polemarch CALLIMACHUS (1), who appears to have supported Miltiades' wish to confront the invading Persian force and fight it out. Much embroidery undoubtedly surrounds the traditional account of the part he played in the victory, but it must have been crucial in persuading the wavering Athenian leaders to attack. After the battle, at his request, he was entrusted with a command of seventy ships which he used to attack the island of Paros and besiege the city, despite continued Persian naval superiority. However, he raised the siege of Paros after twenty-six days, perhaps because of a serious injury he had sustained in a leg, and returned to Athens to be prosecuted on a capital charge by XANTHIPPUS (1) for deceiving the people, and was condemned to pay the huge fine of fifty talents. He died of gangrene shortly thereafter, and his son CIMON paid the fine. See J.F. Lazenby (1993) *The Defence of Greece*, Warminster, England: Aris & Phillips.

Mimnermus (C7 BC) A lyric poet from Smyrna, though Colophon, whose foundation he described in a poem, also later claimed him. We know his work from a few fragments. He wrote two books, *Nanno*, which contains shorter poems on various themes, and *Smyrneis*, on the myths and history of Smyrna and especially the war against GYGES. *Nanno* appears to have contained much erotic poetry about girls and boys, as well as a rousing call to arms. CALLIMACHUS (3) admired Mimnermus' shorter lyrical poetry. He flourished in the late thirties and twenties of the seventh century, but was dead by 600 BC when ALYATTES destroyed Smyrna. He refers to an eclipse of the sun in April 648. See M.I. West (1974) *Studies in Greek Elegy and Iambus*, Berlin; New York: de Gruyter.

Mindarus (died 410 BC) A Spartan admiral who in 411 moved his fleet from Chios to the Hellespont to impede Athenian grain shipments. He was defeated at Cynossema and Abydos. Early in 410 he recaptured Cyzicus, but then suffered a disaster when a larger Athenian fleet, under ALCIBIADES, caught his fleet in the open sea and destroyed it. He died trying to defend it.

Mithridates The name of six Hellenistic kings of Pontus, a kingdom in northern Anatolia.

1. I (reigned 302–266 BC) Originally a king of Cius on the Sea of Marmara, he was of Persian extraction. After a period of exile in Paphlagonia, he created the kingdom of Pontus around Amastris on the Black Sea. He was named 'The Founder' (*Ctistes*), and was succeeded by his son, ARIOBARZANES (2).

2. II (reigned *c*.250–*c*.220 BC) Son of ARIOBARZANES (2), he allied himself by marriage with the Seleucids and married a sister of SELEUCUS (2) II. His daughter, LAODICE (2), married ANTIOCHUS (3) III. However, in the War of the Brothers he supported ANTIOCHUS (14) the Hawk against his brother-in-law, Seleucus. He and his wife were generous in sending relief to Rhodes after the earthquake of 227.

3. III (*c*.220–*c*.189 BC) His existence is presumed from the tradition that there were six kings of the name. His eldest son and heir was PHARNACES (1) I.

4. IV (155–151 BC) Second son of MITHRIDATES (3) III, officially styled 'Philopator Philadelphus' ('Father- and Brother-Loving'), he succeeded his aggressive brother whose policy he modified. He developed friendship with Rome and aided Pergamon against Bithynia.

5. V Euergetes ('Benefactor') (151–120 BC) Probably the son of PHARNACES (1) I, he continued the policy of his predecessor of friendship to Rome and lent support to her during the Third Punic War (149–146) and in the war with ARISTONICUS (2) of Pergamon. He was rewarded with Phrygia. He increased his influence by invading Cappadocia and marrying his daughter, Laodice, to its king, ARIARATHES (6) VI. He was keen on Greek ways and attempted to hellenize his kingdom. He gave financial support to Delos and Athens, and was honoured by those states. Apollo was the object of his special devotion and he portrayed the god on coinage. He was murdered at Sinope in 120, perhaps by members of his family. His wife, Laodice, a Seleucid princess, perhaps through a forged will, claimed the succession for herself and her younger son.

6. VI the Great (Eupator Dionysus) (reigned 120–63 BC) His first task was to gain the throne despite his mother's intrigues (see MITHRIDATES (5) V). He inherited the throne at the age of 12, but had to flee from the court and lie low for some years. He then raised a force and captured Sinope, his mother's capital, and killed his mother and brother. He set about the conquest of the Crimean Peninsula and other parts of the northern coastlands of the Black Sea, which furnished him with wealth and troops. He extended his power and influence in Asia Minor, causing in 116 the assassination of his brother-in-law, ARIARATHES (6) VI of Cappadocia by means of his agent, a Cappadocian nobleman named Gordius. He then worked through his nephew ARIARATHES (7) VII whom he replaced in 101 with his own 8-year-old son, ARIARATHES (9) IX. He also took over Inner Paphlagonia, using NICOMEDES (3) III of Bithynia as his ally. Though warned by the Roman statesman C. Marius in 99 that he risked falling foul of Rome, yet irritated by Sulla's intervention in Cappadocia in 95 when he installed ARIOBARZANES (1) as king, Mithridates took over Cappadocia and Bithynia during the Social War in Italy (91–87), trading on Rome's weakness.

In 89, after the intervention of the commission under M. Aquillius, who ordered Mithridates to withdraw from Cappadocia and Bithynia, which he did, the First Mithridatic War broke out. Aquillius persuaded NICOMEDES (4) IV to attack Pontus, with disastrous results. Aquillius divided his small force into three and was routed and killed. Mithridates sought to secure as much of Asia Minor as he could, calling himself the 'Deliverer' and winning much support from the local people on account of the exactions of the Roman tax gatherers. In the province of Asia in late 88 he ordered the cities to round up the Italian community, consisting of 80,000 people, and massacre them. Rhodes resisted his fleet, but Athens

invited him (see ARISTION) and he sent a force commanded by his general, ARCHELAUS (3), to invade Greece. Sulla responded by moving into Greece in 87 with five legions. He blockaded the Piraeus and Athens, and won significant victories at Chaeronea and Orchomenus. He then moved into Asia, where Mithridates had lost his popularity, and inflamed hostility by taking reprisals. Mithridates was forced to capitulate at Dardanus in 85 on the terms which Sulla dictated (Mithridates had to pay an indemnity of 2,000 talents, surrender seventy warships and was to be recognised as a 'Friend and Ally of Rome'), and was confined to his own kingdom of Pontus. In 83 Sulla's legate, L. Murena, against orders, provoked Mithridates with incursions into his territory. Fighting took place in which Mithridates repelled the invader (Second Mithridatic War). During the next few years, Mithridates consolidated his hold on Pontus and his territories to the north of the Black Sea, and prepared for war, enlisting the aid of the pirates.

In 75 NICOMEDES (4) IV of Bithynia died, leaving his kingdom to the Roman Senate, and the next year the Senate decided to accept the gift. Mithridates, unwilling to see Rome in command of the straits and the balance of power disturbed, made an alliance with Sertorius, the Spanish leader, and in spring 73 invaded Bithynia, thus starting the Third Mithridatic War. He was unable to take Cyzicus, however, and the Roman commander L. Lucullus, governor of Cilicia and Asia, cut him off from his supplies and during bitter fighting forced Mithridates to retreat and finally in 72 to take refuge in Armenia with his son-in-law, Tirganes II, whose new capital of Tigranocerta Lucullus in 69 briefly captured. By 70 Lucullus had conquered the whole of Pontus. Mithridates was unable to return to his kingdom until 68 when a Roman army mutiny against Lucullus relieved the pressure. Even so, he had a hard time defeating the Roman garrison under Triarius in 67. But Pompey succeeded Lucullus in 66 and with superior forces defeated Mithridates at Nicopolis. Mithridates' only recourse was to flee to the Crimea, where he seized his lands from his rebellious son, Machares, and conceived the ambitious plan to invade Italy by a land offensive from the north. However, this was too much for his subjects who, led by his eldest son, PHARNACES (2) II, rebelled. At the age of 69 Mithridates had himself killed by his bodyguard, having proved unable to kill himself by poison, so inured was he by his constant taking of antidotes.

Mithridates was Rome's most dangerous enemy in the last century BC, but he suffered from defects which made his task impossible: he was too cruel to win unwavering support from his subjects and allies, and he was an indifferent general. He was passionate in his opposition to Rome and saw himself as pro-Greek and a liberator of Rome's Greek subjects (he liked to see himself as an Alexander-figure). But for all his talents (he could, for example, speak twenty languages) and energy, in taking on the might of Rome he set himself a task that was beyond his ability or resources. See B.C. Mc Ging (1986) *The Foreign Policy of Mithridates VI Eupator*, Leiden: EJ Brill.

Mnasalces (C3 BC) An epigrammatist from Sicyon. Eighteen of his poems are in the *Greek Anthology* and two more have been found on papyrus. He was attacked as a crude imitator of SIMONIDES in a mock epitaph by THEODORIDAS of Syracuse.

Moderatus (C1 AD) A Neopythagorean philosopher and writer in Greek from Cádiz in Spain. He followed a way of life involving ascetic and vegetarian practices like his contemporary APOLLONIUS (6) of Tyana. He wrote a series of lectures on the subject of Pythagorean philosophy and life-style in eleven books, which have

not survived. He strove to link the teachings of PLATO (1), especially the Theory of Ideas, with a Pythagorean origin, and ascribed a metaphysical significance to the Pythagorean theory of number. He was very influential on the development of Neopythagoreanism and of Neoplatonism. See PYTHAGORAS (1)

Moero (*c*.300 BC) A poetess from Byzantium who wrote a hexameter work entitled *Memory*, of which ten lines survive; a summary exists of a poem named *Curses*; two epigrams also survive.

Molon *see* Antiochus (3) III.

Morsimus (C5 BC) An ophthalmologist and writer of tragedies. He was a great-nephew of AESCHYLUS, and was lampooned by ARISTOPHANES (1) for his inferior plays.

Moschus (mid-C2 BC) A Hellenistic poet from Syracuse. He is described in ancient sources as a grammarian and a pupil of ARISTARCHUS (3). ATHENAEUS reports a Moschus who wrote a treatise on words found in the Rhodian dialect, which may be a reference to the same Moschus. The *Suda* recognises him as the second of three bucolic poets of whom the others were THEOCRITUS and BION (2). We have several of his works, though the bucolic element is slight. The longest is an epyllion in 166 hexameter lines, entitled *Europa*, telling the myth of Europa's rape by Zeus, with an elaborate description (*ekphrasis*) of her basket in the Alexandrian style. It is a highly polished poem, which shows influences from HOMER, the Homeric Hymn to Demeter, Theocritus and APOLLONIUS (1). Three fragments of Moschus' *Bucolics* also survive, though two of them are erotic *jeux d'esprit*. *Eros the Runaway* is a light-hearted piece in twenty-nine hexameters which is presented like a 'wanted' poster by the goddess Aphrodite, the mother of Eros, god of love. Of doubtful authorship is *Megara*, a dialogue between Heracles' wife Megara and his mother Alcmena, bewailing his disappearance. A *Lament for Bion* is definitely not his. See N. Hopkinson (1988) *A Hellenistic Anthology*, Cambridge: CUP.

Myron (mid-C5 BC) A sculptor from Eleutherae in northern Attica, a pupil of AGELADAS and a rival of PYTHAGORAS (2) of Samos. Myron led the movement of exploration in bronze statuary after the end of the archaic period and was greatly interested in symmetry and proportion. The identification of his *Discus-thrower* was made possible by LUCIAN's careful description (several copies of it are extant). His *Athena and Marsyas*, described by the Roman writer Pliny the Elder, *Heracles* and *Perseus* are also known from copies and coins. Statues of athletes, including an *Anadumenos* (a youth tying a headband) are attested, and an image of a cow is preserved in several copies. Myron is referred to in some Greek epigrams. See J. Boardman (1985) *Greek Sculpture: the Classical Period*, London: Thames & Hudson.

Myronides (mid-C5 BC) An Athenian general and son of Callias. He was an ambassador to Sparta in 480 and a general at the battle of Plataea in 479. In 458 he led a force of the oldest and youngest men in the territory of Megara, where he badly mauled a Corinthian army, and in 457, after the defeat of Tanagra, at the head of a hoplite army he won the victory of Oenophyta over the Boeotians. He then disbanded the Boeotian League and encouraged the foundation of democracies in the Boeotian states. He was portrayed in EUPOLIS' comedy *Commons* (*Demoi*), staged *c*.412, as representing the good old days.

Myrtis (early C5? BC) A poetess from Anthedon in Boeotia who is connected in later tradition with CORINNA and PINDAR, the former of whom (in a fragment) criticises Myrtis for trying to compete with Pindar. PLUTARCH paraphrases her poem on the hero Eumostus, but otherwise her work is lost.

N

Nabis (reigned 207–192 BC) A king of Sparta. His father's name, Demaratus, suggests possible descent from the Eurypontid king DEMARATUS. In 207 he succeeded Machanidas as guardian of the young King Pelops on whose death that year he seized the throne. He engaged the support of a guard of mercenary soldiers and Cretan pirates. He may have been maligned by the tradition that he tried to reimpose the reforms of CLEOMENES (2) III in a brutal manner. He was sole king and conducted an active foreign policy of opposition to the Achaean Confederacy. He raided Megalopolis in 204, failed to take Messene in 201 and was defeated by the Achaean general PHILOPOEMEN in 200. In the Second Macedonian War which followed he at first supported PHILIP (3) V, who betrayed Argos to him, but then attempted to change sides. However, the Roman general Titus Flamininus in 195 accused him of tyranny and compelled him to renounce his claim to Argos and the ports of Laconia. He tried to regain his lost ports in 193 with the help of Aetolia, but was defeated by Flamininus and Philopoemen. The following year he was murdered by Aetolians when they took over control of Sparta. See P. Cartledge and A.J.S. Spawforth (1989) *Hellenistic and Roman Sparta*, London: Routledge.

Nausiphanes (C4 BC) An atomist philosopher and a pupil of the Sceptic PYRRHON, with whom he may have served in the campaigns of ALEXANDER (3) III the Great. However, he was also an adherent of DEMOCRITUS' atomist philosophy. He settled on Teos, where *c.*324 he taught EPICURUS the atomic theory of Democritus. Epicurus, however, decried Nausiphanes' teaching, probably because he wished to obscure the debt he owed to Democritus. Nausiphanes wrote a lost work, *Tripod*, which was said to have had an influence on Epicurus' *Canon*. His theory of rhetoric, according to which the study of physics leads to success in political life, and his advocacy of participation in public life, were attacked by Epicureans such as PHILODEMUS.

Neanthes (C3 BC) A historian from Cyzicus and a pupil of PHILISCUS (1) of Miletus. He wrote copiously, including a history of Greece in six or more books, and works on Cyzicus. Among his biographical writings was a life of TIMON (1) the misanthrope of Athens. Only fragments survive.

Nearchus (died *c.*312 BC) A Cretan navigator and a boyhood friend of ALEXANDER (3) III the Great. After serving as satrap of the provinces of Lycia and Pamphylia from 334–329, he commanded the fleet for Alexander in his campaign in India on the River Hydaspes in 326 and then explored the coast between southern India and the Tigris. After taking an active role in Babylon at the time of Alexander's death, he supported ANTIGONUS (1) I, on whose staff he was from 317 to his death, which may have occurred at the battle of Gaza. He wrote a memoir of his travels which was used by ARRIAN and STRABO, of which some passages are known.

Nechepso (C2 BC) The pseudonym of a Hellenistic writer on astrology. The name, together with that of Petosiris, is used by an unknown author to lend an Egyptian flavour to his work, of which a number of fragments survive. It was written in Greek and consisted of at least fourteen books. Its author may have invented the astrological significance of the signs of the zodiac and the work was very influential.

Neophron (late C5 BC) A writer of tragedies from Sicyon who is said to have written 120 plays. Some fragments of a *Medea* survive, which suggests that he wrote his play under the influence of EURIPIDES' play of that name.

Nestor, Lucius Septimius (C2–3 AD) A poet from Laranda in Asia Minor who wrote in Greek a version of the *Iliad* in each book of which a letter of the alphabet did not occur. He also wrote *Transformations*: these works are lost. He left inscriptions at Ostia containing oracular responses which show that he was friendly with important Romans.

Nicander (C2 BC) A poet from Colophon who was also a priest of Apollo at Claros. He left two extant didactic poems in hexameters on poisons and drugs, as well as two epigrams, though neither the science nor the poetry is of high quality. His *Animal Matters* (*Theriaca*), in 958 lines, is on the stings of various creatures and remedies for them; and *Remedial Drugs* (*Alexipharmaca*), in 630 lines, is

on the treating of poisons and their antidotes and contains some useful information culled from earlier authorities such as APOLLODORUS (5). He wrote much other poetry which is lost or preserved only in fragments: *Changes of Shape* (*Metamorphoses*), which influenced the Roman poet Ovid; various epics, including *The Theban Tale*, *The Tale of Oeneus*, *Europa*, *Sicily* and *The Cimmerians*; in elegiac metre he wrote *Hunting to Hounds* and *Snake Legends*; and his *Georgics* inspired Virgil, as did his *Bee-Keeping*. He also wrote a *Collection of Remedies*; *Prognostics*; a *Hymn to Attalus*; *Poets from Colophon* (which may have been in prose, as were his glosses) and a work entitled *Temple Tools*. See A.S.F. Gow and A.F. Schofield (eds) (1953) *Nicander*, Cambridge: CUP.

Nicanor 1. (C3 BC) An agent of ALEXANDER (3) III the Great from Stagirus. He married the daughter of his fellow townsman ARISTOTLE, whom he knew well. Alexander appointed him to proclaim a decree at the Olympic Games in 324 that all exiles might return to their cities with impunity. He carried out negotiations with DEMOSTHENES (2) and was given honorary citizenship of Ephesus. He may be the Nicanor who subsequently served CASSANDER in 319/8 when he captured Munichia and the Piraeus. The next year he defeated CLEITUS (2) on the Bosporus, but quarrelled with Cassander and was executed.

2. (C2 AD) An expert in the punctuation of Greek literature. He wrote influential works, of which fragments have survived, on *Punctuation* in general and on the punctuation of the Homeric poems and those of CALLIMACHUS (3) in particular.

Nicias 1. (*c*.470–413 BC) An Athenian general during the Peloponnesian War. After the death of PERICLES, he represented the chief opposition to CLEON and was elected general a number of times. He first appears in 427 when he occupied the island of Minoa off Megara. In 425, with two colleagues, he led an expedition into the territory of Corinth and then fortified the peninsula of Methana in Argolis. In 424 he occupied the island of Cythera off Sparta. Then, Cleon having been killed, he helped to negotiate an armistice and a year later the fifty-year peace with Sparta which bears his name. His policy was to encourage a moderate attitude towards Sparta and to discourage the extreme imperialism of the democrats. During the period which followed the conclusion of the Peace of Nicias (421), he advocated retrenchment, but was opposed by ALCIBIADES, who sought to pursue an aggressive policy, first in the Peloponnese and then against Syracuse in Sicily. In 415 the Athenians, persuaded by Alcibiades, dispatched the great expedition to Sicily, the three commanders being Alcibiades, Nicias and LAMACHUS. To discredit the operation, Nicias demanded an unusually large force, but the Assembly accepted his proposal. After the expedition sailed, Alcibiades deserted before it reached Sicily. A siege of Syracuse was begun thanks to Lamachus, who was, however, killed in 414. Nicias was ill and discouraged, and the arrival of the Spartan general GYLIPPUS reversed the situation. The Athenians were reinforced by DEMOSTHENES (1) in 413, but were soon overwhelmed. Nicias' superstitious fears and poor leadership prevented a sea-borne withdrawal of the troops and he, his colleague and his men were caught as they fled westwards through Sicily. Many of them were killed in the valley of the Assinarus and the generals were executed. Nicias was a rich man who gave his city excellent financial support, was scrupulously religious and was described by THUCYDIDES (2) as being too good for such a fate. See D. Kagan (1981) *The Peace of Nicias and the Sicilian Expedition*, Ithaca, NY; London: Cornell University Press.

2. (C4 BC) An Athenian painter, a pupil of Antidotus, who was employed by PRAXITELES to paint some of his statues. He gained a reputation for his success in painting female figures, his Andromeda, Calypso and Io being known from fresco copies at Pompeii. He recommended the painting of large scenes and is said to have painted the scene of the Book of the Dead (*Homer, Odyssey*, 11), Heracles' struggle with the Nemean lion, and an exploit of ALEXANDER (3) III the Great.

Nicomachus (C1–2 AD) A writer on arithmetic and harmonics from Gerasa (Jerash in Jordan). His *Introduction to Arithmetic* in two books was based on Pythagorean ideas of number and was translated into Latin by Apuleius. It became important in the Middle Ages. IAMBLICHUS (2) and Philoponus wrote commentaries on it and Boethius drew heavily on it for his *Teaching Arithmetic*. Nicomachus also composed a *Handbook of Harmonics*, a lost *Introduction to Geometry*, and a partly preserved *Mystical Properties of Number*.

Nicomedes The name of four kings of Bithynia, a kingdom in north-western Anatolia.

1. I (reigned *c.*279–*c.*255 BC) The second king of Bithynia and the son of Zipoetes. He declared himself king of Bithynia in 298 and continued the struggle against ANTIOCHUS (1) I for independence. He allied himself with his neighbour MITHRIDATES (1) I of Pontus, returned Cierus to Heraclea Pontica in order to win that city's support, and allowed the Galatians to settle in Phrygia. He founded Nicomedia as his capital (*c.*265) and issued Greek coinage. His will, which favoured his younger children, was upset after his death by his eldest son Ziaëlas who seized the throne but continued to hellenize his kingdom.

2. II (reigned 149–*c.*127 BC) He succeeded his father, PRUSIAS (2) II, after encompassing his death with the help of

ATTALUS (2) II and the connivance of the Romans. He won the favour of the Greek cities and was an ally of Rome, assisting in the war against ARISTONICUS (2), the pretender to the throne of Pergamon, from 133–129. He was disappointed by the refusal of the Romans to extend his frontiers in Phrygia.

3. III (reigned c.127–c.94 BC) The son of NICOMEDES (2) II, he was generous in his munificence to Greek cities from which he earned the title 'Benefactor' (*Euergetes*). The Roman general C. Marius asked him for troops for his war against the Cimbri in 104, but Nicomedes claimed that many Bithynians had been enslaved by the Roman tax gatherers. The Roman Senate then put an end to such enslavement of citizens of allied states for debt. He intrigued with MITHRIDATES (6) VI of Pontus, hoping to share Paphlagonia with him, and intervened in Cappadocia, marrying the queen mother, Laodice, in the hope of extending his rule there, but was prevented by Roman action.

4. IV (reigned c.94–c.74 BC) The last king of Bithynia, son of NICOMEDES (3) III, he was expelled from his kingdom c.92 by MITHRIDATES (6) VI who preferred his brother, Socrates. Rome, represented by Manius Aquillius, restored him a couple of years later and, by demanding a large fee, persuaded him to attack Pontus, thus precipitating the First Mithridatic War, a disaster for Bithynia, during which he lived in exile (see

MITHRIDATES (6) VI). He was restored by Sulla in 85, but found his kingdom, now an ally of Rome, little more than a dependency. When Julius Caesar carried out a mission in 81 to ask him to supply ships for a siege of Mytilene, the two were said to have become lovers. At his death he bequeathed his kingdom to the Roman Senate as he had no children.

Nossis (c.300 BC) A poetess from Locri in southern Italy. She wrote epigrams and love poems; a dozen of her epigrams survive in the *Greek Anthology*, but her love poetry is lost.

Numenius (later C2 AD) A writer on Platonic philosophy from Apamea in Syria. We only know him from two works, of which large fragments are extant: *On the Good* and *A History of the Academy*. His line was that the school had departed from the original teachings of PLATO (1) and, behind him, PYTHAGORAS (1). He saw connections between the original teaching and the Indian Brahmins, Iranian Magi, Egyptians and Jews. He also drew upon gnostic teachings and the *Chaldaean Oracles*, a mystical anonymous work of his own time. He was very influential on PLOTINUS, Origen, PORPHYRY and the Neoplatonists. He postulated two gods, the first being transcendent and called 'The Good', the second being concerned with the world. He considered the material world, and corporeal life, to be evil.

O

Oenomaus (early C2 AD) A Cynic philosopher from Gadara in Syria. Reference to him as Abnimos in the Talmud may indicate that he was a Jew. In imitation of his fellow citizen, MENIPPUS (1), he wrote *Against Oracles*, which is known to us mainly from Eusebius, who attacked his thesis quoting his work extensively. Influenced by DIOGENES (2), he wrote lost tragedies and a political treatise. Like CRATES (2), he composed lost parodies in verse, and he influenced the writings of LUCIAN.

Olympias (C4 BC) The wife of PHILIP (1) II and mother of ALEXANDER (3) III the Great, both kings of Macedonia. She was a Molossian from Epirus, the daughter of Neoptolemus and an imperious, passionate woman who revelled in the ecstatic worship of Dionysus. She married Philip in 357 and bore Alexander the next year and CLEOPATRA (1) c.354. When Philip took a second wife (also Cleopatra) in 337, she went home to Epirus, but returned to Macedonia after Philip's death to support her son's claim to be king. She murdered Philip's widow and her child. She gave ANTIPATER (1), Alexander's viceroy, much trouble after Alexander had left for the East. However, as the king supported his viceroy, Olympias returned in 331 to Epirus, of which her daughter was queen and which Olympias treated as her own personal domain, until in 319 she gave her support to POLYPERCHON in his struggle against CASSANDER, son of Antipater. In 317 she invaded Macedonia, seized EURYDICE, the wife of PHILIP (2) III Arrhidaeus, had them both killed, and massacred her enemies. She thus intended to confirm the inheritance of ALEXANDER (6) IV, her grandson. But her cruelty had cost her much support and Cassander was too strong an opponent. In 316 Cassander besieged her at Pydna, where she gave herself up. Cassander argued before the Macedonian assembly for her execution and she was put to death by the kinsfolk of her victims.

Olympiodorus (C4/3 BC) An Athenian general and statesman who supported the democracy and opposed the Macedonian intervention under CASSANDER. In 306 he obtained help from the Aetolian Confederacy to repel Cassander from Athens and the next year drove his forces from Elatea in Phocis. He supported LACHARES in 296 while Athens was blockaded by DEMETRIUS (3) I the Besieger. After the fall of Athens, he was archon for two years running (294–292), and in 287 he rebelled against the Macedonians, throwing their garrison off Museum Hill. He aided DEMOCHARES to drive the forces of ANTIGONUS (2) II Gonatas out of Eleusis, and c.280 liberated the Piraeus.

Onasander (C1 AD) A writer in Greek on the art of generalship. His work, *Generalship*, which survives, was popular during the Renaissance. He dedicated it to Quintus Veranius, Roman governor of Britain 57–8.

Onesicritus (C4 BC) A writer on ALEXANDER (3) III the Great from Astypalaea, a pupil of the Cynic DIOGENES (2). He was also a sailor and in 326 steered Alexander's flagship on the River Jhelum and later acted as helmsman for NEARCHUS, with whom he quarrelled, on the voyage from India to the Persian Gulf. He wrote a lost encomium on Alexander which appears to have contained many fantasies about India and which was used by STRABO: fragments survive on the Brahmins and on the kingdom of Musicanus. He also gave the first known information about Taprobane (Ceylon).

Onomarchus (died 353 BC) A military and political leader of Phocis in central Greece. In 355 he served under PHILOMELUS in the Third Sacred War and rescued the survivors of the defeat at Neon. He succeeded Philomelus as sole commander and plundered the treasures of Delphi to bribe the Thessalians into inactivity and to raise a new army. Having stamped out opposition at home and in neighbouring cities, he invaded Boeotia and restored Orchomenus. He intended to attack Thebes with the help of Athens and Sparta, but had to face PHILIP (1) II of Macedonia in Thessaly, who was provoked by the alliance that Onomarchus had made with LYCOPHRON (3) of Pherae. In 353 he defeated Philip twice and forced him out of Thessaly, but in the next year he was again confronted by Philip near the Thessalian port of Pagasae and suffered a massive defeat at the battle of the Crocus Field, in which he was killed. See J. Buckler (1989) *Philip II and the Sacred War*, Leiden: EJ Brill.

Ophellas (died *c*.309 BC) A Macedonian officer of ALEXANDER (3) III the Great and governor of Cyrene. He was a member of Alexander's Companions and entered the entourage of PTOLEMY (1) I (later king of Egypt), who as satrap in 322 sent him to seize Cyrene from THIBRON (2) which he proceeded to rule as governor until his death. Little is known about his rule, which was virtually independent of Egypt, and his part in constitutional reforms and the rebellion of 313 is unclear. In 310 he joined AGATHOCLES (1) of Syracuse in a campaign in North Africa, where he hoped to capture Carthage, assembling many would-be settlers, including Athenians – he was married to a noble Athenian woman named Euthydice – but his force suffered hardships and many losses in a desert march and, though it reached Agathocles' army, the expedition was a failure: Agathocles murdered Ophellas and took over his troops.

Oppian (C2 AD) A poet from Cilicia and the author of a didactic poem in Greek, *Halieutica*, in the epic style in five books on fishing and the creatures of the sea. He makes stylish use of myth and simile, and introduces a note of drama in his depiction of the struggle between man and the sea. It was dedicated to an emperor and his son, probably Marcus Aurelius and Commodus.

There is another, inferior, poem in four books about hunting, the *Cynegetica*, ascribed to Oppian in the manuscript. Its style, language and use of myth suggest a different authorship, however, and the poet mentions his home as Apamea in Syria. His dedication of the poem to the Emperor Caracalla puts its date in the third century.

Oxyrhynchus Historian *see* Cratippus (1).

P

Paeonius (C5 BC) A sculptor from Mende in Thrace. His only known work, which dates from c.420, is a marble statue of a flying Victory supported on a high triangular base, found at Olympia to the east of the temple of Zeus. The inscription on the base states Paeonius as the sculptor and that the dedication was made by the Messenians of Naupactus. It also tells us that he made the acroteria for the temple of Zeus. PAUSANIAS (3)'s *Description of Greece* (5. 26) recalls that the Messenians believed that the statue commemorated the defeat of the Spartans at Sphacteria in 425.

Palladas (C4 AD) A writer of Greek epigrams from Alexandria. About 150 of his poems are in the *Greek Anthology*. He revived the genre after years of neglect. He has been considered to be an atheist or agnostic, but his poems are philosophically non-committal. His work is, however, pessimistic, sometimes bitter or cold with black humour. He was an impecunious schoolteacher, and describes his wife as a shrew. Most of his poems are in elegiac couplets, though there are some hexameter and iambic compositions.

Pamphila (C1 AD) A writer of anecdotal history in Greek from Epidaurus. She worked in the reign of Nero and of her thirty-six books, entitled *Historical Notes*, some ten extracts are preserved by DIOGENES (5) Laërtius and Aulus Gellius. Her work may have been summarised by Favorinus.

Pamphilus 1. (C4 BC) A painter from Amphipolis who was taught by Eupompus of Sicyon, where he worked for the rest of his life. Pamphilus was himself the teacher of APELLES, PAUSIAS and MELANTHIUS (2). One of his paintings, *The Descendants of Heracles*, is referred to by ARISTOPHANES (1) in *Wealth*. He painted c.367 a scene of the *Battle of Phlius*. He was an influential and successful teacher of art, charging his pupils a whole talent for a twelve-year course, and making them learn mathematics. He had painting on panels included in the school curriculum at Sicyon.

2. (C1 AD) A lexicographer from Alexandria whose lost dictionary of the Greek language, in ninety-five books, was entitled *Terms and Expressions* and included much work compiled from his predecessors. His dictionary, which ATHENAEUS used, was abridged by Vestinus and the abridgement was epitomised by DIOGENIANUS (2). HESYCHIUS, whose lexicon is extant, used the epitome as a source. Pamphilus also wrote books on physics, botany, and the art of criticism.

Panaenus (mid-C5 BC) An Athenian painter who was closely related to PHIDIAS (perhaps his brother). He assisted Phidias in the tinting of the statue of Zeus in the temple of Zeus at Olympia and painted scenes which were displayed between the legs of the throne. He used saffron to colour the plaster work of the temple of Athena at Elis. He also painted, or collaborated in painting, the *Battle of Marathon* in the Painted Portico at Athens.

Panaetius (*c*.185–109 BC) A Stoic philosopher from Rhodes, the son of Nicagoras. Of noble and priestly birth (he was priest of Poseidon at Lindos), he studied under CRATES (4) at Pergamon and later at Athens under DIOGENES (3) and ANTIPATER (3). He moved to Rome *c*.140 where he became a member of the circle of Scipio Aemilianus. He travelled in the East with Scipio (*c*.144) and made his home alternately in Rome and Athens. In 129 he became the head of the Stoic school at Athens in succession to Antipater; POSIDONIUS was his pupil there. He had much influence and Cicero based his major ethical treatise, *Duties*, on Panaetius' lost work of the same name. He represents a mildly reformist element in the development of Stoic thought: he was open to ideas taken from the works of PLATO (1) and ARISTOTLE, and rejected astrology and prophecy, though he accepted the traditional Stoic doctrine of Providence. He seems to have been more concerned with the practical morality of active Roman citizens than with the ideal of the Stoic sage. Some fragments of his works survive.

Panyassis (C5 BC) An epic poet from Halicarnassus who was related to HERODOTUS. He wrote an epic about Heracles in fourteen books, of which fragments survive.

Pappus (early C4 AD) A writer on mathematics and geography from Alexandria, parts of whose works survive either in Greek or in translation. He wrote commentaries on EUCLID's *Elements* and on part of PTOLEMY (17)'s *Almagest*, parts of which are extant, the former in Arabic. A major work in eight books entitled *A Collection*, consisting of eight of his own treatises and probably compiled after his death, provides a valuable account of Greek mathematics and astronomy, including higher geometry and mechanics, and gives precious information about the contributions to knowledge made by earlier writers, such as APOLLONIUS (2), ARCHIMEDES, ARISTARCHUS (2), HERON, MENELAUS, Nicomedes and THEODOSIUS. Book 1 and part of 2 are lost, but what survives has been highly influential on later study. Pappus produced little that was original in mathematics. His *Universal Geography*, based on Ptolemy's map of the world, is lost, but an extant Armenian work by Moses Chorençai is based on it. See T.L. Heath (1921) *A History of Greek Mathematics*, Oxford: OUP.

Parmenides (born *c*.515 BC) A philosopher from the Greek colony of Elea (Velia) in Lucania, Italy. Little is known of his life save that he made laws for Elea and *c*.450, when he was 65, visited Athens. PLATO (1) named a dialogue after him, inventing for it a meeting between him and a youthful SOCRATES. Considerable fragments of his philosophical hexametric poem, *Nature*, survive, which marked one of the most important stages in the history of philosophy, in which he sought to use language both to contradict pluralist theories and to develop the monist theory that had been adumbrated by the Milesian cosmologists, THALES, ANAXIMANDER and ANAXIMENES, who taught that the world had developed from a single element. In the poem he describes himself driving a chariot from everyday life into a strange place where night and day meet, where he is received by a goddess who speaks to him, and her speech forms the rest of the poem. Her address is divided into two parts: *The Way of Reality* and *The Way of Appearance*. The goddess' argument is dense and rational: though religious language is used in the introductory section, its purpose seems to be to suggest the initiation of the reader into a rigorous use of logic. Linguistic usage lies at the heart of the argument: for Parmenides, the only legitimate use of the verb 'to be' entails that what is must perforce always be, and cannot come into existence or perish. The universe, therefore, that which exists must be singular, entire, unchanging, perfect and in eternal equilibrium like a solid sphere. The opposite, things that are temporary, imperfect or even non-existent, cannot legitimately be spoken of or conceived. Consequently, that which the senses perceive has no validity: plurality, change, the world of multiplicity and variety we think we know, is a deception. Thus, the apparent world (described in *The Way of Appearance*) is simply a delusion, and humanity is in error to contrast seeming opposites like night and day. Parmenides' work led to the foundation of the Eleatic school of philosophy, in which he was succeeded by ZENO (1), who supported Parmenides' theory with his famous paradoxes, and MELISSUS. Parmenides' theory was opposed by later pluralists and atomists, but only confronted by Plato in his dialogue *The Sophist*. A later medical society at Elea commemorated Parmenides as their founder under the name Ouliades ('Son of Apollo Oulios'). See G.S. Kirk, J.E. Raven and M. Schofield (1982) *The Presocratic Philosophers*, Cambridge: CUP; D. Gallop (1984) *Parmenides of Elea*, Toronto: University of Toronto Press; A. Mourelatos (1970) *The Route of Parmenides*, New Haven, Conn.: Yale University Press; and Karl Popper (1998) *The World of Parmenides*, A.F. Petersen (ed.) London: Routledge.

Parmenion (C4 BC) A Macedonian general under PHILIP (1) II and ALEXANDER (3) III the Great. Of noble birth, the son of Philotas, he had an impressive career under Philip, commanding the army that invaded Asia Minor in 336. He supported Alexander's accession after Philip's assassination and overcame the objections of his fellow general, Attalus. He was Alexander's second-in-command at the outset of his expedition into Asia in 334. During the first three years of the campaign he was at all the major battles, commanding the left wing of the army, besides leading independent commands. Two of his sons commanded important units, the hypaspists and the cavalry, but a third, PHILOTAS, was accused of treason and condemned to death in autumn 330, and Alexander had Parmenion assassinated before he could hear of his son's disgrace. In fact, Parmenion had disputed with Alexander as to where the limits of his conquests should be set, and Alexander could not bear the presence of a man to whom he owed his throne – so he had isolated Parmenion at Ecbatana in charge of the Persian state treasure far from the area of fighting.

Parrhasius (late C5 BC) A painter and writer on painting from Ephesus, the son and pupil of Evenor, and contemporary with his rival, ZEUXIS. According to the Roman writer Pliny the Elder he worked most of his life in Athens, of which he became a citizen, and where he displayed his arrogance by dressing outrageously in purple. Among his famous paintings (mostly on mythological subjects), which are all lost, were a portrait of *Theseus*, said for its richness to be 'fed on roses', which later adorned the Capitol at Rome; *The People of Athens*; a *Healing of Telephus*; *Philoctetes*; and *The Madness of Odysseus*. XENOPHON (1) presents him as a character in his *Memoirs of Socrates* and shows him discussing his technique with the philosopher. His drawings were still copied in Pliny's day.

Parthenius (C1 BC) A scholar and poet from Nicaea in Bithynia who was captured in the Third Mithridatic War and brought to Italy. He was freed and lived in Naples, where he wrote and taught.

Most of his poetry, highly regarded by the ancients, is lost except for fragments found on papyri. A strong influence of EUPHORION (2) is detectable. He wrote three books in elegiacs in praise of his wife Arete; he also wrote hexameters. However, a prose collection of outline versions of love stories (*Erotic Experiences*) is extant. It was dedicated to the Roman poet Cornelius Gallus, with the intention that he would versify the stories. Parthenius also influenced Cinna, who may have been responsible for bringing him to Italy, and the other neoteric poets, making the works and techniques of CALLIMACHUS (3) and Euphorion more widely known, and taught Virgil Greek.

Pasion (died 370 BC) An Athenian banker and benefactor of the city who started life as a slave in the Piraeus firm which he eventually took over as owner. He acquired citizenship and married Archippe by whom he had two sons, APOLLODORUS (2) and Pasicles. He also owned a shield factory. We know something of his activities from a speech (no. 17) by ISO-CRATES, who wrote it for a customer of Pasion's who wished to prosecute him. Speeches by Apollodorus, wrongly attributed to DEMOSTHENES (2), also throw light on his career. He left a fortune of some sixty talents, and his former slave, PHORMION (2), continued his business and married his widow.

Pasiteles (first half of C1 BC) A sculptor and writer on sculpture from southern Italy who obtained Roman citizenship in 90. None of his works survives. He wrote *Notable Artistic Works throughout the World*, in five volumes, which was known to the Roman writer Pliny the Elder. He made an ivory statue of Jupiter for the temple built by Metellus Macedonicus. He was famous for his metalwork and for his studies from nature (Pliny tells a story that he was almost killed by a panther when sketching a lion). He founded a workshop from which two

works are extant: an athlete signed by his pupil Stephanus and a pair of figures, Electra and Orestes, signed by Stephanus' pupil, Menelaus. Pasiteles seems to mark a significant point in the adaptation of Greek sculpture to Roman taste.

Patrocles (*c*.345–*c*.275 BC) A Macedonian general who served the Seleucid rulers of western Asia. He commanded Babylon for SELEUCUS (1) I from 312, when he had to defend it from an attack by DEMETRIUS (3) I, and fought in his wars against ANTIGONUS (1) I and Demetrius. He was later appointed to govern the eastern section of Seleucus' empire. He wrote a geographic description of the Caspian Sea area, which he explored *c*.285, though he wrongly believed it was part of the Ocean and he made the further mistake of believing that the Oxus and Jaxartes rivers flowed into the Caspian. According to Pliny the Elder, he claimed that he had sailed from the Caspian to India. Little of his work survives, though it was used as a source by STRABO. He was sent by ANTI-OCHUS (1) I *c*.279 to deal with the increasingly difficult situation in Bithynia, but failed to restore Seleucid rule there.

Pausanias 1. (C5 BC) A Spartan general and regent for King Pleistarchus. Pausanias was an Agiad, the son of CLEOMBRO-TUS and the younger brother of LEONIDAS (1) I. He commanded the Greek army which decisively defeated the Persians at Plataea in 479, and boasted of his success. The following year he was commander of the Greek forces which took much of Cyprus and Byzantium from the Persians. Thanks to his arrogance a mutiny of many Greek forces occurred, and he was also accused of having dealings with the enemy. He was recalled to Sparta for trial but acquitted of treason, and returned in 477 to Byzantium as a private citizen though claiming official backing. The other Greeks refused to recognise him and CIMON the Athenian commander expelled him from the town in 476. Pausanias then settled at Colonae in the Troad and, again under suspicion of dealings with Persia, he was recalled to Sparta *c.*470. He was tried, but acquitted of treason, though he was also suspected of having plotted with the helots (the slave community the Spartans used as serfs). He was finally caught out as being in communication with the Persian king and before he could be arrested he fled for sanctuary to a temple of Athena, where he was starved to death. The ephors moved his body out of the temple just before he died so that the place should not be polluted. The Spartans later celebrated his achievements by dedicating a shrine to him as a hero. See Thucydides, *History*, 1. 95 and 131–4.

2. (reigned 445–426 and 408–395 BC) An Agiad king of Sparta, the son of Pleistoanax and grandson of PAUSANIAS (1). His first reign was nominal as he was a minor during his father's exile and his uncle Cleomenes was regent. He returned to the throne on his father's death and in 403, after the fall of Athens, persuaded the ephors to appoint him in place of LYSANDER as commander of the Spartan force besieging THRASYBULUS (2) in Piraeus. He avoided a confrontation and by negotiation brought about a restored Athenian democracy that was allied with Sparta. He was tried in Sparta for this leniency with the enemy, but was acquitted. In 395 he was ordered to lead an army to assist Lysander in invading Boeotia, but arrived at Haliartus after Lysander's defeat and withdrew without fighting, for which he was sentenced to death by the ephors. He escaped to Tegea, where he lived the rest of his life. He tried to persuade his son, King Agesipolis, to spare the democrats of Mantinea in 385. In exile he wrote a political pamphlet, which was influential on contemporary thought, criticising Spartan constitutional arrangements, including much information about Sparta, and advocating the abolition of the ephorate. Fragments of this work survive.

3. (C2 AD) A travel writer from Magnesia in Lydia who wrote an extant *Description of Greece* in ten books in Greek for Roman tourists covering southern and central mainland Greece. His purpose was, he states, to describe 'all things Greek', and he had himself visited the places he described. It is a highly detailed account and has proved most useful to archaeologists in their excavations of the sites described. In his book he pays attention to buildings, sculptures and other works of art, such as paintings, with emphasis on the archaic and classical periods. He includes information on the historical and religious significance of the sites with which he is concerned. Though he was uninterested in scenery, he gives some information about social life and economic activity. He offers a mostly accurate and only occasionally confused account of his subject.

Pausias (C4 BC) A painter from Sicyon who was the first master of encaustic technique. He was the son and pupil of Bryes and became a pupil of PAMPHILUS (1). He painted *Methe* (Drunkenness), with her face visible through the glass, in the Tholos at Epidaurus. He also painted an ox viewed from the front being sacrificed. He was a pioneer in still life painting and was one of the first to paint ceiling panels.

Pelopidas (died 364 BC) A Theban statesman, general, and leader of the Sacred Band. He was born into a noble family *c.*410 and was a defender of Mantinea at the Spartan siege in 386. He was associated with the democratic party, led by ISMENIAS, and in 382 fled to Athens when the Spartans seized the Cadmeia and executed Ismenias. In 379 he led the force that freed Thebes from the pro-Spartan oligarchs, and was elected Boeotarch for 378 – an office he held thirteen times. In 375 he inflicted a sharp defeat on Sparta at Tegyra and led the Sacred Band to victory at Leuctra in 371. He worked closely with EPAMINONDAS in the Theban invasion of Spartan territory in winter 370/69. The two were unsuccessfully impeached on their return to Thebes on the pretext that they had exceeded their powers. In 369 Pelopidas led an expedition into Thessaly against ALEXANDER (4) of Pherae, freed Larissa from ALEXANDER (2) II, king of Macedonia, and took his nephew PHILIP (1) II hostage. On a second expedition the following year he negotiated with Ptolemy of Alorus, who had murdered Alexander II, but Pelopidas was imprisoned by Alexander of Pherae while on an embassy. Epaminondas secured his release with a show of force. In 367 Pelopidas conducted a mission to ARTAXERXES (2) II, persuading him to cease favouring Sparta. He was killed at the battle of Cynoscephalae while defeating Alexander of Pherae. See J. Buckler (1980) *Theban Hegemony*, Cambridge, MA; London: Harvard University Press.

Perdiccas 1. II (reigned *c.*450–413 BC) A king of Macedonia and son of ALEXANDER (1) I. During his long reign, he consolidated the kingdom and was an ally of Athens until 436, when she colonised Amphipolis. In 432, when Athens supported two rivals for his throne, his brother, Philip, and Derdas, prince of Elimiotis, he negotiated with Sparta and urged her to invade Athenian territory. He also encouraged the revolt of Potidaea and the unification of the Bottiaeans and Chalcidians, whom he urged to concentrate their forces at Olynthus. The Athenian general Archestratus, allied with the pretenders, captured Therme (later Thessalonica) and forced Perdiccas to terms. He could not prevent the Athenian siege of Potidaea, whose citizens he assisted as well as he could. The following year the Thracian king, SITALCES, brokered a new treaty by which Athens returned Therme and Perdiccas abandoned Potidaea. In the face of an invasion of Bottiaea and Chalcidice in 429 by Sitalces, his cavalry won a decisive battle and he formed an

alliance with the Thracian by marriage. In 424 he gave assistance to a Spartan army under BRASIDAS which won over several cities and took Amphipolis. He did not, however, gain the success he hoped for in attacking Arrhabaeus, the king of Lyncus on the border with Epirus, and deserted the Spartans for a new Athenian alliance. In 417 he joined a Peloponnesian coalition under Sparta. In the winter of 415, however, the Athenians forced him to return to their alliance and the next year he joined an unsuccessful attack on Amphipolis.

2. (died 321 BC) A Macedonian general who was second-in-command to ALEXANDER (3) III the Great. He was of noble birth, the son of Orontes and, at the outset of Alexander's campaign in Asia, an infantry commander (*taxiarch*). He was made a member of the royal bodyguard by 330 and, after the departure of CRATERUS (1) for Europe and the death of HEPHAESTION, he was second in rank (*Chiliarch*) to the king. After Alexander's death in 323, the assembly of the army at Babylon confirmed his right to be 'regent', and, as such, the protector of Alexander's half-brother, PHILIP (2) III Arrhidaeus, and unborn son, ALEXANDER (6) IV, and also supreme commander. He proceeded to conquer Cappadocia (see ARIARATHES (1) I) in 322, but his claims were soon questioned by ANTIPATER (1) and Craterus, though he was supported by EUMENES (1). However, he was alarmed by the independence of PTOLEMY (1) I, whose satrapy (province) of Egypt Perdiccas invaded in 321. His own troops, however, were suborned by Ptolemy's enticements and, tired of his arrogance, the satrap of Media, Peithon, aided by SELEUCUS (1) I and Antigenes, murdered him in his tent.

Periander (ruled *c.*627–586 BC) A tyrant of Corinth and the son of CYPSELUS. Two contrasting traditions exist about him: one is that, unlike his gentler and more popular father, he was a ruthless despot with a bodyguard, a man who murdered his wife, Melissa, made love to her corpse, had 300 youthful Corcyrean hostages castrated, and stripped the clothes off the ladies of Corinth and burnt them; the other tradition is favourable and reveals a forward-looking and energetic imperialist and promoter of trade who took back the Corinthian colony of Corcyra, installed his son, Lycophron, as its tyrant, and along with Corcyra founded Apollonia and Epidamnus on the Illyrian coast. He founded Potidaea in Chalcidice, was allied to THRASYBULUS (1) of Miletus and ALYATTES of Lydia, and established relations with Athens and Egypt. He built up the navy of Corinth and is said to have suppressed piracy. He built the *diolkos* (a facility for transporting ships and cargoes across the Isthmus) and the harbour of Lechaeum. He is associated with the flowering of Corinthian art as witnessed by pottery and architectural remains, and he received the poet Arion at his court. He was depicted by PLUTARCH as one of the SEVEN SAGES, the host of a fictitious banquet for the other six. He married a daughter of Procles, the tyrant of Epidaurus, whom he later deposed. All his sons died before him (Lycophron was murdered by the Corcyreans) and he was succeeded by his nephew Psammetichus, also known as Cypselus, who was overthrown and killed in 582. The harsh treatment that ensued of the remains of the tyrants and memorials of their reigns suggests that by the end of his reign Periander was deeply unpopular. See J.B. Salmon (1984) *Wealthy Corinth*, Oxford: Clarendon Press.

Pericles (*c.*495–429 BC) An Athenian statesman, the son of XANTHIPPUS (1) and Agariste, an Alcmaeonid woman who was a niece of the sixth-century statesman CLEISTHENES (2). He financed the chorus for AESCHYLUS' play *The Persians* in 472. In 463 he entered politics by being elected a prosecutor of the conservative CIMON for corruption, and

allied himself with the radical EPHIALTES (2) in attacking the powers of the ancient council of the Areopagus. From 461, with Ephialtes dead and Cimon in exile, he was at the fore, but solid evidence of his activities is lacking. In 454 he proposed that Cimon be recalled. He was commander of an expedition to the Gulf of Corinth *c.*454 and organised the sending of Athenian settlers to several places in the Delian Confederacy (a policy of imperial domination that he developed), especially the Hellespontine region. He introduced the principle of paying jurymen in trials and in 451 confined citizenship to those qualified through both parents. He proposed *c.*448 a congress of all the Greeks to consider a series of measures whose agenda was the glorification of Athens: the rebuilding of temples destroyed by the Persians, the chief of which were on the Acropolis at Athens, freedom for all to sail the seas, and perhaps a new panhellenic confederacy led by Athens. Sparta declined to attend. In 446 he put down a dangerous revolt in Euboea and led resistance to a Spartan invasion of Attica. The following winter he negotiated the Thirty Years Peace with Sparta and her allies. In 447, failing general Greek support, he inaugurated a building programme at Athens to restore the temples with the money contributed by the Delian Confederacy for defence against Persia, no longer needed now that peace had been made. Among the masterpieces of art and architecture for which he was ultimately responsible were the buildings on the Acropolis of Athens, the Parthenon, the Erechtheum, the Propylaea and the Odeon: the visible part of the Athens he later described as 'A School for Hellas'. This programme was opposed for its extravagance by THUCYDIDES (1), who had upper-class support, but was ostracised, i.e. exiled, *c.*443.

Pericles was instrumental in establishing the panhellenic colony of Thurii in southern Italy in 444. From 443 he was elected general (the only important elective office in Athens) every year until his death. In 440 he besieged Samos, which wished to leave the Delian Confederacy, and after a nine-month siege he forced it to accept Athenian terms. In 437 he founded a colony at Amphipolis in Thrace and about that time led an expedition to reinforce Athenian influence in the Black Sea region. He was firmly opposed to the Peloponnesian League led by Sparta. He allied Athens with the Corinthian colony of Corcyra in 433, proposed in 432 a decree to ban Megara's ships from all ports in the Confederacy, and in 431 seized Aegina, from which he expelled the citizens and replaced them with Athenian settlers. He formed the strategy which Athens followed when the Archidamian War broke out in 431 (see ARCHIDAMUS 1) of abandoning the countryside of Attica and relying on the fleet to defend shipping routes and to attack the Peloponnesians where possible, hoping that the enemy would tire. It lacked appeal, however, as it brought few tangible results, and Pericles became unpopular, especially when in 430 a virulent plague broke out in Athens, where conditions were already bad because of the overcrowding of the rural population as refugees camped in the open spaces in the city. He was deposed from his office and fined for embezzlement, and the Athenians tried to negotiate peace with Sparta. He was soon re-elected, however, and died in harness, a late victim of the plague.

He married a cousin, Dinomache, the mother of ALCIBIADES by her previous husband, Cleinias, but the union was unhappy. Their two sons died in the plague. His mistress was ASPASIA, a woman of Miletus, by whom he had a third son, also called Pericles, who being of mixed and therefore illegitimate birth was granted citizenship so that his father might have an heir. Pericles was a fine orator but, despite his democratic principles, he kept aloof from the citizens. He was an imperialist and of noble blood,

and his policies were popular in the Athens of his day. He generally wore a helmet in public to disguise his misshapen head. He associated with intellectuals and artists, and ANAXAGORAS, PHIDIAS and Aspasia were prosecuted by his enemies. He defended them, but Anaxagoras and Phidias were expelled from Athens. He was a friend of the tragedian SOPHOCLES. The historian THUCYDIDES (2) saw him as a brilliant leader of complete integrity and PLUTARCH wrote his biography. See G.E.M. de Ste Croix (1972) *The Origins of the Peloponnesian War*, London: Duckworth; D. Kagan (1969) *The Outbreak of the Peloponnesian War*, Ithaca, NY: Cornell University Press; A.J. Podlecki (1998) *Perikles and His Circle*, London: Routledge.

Persaeus (*c.*306–243 BC) A Stoic philosopher from Citium in Cyprus, the son of Demetrius. Persaeus was a pupil of ZENO (2), the founder of Stoicism, who also reared him at his house in Athens. Zeno sent him in 277 to the court of King ANTIGONUS (2) II Gonatas at Pella in Macedonia to teach philosophy. Persaeus became very influential and taught the king's son, Halcyoneus. He wrote on a variety of topics (although his works are lost), such as *Kingship*, *The Spartan Political System*, *Dialogues* and a criticism of PLATO (1)'s *Laws*. He defended orthodox Stoicism against deviants such as HERILLUS and ARISTON (1). In 244 he was given command of the Acrocorinth, the fortress of Corinth, but the following year was expelled by ARATUS (2) of Sicyon and killed himself for shame.

Perseus (reigned 179–168 BC) The last king of independent Macedonia who was the elder of the two sons of PHILIP (3) V and acceded at the age of 33. He opposed his younger brother Demetrius' pro-Roman stance and claim to the throne (there was a false rumour that Perseus was a slave's son) and, after plotting against him for two years, engineered his execution in

180. He did, however, fight against the Aetolians in his father's alliance with Rome, and renewed the treaty after his accession. He strengthened the power and influence of his kingdom by dynastic marriage – he took Laodice, daughter of SELEUCUS (4) IV, as his wife, and married his sister to PRUSIAS (2) II of Bithynia. He won the friendship of Rhodes and conquered Dolopia in Thessaly. He also interfered in conflicts in Aetolia and Thessaly, and visited Delphi with an armed force, restoring Macedonia to the leadership of the council of states centred on Delphi (the Amphictions). His energetic policy, however, was at the expense of Pergamon, whose king, EUMENES (3) II, complained in 172 to Rome. In the following winter he met Q. Marcius Philippus who tricked him into thinking that Rome would not attack him before he had time to negotiate. However, he faced up to the coming conflict (the Third Macedonian War) and won a frontier skirmish in 171. He tried to rally support in Greece, but with little success. His one ally, Genthius, an Illyrian king, collapsed before the Romans as they attacked from the west, and Perseus fought L. Aemilius Paullus at Pydna on the Thermaic Gulf in June 168. After being routed, he burnt his archives and fled to Samothrace, where he was captured. He marched in Paullus' triumph and died two years later in confinement at Alba Fucens in Latium.

Peucestas (C4 BC) A Macedonian satrap of Persis in Iran. He accompanied the expedition of ALEXANDER (3) III the Great to Asia in 334 and in 325 saved his king's life at Multan in the southern Punjab when Alexander was fighting the Malli. Though a commoner, he was made a member of the king's bodyguard and in 325 he was made satrap of Persis where he pleased Alexander by learning the Persian language and wearing Persian clothes. He also raised Persian troops in 323 to serve with the Macedonian army. After Alexander's death he supported

EUMENES (1) and led a group of satraps who resisted ANTIGONUS (1) I the One-eyed, but he was deposed by Antigonus in 316. He was in Caria c.312. The date of his death is unknown.

Phaedo (C5/4 BC) A friend of SOCRATES from Elis. He was brought to Athens as a prisoner of war and worked as a bath-slave. He was set free and became a devoted hearer of Socrates. PLATO (1) made him the narrator of the dialogue that recounts the last hours of Socrates' life in 399. He returned to Elis where he founded a philosophical school and wrote dialogues of which a fragment or two have survived.

Phaedrus 1. (C5 BC) A member of SOCRATES' circle who figures in three dialogues of PLATO (1). He is presented as a naïve enthusiast.

2. (early C3 BC) An Athenian of the deme Sphettos, a moderate politician and general, the son of Thymochares who was a rich mine-owner. He served as general under the tyrant LACHARES, commanding both mercenaries and the Athenian home guard. In 287 he collaborated with his brother, CALLIAS (4), in obtaining Egyptian help for the expulsion of the troops of DEMETRIUS (2) of Phaleron from Athens, and took part in negotiating the peace treaty and recommending it to the Assembly. He was elected general by the restored democracy the following year and obtained a subsidy of fifty talents from the Egyptian king, PTOLEMY (1) I. See T.L. Shear (1978) *Kallias of Sphettos and the Revolt of Athens*, Princeton, NJ: American School of Classical Studies at Athens.

3. (c.140–70 BC) An Epicurean philosopher of Athenian origin who taught in Rome, where he was head of a philosophical school. He taught Cicero who admired him as a philosopher and as a writer.

Phaenias (late C4 BC) A pupil of ARISTO-
TLE. His writings on history were used by
PLUTARCH. His lost works included *Ven-
geance in the Liquidation of Tyrants* and
The Tyrants of Sicily. Plutarch also used
his works to support his biographies of
SOLON and THEMISTOCLES.

Phalaecus (died *c*.345 BC) A Phocian
general who was probably the son of
ONOMARCHUS and the nephew of PHAYL-
LUS, whom he succeeded as ruler of
Phocis in 351. In the Third Sacred War
he captured Orchomenus, Coronea and
Corsiae, but drew upon himself the hostility of Macedonia. He was ousted by his
compatriots, but regained power and in
346 negotiated a safe passage out of
Nicaea on the Malian Gulf which ended
the war. With his mercenary army he
withdrew to Crete, where he was burnt
to death in an accident.

Phalaris (ruled *c*.570–554 BC) A tyrant of
Acragas (Agrigento) in Sicily. About ten
years after the city was founded, this
Rhodian settler gained power by seizing
the Acropolis with a band of followers.
He fought against the native people, the
Sicans, and the Phoenicians who had
settled to the west, and took possession
of Himera on the north coast of the
island. He fortified Acragas and expanded
its territory. He was violently overthrown
by an ancestor of THERON. Tales of
depraved cruelty were later told of his
reign: he was said to kill his victims by
roasting them alive in a bronze bull.

Phanocles (C3? BC) A Greek elegiac poet
of whose poem, *Love Affairs or Lovely
Boys*, some half-dozen fragments survive.
The poem told of the pederastic amours
of gods and heroes, and the largest fragment is concerned with the murder of
Orpheus. He owed a debt to HOMER for
his direct and simple style, and to CALLI-
MACHUS (3) for his interest in aetiology.

Phanodemus (mid-C4 BC) An Athenian
historian and politician, the son of Diyllus. He wrote a history of Athens in nine
books, exaggerating the part played by his
native city in events. Some fragments of
this work survive, mostly on myth, but
the latest is concerned with the death of
CIMON. He was keenly interested in religion and cult, and led an Athenian
pilgrimage to Delphi in 330. In 343 and
in several later years he was crowned for
his political services to Athens: he co-
operated with LYCURGUS (3) after the
battle of Chaeronea in his attempts to
restore Athens' power. His son DIYLLUS
was a historian.

Pharnabazus (ruled *c*.413–388 BC) A Persian satrap of Phrygia, the territory
known as Dascylium, south of the Hellespont, an office which he inherited from
his father, Pharnaces. He followed the
Persian policy of recovering the maritime
states which the Greeks had freed, and in
the Peloponnesian War played the Greek
states off against each other, rivalling his
fellow satrap TISSAPHERNES. He supported Sparta's attempts to destroy Athenian sea power, and went in person to
Abydus, Cyzicus and Chalcedon. He then
supported Athens' efforts to gain peace
with Persia which were foiled in 407 by
CYRUS (2). In 404 he organised the murder of ALCIBIADES for LYSANDER, and in
398 his satrapy was invaded by DERCYLI-
DAS and again by AGESILAUS II, who in
395 met him and invited his co-operation.
However, Pharnabazus preferred to stay
loyal to his king. He then collaborated
with CONON with whom he won the
decisive battle of Cnidus in 394 against a
Spartan fleet. He removed the Spartan
governors from many island states and the
next year led the Persian fleet across the
Aegean as far as the Isthmus of Corinth,
attacking Sparta and her allies and dis-
tributing Persian cash to the Athenians. In
388 he was recalled to Susa and married a
daughter of ARTAXERXES (2) II. Two years
later he led an unsuccessful attempt to

reconquer Egypt. He was succeeded as satrap by Ariobarzanes.

Pharnaces 1. I (ruled *c*.189–*c*.155 BC) A king of Pontus and the son of MITHRIDATES (3) III. He captured Sinope *c*.183 and tried to expand his kingdom in Asia Minor, but was unable to defeat an alliance of Rhodes, ARIARATHES (4) IV of Cappadocia, PRUSIAS (2) II of Bithynia and EUMENES (3) II of Pergamon, and made peace reluctantly in 179. He was forced to surrender many of his conquests, but kept Sinope. He was the first king of Pontus to become a Friend of the Roman People. He was honoured at Athens for his generosity to that state, and was succeeded by his brother MITHRIDATES (4) IV.

2. II (ruled 63–47 BC) A king of Bosporus in the Crimea, the son of MITHRIDATES (6) VI of Pontus. He led the rebellion that brought about his father's death and was awarded the kingdom of Bosporus (Crimea) by Pompey. In 48 he took advantage of the civil war among the Romans to seize Colchis, Lesser Armenia, Cappadocia and part of Pontus, and defeated a Roman army under Gnaeus Calvinus at Nicopolis. The following year, in a lightning campaign, Caesar defeated him at Zela (which Caesar reported with *veni, vidi, vici* – 'I came, I saw, I conquered') and he returned to Bosporus where he was killed in an insurrection by Asander.

Phayllus (mid-C4 BC) A Phocian general in the Third Sacred War. From 354 he assisted his brother, ONOMARCHUS, and was defeated in Thessaly by PHILIP (1) II in 353. He took over his brother's generalship after the defeat of the Crocus Field in the following year. He then took time to recover the forces of Phocis and raise new mercenaries by doubling their pay. He occupied Thermopylae against Philip and in 352 suffered a series of defeats in Boeotia. He invaded the

Peloponnese in 351, but fell ill and died that year. He was succeeded by PHALAECUS.

Pheidon (C7 BC) A king of Argos who instituted a system of weights and measures that became standard in the Peloponnese. He defeated Sparta at Hysiae *c*.669 and, according to a tradition preserved by HERODOTUS, interfered in the affairs of Corinth and Aegina, the latter of which he occupied. He is also credited, perhaps falsely, with striking the first Aeginetan coins. He took over the presidency of the Olympic Games from the Eleans. He gained a reputation for despotic behaviour and ARISTOTLE considered him to have turned his monarchy into a tyranny. He is reported to have been killed while intervening in a civil war in Corinth; his example led to the tyrannies of Corinth and Sicyon.

Pherecrates (C5 BC) An Athenian comic poet. His work has not survived apart from 300 fragments (we know the titles of nineteen plays). He was active between 440–420 and won several prizes at the City Dionysia and Lenaea festivals. His plays show much originality of plot and treatment, and we have substantial insights into *Deserters*, *Wild Men*, *Miners*, *Persians*, *Ant-men*, *Tyranny* and *Chiron*. In a fragment from *Chiron*, Music makes a speech of complaint against contemporary musicians.

Pherecydes 1. (mid-C6 BC) A philosopher from Syros. The first Greek prose-writer, he wrote (*c*.544) a prose treatise, entitled *The Seven Recesses*, on the origin of the universe and the birth of the gods, of which we know something from fragments and references. He postulates that Zas, Chronos and Chthonie (cf. Zeus, Cronos and Gaia, the Earth) are the original trinity of eternal gods; other gods originated from 'recesses'; Zas married Chthonie; and Chronos had a war with a snake-creature (Ophioneus). There is apparent similarity to the Orphic cosmogeny and some community with HESIOD's *Birth of the Gods*. Nothing is known of his life, though there was a tradition of mystical powers and a strange death. He was also credited implausibly with teaching PYTHAGORAS (1) the doctrine of metempsychosis (transmigration of souls).

2. (mid-C5 BC) An Athenian historian who composed copious, lost historical accounts based on myth and genealogy. He is praised by DIONYSIUS (7) of Halicarnassus (*Rom. Ant.* 1. 13, 1).

Phidias (Pheidias) (*c*.490–*c*.425 BC) An Athenian sculptor, the son of Charmides, probably the most famous sculptor of antiquity. He is reported to have been the pupil of Hegias and AGELADAS. Early in his career *c*.456 he created a huge bronze statue of Athena Promachos which stood in the open on the Acropolis at Athens; a bronze group at Delphi commemorated the battle of Marathon (the Riace bronze warriors may have belonged to this group); and the Lemnian Athena, which a Roman copy is thought to represent. He was best known in antiquity for his two great statues, to outward view of gold and ivory, of Athena in the Parthenon and Zeus at Olympia. According to PLUTARCH's *Life of Pericles*, PERICLES entrusted Phidias with the direction of his whole building programme. He was certainly responsible for the carvings on and in the Parthenon. The gold and ivory statue of Athena Parthenos was begun in 447 and installed in the *naos* (inner chamber) of the Parthenon in 438. We have detailed knowledge of it from PAUSANIAS (3) and Pliny the Elder. It was a standing figure about 12 metres high. In her right hand Athena held a figure of Victory, in her left hand she held a spear and a shield which was carved with the battle of the Amazons on the outside and the battle of the giants on the inside. Her sandals were decorated with Lapiths and centaurs. The base was carved with a relief of the birth of Pandora. Her Aegis

showed a Gorgon's face, and her helmet was adorned with a sphinx and two carvings of Pegasus.

According to Plutarch, Phidias was prosecuted by Pericles' enemies for stealing some of the ivory for the statue and for impiously representing himself and Pericles in the images on the shield. He was found guilty on the second charge and escaped to Olympia, where he was commissioned to design the gold and ivory seated statue of Zeus, which was even larger than the statue of Athena Parthenos. The god held a Victory in his right hand and a sceptre in his left, and his throne was decorated with Graces, Hours and Victories and other figures, including the children of Niobe. The base of the statue showed the birth of Aphrodite and on screens between the legs were painted scenes from mythology by PANAENUS. The remains of Phidias' workshop at Olympia have been excavated. He also took part in a competition at Ephesus for which he made a statue of an Amazon. PHILOCHORUS says that he was killed by the Eleans after he finished his work on the Zeus.

Phidias' versatility as a plastic artist was unsurpassed: besides sculpture, he was a painter, engraver and metal-worker. He left a school of sculptors who led the field for years to come. He was regarded by Hellenistic and Roman artists as their supreme classical model. We can appreciate his work in the Parthenon sculptures, which he designed even if he did not execute them himself. See A.F. Stewart (1990) *Greek Sculpture*, New Haven, Conn.; London: Yale University Press; and G.M.A. Richter (1970) *The Sculpture and Sculptors of the Greeks*, New Haven, Conn.; London: Yale University Press.

Phidippides (Pheidippides, Philippides) (early C5 BC) An Athenian messenger and long-distance runner who in 490 at the time of the Persian landing at Marathon took a request for assistance from Athens to Sparta, 240 kilometres

(149 miles), in two days. The story was told by HERODOTUS (6. 105), who also says that he saw Pan on the mountains of Arcadia who asked him why the Athenians did not grant him state worship. The omission was rectified after the battle.

Philemon (c.361–c.264 BC) A writer of the New Comedy from Syracuse or from Soli in Cilicia who migrated to Athens, where he started to compose for the stage c.330 and was granted citizenship in 307/6. In a life of about a 100 years he wrote ninety-seven plays of which we know the titles of some sixty. None of his work survives in full, though we have nearly 200 fragments. He was a contemporary of ME-NANDER (1), with whose work he often competed and whom he quite often beat into second place. He won a victory at the City Dionysia in 327, as well as three victories at Lenaea festivals. He was invited to the court of PTOLEMY (1) I of Egypt (we do not know if he went there) and attended the court of King MAGAS of Cyrene. Of the titles we possess, only a couple imply mythical subjects. Posterity was less kind to him than to Menander, and the surviving fragments suggest a tendency to verbosity and moralising. However, we have a parody, spoken by a cook, of part of EURIPIDES' *Medea*. Plautus adapted three of Philemon's plays for the Roman stage, *The Merchant*, *The Treasure*, to which he gave the Latin title *Trinummus* ('Three Quid'), and possibly *The Ghost*, under the title *Mostellaria*. There is a certain tendency to moralise in these adaptations, as well as the usual characteristics of the New Comedy, such as wit, surprise, recognition, some sexual reference including seduction, and realism of characterisation. Philemon was popular after his death and his plays continued to be performed, but no papyrus fragments have turned up. See T.B.L. Webster (1970) *Studies in Later Greek Comedy*, Manchester: Manchester University Press.

Philetaerus 1. (early C4 BC) An Athenian poet of the Middle Comedy who wrote twenty-one comedies of which we know the titles of thirteen. A few are burlesques based on myth, but many refer to topical events. He won two first prizes at Lenaea festivals.

2. (c.343–263 BC) A Macedonian ruler of Pergamon in western Asia Minor. The son of Attalus and a woman from Paphlagonia, he served under ANTIGONUS (1) I the One-eyed and was appointed commander of Pergamon by LYSIMACHUS, who used the place as a treasury. In 282 he changed allegiance to SELEUCUS (1) I and after Seleucus' death in 281 ruled under nominal Seleucid sovereignty. He expanded the territory of Pergamon and gave generous benefactions to some Greek cities. He successfully defended Pergamon from the Galatian invasion of Asia Minor 278–276 and founded a dynasty (the Attalids) by adopting his nephew, EUMENES (2) I.

Philetas (Philitas) (c.340–c.280 BC) A Greek poet and scholar from Cos, the son of Telephus. He became the tutor of PTOLEMY (2) II while the latter was a child on the island, and may have taught THEOCRITUS, ZENODOTUS and HERMESIANAX. Whether he left Cos for any substantial time is uncertain. He wrote hexameter and elegiac poetry, including epigrams, which was influential on Hellenistic and Roman poetry, especially CALLIMACHUS (3) and Propertius, though little of his work survives. We have the titles of five works in verse: *Demeter*, *Hermes*, *Telephus*, *Epigrams* and possibly *Playthings*. He also wrote prose: thirty fragments of a work entitled *Miscellaneous Glosses* survive. There may be a connection with the character Philetas in the novel *Daphnis and Chloe* by LÓNGUS. A bronze figure commemorated him in Cos.

Philicus (C3 BC) A Greek poet and tragedian from Corcyra who spent his life in

Alexandria, where he became a member of the Pleiad and a priest of DIONYSUS. He wrote forty-two tragedies of which nothing, not even the titles, survives. However, part of his *Hymn to Demeter* in choriambic hexameters is extant. It is dedicated to contemporary grammarians and tells of the consolation of the grieving goddess by the promise of a cult at Eleusis, and of the old peasant woman, Iambe, who cheered the goddess up with her jests. The fragments show Philicus to have been a master of the Hellenistic epyllion.

Philinus (mid-C3 BC) A Greek writer on medicine from Cos and the founder of the Empirical school of medicine. He was a pupil of HEROPHILUS, but broke away from his master's school and disputed with him his use of signs from the pulse as diagnostic tools. He was critical of the dictionary of Hippocratic medical terms by Bacchius, another of Herophilus' pupils, and produced his own lexicon in six books. He made a serious contribution to pharmacology as is witnessed by GALEN and others.

Philip 1. II (382–336 BC) A king of Macedonia, the youngest son of AMYNTAS (2) II and brother of ALEXANDER (2) II and Perdiccas III, for whose young son Amyntas he may have acted as regent. Alexander had been murdered by a usurper and Perdiccas had been killed in battle with the Illyrians in 360. Philip had probably been imprisoned as a hostage in Thebes from 369–367, and when he came to power he was confronted by the task of rescuing the kingdom from collapse. One of his first acts when he took power in 359 was to claim the crown and dispossess his nephew. He defeated the Athenians, who were supporting his rival Argaeus near Aegae, and made peace with them. He also paid the Thracians to refrain from attacking him. Meanwhile, he built up an army of Macedonian citizens, mostly of the lower class, whom

he trained in the use of a new elongated pike in the context of the phalanx (a flexible military formation used in conjunction with cavalry). This army won an important victory over the Illyrians at Lake Lychnitis and he absorbed the independent states of upper Macedonia into his kingdom. In 357 he captured the Athenian colony of Amphipolis and seized Pydna. The next year he took Potidaea, which he handed to Olynthus and its allies, the Chalcidic Confederacy, with whom he made an alliance. He advanced eastwards and took Mt Pangaeus in 356, establishing a new, fortified city at Crenides which he named Philippi after himself. The produce of the gold mines there allowed him to hire a large number of mercenary soldiers and to bribe many Greek politicians. In 354 he took Methone, in the siege of which he was wounded in the face and lost his right eye. He made marriage alliances with the Molossian royal family of Epirus (see OLYMPIAS) and the ALEUADAE of Thessaly. He became involved in the Third Sacred War of Central Greece in which he was driven from Thessaly in 353 by ONOMARCHUS of Phocis whom he defeated, together with LYCOPHRON (2) of Pherae, and killed the following year in the battle of the Crocus Field. This resulted in Philip's acquisition of Thessaly and its excellent cavalry forces. In 349 and 348 he besieged Olynthus, which had given refuge to his dissident kinsfolk, and took it through treachery. DEMOSTHENES (2) was unable to raise Greek resistance to Philip, despite his harsh treatment of the Olynthians, and made terms with him in spring 346 (the Peace of PHILOCRATES). However, Philip was asked to lead an Amphictionic force against Athens' ally, Phocis. He occupied Thermopylae and prevented Athenian reinforcements from reaching the Phocians, whom he subdued, destroying their cities and sending many of them to settle in Thrace. He delayed his ratification of the Peace until July. He then took Phocis' seat on the Council of the Amphictiony of Delphi.

ISOCRATES had urged Philip to lead a Greek expedition against Persia, but instead he turned northwards and eastwards, and by 340 he had subdued the Dardanian and Taulantian Illyrians and taken over Odrysian Thrace. He also intervened in the Peloponnese to lend support to the Messenians against Sparta and sent mercenaries to Euboea. Athens responded in 341 by invading Euboea and driving out pro-Macedonian governments at Eretria and Histiaea. In 340 Philip besieged Perinthus and Byzantium, and seized ships carrying grain to Athens. This led to open hostilities that culminated in August 338. Athens had allied herself with Thebes and the two states resisted an attack on Amphissa by Philip at the head of an Amphictionic force. At Chaeronea in Boeotia the two armies met Philip, whose forces were a fraction of those he had at his disposal. However, he crushed the allies and thus ended Greek independence. He stationed Macedonian garrisons at strategic positions in Greece and summoned a congress of Greek states to Corinth in summer 337 where he established a federal constitution for Greece (the League of Corinth) with himself as its head in the position of *Hegemon* (leader). Constitutional change was henceforth forbidden and the Greek states were prevented from declaring war on each other (Sparta and Crete alone escaped his net). The congress determined to attack Persia and commissioned Philip to lead the expedition. In autumn 336, after an advance party had crossed into Asia, Philip was assassinated at Aegae by a young Macedonian named Pausanias at the wedding of Cleopatra, his daughter by Olympias, to ALEXANDER (5) of Molossia. Philip had himself married a woman named Cleopatra, niece of a Macedonian nobleman Attalus, some months earlier, and Olympias had angrily departed for home in Epirus. Her son, ALEXANDER (3) III, had been in Illyria

until his recall shortly before his father's death. There had also been something of a reconciliation with Olympias, who attended the wedding.

Philip not only saved the Macedonian kingdom, but also brought it to greatness. Despite the venomous attacks of Demosthenes, accusing him of trickery and bribery, he was a great statesman, a subtle diplomat, and a skilful general and organiser of armies. He was succeeded by his son, Alexander, whom he had trained in warfare and who was well able to take on the project of conquering Persia. See G.L. Cawkwell (1978) *Philip of Macedon*, London: Faber & Faber; and J.R. Ellis (1976) *Philip II and Macedonian Imperialism*, London: Thames & Hudson.

2. III Arrhidaeus (*c*.358–317 BC) A son of PHILIP (1) II by Philinna, a Thessalian dancing-girl. He was considered to be mentally defective and so was not put to death by ALEXANDER (3) III on his accession as were some of his siblings. However, in June 323, on Alexander's death, the army proclaimed him king jointly with Alexander's son, but he was never more than a tool of cleverer men, such as PERDICCAS (2), ANTIPATER (1) and POLYPERCHON. Perdiccas as regent made him marry his half-niece, EURYDICE, who in a *coup* in 317 overthrew Polyperchon, and was herself defeated in a *coup* by OLYMPIAS. That autumn he and his wife were murdered by Olympias.

3. V (238–179 BC) A king of Macedonia, the son of King DEMETRIUS (5) II and adopted son of King ANTIGONUS (3) III Doson. He succeeded the latter in summer 221 at the age of 17 and quickly made an impression of energy and strength. After campaigning against the Illyrians (see SCERDILAIDAS), he met ARATUS (2) of Sicyon and, at his instigation, led the forces of the Hellenic Confederacy in the Social War against Aetolia and her allies, Sparta and Elis. The war was successfully ended in 217 by the Peace of Naupactus which gave Philip the opportunity to strike to the north and take over Illyria and the Dalmatian coast from the Romans, who were embroiled in the Second Punic War. Philip was instigated to embark on this First Macedonian War by the exiled DEMETRIUS (10) OF PHAROS. He made a treaty with Hannibal in 215, to little effect, and lost his Adriatic fleet in 214 when Laevinus brought a Roman force to Apollonia, but was more successful by land. He then turned to the Peloponnese, where he dealt harshly with Messene and alienated the Achaean Confederacy. In 212 the balance of power swung against him as Rome allied herself with Aetolia and Pergamon. He then supported the Achaeans in their war with Sparta and showed skill in resisting Aetolian and Roman aggression. The Romans retired in 207 and Philip sacked Thermum, the capital of Aetolia. The war finally fizzled out when the Aetolians made peace in 206 and, by the Peace of Phoenice in 205, Rome accepted terms granting Philip access to the Adriatic.

Philip now turned to the Aegean where he employed a pirate, Dicaearchus, as his admiral in an attack on shipping and the possessions in Asia Minor of the youthful Egyptian king, PTOLEMY (5) V. The extent of involvement of ANTIOCHUS (3) III, with whom he made a treaty in 203, is uncertain. He turned the Greeks against him by the cruelty of his treatment of prisoners and captured cities, and Rhodes, a formidable sea-power: and ATTALUS (1) I, king of Pergamon, defeated him at the battles of Chios and Lade in 201, themselves, however, suffering heavy casualties. Attalus and the Rhodians requested help from the Roman Senate, which was now free of the war with Hannibal. In 200 Philip attacked Athens and the Thracian Chersonese, learning of the Roman ultimatum and declaration of war while at Abydos. In the Second Macedonian War Philip fought the Romans in Macedonia and Thessaly, but was defeated decisively by Flamininus at Cynoscephalae in 197. The Romans dictated terms: he

was confined to Macedonia, had to pay an indemnity of 1,000 talents, surrender his fleet and give hostages, including his younger son, Demetrius. Philip realised how weak he then was and co-operated with Rome in her dealings with the Greeks, assisting her in 195 against NABIS, tyrant of Sparta, and against the alliance of Antiochus with the Aetolians in 192 and the years following. He helped the Scipios to cross his kingdom with their forces in 190 for which his debt to Rome was remitted and his son returned. In the following five years he gave his attention to the prosperity of Macedonia, but after 185, suspecting that Rome would interfere again, he asserted his supremacy in the Balkans, where he worked by force and diplomacy. In 180 the differences between his sons over Demetrius' friendship with Rome, which fostered in him hopes of succeeding to power, flared up and Philip reluctantly executed Demetrius for treason. He died at Amphipolis the following year while trying to engineer further disruption in Illyria. Like PHILIP (1) II he was a brilliant general, but was unable to maintain a consistent policy and was faced with a rising power he could not match.

Philippides (late C3 BC) An Athenian poet of the New Comedy. He wrote forty-five plays, of which some fragments survive: we have fifteen titles. He won first prize at the City Dionysia festival in 311, and other prizes at various Lenaea festivals. Philippides was a friend of LYSIMACHUS, and he was honoured in a decree passed by STRATOCLES in 292.

Philippus (mid-C4 BC) An astronomer from Opus in Locris who made an astronomical calendar. A pupil of PLATO (1), he was credited by DIOGENES (5) Laërtius with copying out Plato's *Laws* on to papyrus and writing an *Appendix to the Laws* (*Epinomis*), which, however, is more likely to be Plato's own work.

Philiscus 1. (C4 BC) A Milesian pupil of ISOCRATES who, like his master, wrote political pamphlets, as well as a handbook of rhetoric and a biography of LYCURGUS (3). Fragments of his work survive.

2. (C4 BC) A Middle Comedy writer whose works were based on myth. A papyrus fragment of his play, *The Birth of Zeus*, survives.

3. (C4 BC) A Cynic philosopher from Aegina who studied under DIOGENES (2) at Athens and wrote lost tragedies.

Philistion (C4 BC) A physician and writer on medicine from Locri in southern Italy. He taught EUDOXUS of Cnidus. GALEN ascribed him to a group of Sicilian doctors and regarded him as adopting EMPEDOCLES' theory of the four elements, to each of which he opposed a related quality: earth to moist, water to dry, air to hot and fire to cold. He thought that disease was caused either by an imbalance of the elements in the body or by external injury or problems arising from difficulties with respiration, which he saw as a cooling system. He wrote books on diet and other treatments, but none of his works survives. It seems likely that he knew PLATO (1), who is thought to have derived from him his ideas on pathology expounded in *Timaeus*.

Philistus (c.430–356 BC) A Syracusan politician and historian, and a supporter and friend of the tyrants DIONYSIUS (1) I and DIONYSIUS (2) II. He helped the former in his seizure of power in 405 and held the post of commander of the garrison of Ortygia for many years. In 386 he was banished by Dionysius for personal reasons and lived in Epirus, where he wrote his *History of Sicily* in thirteen books. He was recalled by Dionysius II in 366 and was appointed admiral. He was hostile to the attempts of PLATO (1) to reform the constitution and assisted in the banishing of DION. While Dionysius was in Italy in 357, Philistus guarded the sea route from Greece, but Dion eluded him and landed in Sicily. The following year, when HERACLIDES (2) brought Dion naval reinforcements, Philistus was defeated and killed, perhaps by his own hand.

His history was widely respected and to some extent followed the methods of THUCYDIDES (2). Although it has perished apart from scanty fragments, we know it was used as a source by DIODORUS (3) Siculus and is referred to by PLUTARCH, DIONYSIUS (7) of Halicarnassus and PAUSANIAS (3).

Philochorus (c.340–260 BC) A Hellenistic historian and writer on religion from Athens. A professional seer, he was official augur in 306. An Athenian patriot, he wrote a history of Attica (*Atthis*) in seventeen books, the 170 fragments of which allow an understanding of its method and scope: after dealing with earlier times in chronological order, he covered his own lifetime in great detail, though none of his work on that period survives. He also wrote on chronology, festivals and on literature, ALCMAN and EURIPIDES (twenty-seven titles are known). His chief source for the fourth century was the work of ANDROTION, and he was familiar with earlier historians, such as HERODOTUS and THUCYDIDES (2). He was executed at about the age of 80 by King ANTIGONUS (2) II Gonatas of Macedonia for supporting PTOLEMY (2) II in the Chremonidian War.

Philocles (C5 BC) An Athenian tragic poet, a nephew of Aeschylus. Nothing of his work survives, but we learn that he composed 100 plays and defeated SOPHOCLES' masterpiece, *King Oedipus*, for the prize at its first showing. He was the butt of the comic poets, who mocked his harshness of style. He wrote a tetralogy of plays entitled *Pandionis*, including *Tereus*.

Philocrates (mid-C4 BC) An Athenian politician who negotiated the peace named after him with PHILIP (1) II in 346 after the fall of Olynthus in 348. He had been frustrated in an earlier attempt by a writ of illegality, which DEMOS-THENES (2) succeeded in rebutting. In 346 he led two embassies on which both Demosthenes and his rival AESCHINES (2) served, and himself proposed the acceptance of the terms of peace and alliance with Philip to the Assembly. While Demosthenes turned against the treaty, Philocrates stood by it even when Philip entered Phocis to bring the Third Sacred War to an end. In 343, the peace now being unpopular, HYPERIDES prosecuted him for corruptly accepting bribes and favours from Philip and he fled into voluntary exile. He was condemned to death in his absence. See G.L. Cawkwell (1978) *Philip of Macedon*, London: Faber & Faber.

Philodemus (*c*.110–*c*.37 BC) An Epicurean philosopher and poet from Gadara in Syria, educated at Athens, who *c*.75 moved to Italy, where he enjoyed the friendship and protection of the Piso family. He passed much time in a splendid villa at Herculaneum, probably owned by Lucius Piso Caesoninus, and there taught Greek literature and philosophy and wrote. His library of some 1,200 papyrus scrolls, preserved in the eruption of Versuvius in AD 79 by the fall of ash, were rediscovered there. His poems are of erotic character and some thirty-five are preserved in the *Greek Anthology*. They were admired by Cicero and imitated or alluded to by the Roman poets Horace, Virgil, Propertius and Ovid. He composed books on philosophy and the history of philosophy for the Piso family. He also wrote works of literary criticism, psychology and aesthetics, and he elaborated a theory of art that by-passed moral and logical philosophy. His prose works did not survive antiquity, but now a library of papyri, rediscovered in the villa, is being slowly deciphered despite the charred and damaged state of the papyri. See also

ZENO (5). See J. Annas (1992) *Hellenistic Philosophy of Mind*, Berkeley, CA: University of California Press; M. Gigante (1995) *Philodemus in Italy*, Ann Arbor, Mich.: University of Michigan Press; and D. Obbink (ed.) (1995) *Philodemus and Poetry*, New York; Oxford: OUP.

Philolaus (*c*.470–390 BC) A Greek philosopher of the Pythagorean school from Croton or Taras (Tarentum). He is mentioned in the *Phaedo* of PLATO (1) as regarding suicide as immoral. He lived and worked in Thebes, where SIMMIAS (1) and CEBES were his disciples. He wrote a work on scientific theories, including cosmology, in which he postulated that the Earth is a planet that revolves around a central fire (not the sun), and had a theory of matter in which everything consists not only of infinite materials, like earth or void, but also of limiting factors, such as shapes. He believed that elements are united by harmony in pleasing mathematical arrangements. Some of the fragments attributed to Philolaus are considered genuine, and show that ARISTOTLE drew on his work when researching Pythagorean doctrine.

Philomelus (died 354 BC) A Phocian general, the instigator of the Third Sacred War. After a period of turmoil in which the Delphic Amphictiony under Theban leadership had fined Phocis heavily for the cultivation of sacred land at Delphi, the Phocians, ejected from the sanctuary, elected Philomelus general with supreme power. In the summer of 356 Philomelus hired mercenaries and used them and Phocian troops to seize Delphi. Philomelus, claiming Delphi for Phocis, made alliances with Athens and Sparta. Thebes reacted by persuading the Amphictionic council in autumn 355 to declare a sacred war against Phocis. Philomelus felt free to steal the treasures of Delphi to hire more men and in spring 354 defeated the Boeotians with the Locrians and then the Thessalians. But in the autumn of that year the Boeotians rallied and heavily defeated Philomelus at Neon in Phocis, after which he killed himself. See J. Buckler (1989) *Philip II and the Sacred War*, Leiden: E.J. Brill.

Philon (Philo) 1. (C4 BC) An architect and writer on buildings from Eleusis who built the arsenal at Piraeus and the porch of the Telesterion at Eleusis. His books are lost, but an inscription gives a detailed specification of the arsenal.

2. (C4/3 BC) A writer on logic and a pupil of DIODORUS (1) Cronus. A dialectician like his teacher, he created new and important theories in logic.

3. (late C3 BC) A writer on technology from Byzantium. He borrowed ideas from CTESIBIUS and wrote a *Compendium of Mechanics*, which is about artillery, hydraulics, war-machines and siege-craft, of which two complete books and parts of two others are preserved (HERON refers to a lost book on automata).

4. (159–83 BC) A philosopher from Larissa and the last head of the Academy of PLATO (1). He studied at Larissa under Callicles, a pupil of CARNEADES, and at the age of 24 went to Athens to study under Clitomachus, whom he succeeded as head in 109. He migrated to Rome in 88 and taught there; his pupils included Cicero, who refers to his teachings in his *Former Academics* and in *Lucullus*, and we know something of them from an account in the works of John of Stobi. We know nothing, however, of his writings – not even the titles. He was challenged for the headship of the Academy by his pupil ANTIOCHUS (15) OF ASCALON, who seized it, condemning his old master for being too sceptical, and himself turning to dogmatic ideas of a Stoic type: he wrote a work, *Sosus*, against Philon. Philon appears to have had little influence on later Platonism. See H. Tarrant (1985) *Scepticism or Platonism?*, Cambridge: CUP.

5. Herennius (*c*.AD 70–*c*.160) A historian of Phoenicia from Byblos who wrote in Greek. Eusebius preserved a considerable amount of his history by quoting it in his *Preparation for the Gospel*. Philon gives an account of Phoenician religion which owes something to EUHEMERUS, accounting for gods as originally heroes of past times. How much of his work is derived from genuine Phoenician sources is uncertain: he claimed to have translated a considerable amount from an ancient Phoenician author named Sanchuniathon, and some of his work is in agreement with material found in texts from Ugarit. He also wrote on grammar and synonyms, cities, bibliography and a work on the reign of the Roman emperor Hadrian.

Philonides 1. (C5 BC) An Athenian poet of the Old Comedy and producer of plays. He produced the extant plays of ARISTOPHANES (1), *Wasps* and *Frogs*, as well as the lost *Amphiaraus* and probably the *Proagon*. Very little is known of his own plays.

2. (early C2 BC) An Epicurean philosopher and mathematician from Laodicea in Syria who was elected an honorary citizen of Athens. He knew APOLLONIUS (2) of Perge and the mathematician ZENODORUS.

Philopappus (C2 AD) A Commagenian prince of Seleucid descent whose name was Gaius Julius Antiochus Epiphanes. The title, Philopappus ('loving his grandfather'), refers to his grandfather, ANTIOCHUS (18) IV, the last king of independent Commagene. He was suffect consul at Rome in 109 and settled in Athens, where he was a citizen and was elected archon. As benefactor of his adopted city he was allowed to build a splendid memorial on Museum Hill.

Philopoemen (*c*.253–182 BC) A general and statesman of the Achaean Confederacy, the son of Craugis of Megalopolis in

Arcadia. In 223 he took part in the defence of Megalopolis when it was attacked by CLEOMENES (2) III of Sparta. After playing a major role in the battle of Sellasia in 222 he went to Crete, where he became captain of a force of mercenary soldiers. He returned to the Peloponnese c.209 and was elected cavalry commander of the Achaean Confederacy and 'general', the title of the chief magistrate, the following two years. During this time he reformed the army. He led the Achaeans successfully at the battle of Mantinea against Sparta in 207, when he overthrew the tyrant, Machanidas, and from 202–199 he opposed the Spartan King NABIS, first as a citizen and later as general, joining forces with the Romans to do so; but he then returned to Crete for six years. In 193, after the Romans had withdrawn, he began a further period as general and, after the assassination of Nabis, he brought Sparta into the Confederacy despite the opposition of the Roman general Flamininus. In 191 he annexed Messene and Elis to the Confederacy. He was general from 191–188 when he annulled the Spartan constitution, destroyed its walls and abolished its military system. He did this despite the opposition of the Roman Senate, whose right to oversee the Confederacy Philopoemen consistently rejected. He held two further years of office, 187/6 and 183/2, and during the latter was captured in the rebellion of Messene and killed by poison. His funeral was led by POLYBIUS the historian, who wrote a lost biography of Philopoemen, the last great independent Greek statesman. Effectively, his heir as leader of the Confederacy was CALLICRATES (2), who, however, yielded to Roman authority.

Philostratus, Lucius Flavius (died c.AD 245) A Greek biographer whose family originated from Lemnos, though he lived mostly in Athens. The Roman empress, Julia Domna, asked him to write the life of APOLLONIUS (6) of Tyana for her. He also wrote biographies of Sophists, providing useful information about the 'Second Sophistic', and probably works entitled *Athletic Training*, *Erotic Letters* and *Hero-cults* (the last being a dialogue on the heroes of the Trojan War). These works are extant. Two other members of the family of Philostratus wrote surviving works which describe paintings: both works are named *Pictures*.

Philotas (died 330 BC) A Macedonian general, the son of PARMENION. He commanded the Companion Cavalry for ALEXANDER (3) III the Great with much distinction. However, he was embroiled in a conspiracy against the king to the extent that, having some knowledge of it, he failed to denounce the plotters and, accused of this, he was executed by the army. Alexander had his father assassinated without being told of his son's disgrace. Nothing is known of the actual plot.

Philoxenus 1. (c.435–380 BC) A dithyrambic poet from Cythera who was at the court of DIONYSIUS (1) I of Syracuse and was imprisoned in the stone quarries there. He was a musical innovator, introducing solo singing into the dithyramb. His *Cyclops*, in which the eponymous character sings a solo, was parodied by ARISTOPHANES (1) in his *Wealth*.

2. (early C4 BC) A poet from Leucas who composed a surviving poem, *The Banquet*, in the dithyrambic style and in dactylo-epitrite metre. He was probably the author of *The Cook-book*, a poem in hexameters quoted by PLATO (2).

3. (late C4 BC) A painter from Eretria. He painted a scene of ALEXANDER (3) III the Great confronting DARIUS (3) III in battle. It was commissioned by CASSANDER, and was probably the original of the famous mosaic of the scene, which was found at Pompeii and is now in the Naples museum.

Philumenus (late C2 AD) A writer on medicine from Alexandria. He wrote *Poisonous Animals*, used as a source by Aelianus, a partly extant work on bowel disease, and a lost work on gynaecology.

Phocion (402/1–318 BC) An Athenian general and statesman, the son of Phocus. He was a pupil of PLATO (1) and a friend of XENOCRATES. He was elected general forty-five times – more often than any other Athenian. Of noble birth, he was incorruptible and held patriotic and conservative views. He was also a fine extempore speaker and despised the demagogues. He supported the policies of EUBULUS (1) and opposed DEMOSTHENES (2) in his crusade against the growing power of PHILIP (1) II of Macedonia. He was, however, involved in successful military action against Macedonia in Euboea in 348, and again in 341 when he expelled Cleitarchus from Eretria. In 342/1 he attacked Megara and installed a democracy there, and in 340 he assisted in the defence of Byzantium, which Philip was besieging. In summer 338, before the battle of Chaeronea, Phocion urged the Athenians to accept Philip's peace overtures, and, after the battle, he was appointed general by the Areopagus in place of CHARIDEMUS and negotiated terms for Athens. In 335 he led a successful embassy to ALEXANDER (3) III the Great after the destruction of Thebes to ask him to forbear from punishing Athens for her complicity and turn instead against Persia. In 322, when nearly 80 years old, he was involved in the Lamian War, which he opposed, and drove off a Macedonian raid on Rhamnus. After the battle of Crannon, when Athens had no allies left, Phocion was a member of the embassy on which he and DEMADES negotiated peace with ANTIPATER (1). He collaborated in the establishment of an oligarchic regime and the occupation of Munichia by a Macedonian garrison whose commander was replaced in 319/8 by NICANOR (1). The next year POLYPERCHON brought

about a brief restoration of democracy at Athens, and he handed the old man to his compatriots for trial. The Assembly, packed with extreme democrats (many of whom had no right to be present), took out its spite on Phocion and condemned him to drink hemlock, though they were persuaded to stop short of torturing him. His calm death was compared to that of SOCRATES. See PLUTARCH's *Life of Phocion*; and L. Tritle (1988) *Phocion the Good*, London; New York: Croom Helm.

Phormion 1. (C5 BC) An Athenian admiral. He first appears as one of the commanders of the fleet sent against Samos in 440, and a few years later he led a squadron to the Gulf of Ambracia, where he handed the city of Abracia to the Acarnanians and Amphilochians. In 432 he was sent to besiege Potidaea. In the winter of 430/29 he was put in command of a fleet based at Naupactus on the Corinthian Gulf, and blockaded Corinth. The following summer he won two brilliant victories over superior Peloponnesian fleets led by Cnemus and restored Athenian power in Acarnania. Some time after his return in 428 he was accused of embezzlement and fined.

2. (C4 BC) An Athenian banker, formerly a slave of PASION, who leased the bank from his former master shortly before his death. After Pasion's death, he married his widow, Archippe. His stepson APOLLODORUS (2) prosecuted him unsuccessfully *c.*349 for embezzling money belonging to the business. He obtained citizenship, as Pasion had, through benefaction to the state.

Phrynichus 1. (C6/5 BC) An Athenian writer of tragedies who is said to have first introduced female characters into tragedies. He won a first prize *c.*510, and in a victorious play of 476 THEMISTOCLES was his chorus-leader. Like his younger contemporary, AESCHYLUS, he wrote on themes of current history as well as on myth. He produced *c*.492 a tragedy, *The Fall of Miletus*, for which he was fined 1,000 drachmas for upsetting his fellow citizens, who felt deeply worried and guilty about the Persian suppression of the Ionian Revolt that had just ended in failure. He also wrote plays entitled *Phoenician Women*, *The Egyptians*, *The Danaids*, *Alcestis*, and plays on other mythological subjects.

2. (C5 BC) An Athenian writer of the Old Comedy whose career began *c*.430. He won two victories at the Lenaea festival and one at the City Dionysia. Nine titles of his plays are known, and nearly 100 fragments.

3. (died 411 BC) An Athenian general in the fleet at Samos in 411 who was hostile to ALCIBIADES. When the latter offered to gain the support of TISSAPHERNES if an oligarchy was established at Athens, Phrynichus was sceptical of his intentions. After PISANDER had persuaded the Assembly to accede to Alcibiades' plan, he had Phrynichus deposed from his command on account of his known hostility to Alcibiades. He returned to Athens, where he joined the group of radical oligarchs who set up the rule of the Four Hundred at Athens in 411. He was sent on an embassy to Sparta, together with ANTIPHON (1) and Pisander, to offer peace on any terms. On his return, he was assassinated and his killer was rewarded with Athenian citizenship.

4. **Arabius** (late C2 AD) A Greek lexicographer and rhetorician from Bithynia. He wrote a dictionary of Attic words entitled *A Preparation for Learning* in thirty-seven books of which a summary by the ninth-century scholar Photius is extant. There is also an abridgement (entitled *A Selection*) of a work entitled *The Atticist*, with the subtitle, *The Choice of Good, Reputable Substantives*. He took as his authority for 'good' Greek usage the Classical tragedians and prose-writers of Athens, though he considered

even them to be fallible. He accepted that diverse stylistic levels are permissible. He failed to obtain the chair of rhetoric at Athens and criticised its occupant, POLLUX.

Phylarchus (mid-C3 BC) A Greek historian from Naucratis who worked in Athens, where he wrote a work covering the period from 272 (the death of PYRRHUS) to 220 (the death of CLEOMENES (2) III) in continuation of the work of DURIS (2) of Samos and the *History of the Successors* by HIERONYMUS (1) of Cardia. He adopted the sensational approach to his subject of the former rather than the dispassionate style of the latter. Phylarchus' admiration of Cleomenes and disparagement of the Achaean Confederacy biased his work and earned him the reprobation of POLYBIUS. His work is marred by digression, reporting of miracles, love stories and various anecdotes. Sixty fragments remain to confirm this view of his work. PLUTARCH, however, used him as his chief source for the *Lives* of Cleomenes, AGIS (3) IV, and a source for those of ARATUS (2) of Sicyon and PYRRHUS. His other lost works were *A History of Antiochus III and Eumenes II of Pergamon*, *Epitomes of Myths*, *Inventions*, and *Unwritten Matters*.

Phyromachus (*c*.200 BC) An Athenian sculptor and painter who was among those who introduced Pergamene baroque. Pliny the Elder reports that he contributed to scenes of the Pergamene battles with the Galatians.

Pindar (518–*c*.438 BC) A lyric poet from Cynoscephalae in Boeotia near Thebes. Of noble family, the Aegeidae, he was the son of Daiphantus and Cleodice. His talent manifested itself early, and at the age of 20 in 498 he was commissioned by the ALEUADAE to compose a victory ode (*Pyth.* 10) for the Thessalian youth Hippocleas. From then on he was regularly asked to compose odes celebrating the achievements of athletes from the length and breadth of the Greek world. He wrote far more than has come down to us, though the four extant books of victory odes, composed to celebrate the athletic and chariot-racing triumphs of winners of the four major festivals of the Greek world, the Olympic, Pythian, Nemean and Isthmian games, are a mighty achievement sufficient to justify his place as the foremost Greek lyric poet.

The Alexandrian editors formulated seventeen books of his works: four of victory odes (*epinikia*), two of dithyrambs, two of processional hymns, three of 'maiden songs', two of lyrics for dances (*hyporchemata*), one each of paeans, encomiums, dirges and hymns. Fragments of the lost books, some quite long, principally the dithyrambs and paeans, also exist. He travelled widely and knew Athens well. Some of his major patrons were kings or tyrants of Macedonia, Cyrene, Thrace, Italy, Sicily, Rhodes and Asia Minor. The odes he composed for the victors reflected Pindar's belief, shared by the majority of his Greek contemporaries, in the nobility of athletic skill and prowess. His odes were sung by choirs at the celebrations after the victory or on the athlete's return to his home. The odes normally contained a story based on a familiar myth – very often one that was relevant to the victor's native city. Pindar usually dwelt on a single facet or episode in a myth and sketched in the rest. He would begin his odes with information about the victor, his family and ancestry, his city and previous victories associated with these. He also frequently included praise of himself. Pindar placed high importance on the opening words of the odes and made them as striking as possible to capture the hearer's attention. Pindar's genius lay in his brilliant use of language and imagery: he was a master of rhythm and scarcely ever used the same metrical pattern again in later odes. He also moralised in a conventional way, though he did so with grace and magnifi-

cence of phrase. Consequently, the odes often take on a pronounced didactic tone. He seems to have accepted the neutral stance of his city Thebes in the Persian wars. However, shortly after the Greek victory, he wrote an ode celebrating Aeginetan courage at the battle of Salamis. His admiration for Athens was such that he felt he should defend it to his compatriots in *Pyth.* 9. However, after *c*.460 he cooled towards Athens as it embarked on a policy, associated with PERICLES, of imperialism. He accepted and praised the traditional Olympian gods, but also felt the power of Orphic mystery cult and Pythagorean teachings. He believed implicitly in the truth of the ancient myths. See C.M. Bowra (1964) *Pindar*, Oxford: Clarendon Press; E.L. Bundy (1962) *Studia Pindarica*, Berkeley, CA: University of California Press; and W.H. Race (ed.) (1997) *Pindar*, Loeb Classical Library, Cambridge, MA: Harvard University Press.

Pisander (C5 BC) An Athenian politician who was involved in the investigation of the mutilation of the Herms in 415 (see ANDOCIDES 2). In 412 he joined the oligarchs and helped to organise the revolution of 411, proposing the motion in the Assembly to establish the Council of Four Hundred. He travelled to Samos to try to convince the troops there to support the move, and only got away with his life thanks to the intervention of ALCIBIADES. He was a member of an embassy of leading oligarchs who went to Sparta to negotiate peace on any terms. Shortly after his return, when the narrow oligarchy fell, he fled to AGIS (1) II at Decelea and thence to Sparta. He was condemned to death in his absence. He was the butt of the writers of comedy for his corrupt dealings and for his fatness.

Pisistratus (*c*.595–527 BC) A tyrant of Athens, born at Brauron, the son of Hippocrates. His mother was said to be a cousin of SOLON's mother. He claimed descent from the mythical family of the Neleids of Pylos. One of his ancestors was archon in 669/8. In 565 Pisistratus was polemarch and fought a successful campaign against Megara in which he took her port of Nisaea and reinforced Athenian ownership of Salamis. In the period of factional disputes that followed, he founded a party of 'Hillsmen' for the less affluent or noble people who were disaffected with the two aristocratic parties, namely the 'Plain' led by LYCURGUS (1) and the 'Coast'. In about 561 he complained to the Assembly that he had been assaulted by his enemies, and was granted a bodyguard, whom he used to seize power. He was soon removed by a combination of the other two parties and *c.*556 made another attempt, supported by Megacles, head of the ALCMAEONIDS and leader of the Coastal party, whose daughter Pisistratus married. He is said by HERODOTUS to have advanced his cause by dressing a tall, handsome girl as Athena, riding into Athens in her company, and thus claiming the goddess' patronage. His bid for power failed as he fell out with Megacles, and he lived in exile in Macedonia for ten years, building up a power base with money from Thracian silver mines, in which he had an interest, and with which he recruited mercenary soldiers. He also cultivated close relations with Eretria, Thebes, Argos, Thessaly and Naxos. In 546 he landed with his army near Marathon and defeated his opponents at Pallene.

This time he established his rule firmly with the support of his mercenaries, whom he paid with cash raised from his mines in the Strymon area of Thrace and in Attica, and with the help of a tithe, later a 5 per cent tax, on produce, as well as a tax on trade. He ruled continuously from 546 until his death. His rule was peaceful and benevolent, and he respected the laws and constitution as established by Solon, manipulating the system by nomination. He was keen to conciliate his former enemies, and he did not

confiscate their estates, though one or two went into exile for a time. During his tyranny, the prosperity of Athens grew rapidly and Athenian pottery, the black-figure ware, took the lead in volume of production. He lent money to farmers on marginal land to encourage its cultivation. His interest in rural matters also led him to establish a system of travelling judges, and he himself often travelled through the countryside. He encouraged the development of the market-place (*agora*) in Athens: a number of its buildings date from his time. He supported certain cults, notably that of Apollo, and he purified Delos and started a festival of Apollo on the island. He built a temple to Apollo Patroos in the market-place. He encouraged the arts, and had the works of HOMER recited at the Panathenaic festival and written out in a definitive text. He also encouraged the development of the theatrical festivals of Dionysus. Attic coinage spread during his rule. He regained Sigeum near Troy for Athens, to complement the rule of the Thracian Chersonese by Miltiades of the Philaid family, the uncle of the victor of Marathon, and installed his son Hegesistratus as tyrant there. He was also closely allied with LYGDAMIS, tyrant of Naxos. He was succeeded by his elder son, HIPPIAS (1).

Pittacus (*c.*650–570 BC) A constitutional ruler and general of Mytilene in Lesbos. In 606 he led a force to contest the possession of Sigeum with Athens; PERIANDER, the tyrant of Corinth, later arbitrated the matter in favour of Mytilene. He was instrumental *c.*590 in expelling the tyrant Melanchros, and repelled an attempt by exiled aristocrats, led by the poet ALCAEUS and Antimenides, to return and take over the state. He was elected *aesymnetes* ('arbitrator') for ten years with dictatorial powers to restore order. Alcaeus accused him of being a tyrant, but he duly retired at the end of his term of office. He imposed a moderate constitution like the one of his contemporary,

SOLON, at Athens and became famous for his wisdom. He declared that the law code was the best protector of the city. He doubled the penalty for any crime committed by an offender while drunk. He was accounted one of the SEVEN SAGES of Greece.

Pixodarus (ruled 341–334 BC) A satrap of Caria and Lycia, the youngest brother of MAUSOLUS. He expelled his sister ADA from the throne in 341 and, after failing to ally himself with Macedonia by a dynastic marriage, he was assisted in his administration by Orontobates, a Persian. When ALEXANDER (3) III the Great arrived in 334 after the battle of Granicus, he reinstated Ada.

Plato 1. (c.427–347 BC) An Athenian philosopher, one of the most original and seminal of ancient thinkers. He was of distinguished family on both sides: his father, Ariston, died when he was a child; his mother, Perictione, sister of CHARMIDES and cousin of CRITIAS, remarried. Plato's stepfather, Pyrilampes, was a man of political importance and had been a close associate of PERICLES. Plato's parents had three other children, Adeimantus, Glaucon and Potone. Pyrilampes, Perictione's uncle, already had a son, Demus, as well as another son, Antiphon, by Perictione. Plato (a nickname meaning 'stocky'; his real name was Aristocles) was therefore greatly aware of Athenian politics in his youth and also deeply influenced by his friendship with SOCRATES, whom he frequently heard discussing philosophical questions in the most receptive years of his youth. His first tutor in philosophy was the Heraclitean CRATYLUS. When he was about 28, he attended the trial of Socrates and, after the verdict, urged his friend to increase the amount of the fine he proposed to thirty mnas and offered his own security. He could not attend Socrates' execution through illness.

Although he had originally wished to enter politics, he became increasingly disillusioned: the behaviour of the oligarchs in 404/3 disgusted him, especially when they tried to implicate Socrates in their crimes by making him their accomplice in the arrest of Leon of Salamis. After the restored democracy took Socrates' life, Plato with some other friends of Socrates withdrew to Megara where he lived with EUCLIDES (1) and then apparently travelled widely. He is said to have visited Egypt and Cyrene, and in 387 visited Italy and Sicily where the luxurious living of the rich repelled him. However, he made friends with the Syracusan DION, son-in-law of the tyrant DIONYSIUS (1) I, who is said improbably to have kidnapped Plato and sold him into slavery. Plato also visited ARCHYTAS of Tarentum, the leading Pythagorean of the day, who, like him, was trying to establish a school. At some date after that he founded a college at Athens for teaching and research, the Academy, based on his house adjacent to a public gymnasium in a grove sacred to the hero Academus, a mile outside the walls. In 367, after the death of Dionysius, he reluctantly returned to Syracuse at Dion's invitation so that he could instruct the tyrant's son and thus make him fit to rule a state that was seriously threatened by the external threat from Carthage. DIONYSIUS (2) II, however, soon grew jealous of the friendship between Plato and Dion and banished the latter, asking Plato to stay. Plato, however, returned home. He went back to Dionysius' court with his nephew SPEUSIPPUS in 361 at the tyrant's invitation, which had been given with a promise to take Plato's teaching seriously, and work was done on a constitution for a new federation of Greek states, but opposition to the project was too strong: Plato found himself in detention and was able to leave for home only after the intervention of Archytas. Having completely failed to influence the affairs of Sicily, he spent the rest of his life in Athens teaching and writing in the

Academy. His most distinguished pupil at that time was ARISTOTLE. He was succeeded as head of the Academy by his nephew Speusippus.

Plato was a copious writer of philosophical works, all of which, together with one or two works falsely attributed to him, have survived. His friend Socrates was the greatest inspiration of his thought, and, as he preferred to write philosophy in the form of dramatic dialogues, he made Socrates the leading figure in them. He differed, however, from the historic Socrates in three ways: he did not marry, he left his philosophical arguments in written form, and he founded a school. A small collection of his elegiac poetry is preserved in the *Greek Anthology*, the most famous being a brief elegy commemorating Dion; however, the authenticity of these poems is dubious. Thirteen letters were attributed to him, of which the first is certainly a forgery. The rest may be pseudonymous (we know there was a flourishing industry in such documents). However, some or all the rest may be authentic and, if so, they supply interesting biographical information. The life and experiences of Plato, however, have no bearing on the substance of his philosophical writings: in the dialogues he is entirely self-effacing and wishes us to concentrate on their stimulus to thought, paying no heed to the personality and life of the author. Besides the published writings, Plato's 'unwritten teachings', of which we only have tantalising glimpses from brief notes in Aristotle's writings, were known to his intimate friends and pupils, such as Aristotle and XENOCRATES, who heard them in Plato's lectures. DIOGENES (5) Laërtius wrote a life of Plato, including details of his will.

His philosophical works are mostly written in dialogue form, in which various speakers express differing approaches to the subject from their own point of view. Even his account of the trial of Socrates in 399, *The Defence Speech of Socrates (Apology)*, is presented as a first-person verbatim account. Plato himself, however, never figures in his dialogues. Though his works are impossible to date, they are usually recognised as falling into three broad periods. The early group, in which Socrates is always a leading participant (the 'Socratic' dialogues), which seems to represent a genuine record of Socrates' philosophical method in which he questions other people about their views, but rarely argues for his own view. The general Socratic axiom that virtue is knowledge emerges in these debates. Besides the *Apology*, this group includes *Crito*, *Euthyphro*, *Ion*, *Lesser Hippias*, *Greater Hippias*, *Laches*, *Lysis*, *Menexenus*, *Protagoras*, *Euthydemus*, *Charmides*, *Lovers*, *Hipparchus*, *Clitophon* and *First Alcibiades*. The middle and late groups are radically different in being longer, expressing positive statements of philosophical theories, and often lacking the dramatic setting of the earlier dialogues. In these later dialogues, the figure of Socrates is used by Plato to express his own views. The middle group consists of *Gorgias*, *Meno*, *Phaedo*, *Drinking Party (Symposium)*, *The Republic* (though Book 1 is clearly much earlier and offers a picture of the historic Socrates) and *Phaedrus*. A transitional group is *Timaeus*, *Critias* and *Theaetetus*. The late works are *Cratylus*, *Parmenides*, *The Sophist*, *The Statesman*, *Philebus* and *The Laws*. Plato's use of the dialogue with its dramatic overtones, humorous moments and even poetic language was an inspired means of sugaring the philosophic pill. Consequently, he is one of the most accessible, indeed charming, of all philosophic writers. However, the method became something of a straitjacket and in his later work it detracts from the clear exposition of argument. He never commits himself to any theory or doctrine nor does he build a hierarchical system of tenets. It is in fact impossible to conclude which, if any, of the views expressed in the dialogues were really owned by Plato. In the middle group, especially *The Republic*, his best-known work, he develops the theory of 'forms' or 'ideas', existing separately in an ideal universe, upon which all material objects are modelled. This theory is itself subjected to criticism in later dialogues. Plato owed a great deal to the Pythagoreans and their interest in mathematics. He was also greatly influenced by PARMENIDES and ZENO (1), whom he presents unhistorically in his dialogue *Parmenides* in argument with a youthful Socrates. It appears that the late dialogues were the product of a man whose experience in trying to teach philosophy in the Academy had made him understand the need to explore philosophical questions in a more positive way. In these discussions, the figure of Socrates becomes an anachronism. In *The Republic*, as he pursues the definition of justice, Plato explores political ideas and draws an interesting analogy between the state and the individual. A much more realistic approach to political philosophy is found in the later dialogues, in particular in *The Statesman*, *The Laws* and *Critias*, in which he returned to the concerns of the previous century and the problems discussed by the earlier pre-Socratic philosophers.

The enduring value of Plato's writings lies in their variety of approach, brilliance of style, depth of subject matter, and in the originality and seriousness of their treatment of the profoundest issues, despite the elusive nature of their author. See R. Kraut (ed.) (1992) *The Cambridge Companion to Plato*, Cambridge: CUP; G. Vlastos (1994) *Platonic Studies*, Cambridge: CUP; and G. Vlastos (1991) *Socratic Studies*, Cambridge: CUP; R.E. Allen (ed.) (1965) *Studies in Plato's Metaphysics*, London: Routledge & Kegan Paul; and I.M. Crombie (1962–3) *An Examination of Plato's Doctrines*, London: Routledge & Kegan Paul, 2 vols.

2. (late C5 BC) An Athenian poet of the Old Comedy who won first prize at the City Dionysia festival in 410. Though his works are lost apart from brief quotations, we know of thirty titles of his plays, many of which are named after prominent politicians (his *Envoys* dates from an actual Athenian embassy to Persia in the 390s). He also appears to have composed burlesque based on myth and to have satirised artistic innovations.

Plotinus (AD 205–269/70) A philosopher from Lycopolis in Egypt, the founder of Neoplatonism. His life is known to us from a memoir by his pupil PORPHYRY. He began attending lectures given by Ammonius Saccas at Alexandria *c*.233. In 242 he accompanied the unsuccessful expedition against Persia of the Roman emperor Gordian III to Mesopotamia in the hope of learning about oriental philosophy. He went to Rome in 244 where he founded a school and taught philosophy until *c*.262 when he retired to Campania where he died. At the age of 50 he started writing philosophical essays, which Porphyry collected by subject into six groups of nine (the *Enneads*), generated by discussions with his pupils. They are difficult reading and were unrevised by Plotinus, who had bad eyesight.

In the works of Plotinus we have the largest and most complete ancient philosophical system after that of ARISTOTLE. His idealist philosophy is focused on the concept of the One (cf. PARMENIDES), which he identifies with the 'Good' of PLATO (1). His philosophy was that existence depends upon the One and all values derive from it; all reality may be compared by analogy with a series of concentric circles set around the One, resulting from its expansion; each circle depends logically on the one inside it (its 'cause') and matter exists on the edge of the outermost circle. There are three grades of reality starting from the One and proceeding outwards: Mind, Soul and Nature. As a person moves outwards, he or she finds lessening unity and increasing individuality. 'Mind' contains the Platonic 'ideas', which it perceives beyond the realm of change and time, where the known and the knower are only distinguished logically. 'Soul' apprehends its objects of perception in a chronological sequence and as distinct from each other. 'Nature' resembles the 'World-soul' of the Stoics: the perceived physical world is, according to Plotinus, a faint dream perceived by Nature. Man may momentarily attain 'ecstasy' and union with the One by a supreme effort of intellectual activity. It is here that Plotinus shows affinity with oriental mysticism. He also contributed in important ways to psychology in the areas of memory, perception and consciousness, as well as to aesthetics and ethics. He makes no mention of Christianity, though later Christian thinkers used his ideas. He was opposed to Gnosticism. See R.T. Wallis (1972) *Neoplatonism*, London: Duckworth; J.M. Rist (1967) *Plotinus*, Cambridge: CUP; and A.H. Armstrong (1940) *The Architecture of the Intelligible Universe in the Philosophy of Plotinus*, Cambridge: CUP.

Plutarch (L. Mestrius Plutarchus) (*c*.AD 46–*c*.121) A biographer and moral philosopher from Chaeronea in Boeotia where he lived most of his life, though he travelled as far as Egypt. He was the son of Autobulus and grandson of Lamprias, both of whom he introduces as characters in his dialogues. In the reign of Domitian he lectured on philosophy in Rome and acquired influential friends there: his patron, the ex-consul L. Mestrius Florus, C. Minicius Fundanus, Q. Sosius Senecio and the Syrian-Athenian PHILOPAPPUS (like Philopappus he too was a lover of Athens). He was appointed *c*.90 as a priest of the shrine at Delphi, whose influence he enhanced, and he was later commemorated there with a bust dedicated by the Delphians and Chaeroneans. He was a pious believer in the old gods and in the collaboration between Rome and her teacher, Greece. He may have held a procuratorship in Achaea, though the evidence for this is weak.

Towards the end of his life he was a magistrate at Chaeronea.

Plutarch was a prolific writer and produced over 200 books. Of these, most of the biographies and many miscellaneous works survive: fifty *Lives*, consisting of twenty-three pairs of 'parallel' lives of famous Greeks and Romans, such as ALEXANDER (3) III the Great and Caesar, Theseus and Romulus, comprising nineteen 'comparisons', and four other lives, including two emperors, Galba and Otho. These biographies are not straightforward accounts of men's lives on historical lines, they were written with a moral purpose: to present useful patterns of behaviour for readers to follow or examples of what to avoid. Plutarch is keen to record certain features of his subjects' lives, for instance their education, entry into public life, points of climax, changes of fortune and latter years. He was glad to introduce anecdotes, especially those with the effect of revealing character. Consequently, the usefulness of the *Lives* for historians is limited.

The rest of his works, loosely entitled *Moralia* or *Moral Essays*, are very mixed in subject matter, for instance rhetorical eulogies of great cities, pleas for good behaviour, advice for the young, advice on marriage, and a consolation written for his wife on their daughter's death. He wrote nine books of witty and learned *Table Talk*. He was a Platonist, though his manner of composition can appear more Aristotelian: his dialogues tend to long speeches and he is often himself a participant. He was interested in prophecy and set four dialogues in Delphi in which he expounded his philosophical and religious views. His aim appears to have been to reconcile Plato's monotheism with the traditional Greek cults to which he was devoted. Though he was well versed in Roman history, his knowledge of Latin may have been weak and he shows little acquaintance with Latin literature. He wrote essays that were critical of Stoic and Epicurean philosophy, and attacked

HERODOTUS in *Herodotus' Spitefulness* for his hostile account of Thebes in the Persian wars. Several spurious works were included in the body of Plutarch's works and some of these are important in their own right: on education, on fate in Platonic thought, and on music. He has always been a popular writer with a flowing, graceful style. He greatly appealed to Byzantine teachers, was influential on Montaigne and Francis Bacon, and was an important source for Shakespeare. He was translated into French by Amyot in the sixteenth century and a little later into English. See C.P. Jones (1971) *Plutarch and Rome*, London: Clarendon Press; and D.A. Russell (1981) *Plutarch*, London: Duckworth. Much of Plutarch's *oeuvre* is translated in the Penguin Classics series.

Polemon 1. (*c*.351–*c*.270 BC) An Athenian philosopher who headed the Academy from *c*.314 until his death. He was converted by his predecessor XENOCRATES from a dissolute life and became a moralist, finding theoretical philosophy sterile. He was a teacher of ZENO (2), the founder of Stoicism, who adopted Polemon's doctrine of living according to nature. Though he wrote much, he contributed nothing new to philosophy. He was succeeded by CRATES (3).

2. (early C2 BC) A Stoic from Ilium who published a book of inscriptions found on dedications and monuments in Athens, Sparta and Delphi. He also published a work attacking ERATOSTHENES.

3. (ruled 37–8 BC) A king of Pontus and the Crimea, the son of Zeno, a rich rhetorician of Laodicea on the Lycus in Asia. He appears to have gained Roman support and citizenship by leading (with his father) the defence of the city against the Parthian invasion of 40. Marcus Antonius, the triumvir, appointed him prefect (governor) of part of Cilicia and Lycaonia in 39, but in 37 transferred it to Cleopatra and sent him to rule Pontus as king instead. He accompanied Antonius on his expedition via Armenia against Parthia in 36 and was captured. He was ransomed and in 35 he assisted at the negotiations between Antonius and his former captor, Artavasdes of Media Atropatene (Azerbaijan). In 34 Antonius added Lesser Armenia to Polemon's kingdom, which he lost in 31 after supporting Antonius in the Actium campaign. Octavian allowed him to keep Pontus and added the Bosporan kingdom (Crimea), which Agrippa helped him to seize. He was killed in 8 by rebels in the Crimea and succeeded in Pontus by his widow Pythodoris.

4. Marcus Antonius (*c*.AD 88–144) A sophist and physiognomist from Laodicea who was distantly related to POLEMON (3). In 130 he was selected to deliver the opening speech of Hadrian's temple of Olympian Zeus at Athens. He published speeches, of which two are extant, imaginary pleas delivered by the fathers of two heroes of the battle of Marathon for the award of a prize of valour to their sons. He also published a work on physiognomy known from translations into Latin and Arabic.

Pollux, Julius (C2 AD) A Greek scholar and rhetorician from Naucratis in Egypt. He wrote an orator's handbook in ten books giving terms that might be used in referring to all kinds of topics in public speaking, entitled *A Glossary* (*Onomasticon*). Each book was prefaced with a letter of dedication addressed to the Roman emperor Commodus. From the eighth book we learn of Pollux's appointment as professor of rhetoric at Athens, and in the last three books he answered the criticisms of his rival, PHRYNICHUS (3). LUCIAN lampooned him in the *Teacher of Rhetoric*. Only an interpolated abridgement of his work has survived, including the story of Heracles' discovery of purple dye. The work is useful for particles of information we would not otherwise have on a variety of subjects, including the Athenian constitution and stage production.

Polyaenus (C2 AD) A Macedonian rhetorician who wrote an extant work on military practice entitled *Stratagems*, which he dedicated to Marcus Aurelius and Lucius Verus with the purpose of helping them plan their campaign against the Parthians (162–6). It is a strange mixture of fact and fiction, but the main purpose is didactic and examples of military successes are taken from Greek and Roman history. It shows signs of the haste with which it was compiled.

Polybius (*c*.200–*c*.118 BC) A Greek historian of Rome, the son of LYCORTAS of Megalopolis. In 180 Polybius carried the ashes of PHILOPOEMEN to burial. Hence in his youth he was at the centre of the politics of the Achaean Confederacy, in which he quickly rose to prominence. He was sent to Alexandria as an envoy in 180, and ten years later was elected *hipparch* ('master of the horse') of the Confederacy. After the Roman victory in 168 at Pydna over Macedonia, Polybius was one of a thousand Achaean noblemen deported to Italy for having failed to assist Aemilius Paullus. Whereas the other captives were scattered through Etruria, Polybius was kept in Rome and befriended by Scipio Aemilianus (the son of Paullus) and became attached to the Scipionic Circle. Scipio took him in 151 to Spain and Africa, where he met Masinissa. In 150 the captives were released and in 146 he was again in Africa and witnessed the destruction of Carthage. He took part in a voyage of exploration on the Atlantic and then returned to Greece, where he helped the Romans to organise the province of Macedonia. He subsequently visited Alexandria and Sardis. In 133 he was present at the siege and fall of Numantia.

Most of his writings are lost, including his biography of Philopoemen, a book on

military tactics, an account of the siege of Numantia and a treatise on the equatorial region of the earth. Substantial parts of his *Histories* (in forty books) survive however, including the whole of Books 1–5. The work covered the period from 220–168 and set out to show how Rome conquered so much of the known world in so short a time, as well as the nature of her constitution. There is an introductory section that starts with the First Punic War, 264–220 (the former date being the end of the *History* of TIMAEUS 2). The first thirty books were published *c*.150, and he later added ten more books to continue the period to 146 and included, in Book 34, a geographical conspectus. Some books are entirely lost, some are known from epitomes and there exist quotations of others of varying lengths. His method involved a temporal progression by Olympiads, as well as a geographical progression from west to east in four blocks (Rome and the west, Greece and Macedonia, Asia, and Egypt). His approach was pragmatic and he used carefully collected and assessed primary evidence, interviewed eye-witnesses, visited sites of important actions and studied public and private records (he had access to Roman official documents through his association with Scipio). He was particularly interested in political and military history, and described the Roman constitution as a mixture of monarchic, oligarchic and democratic features. He was keen to account for actions by determining their causes in the broadest way. Not without bias himself, he criticised other historians for their bias and inaccuracy. However, he was a writer of integrity and strove to record faithfully what was actually done and said. He was used as a source by the Roman historian Livy. See F.W. Walbank (1990) *Polybius*, Berkeley, CA; London: University of California Press; and S. Hornblower (ed.) (1996) *Greek Historiography*, Oxford: Clarendon Press.

Polycles (C2 BC) An Athenian sculptor who settled and worked in Rome. His ancestors had been active sculptors in Athens, and he himself is said by Pliny the Elder to have revived bronze-casting in 156. He made bronzes for Roman patrons, including statues of gods for temples. His brother Dionysius helped him cast a *Jupiter*, and the head of his *Heracles* survives. A *Hermaphrodite* of his has been recognised in the Capitoline type. His style was a revival of that of PRAXITELES.

Polyclitus (*c*.480–*c*.410 BC) A sculptor from Argos who was a pupil of AGELADAS. He mostly worked in bronze, though he made a renowned gold and ivory statue of Hera for the Heraeum (temple of Hera) at Argos. His most famous work was a spear-bearer (*Doryphorus*) of which many copies are believed to exist. He seems to have based his lost technical treatise on sculpture, the *Canon*, on this statue. In this work he explained the mathematical relations between the different parts of the body as applied to the creation of a sculpture. This work was highly influential and remained in vogue until Roman imperial times. Pliny the Elder says its principles were observed like a law. Varro criticised his work for being stereotyped as a result of the rigorous application of his Canon. Polyclitus also made a *Diadumenos* (victor binding on a headband), a *Discus-Thrower* and an *Amazon*, of which copies are identified. The *Westmacott Boy* may be a copy of his bronze of the boxer Cyniscus at Olympia. See J. Boardman (1985) *Greek Sculpture*, London: Thames & Hudson; and A.F. Stewart (1990) *Greek Sculpture*, New Haven, Conn.; London: Yale University Press.

Polycrates 1. (ruled *c*.535–522 BC) A tyrant of Samos, the son of a previous tyrant, Aiaces. Around 535 he seized power with little opposition in company with his two brothers, Pantagnotus and Syloson, but soon took sole power. He made Samos a formidable naval power and annexed some nearby islands, including Rheneia, which he dedicated to Apollo. Polycrates made himself rich through his naval supremacy in the Aegean Sea which allowed him a free hand at piracy. He allied himself with AMASIS (1) of Egypt, but in 525 supported CAMBYSES' invasion of Egypt by supplying him with ships. His sailors, however, mutinied and joined an attempt by Samian aristocrats, with the help of Sparta and Corinth, to unseat him. He survived the revolt, but in 522 was lured to the Asiatic mainland by Oroetes, satrap of Sardis, who deceived Polycrates by pretending to be plotting a revolt from DARIUS (1) I, and crucified him. Samos prospered under Polycrates' rule, and he patronised the arts, receiving ANACREON, IBYCUS and THEODORUS (1) at his court. He improved the harbour with a mole, and may be credited with supplying the city with water by mining a tunnel beneath a mountain. He also constructed the great temple of Hera. See G. Shipley (1987) *A History of Samos, 800–188 BC*, Oxford: Clarendon Press.

2. (*c*.440–*c*.370 BC) An Athenian sophist who wrote a *Prosecution Speech against Socrates*, which he fictitiously assigned to ANYTUS. It is possible that the two *Defence Speeches of Socrates* by PLATO (1) and XENOPHON (1) were responses to Polycrates' work. LIBANIUS also wrote a reply to it, but since his time the work has been lost. Polycrates, who later moved to Cyprus, made paradoxical writings his speciality and wrote works in praise of Clytaemestra and the xenophobic pharaoh Busiris.

Polygnotus (*c*.500–*c*.440 BC) A Greek painter from Thasos who settled in Athens *c*.462 and was befriended by CIMON. In company with MICON, he painted scenes from the Trojan War (*Battle of Amazons* and *Battle of Marathon*) on panels in the Painted Portico (*Stoa*

Poikile) and refused a fee for his work. He was awarded Athenian citizenship for his work. He also painted *The Rape of the Daughters of Leucippus* in the temple of the Dioscuri, and helped in the decoration of the temple of Theseus. At Delphi he painted a *Sack of Troy* and *Odysseus in the Underworld* in the clubhouse of the Cnidians. His pictures of *Odysseus Slaying the Suitors*, *Achilles on Scyros* and *Nausicaa* were in the art gallery of Athens. His works, which are all lost, were described by ARISTOTLE, THEOPHRASTUS and PAUSANIAS (3) from whom we learn of his excellence in delineating character in the human face. Pliny the Elder attributed to him the first representation of transparent drapery. LUCIAN admired his lively facial expressions, though to Theophrastus his style, without shading, seemed old-fashioned. See R. Kebric, *The Paintings in the Cnidian Lesche at Delphi*, Leiden: E.J. Brill.

Polyperchon (*c*.380–*c*.303 BC) A Macedonian commander of ALEXANDER (3) III the Great, the son of Simmias. He commanded a brigade of infantry from his native district of Tymphaea until 324 when he returned home with CRATERUS (1) and the veterans. He acted as governor of Macedonia during the Lamian War and won the trust of ANTIPATER (1), who appointed him regent on his deathbed in 319. He was then confronted by Antipater's son, CASSANDER, as a result of which his position quickly deteriorated. He assisted Athens to a democratic revolution in 318 (against PHOCION), but lost the Peloponnese and returned to Macedonia. In early 316, however, having allied himself with OLYMPIAS against EURYDICE, who was supported by the army, he was driven out. He returned to the Peloponnese and in 315 yielded the regency to ANTIGONUS (1) I the One-eyed. In 309 he again invaded Macedonia, intending to install Alexander's bastard son, Heracles, as king. However, he came to terms with Cassander and in return for recognition as ruler of the Peloponnese he killed Heracles. The end of his career is obscure. See N.G.L. Hammond and F.W. Walbank (1972–1988) *A History of Macedonia* Oxford: Clarendon Press, vol. 3.

Polystratus (early C3 BC) An Epicurean philosopher who was a disciple of EPICURUS and succeeded HERMARCHUS as the third head of the Garden. One work of his survives through preservation in Piso's villa at Herculaneum, *Contempt for the Irrational*. He wrote a lost *On Philosophy* and attacked the Sceptics for their refusal to accept knowledge derived from the senses as reliable.

Polyzelus (late C5 BC) An Athenian poet of the Old Comedy who won four victories at Lenaea festivals. From their titles his plays appear to have ranged from satire of myth to political satire.

Porphyry (AD 234–*c*.305) A Greek-speaking Neoplatonist scholar from Tyre who was originally named Malchus ('king'), but adopted the Greek name, Porphyrius ('purple'). He studied at Athens under Cassius Longinus after which he moved in 263 to Rome and became a disciple of PLOTINUS, whose *Enneads* he edited and whose extant biography he wrote. He was scarcely an original thinker, but, because of his wide interests and habit of quoting his sources, his works, many of which have survived whole or in part, offer useful information from earlier authorities. Seventy-seven titles are known (a few pre-dating his conversion to Plotinism). We have considerable fragments of *Philosophy from Oracles*, giving information about ritual; *Statues*; and a *History of Philosophy* of which only a *Life of Pythagoras* survives complete. His works on Plotinian thought include *Subjects for Reflexion*, an extant random collection of Plotinian propositions, *On Abstinence*, a plea for vegetarianism in four books (written because of the apostasy of his friend Firmus Castricius) which survives whole, as do two letters, *To Anebo*, a critical discussion of religious ritual rejecting animal sacrifice, and *To Marcella*, his wife, giving moral advice. Some fragments of his polemic in fifteen books, *Against Christians*, survive, though the work was officially destroyed in 448 (the critical method he employs in it is based on historical arguments). He also proved the *Book of Zoroaster* to be a forgery. He wrote many commentaries on the classical philosophers – a short commentary on ARISTOTLE's *Categories* survives complete and there are fragments of a longer one. His *Intoduction to Aristotle's Categories* was widely used in the Middle Ages as a textbook on logic. Other philosophical commentaries on PLATO (1), THEOPHRASTUS and PLOTINUS are lost. He wrote an influential commentary on the incomplete *Harmonics* of PTOLEMY (17) and another on his *Tetrabiblos* on astrology. He also wrote a treatise on the quickening of the embryo; *The Cave of the Nymphs in the Odyssey*, an extant, allegorising interpretation of its subject; *Homeric Enquiries*, a landmark study of Homer; and other works about language. See R.T. Wallis (1972) *Neoplatonism*, London: Duckworth; and G. Clark (1999) *Porphyry on Abstinence*, London: Duckworth.

Porus (C4 BC) An Indian king named after the nation (Pauravas), he ruled in the Punjab between the rivers Jhelum and Chenab. He met the invasion of ALEXANDER (3) III the Great with resistance, but was defeated in spring 326 at the River Hydaspes despite his use of elephants in battle. He was a tall, imposing figure and his courage impressed Alexander, who made him an ally and increased the size of his kingdom. He was assassinated in 317 by a Macedonian satrap, Eudamus, and his kingdom was taken by Chandragupta (SANDRACOTTUS), founder of the Maurya kingdom in northern India.

Posidippus 1. (C3 BC) A poet of the New Comedy, born in Macedonia, fragments of whose work survive. He won four victories in the dramatic festivals at Athens from 289. His *Girl Locked Out* was revived a century later and his works influenced Roman comedy. His portrait statue exists. See G. Sifakis (1967) *Studies in the History of Hellenistic Drama*, London: Athlone Press.

2. (C3 BC) A composer of epigrams from Pella in Macedonia who was writing in the 270s. Twenty of his poems, on erotic subjects treated with realism and irony, are in the *Greek Anthology*. He appears to have been regarded with hostility by CALLIMACHUS (3) who nevertheless influenced his work, as did ASCLEPIADES (1). A poem on old age survives on tablets and a further 100 epigrams on various subjects have been preserved on a papyrus roll. See A.D.E. Cameron (1993) *The Greek Anthology*, Oxford: Clarendon Press.

Posidonius (*c*.135–*c*.51 BC) A Stoic philosopher, historian and scientist from Apamea in Syria. He studied philosophy under PANAETIUS in Athens and settled in Rhodes, where he acquired citizenship and set up a school. He travelled extensively for scientific research in Italy, Gaul and Spain, and in late 87 served on an embassy to Rome to represent the Rhodians and had dealings with C. Marius, whom he came to detest. Thereafter, several noted Romans visited him, including Cicero, who studied at the school, and Pompey, of whom Posidonius approved and whose eulogy he wrote.

He wrote *Histories* in fifty-two books starting from 146, the close of POLYBIUS, to the dictatorship of Sulla in 85, possibly incomplete, of which we have some brief quotations by ATHENAEUS. The work, which was centred on the development of Rome, rested on a moralistic theory of historical explanation. As he accepted a unitary theory of history and considered character important in determining events, Posidonius showed a special interest in ethnology, national characteristics and the relationships between the ruling class and the ruled. He decried the Gracchi, Marius, the equestrians and the Greek independence movement, and praised the Roman nobility, the empire and, above all, Pompey. To satisfy himself on his view of the world he did much observation and research of a 'scientific' nature, and wrote extensively about his findings. Though little of his work has survived, we know of works on astronomy, mathematics, geography, meteorology, seismology, zoology, botany and anthropology (some thirty titles are known). He invented a theory connecting the tides and the phases of the moon, and worked out a method to measure the circumference of the earth. He also constructed a globe and made a map. His book, *Oceans*, explored the effects of ocean currents on climate, the connection between astronomic observations and the geographical zones, and human geography.

His Stoicism was orthodox, though he believed that philosophical ideas were capable of development in the light of fresh criticism. He reacted against the ethical teachings of CHRYSIPPUS and preferred to recognise the irrational, natural forces in the mind: the main arguments of his *Emotions* can be recovered from GALEN. He also wrote on logic and natural philosophy, poetry and rhetoric. He had an enormous influence both on his contemporaries and on posterity until the Dark Ages. He was more appreciated and studied for his work in history and the sciences than for his philosophical system. However, when Cicero asked him to write a history of his consulship, Posidonius tactfully declined. See A.A. Long (1971) *Problems in Stoicism*, London: Athlone; and J. Barnes and M.T. Griffin (eds) (1997) *Philosophia Togata*, Oxford: Clarendon Press.

Pratinas (C5 BC) A playwright from Phlius who worked in Athens at the time of AESCHYLUS and who composed tragedies, dithyrambs and satyr plays (the majority of his works were satyr plays). Only one fragment survives in ATHENAEUS (14. 617).

Praxagoras (C4 BC) A Greek physician from Cos. He was an anatomist who had studied the Sicilian medical tradition (see PHILISTION). He first distinguished between veins and arteries, rejecting the theory that respiration is a cooling system for the body: he taught that *pneuma* (breathed air) is conducted by the arteries to the extremities of the body by way of *neura* (fine arteries). He held that blood, circulated round the body by the veins, is a product of digested food. He considered the pulse important for diagnosis of diseases, most of which he considered to be caused by an imbalance in the humours owing to a failure of digestion. He seems to have used this theory in formulating treatments that consisted of purges and regulating the diet. He probably taught HEROPHILUS. He marks a transition between old medicine and the new medicine of Alexandria, and GALEN recognised his importance. His work survives only in fragments. See J. Longrigg (1994) *Greek Rational Medicine*, London: Routledge.

Praxiteles (*c*.400–330 BC) An Athenian sculptor, the son of the sculptor CEPHISODOTUS. He worked in bronze and marble, preferring the latter. In a long career he produced about eighty statues, making figures of youthful gods his speciality. However, no work of his is known to survive. His most famous statue was the *Aphrodite* of Cnidus which we know from copies (it portrayed the goddess nude and ready for a bath, holding her dress in her left hand, with a water jug beside her). His model was said to be Phryne, who also modelled for APELLES. He was careful with the finish of the surface of his marbles, many of which NICIAS (2) painted. Other works known from copies are *Apollo Killing a Lizard*, *Eros* of Thespiae, *Eros* of Parium, *Satyrs*, *Aphrodite* of Arles and *Apollo Lynceus*.

The famous *Hermes and Dionysus*, found at Olympia, is probably too late to be his (despite what PAUSANIAS (3) says). Praxiteles was very influential and his style was often imitated, especially by Alexandrian artists. He set a pattern for the female nude which lasted throughout ancient times. He had a son, CEPHISODOTUS, who worked with him. See A.F. Stewart (1990) *Greek Sculpture*, New Haven, Conn.; London: Yale University Press; and B.S. Ridgway (1989) *Hellenistic Sculpture*, Madison, WI: University of Wisconsin Press.

Proaeresius (AD 276–367) A Greek rhetorician from Cappadocia who became professor of the subject at Athens, where he taught the Christian writers Basil and Gregory, and the Roman emperor Julian. He spent some time in Gaul at the court of the emperor Constans, and was offered and refused a chair of rhetoric at Rome. He resigned his chair in 362 when Julian forbade Christians to teach, even though he was exempted from the rule, and resumed it after Julian's death.

Prodicus (C5 BC) A Greek sophist and teacher of rhetoric from Ceos, an acquaintance of SOCRATES. He took advantage of diplomatic missions, which he was appointed to carry out, to advance his career as a teacher, offering instruction for which he charged high fees. PLATO (1) introduces him as a character in his *Protagoras* where his concern with the correct application of words is introduced with a hint at his pedantry. His writings are lost, though we have in XENOPHON (1) a retelling of his myth of the *Choice of Heracles*. His accounts of the origin of religion relied on naturalism.

Protagoras (*c.*490–420 BC) A Greek sophist from Abdera who travelled among the Greek states and spent much time at Athens. He was the first to call himself a sophist and to teach for payment. He was highly respected at Athens, where he

spent much time and where PERICLES invited him in 444 to draw up a constitution for the colony of Thurii. The story of his trial and banishment is a later invention, which is inconsistent with the evidence of PLATO (1). He wrote two lost books: *Truth*, in which he pronounced his famous principle that 'Man is the measure of all things'; and *The Gods*, in which he professes an agnostic approach to religion. His underlying teaching seems to favour a relativist attitude to knowledge (that sense-impressions and beliefs are true only for the person who holds them), thus rejecting objectivity. Plato refuted this doctrine in the *Theaetetus*, and DEMOCRITUS attacked it. We have a portrait of Protagoras as a thinker in Plato's dialogue of that name, in which he is shown proposing a doctrine of human society in which justice is based on a social contract between the citizens. He rejects the principle of retribution as the justification for punishment in favour of deterrence. See G.B. Kerferd (1981) *The Sophistic Movement*, Cambridge: CUP; and C. Farrar (1988) *The Origins of Democratic Thinking*, Cambridge: CUP.

Protogenes (late C4 BC) A Greek painter and writer on art from Caunus in Caria who worked mostly on Rhodes. He was acquainted with APELLES, who is said to have considered that his work lacked grace. His masterpieces were a portrait of an imaginary Ialysus, the founder of Rhodes, and of a resting satyr. He also painted portraits of contemporaries, for instance, ARISTOTLE's mother, ANTIGONUS (1) I and PHILICUS. He wrote two lost books on painting. See M. Robertson (1975) *History of Greek Art*, Cambridge: CUP, vol. 1.

Prusias 1. I (reigned *c.*230–182 BC) A king of Bithynia, known as *Cholos* ('The Lame'), the son of Ziaëlas and grandson of NICOMEDES (1) I. In 220 he made war on Byzantium and in 216 he defeated the invading Galatians. He made a marriage alliance with PHILIP (3) V of Macedonia and supported him in his wars against Pergamon. During the First Macedonian War in 208, he attacked Pergamon when its king, ATTALUS (1) I, was engaged in Greece on the side of Rome against Macedonia, and was included as an ally of Macedonia in the treaty of Phoenice in 205. In 202 he was given Cius and Myrlea on the south coast of the Sea of Marmora by Philip, which he renamed respectively Prusias and Apamea. He took parts of Mysia and Phrygia from Pergamon in 198 and attacked Heraclea on the Black Sea from which he took Cierus, renaming it Prusias-on-the-Hypius, and Tieum on the Black Sea. In 191, when war broke out between Rome and ANTIOCHUS (3) III, he remained neutral, having received assurances from the Scipios, who conducted the Roman campaign. He gave refuge c.188 to the fugitive Hannibal, whose services he used as his admiral. In 188 he began a war with EUMENES (3) II of Pergamon which he lost in 183 when he was forced to return territory he had earlier taken from Attalus. Flamininus then demanded the surrender of Hannibal, who preferred to kill himself. Prusias was succeeded by his son, PRUSIAS (2) II.

2. II (reigned 182–149 BC) A king of Bithynia, known as *Cynegetes* ('The Hunter'), the son of PRUSIAS (1) I. He refrained from conflict with Rome and in 181 joined EUMENES (3) II of Pergamon in an attack on King PHARNACES (1) I of Pontus. He married a sister of PERSEUS, king of Macedonia, but did not help him against Rome. In 168, after the fall of Perseus, he went to plead with the Senate at Rome (his abject attitude to the Romans earned him the contempt of the Greeks). He made war on Pergamon (156–154) against the orders of Rome and was defeated. Rome imposed an indemnity and Prusias sent his eldest son, NICOMEDES (2) II, to Rome to plead for release. Nicomedes, however, revolted, believing that his father meant to kill him

if he failed and replace him with a half-brother. He returned to Bithynia and with help from ATTALUS (2) II of Pergamon caused his father to flee to Nicomedia where the citizens, who had no love for Prusias, were permitted to stone him.

Ptolemaïs (early C1? AD) A musicologist from Cyrene: she wrote a lost introduction to Pythagorean musical theory which was used by PTOLEMY (17).

Ptolemy (Ptolemaeus) The name of all fifteen Macedonian kings of Egypt.

1. I Soter ('Saviour') (367–282 BC) A Macedonian general and childhood friend of ALEXANDER (3) III the Great, the son of Lagus and ARSINOË (1), and later the satrap and king of Egypt. He served as a member of the 'Companions', an elite corps, and took part in the marriage of Macedonians with Persian women at Susa in 324, marrying Apame, the daughter of ARTABAZUS, but he soon divorced her. Shortly after Alexander died in 323, Ptolemy gained the satrapy of Egypt. In 322, when PERDICCAS (2) was conveying Alexander's embalmed corpse to Macedonia, Ptolemy seized it at Damascus and took it to Egypt to bury in the city of Alexandria, which the king had planned but never seen. He executed CLEOMENES (3), who had illegally enriched himself, and also attacked and took Cyrene which was in the hands of Greek mercenaries. The next year, when Perdiccas, his superior, invaded Egypt, he avoided fighting him but contrived his assassination. In 315 he joined a league of the 'successors' (*diadochi*) of Alexander to oppose the claims of ANTIGONUS (1) I the One-eyed, who was finally defeated in 301 at Ipsus. In 312 he forestalled an invasion by DEMETRIUS (3) I the Besieger by his victory at the battle of Gaza, but lost control of Cyprus to him in 306. In 305, following Antigonus' precedent, he took the title of king, ruling Egypt from Alexandria and Ptolemais, a city he founded in

Upper Egypt. Though his administration was Greek in language and culture, he consulted Egyptian experts, and in Egypt proper he and his descendants assumed the character and powers of the pharaohs. He developed the worship of a new, composite god, Sarapis, previously established by Nectanebo at Saqqara, to unite native and Greek settlers in devotion to a common deity, for whom he built a shrine at Alexandria. In 304 he rescued the Rhodians from a siege by Demetrius and won the title 'Saviour'. In 301, after Ipsus Ptolemy reoccupied southern Syria and Palestine, and in 295 he recovered Cyprus and advanced his influence into the Cyclades and Asia Minor. The Macedonian kingdom he established in Egypt lasted until the Roman conquest by Augustus in 30.

Shortly after his arrival in Egypt, Ptolemy married Eurydice, daughter of ANTI-PATER (1), by whom he had six children. However, he divorced her at an unknown date and took his half-sister, BERENICE (1) I, already his mistress, as his wife: she was the mother of PTOLEMY (2) II and ARSI-NOË (2) II. Ptolemy was also the writer of a lost history of the reign of Alexander the Great, of which little is known apart from a quotation in STRABO, and which ARRIAN used as a main source for his extant *Anabasis*. It was almost certainly very favourable to Alexander's image and also showed Ptolemy as a prominent commander. On the advice of DEMETRIUS (2) of Phaleron he also founded the 'Museum', a college of leading intellectuals, and participated in its debates. During his reign the famous library was also established. See P. Green (1990) *Alexander to Actium*, Berkeley, CA; Los Angeles: University of California Press; P.M. Fraser (1962–84) *Ptolemaic Alexandria*, 3 vols, Oxford: Clarendon Press; and L. Pearson (1960) *Lost Histories of Alexander*, New York: American Philological Association.

2. II Philadelphus ('sister-loving') (308–246 BC) A king of Egypt and other territories, the son of PTOLEMY (1) I Soter and his third wife BERENICE (1) I. He was born in Cos and his father showed his preference for him over his older half-brother, PTOLEMY (16) Ceraunus, by making him joint king in 285. He succeeded in 282 and spent much of his reign in conflict with the Seleucid kings. The First Syrian War (274–271 BC) against ANTI-OCHUS (1) I led to expansion into Asia to include Judaea, Peraea and most of Phoenicia, as well as Cyprus, Cilicia, Lycia. He supported Athens in the War of CHREMO-NIDES (266–261 BC), fought in Greece and on the Aegean Sea, and lost some territory as a result. The Second Syrian War (260–253 BC) brought him no further gains and he restored relations with the Seleucids by marrying his daughter, BERE-NICE (2) Syra, to ANTIOCHUS (2) II. In 250 he recovered Cyrene and established trade down the Red Sea to the east. He built the Pharos (lighthouse) on an island off Alexandria, and other buildings. He developed the bureaucracy and tax system of which numerous papyri testify. In 289 he married his niece, ARSINOË (3) I, daughter of LYSIMACHUS, who was the mother of his successor. In 279, accusing her of plotting against him, he exiled her and married his sister, ARSINOË (2) II, formerly the wife of Lysimachus, who added her Aegean territory to his empire and whom he honoured greatly. He had no children by her.

3. III Euergetes ('Benefactor') (284–221 BC) Eldest son and successor in 246 of PTOLEMY (2) II Philadelphus. On his accession he married BERENICE (3) II, daughter of MAGAS of Cyrene and mother of his heir, and brought Cyrene under his rule. He fought the Third Syrian War (246–241) against SELEUCUS (2) II to support the claim of his nephew, the son of his sister, BERENICE (2), to the Seleucid throne, and expanded his possessions in Syria and Asia Minor, but was compelled to make terms. He was involved in Greek affairs, supporting the Achaean League and ARATUS (2) of Sicyon against Macedonia until *c*.227 when Aratus sought help from the Macedonians. After that he supported CLEOMENES (2) III of Sparta whom he allowed to settle in Egypt when he was exiled. He founded the temple of Sarapis at Alexandria.

4. IV Philopator ('father-loving') (*c*.244–204 BC) A son of PTOLEMY (3) III Euergetes and BERENICE (3) II, he acceded in 221 and in 217 married his full sister ARSINOË (4) III. ANTIOCHUS (3) III invaded Palestine in 219 and began the Fourth Syrian War, but in 217 Ptolemy won the battle of Raphia using native Egyptian forces and so restored his possessions in Coele Syria. However, in 207 Upper Egypt, including its capital, Thebes, seceded from the kingdom for some twenty years. He built a tomb complex for his family round the tomb of Alexander in the Palace Quarter of Alexandria. His wife was murdered *c*.205 in a palace *coup* and he himself was murdered a few months later, but his death was kept secret by his ministers, Sosibius and Agathocles.

5. V Epiphanes ('revealed') (210–180 BC) He became king at the age of 6 and was a tool in the hands of the ministers, Sosibius and Agathocles. The result was a sustained attack from both outside Egypt and within: in the Fifth Syrian War Egypt was attacked by ANTIOCHUS (3) III and PHILIP (3) V and lost her territories in the Aegean and Asia Minor, and in 200, after the battle of Phanium, Palestine was also lost. In 197 Ptolemy came of age and was crowned Pharaoh at Memphis by the ancient Egyptian ritual, an occasion commemorated by the inscription on the Rosetta Stone. He made peace with Antiochus in 195 and two years later married his daughter, CLEOPATRA (2) I. He won back Upper Egypt in 186.

6. VI Philometor ('mother-loving') (*c*.191–145 BC) He succeeded in 180 at the age of about 12 and ruled jointly with his mother, CLEOPATRA (2) I, until her death in 176. The following year he married his sister CLEOPATRA (3) II. In 170 ANTIOCHUS (4) IV began the Sixth Syrian War and invaded Egypt twice. He was crowned as its king in 168, but abandoned his claim on the orders of the Roman Senate. From 169–164 Egypt was ruled by a triumvirate consisting of Ptolemy, his sister-queen and his younger brother known as PTOLEMY (8) VIII, but in 164 he was driven out by his brother and went to Rome to seek support, which he received from Cato. He was restored the following year by the intervention of the Alexandrians and ruled uneasily, cruelly suppressing frequent rebellions, until he was killed in Syria, fighting against ALEXANDER (10) Balas.

7. VII Neos Philopator ('new father-loving') A son of PTOLEMY (6) VI Philometor who reigned briefly with his father in 145 BC and for a short time after that. He was murdered by his uncle, PTOLEMY (8) VIII Euergetes II, who succeeded him.

8. VIII Euergetes II (*c*.182–116 BC) The younger brother of PTOLEMY (6) VI Philometor, known familiarly as Pot-Belly (*Physcon*). After ruling jointly with his brother and his sister, CLEOPATRA (3) II, between 169–164, he expelled PTOLEMY (6) VI, but the following year was himself forced to leave Alexandria and take up rule over Cyrene. The Roman Senate, despite his appeal, gave him no material help. However, in 154 he willed his possessions to Rome. In 145 he returned to succeed his brother, eliminated his nephew, PTOLEMY (7) VII Neos Philopator, and married his brother's widow, his own sister, CLEOPATRA (3) II. He later took his niece, Cleopatra's daughter, CLEOPATRA (4) III, as a junior wife. About this time the Roman Senate sent Scipio Aemilianus to investigate the state of Ptolemy's kingdom. In 132 Cleopatra III rebelled and tried to replace Euergetes with the Seleucid king of Syria, DEMETRIUS (7) II, and a long internal war followed. Euergete finally had Demetrius assassinated in 125 and a public reconciliation between the dynasts took place the following year and Ptolemy Euergetes VIII, Cleopatra II and Cleopatra III then ruled together until his death. Euergetes' reign was characterised by its brutality and vindictiveness towards Alexandria, which had supported his brother.

9. IX Soter II (142–81 BC) The elder son of PTOLEMY (8) VIII Euergetes II, known as Chickpea (*Lathyrus*). His mother was CLEOPATRA (4) III who was a dominant force during much of his reign. He married two of his sisters, Cleopatra IV, who bore Berenice IV, and Cleopatra V Selene, who bore two sons. His mother inherited the kingdom in 116 and appointed him to rule jointly with her and his aunt, though the latter died soon after. However, his mother preferred her younger son (PTOLEMY (10) X Alexander. After several rebellions, in 107 she succeeded in driving him out and he became king of Cyprus. He also became involved in the affairs of Syria, and won a victory over the JEWS. He reconquered Egypt in 89/9. He ruled jointly with his daughter, Cleopatra Berenice, until his death.

10. X Alexander (*c.*140–88 BC) Formerly governor of Cyprus (116–107), he joined his mother on the throne of Egypt, exchanging roles with PTOLEMY (9) IX Soter II. Alexander and his mother quarrelled constantly, and when she died in 101 he was believed to have killed her. Alexander married his brother's daughter, Cleopatra Berenice, making her joint ruler.

In 88 the Alexandrians drove Alexander out of Egypt. He made attempts from Syria and Asia Minor to regain his kingdom, but died in a sea-battle.

11. XI Alexander II (*c.*100–80 BC) A son of PTOLEMY (10) X who was installed in power by the Roman general Sulla in 80 with his stepmother, Cleopatra Berenice, as his wife and partner in power. However, he murdered her within days and was himself murdered by the Alexandrians. Thus, the legitimate line of Ptolemy was extinguished. He willed his kingdom to Rome.

12. XII Neos Dionysos ('new Dionysus') (ruled 80–51 BC) An illegitimate son of PTOLEMY (9) IX, popularly known as the Piper (*Auletes*), he was chosen as king by the Alexandrians and married his sister, Cleopatra Tryphaena. In 58, however, the Alexandrians drove him into exile because of his pro-Roman policy but, after three years spent in Rome trying to rouse support, he was restored by the Roman governor of Syria, Gabinius, though he had to pay him a huge bribe which, together with other expenditures to gain Roman support, crippled the Egyptian economy. He left his kingdom to his two oldest children, CLEOPATRA (5) VII and PTOLEMY (13) XIII.

13. XIII (63–47 BC) The elder son of PTOLEMY (12) XII Neos Dionysos, he ruled jointly until 47 with his older sister, CLEOPATRA (5) VII, whom he married. He had Pompey murdered in 48 when he arrived in Egypt fleeing from Julius Caesar, in order to gratify the latter, but greatly offended him. He was defeated in the war that ensued and was drowned in the Nile.

14. XIV (59–44 BC) The younger son of PTOLEMY (12) XII, he replaced his elder brother as king in 47 and married his sister, CLEOPATRA (5) VII. Three years later she had him assassinated.

15. XV (47–30 BC) The son of Caesar and CLEOPATRA (5) VII. His nickname 'Caesarion' means 'Caesar's son', but his official name and style was Ptolemy XV Caesar Theos Philopator and Philometor ('father-loving and mother-loving god'). He was his mother's first child. In 44

Cleopatra made him joint ruler with herself, and in 34 he was given the title 'King of Kings' at the Donations made by Antonius. Octavian regarded Egypt as the principal threat to Rome and, as Antonius declared that Caesar had acknowledged Caesarion as his son, he had Oppius write a pamphlet to disprove the claim. Cleopatra sent him to a place of safety after Actium, but he was tricked into returning to Alexandria and killed on Octavian's order.

16. Ptolemy (Ptolemaeus) Ceraunus ('Thunderbolt') (died 279 BC) A king of Macedonia, the eldest son of PTOLEMY (1) I, king of Egypt. In 285 his father made his younger half-brother PTOLEMY (2) II his heir. Ceraunus left the country and appealed unsuccessfully in turn to SELEUCUS (1) I and LYSIMACHUS to assist him in gaining the throne of Egypt. He was believed to have assassinated Agathocles, eldest son of Lysimachus, to ensure the succession of the son of his half-sister, ARSINOË (2) II, as king of Lysimachus' territories. He moved to the court of Seleucus and joined him in the war that he began in 282 against Lysimachus. Some months after the battle of Corupedium, in 281, he assassinated Seleucus near Lysimacheia in Thrace and proclaimed himself king (namely of the Macedonians). He made agreements with the cities of western Asia Minor and turned his attention to Europe, aiming at the throne of Macedonia. He defeated his rival, ANTIGONUS (2) II Gonatas, in a sea-battle and made his headquarters at Cassandreia, inviting Arsinoë to join him, but after he murdered her children she fled to Egypt. He was killed defending Macedonia from an invasion by the Galatians.

17. Ptolemy (Claudius Ptolemaeus) (c.AD 100–170) A writer in Greek on mathematics, astronomy, geography and music. He was born at Ptolemaïs in Egypt and lived and worked in Alexandria, where he became head of the Museum. His writings on astronomy and geography were very influential for centuries to come, and his work on trigonometry was seminal. He did original research in a number of areas, but adopted as axiomatic the theory of HIPPARCHUS (2) of a geocentric universe (a theory that he refined in detail). His greatest work, known to us by its Arabic title as the *Almagest* (viz. *Megiste* sc *Syntaxis* 'The Great Collection'), was the *Mathematical Collection* in thirteen books, which covers astronomy and related mathematical tables and computations. Ptolemy made the meticulous observations on which this work was based between 127–147. In it he describes the nature of the visible universe, the theory and practice of trigonometry, and his theories regarding the Sun, Moon, eclipses, fixed stars and planets. Though many of the works of earlier writers perished, mainly because of the success of Ptolemy's work, we can still evaluate their contributions to science: he reformed and clarified his predecessors' work and left a lucid, complete and authoritative account of the subject with the mathematical basis required to validate it. This work remained the standard textbook on the subject for 1,300 years. His other works on astronomy were the *Hypotheses of the Planets* in two books, containing instructions for building a planetarium, including the exposition of a theory that the heavenly bodies were fixed upon contiguous concentric spheres, a theory that was widely accepted in the Middle Ages; *Planispherium*, describing the theory of the construction of the astrolabe; *Analemma* (preserved in Latin), on the mathematics underpinning sundials; *Handy Tables*, expanding tables given in the *Almagest*; *Phases of the Fixed Stars*, of which the second book survives, giving the risings and settings of certain bright stars. His earliest work, *The Canobic Inscription*, a list of astronomic constants, is repeated and corrected in the *Almagest*.

Of equal importance was his *Geography* in eight books, perhaps with an atlas appended, in which he tried to collect the information to make maps of the whole known world. Unfortunately his work is blemished by a number of serious errors, including an underestimate of the earth's circumference and an elongation of the Mediterranean Sea, but the method it rests on is fundamentally sound and it was a remarkable achievement that had enormous influence on notions of geography until the age of exploration. He aimed to define the positions of a list of places in terms of latitude and longitude, and gave information about their principal features. He also wrote *Influences* in four books on astrology to complement the *Almagest*, as well as *Optics* (four of the five books are mostly extant in a Latin translation from Arabic), which deals with vision, colour, mirrors, the reflection of light and refraction, and is a considerable advance on the work of EUCLID. His work on musical theory, entitled *Harmonics*, follows not uncritically the mathematical theories of the Pythagoreans and at the same time employs practical methods and tests theory by perception. His book includes invaluable information about the octave, tones and the contemporary tuning of instruments, and describes the experiments and apparatus he used. One philosophical work, a short treatise on epistemology entitled *Judgement and Decision*, is attributed to his pen.

Some lost works are reported by other writers: *Dimension*, proving that there are only three dimensions; *Mechanics*; and *The Elements*. See G.J. Toomer (1984) *Ptolemy's Almagest*, London: Duckworth; G. Grasshoff (1990) *The History of Ptolemy's Star Catalogue*, New York: Springer; and A. Barker (ed.) (1989) *Greek Musical Writings*, vol. 2, Cambridge: CUP.

Pyrrhon (*c.*365–275 BC) A philosopher from Elis who was the founder of Scepticism. He is said to have been poor and to have begun life as a painter, and then to have studied under the Megarian

Bryson, and under DEMOCRITUS' follower ANAXARCHUS, and to have travelled with the latter in the retinue of ALEXANDER (3) III the Great on his expedition into Asia in 334. On this journey he met Indian gymnosophist philosophers and Persian magi, and was influenced by their teachings. He returned to Elis, where he lived quietly, gaining the respect of his fellow citizens, who elected him to a priesthood. He wrote nothing apart from a poem addressed to Alexander, now lost, and his philosophy was put in writing by his disciple, TIMON (2) of Phlius. He taught that tranquillity can be gained by the practice of withholding commitment to the truth or falsity of any proposition; as all organic beings are subject to continuous renewal and change, we are unable to know anything of them but appearances. The wise man, therefore, refrains from passing judgement, accepts appearances without claiming their truth, and tries to attain tranquillity. Timon castigated other philosophers for their concern for unattainable truth and contrasted their anxiety with Pyrrhon's calm serenity.

Pyrrhus (319–272 BC) The most famous Molossian king of Epirus, the son of Aeacides, and cousin of ALEXANDER (3) III the Great. As a youth he was exiled from his kingdom, over which he had reigned as a minor from 307–302, when CASSANDER seized it, and he took refuge with DEMETRIUS (3) I the Besieger. He was present at the battle of Ipsus in 301 and was sent by Demetrius as a hostage to PTOLEMY (1) I, whose stepdaughter Antigone he married. In 295 he won back his kingdom with the help of Ptolemy and AGATHOCLES (1) of Syracuse and ruled jointly with his kinsman, Neoptolemus, whom he quickly liquidated. He tried to gain the throne of Macedonia, but in 294 Demetrius seized it, though Pyrrhus won territory at the expense of that kingdom, namely southern Illyria, Parauaea and Tymphaea, and he also took Ambracia, Amphilochia and Acarnania.

On Antigone's death he remarried, wedding a daughter of Agathocles, and was given Corcyra and Leucas as her dowry. He took other wives in addition, namely the daughters of the Illyrian rulers of Paeonia and Dardania. In 291 war broke out between Pyrrhus and Demetrius, and in 287 the latter was forced to flee. Pyrrhus declared himself king of Macedonia and occupied half Macedonia and Thessaly, but three years later, in 284, LYSIMACHUS, the ruler of Thrace, now freed from the threat posed by Demetrius in Asia Minor, drove him out of Macedonia and established himself as king, and Pyrrhus turned his attention to the west.

Invited by the Tarentines in 281 to help them against Rome, he transported a force of 25,000 men on foot, 3,000 cavalry and 20 elephants to Italy. In 280 he defeated the consul Laevinus at Heraclea, sustaining such huge losses as to coin the phrase 'Pyrrhic victory'. He marched on Rome with a large force of Italians and Greek inhabitants of southern Italy, and, after failing to negotiate peace, won another battle in 279 at Ausculum, again losing heavy casualties. He then diverted his attention to Sicily where he answered an appeal from Syracuse and Messina for aid against the Carthaginians. Though he won some early successes, he quarrelled with his allies and was defeated at Lilybaeum. In 276 he withdrew from Sicily with little to show for his pains, and in 275 was crushed near Malventum (from then on it was renamed 'Beneventum') by the consul, M. Curius Dentatus. He retired to Epirus with a third of those he had led out, and left a small garrison in Tarentum. He successfully attacked Macedonia in 273, drove out King ANTIGONUS (2) II Gonatas and resumed his kingship, but became unpopular when he pillaged the royal tombs at Aegae. He invaded the Peloponnese, attacked Sparta unsuccessfully and was killed in a riot at Argos by a roof-tile which a woman threw at him.

Despite his foreign adventures he did much for Epirus, completing its hellenization and building among other structures the great theatre at Dodona.

Pythagoras 1. (C6 BC) A philosopher and mystic from Samos, which he left c.531 to escape the tyranny of POLYCRATES (1). His wife's name was said to be THEANO, and his daughters were Myia and Arignote. He settled at Croton in southern Italy and gathered round himself a religious community of men and women to live according to a rule he devised: they were bound to secrecy about their doctrines and had to practise a strict regime of abstinence from certain foods, especially animal flesh, in the belief that the souls of men and animals transmigrate at death into other creatures, including plants (cf. PHERECYDES 1). In this community Pythagoras was regarded as sanctified and all discoveries made by his disciples were attributed to him. He taught that the body is a tomb (*Soma Sema* literally 'body tomb') from which man's soul may escape by the practice of asceticism to purify the soul from the corruption of the body so as to enable it to escape from the cycle of reincarnations, to which all impure life was regarded as doomed, and so eventually to lose its individuality by being merged into a universal soul. These ideas and practices must have been unacceptably strange to the people of Croton as they would, for example, have meant the self-imposed exclusion of the Pythagorean community from sacrifices to the gods. The followers of Pythagoras were hounded out of Croton. He himself went to Metapontum, where he died c.497. His companions separated and soon communities of Pythagoreans were established in many places in the Greek world.

Anything that Pythagoras may have written was quickly lost, partly on account of the secrecy adopted by his movement. We are acquainted with some of his ideas through the works of PLATO (1), as well as through a mass of legend that grew up around him – such that the Greeks of the succeeding generations had no reliable knowledge of his life or teachings. It was believed, however, that he made important discoveries about music and mathematics, namely that he discovered the numerical ratios which determine the principal intervals in the musical scale. Pythagoreans thus came to interpret the universe in terms of number and proportion. They used an arithmetic notation that represented numbers as patterns of dots (from which the notion of 'square numbers' is derived), and Pythagoras was believed to have postulated the '*tetraktys* of ten' (the supreme number, ten, being the sum of 1, 2, 3 and 4). The order (*kosmos*), which was displayed by music and mathematics, led the Pythagoreans to a belief in the organised order of the whole universe, to which they first applied the term *kosmos* ('order') with the added sense of 'beauty'. The theorem attributed to Pythagoras by Euclid had been known long before, though he may have refined its proof. The later Pythagoreans adopted a theory of the universe according to which the earth was a sphere and, according to ARISTOTLE, they believed that all the heavenly bodies and the Earth revolve around a central fire following strict rules of geometry. The chief exponents of Pythagorean doctrine were PHILOLAUS and ARCHYTAS, and in the sphere of medicine, ALCMAEON. Plato and (apparently) SOCRATES were much influenced by Pythagorean thought, especially by their mathematics and doctrine of the soul as belonging to an eternal world. The *Phaedo* of Plato exemplifies Pythagorean religious ideas, and his *Timaeus* their cosmology. Some of Pythagoras' teachings are remarkably similar to those of his contemporary, Gautama Buddha. See W.K.C. Guthrie (1962–78) *A History of Greek Philosophy*, vol. 1, Cambridge: CUP; and *The Greek Philosophers*; J. Barnes (1982) *The Presocratic Philosophers*, vol. 1, London: Routledge & Kegan Paul; W. Burkert (1972) *Lore and Science in Ancient Pythagoreanism*, trans. by E.L. Minar, Cambridge, MA: Harvard University Press; and G.S. Kirk, J.E. Raven and M. Schofield (1982) *The Presocratic Philosophers*, Cambridge: CUP.

2. (C5 BC) A Greek sculptor from Samos who settled at Rhegium (Reggio di Calabria) after the failure of the Ionic Revolt in 494. He was a rival of MYRON, and worked only in bronze. Several of his works are mentioned by Pliny the Elder, who credits him with a move towards naturalism, and PAUSANIAS (3).

Pytheas (late C4 BC) A navigator and astronomer from Massilia (Marseille) who explored the Atlantic seaboard of Europe. He wrote two books, *The Ocean* and *The Circumnavigation*, of which little remains, and which were met with disbelief. From later authorities (Pliny the Elder, DIODORUS (6) and STRABO) we learn that he sailed from Cádiz along the coasts of Iberia and Gaul to Britain, passing the island of Ushant and visiting Cornwall, which he called Belerion, and circumnavigating Britain, whose climate and peoples he described in his book. He then sailed north and discovered a country which he named Thule (possibly part of Norway), entered the Baltic, and visited an island where amber was plentiful, probably near the mouth of the Vistula. He was interested in map-making, and used his observations of the stars to determine the latitude of Massilia and other places in Gaul, as well as Britain. See C.F.C. Hawkes (1977) *Pytheas: Europe and the Greek Explorers*, Oxford: Blackwell.

Pythius (C4 BC) An architect from Priene in Asia Minor to whom are attributed the design of the Mausoleum of Halicarnassus and, perhaps on a commission from ALEXANDER (3) III the Great, the temple of Athena Polias at Priene, both of the Ionic order. He wrote a lost work on architecture in which he rejected the use of the Doric order for sacred buildings because of difficulties caused by the spacing of triglyphs. He is referred to by Vitruvius and Pliny the Elder.

R

Rhianus (*c*.275–*c*.210 BC) A Cretan poet and Homeric scholar who was born a slave and worked as an attendant in a wrestling school. He was liberated, educated, and became a teacher. Of his poetry, only eleven epigrams and a couple of fragments of his Messenian epic have survived. He wrote the following lost works: an epic poem in fourteen books on *Heracles*; epics based on the history of Thessaly, Elis, Achaea; and most famously, an epic on the Second Messenian War in at least six books, centred on the story of ARISTOMENES, which PAUSANIAS (3) used. The longest fragment, twenty-one lines in epic metre, may be an entire poem (it is an attack on the folly of mankind). Rhianus also produced an edition of the poems of HOMER: although it is lost, some forty-five references to it show his good sense. His works seem to have displayed much geographical knowledge. Rhianos seems to represent a reaction against the doctrine of CALLIMACHUS (3) that a long poem was inartistic.

Rhinthon (early C3 BC) A writer of farces from Tarentum in southern Italy, the son of a potter. NOSSIS, who wrote his extant epitaph, says that he was a Syracusan. Titles of his lost plays suggest that many were burlesques of works by EURIPIDES. A few fragments, in the Doric dialect, survive. See also SCIRAS

Rhodopis *see* Sappho.

Roxane (*c*.345–*c*.311 BC) A Bactrian princess and daughter of Oxyartes. When ALEXANDER (3) III the Great had conquered Bactria and Sogdiana, in spring 327 he took her as his first wife and married her according to Macedonian ritual. She was pregnant when he died in 323 and her son was recognised and proclaimed as King ALEXANDER (6) IV by the regent, PERDICCAS (2). After his murder in 321, Roxane and her son fell into the hands of ANTIPATER (1), who took them to Macedonia in 320. After his death in 319, she fled with her son to her mother-in-law, OLYMPIAS, but the move ended in disaster when all three were caught by CASSANDER, who hated Alexander's family, at the siege of Pydna in spring 316. Roxane and Alexander were held in wretched conditions in Amphipolis until Cassander had them killed. See R.M. Errington (1986) *A History of Macedonia*, Berkeley, CA; Oxford: University of California Press.

S

Sacadas (C7/6 BC) A musician and poet from Argos who composed for the pipes (*aulos*) and set his own elegiac poetry to tunes. He won three victories in competitions on the instrument at the Pythian Games at Delphi, and helped to revive musical performance at Sparta in the ceremony of the Gymnopaedia.

Sandracottus (late C4 BC) The Greek form of the name Chandragupta, the Indian king who founded the Maurya empire. With the help of his friend and mentor the statesman Kautilya, who planned the *coup*, the low-born general Chandragupta Maurya *c*.324 seized possession of the Nanda kingdom of Magadha which lay around the Ganges river in northern India and expanded it rapidly, building up a huge army of 600,000 men and 9,000 elephants of war. Magadha was immensely rich and powerful and rumours of its strength had deterred the army of ALEXANDER (3) III the Great from proceeding further in his invasion of India. Over a period of twenty years Chandragupta's empire embraced the whole of the north of the Indian subcontinent southwards as far as the site of Indore. SELEUCUS (1) I invaded this empire from the north-west *c*.304, and crossed the Indus, and was almost certainly heavily defeated in a battle fought somewhere near the upper reaches of the Indus. Now that Seleucus had been taught a lesson, Chandragupta

concluded a treaty of friendship with him by which Seleucus ceded all the Indian territories he had claimed including the border satrapies of Gedrosia, Gandhara Paropamisus and much of Arachosia: Chandragupta gave Seleucus a force of some 500 elderly elephants with their keepers, which relieved his purse of expense. There may have been a matrimonial alliance between the two royal families, and Seleucus was allowed to station a resident ambassador, the historian MEGASTHENES, at the Indian court. Chandragupta ruled his empire for about twenty-four years, abdicating *c*.299 to become a Jain ascetic.

Sappho (C7/6 BC) A poetess from Eresus and Mytilene in Lesbos, born *c*.620, the daughter of Scamandronymus and Cleis and a contemporary of the poet ALCAEUS. Out of her substantial *oeuvre* only one complete poem survives together with, thanks to the papyrologists, some substantial fragments. Her poetry is intensely personal, mainly about human relationships and the feelings they engender; her descriptions of those she loves are often passionate and given in very physical terms. Her style is simple, direct and powerful; she uses poignant and effective images, and is a mistress of invective. Like Alcaeus, she wrote in the Aeolic dialect, though with epic variants where admissible. Her work was collected and published at Alexandria in Hellenistic times in nine books according to their metre: the sapphic metre in which her first book was composed, named after her, is frequent in the surviving poems in which predominant themes are the love of woman for woman, hymns to Aphrodite, the Muses and the Graces, and mythical subjects such as the wedding of Hector and Andromache; there are also fragments of a dirge for Adonis and of a poem relating to her brother. She wrote a renowned poem on the physical effects of erotic passion that Catullus paraphrased in Latin, and we have complete a hymn addressed to Aphrodite. Apart from the wedding songs and the dirge, her only compositions designed for public performance, all her poetry is personal and private. The wedding songs (*epithalamia*) display heavy flat humour far removed from the light ribaldry normal in such compositions, and which may have had a satirical purpose. Again, similar poems by Catullus may throw light on what our scraps of Sappho's texts do not reveal.

Our information about her life is limited (the ancient biographies are unreliable and even contradict each other), but certain inferences, mainly from her own works, are possible. She was born into aristocratic society on an island where political turmoil was commonplace, though she herself appears not to have been greatly affected by it. There is evidence of a period of exile, perhaps in Sicily, when Sappho lacked the pleasures which usually surrounded her. She married and had a daughter whom she named Cleis after her mother. She writes of her brother Charaxus, who went to Egypt where he spent his fortune to buy the freedom of a Thracian slave-prostitute known as Rhodopis – a nickname, her real name was Doricha. However, after thus gaining her freedom, Doricha rejected Charaxus and continued to practise her former trade on her own behalf in the commercial port of Naucratis and amassed a huge fortune. Sappho shows

her brother her anger for his stupidity in beggaring himself for such a woman (see Herodotus 2. 134ff.). She had another, younger brother of whom she was fonder. Sappho seems to have been at the centre of a group of female friends, younger unmarried women, the nature of whose relationship with her is controversial: she may have had a role of adviser or elder sister among them, though evidence is lacking. She also had enemies such as Andromeda, Gorgo and Mica, who tried to lead Sappho's friends astray or betrayed her affection, and to whom she shows her anger and contempt. Her favourites were the girls Anactoria and Atthis. The story, told by Ovid in his *Heroines*, that she threw herself off a cliff in desperate love for a man named Phaon, is a fiction derived from the New Comedy: it was, however, to lead to many other fanciful tales about her. Until Christianity caused the burning of her works, they were popular and admired for their resonance and euphony; a poem in the *Greek Anthology* declared her to be the 'tenth Muse'. See D.L. Page (1979) *Sappho and Alcaeus*, Oxford: Clarendon Press; and R. Chandler (1998) *Sappho*, London: Phoenix.

Satyrus (C3 BC) A biographer and anecdotist from Callatis on the Black Sea (in Romania). Quotations of his work are found in DIOGENES (5) Laërtius and ATHENAEUS, and a papyrus of his *Life of Euripides* was found at Oxyrhynchus. He composed lives of famous men such as PHILIP (1) II, DEMOSTHENES (2), and other statesmen as well as poets and philosophers. He took an uncritical, anecdotal approach to his material and could not distinguish fiction from autobiography. A fragment from his lost work *Characters* displays the same faults and shows a moralising tendency.

Scerdilaidas (C3 BC) A king of the Ardiaei of southern Illyria, probably the son of King Pleuratus and younger brother of

King Agron. In 231 Agron died and his widow Teuta acted as regent for her stepson Pinnes: meanwhile, Scerdilaidas led the army in an attack on Epirus. A year later Teuta was defeated by Roman forces in alliance with DEMETRIUS (10) OF PHAROS who became the effective ruler and a 'friend and ally' of Rome, and the Illyrian kingdom was much reduced in size. We do not know what part Scerdilaidas took in these events. Subsequently, in 220, he joined Demetrius and the Aetolians in a naval attack on Pylos and the Aegean islands, but then switched sides and joined the Hellenic Confederacy led by PHILIP (3) V. In 219 Demetrius was expelled from Pharos by Rome and took refuge with Philip. After this Scerdilaidas seems to have co-operated with the Romans, and in 217/6 he warned them of Philip's aggressive preparations and received ten Roman ships to defend his coast. In 213/2 he was attacked by Philip who took Lissus. At some point he abandoned Pinnes and took the kingship and in 211 allied himself with Rome and Aetolia. He died some time before the Peace of Phoenice in 205 and was succeeded by his son, Pleuratus. See J.J. Wilkes (1936–1992) *The Illyrians*, Oxford: Blackwell.

Sciras (C3 BC) Like RHINTHON, a writer of farces from Tarentum. We know of a single title of a work by him, *Meleager*, and have an extract parodying line 75 of EURIPIDES' *Hippolytus*.

Scymnus (*c.*170 BC) A geographical writer from Chios who wrote a lost geographical survey. His name was wrongly attached to another survey of the early first century BC dedicated to NICOMEDES (4) IV of Bithynia, of which a fragment survives. The fragment offers useful historical information on Greek colonies and the coasts of Liguria, Spain and the Black Sea.

Scythinus (C4 BC) A poet and prose writer from Teos who composed an iambic poem, of which fragments survive, expounding the teachings of HERACLITUS, and lost prose works: *Nature*, and an account of the great deeds of Heracles entitled *A History*.

Seleucus 1. I Nicator ('Victor') (*c.*358–281 BC) A Macedonian successor to much of the empire of ALEXANDER (3) III the Great, and the founder of a dynasty prominent in western Asia for more than two centuries. He was the son of Antiochus, a nobleman and commander in the army of PHILIP (1) II, and Laodice. After serving as a page at Philip's court, he became a junior member of Alexander's staff in the invasion of Asia, being a contemporary of Alexander, until the invasion of India in 326 when he was made commander of the royal hypaspists, an élite infantry regiment fiercely loyal to the king. His marriage to the Bactrian princess Apama, contracted at Susa in 324 at the mass union of Macedonians with native women, was reputed to be the only one that lasted. After Alexander's death in 323, Seleucus supported the 'regent', PERDICCAS (2), as his second-in-command, but in 320, by lending support to those suborned by PTOLEMY (1) I to murder Perdiccas, he won the satrapy of Babylonia. Here he showed diplomatic talent, conciliating the Babylonian priests to win popular support. In 315, however, ANTIGONUS (1) I challenged his authority even though he had assisted Antigonus against EUMENES (1). Seleucus escaped from Babylon to Egypt where he cultivated the friendship of Ptolemy: he commanded a section of the Egyptian fleet in a stand-off with the forces of Antigonus and put down a rebellion in Cyprus. After the battle of Gaza in 312, in which Ptolemy's forces defeated Antigonus' son, DEMETRIUS (3), Seleucus was safe to return to Babylon which he did in a dash across the desert with a small, mobile force which proved capable of seizing the Babylonian citadel. He counted the Seleucid Era from 7 October 312 BC, though he did not take the title 'king' until *c*.305, well after the death of ALEXANDER (6) IV. Leaving his faithful general PATROCLES in charge of Babylon, he expanded his area of control to Susiana, Media, Persis, Aria and possibly Parthia. In 310, however, Antigonus captured part of Babylon and fighting continued until summer 308, when a truce was declared. Seleucus took advantage of the peace to consolidate and extend his empire eastwards. In about 304 he invaded the upper Indus region, but met with a severe setback and in 303 negotiated peace with the Maurya king SANDRACOTTUS, to whom he ceded the Indus valley, Gedrosia, Gandhara, the Paropamisus (the Hindu Kush) and the east of Arachosia: in return he was given 500 ageing elephants. About this time he built a new capital, Seleuceia, across the Tigris from Babylon, which he connected to the Euphrates with a canal.

The summit of his career was the battle of Ipsus in early summer 301, in which four surviving rulers of Alexander's empire, Ptolemy, Seleucus, LYSIMACHUS of Thrace and CASSANDER, allied to put an end to the aspirations of a fifth, Antigonos, to rule Alexander's empire. In the battle Seleucus united his force with that of Lysimachus and routed Antigonus' army, killing him and putting his son, Demetrius, to flight. As he had been the senior contestant, Seleucus gained most from the victory, namely Mesopotamia and northern Syria (the southern part of which was occupied by Ptolemy). He exploited his new access to the sea and founded new cities including Antioch and Apamea *c*.300 to establish his control over northern Syria, and encouraged immigration from Greece and Macedonia. In 298, Apama being almost certainly dead, Seleucus married Demetrius' daughter, Stratonice, thus forging a new alliance aimed at Ptolemy and Lysimachus. Around 292, however, Seleucus gave up his wife to his son by Apama, ANTIOCHUS (1) I: she had so far borne a daughter, Phila, who later married ANTIGONUS (2) II

Gonatas. Stratonice bore his son several children. In 285 Seleucus was confronted by Demetrius, who had been expelled from Macedonia and driven over the Taurus mountains by Lysimachus' son, Agathocles, and had entered Syria, but he captured him without a fight. In 282 he attacked the kingdom of his former ally Lysimachus at the battle of Corupedium near Sardis, killed Lysimachus and seized his possessions in Asia Minor. To complete his aim of reuniting Alexander's Macedonian empire of which he claimed to be king, he resolved to invade Europe and conquer his native land, but in September 281, after crossing to Europe, he was assassinated at Lysimacheia by his protégé PTOLEMY (16) Ceraunus, the eldest son of PTOLEMY (1) I, who took the kingdom of Macedonia for himself. Seleucus was succeeded by his son, Antiochus, whom he had appointed in 292 as his viceroy with full royal authority in the eastern provinces beyond the Euphrates. See J.D. Grainger (1990) *Seleukos Nikator*, London: Routledge; S. Sherwin-White and A. Kuhrt (eds) (1987) *Hellenism and the East*, London: Duckworth; and S. Sherwin-White and A. Kuhrt (eds) (1993) *From Samarkand to Sardis*, London: Duckworth.

2. II Callinicus ('Triumphant') (*c*.265–225 BC) A Seleucid king, the eldest son of ANTIOCHUS (2) II and LAODICE (1). He became king in 246 on his father's death, enforcing his claim over that of the infant son of his stepmother BERENICE (1) I, whom his mother murdered; consequently he had to fight the Third Syrian War (246–241) against Berenice's brother PTOLEMY (3) III. Within a few years he had lost Bactria, the furthest east of his provinces, to independence under DIODOTUS (2). He fought against the invading Parthians who were now asserting their power against that of the Seleucids. In order to bring the war with Egypt to an end, he made his younger brother, ANTIOCHUS (14) 'the Hawk', his partner in power, but the latter, who was given Asia Minor to govern, seceded with the support of the Cappadocian king ARIARATHES (3) III, which cost Seleucus his possessions in Asia Minor. ATTALUS (1) I of Pergamon, however, expelled Antiochus from all but Cilicia, and it was Seleucus' son, ANTIOCHUS (3) III, who recaptured these territories. Seleucus sent relief to Rhodes after the earthquake of 227/6. He was succeeded by his son, SELEUCUS (3) III Ceraunus.

3. III Ceraunus ('the Thunderbolt') (c.243–223 BC) A Seleucid king, who after a brief reign of three years (225–223) was assassinated in Asia Minor by members of his army while on campaign against ATTALUS (1) I of Pergamon. He was succeeded by his younger brother ANTIOCHUS (3) III.

4. IV Philopator ('Father-loving') (c.218–175 BC) A Seleucid king, the second son of ANTIOCHUS (3) III. Having served in military command under his father, he was made joint king after the battle of Magnesia in 189 and succeeded in 187. He was severely constrained in policy at home and abroad by the harsh treaty of Apamea which Rome had imposed on his father, involving an indemnity of 15,000 talents; his freedom to move westwards by land or sea was also curtailed by the treaty. He maintained good relations with the independent powers of the east, Macedonia and Egypt. He continued his father's favourable treatment of Judaea, guaranteeing that religious revenues would if necessary be subsidised by his treasury. He was assassinated by his minister Heliodorus, who tried to withdraw the subsidy.

5. V A Seleucid king, the eldest son of DEMETRIUS (7) II, he became king in 126 BC but was killed by his mother, Cleopatra, the next year.

6. VI Epiphanes ('the Glorious') (reigned 96–95 BC) A Seleucid king of Syria, the eldest son of ANTIOCHUS (8) VIII Grypus.

The year after his accession he defeated and killed his uncle, ANTIOCHUS (9) IX, but later in the year was defeated by the latter's son ANTIOCHUS (10) X and expelled from the kingdom.

7. (C2 BC) An astronomer from Seleuceia on the Persian Gulf, whom STRABO describes as an astrologer. According to PLUTARCH he was a supporter (the only one recorded) of the heliocentric theory of the solar system of ARISTARCHUS (2) of Samos and tried to prove its validity. He also studied the tides from his knowledge of the Gulf (then known as the Red Sea), and attributed them to the influence of the moon, which he regarded as resisting the earth's rotation: he refuted the tidal theory of CRATES (4) of Mallus.

8. Homericus (C1 AD) A critic and commentator on Greek literature from Alexandria who attended and perhaps was executed at the court of the Roman emperor, Tiberius. Only fragments survive of his copious writings in Greek: commentaries on the works of most of the Greek poets, biographies of writers, a work on the gods, a treatise on paradoxes, a commentary on Solon's laws, a critique of the symbols used by ARISTARCHUS (3) in the text of HOMER (hence his nickname), works on the Greek language and on literary style, a work on proverbs and a miscellany. A work entitled *Philosophy*, attributed to a Seleucus by DIOGENES (5) Laërtius, may be another's.

Semonides (Simonides) (mid-C7 BC) An iambic poet from the Aegean island of Amorgos, contemporary with ARCHILOCHUS, Semonides appears to have been born in Samos and to have accompanied a Samian colonisation of Amorgos. He is said to have written two books of iambic poetry: most of his work has perished, though a long fragment (118 lines) of a poem in the Ionic dialect, owing something to popular fables and satirising women, who are compared with animals to account for their various characteristics, was preserved by John of Stobi. Other fragments show a tendency to moralise and yet others are from racy and humorous stories. See H. Lloyd-Jones (1975) *The Female of the Species*, London: Duckworth.

Semos (*c*.200 BC) An antiquarian from Delos, about which he wrote a survey in eight books (*The Deliad*) much quoted by ATHENAEUS. He was also the author of works on *Islands*, *Paros*, *Pergamon*, and a collection of *Maps*. From his work entitled *Paeans*, of which Athenaeus also preserves a useful extract, we gain information about the masks, costume, use of improvisation, and the display of the phallus, in performances. The writings of this meticulous scholar have perished, apart from the fragments described.

Serapion (Sarapion) 1. (*c*.200–*c*.150 BC) A physician from Alexandria of the Empiricist school, he wrote a medical work entitled *Therapeutics* from which a number of prescriptions for medicines survive. He placed great emphasis on the priority of observation and experiment in medical practice, and was highly considered by GALEN.

2. (C1 BC) A writer on geography (lost) and astrology (partly extant) from Antioch, known to Cicero, he estimated the size of the sun at eighteen times that of the earth.

Seven Sages of Greece Established by PLATO (1) in his dialogue *Protagoras* (343 BC). See BIAS, CHILON, CLEOBULUS, PERIANDER, PITTACUS, SOLON and THALES.

Sextus Empiricus (late C2 AD) A Greek writer on medicine of the Empiricist school and on philosophy in the Sceptical tradition of PYRRHON, he was the pupil of an otherwise unknown doctor Herodotus who practised in Rome. Three of his philosophical works survive: *An Outline*

of Pyrrhonism in three books, which seeks in the first to define Pyrrhon's doctrine as against similar theories and, in the last two, to refute dogmatic theories under the headings of logic, epistemology, ethics and physics; *Against the Professors* in six books, attacking the disciplines of grammar, rhetoric, geometry, arithmetic, astrology and music; *Against the Dogmatists* in five books, a deeper criticism of these teachings. These latter works were at some time combined into one work. His works on medicine are unfortunately lost. Though not an original thinker, he was an intelligent and conscientious compiler of the works of earlier Sceptical thinkers from AENESIDEMUS onwards and provides an invaluable insight into ancient philosophy, including much, such as Stoic logic, with which he had no sympathy. See J. Annas and J. Barnes (1985) *The Modes of Scepticism*, Cambridge: CUP.

Silanion (*c*.370–*c*.320 BC) An Athenian sculptor who sculpted in bronze both mythological works and portraits. Of the former we know of an *Achilles* (or *Ares*), a *Theseus* and a *Dying Jocasta*. His portrait of PLATO (1) is known from a copy, and was the prototype for many later portraits of philosophers; his CORINNA is also so known. A bronze head of a boxer found at Olympia has been identified with his *Satyrus* (twice victor, in 332 and 328). He also sculpted SAPPHO and a sculptor named *Apollodorus*. He wrote a lost treatise, *On Proportion*.

Silenus (C3/2 BC) A historian from Caleacte in Sicily who wrote a lost history of his native land. He was one of two Greek historians who were invited to join Hannibal's expedition to Italy, and his work, of which very little is left, was used by POLYBIUS and the Roman historian Coelius Antipater. It appears to have been in the tradition of romantic historiography: witness the description of Hannibal's dream as he crossed the Ebro.

Simmias 1. (C5 BC) A Theban follower of
SOCRATES and an associate of CEBES, he is
an important character in PLATO (1)'s
Phaedo where he is said to have been a
pupil of the Pythagorean philosopher
PHILOLAUS. However, the theory he pro-
pounds in the *Phaedo* concerning the
constitution of the soul is not Pythagorean
as it denies the immortality of the soul. In
the *Phaedrus* Simmias is shown originating a philosophical discussion, and is
praised for his ability. According to DIO-
GENES (5) Laërtius he wrote twenty-three
philosophical dialogues, of which nothing
else is known.

2. (early C3 BC) A poet and lexicographer from Rhodes who wrote three books
of glossaries and four of poetry. A few
glosses on the meanings of words are
quoted by ATHENAEUS; fragments survive
of poems in hexameters named *Apollo*,
Gorgo and *The Months*; lyric poetry;
epigrams; and pattern-poems, the latter
named *Wings*, *The Axe* and *The Egg*. He
writes in several dialects, though calling
himself the 'Doric nightingale'.

Simon (C5 BC) An Athenian cobbler who,
according to the fourth-century *Socratic
Letters*, in which he is a prominent
personage, was befriended by SOCRATES
and discussed philosophical questions
with him. DIOGENES (5) Laërtius says
improbably that he wrote memoirs of
Socrates in dialogue form. The site of his
workshop near the Athenian market-place
has been found.

Simonides (*c.*556–468 BC) A lyric and
elegiac poet from Iulis in the Aegean
island of Ceos, he was the son of
Leoprepes and uncle of the poet BAC-
CHYLIDES; Hylichus, mentioned by CALLI-
MACHUS (3), was an ancestor of his. He
spent some time at the court of HIPPIAS
(1) in Athens as a guest of the tyrant's
brother HIPPARCHUS (1). He wrote an
epitaph for Hippias' daughter, Archedice,
and while in Athens competed in dithy-

rambic contests of which he was later said
to have won at least fifty-seven in his
lifetime. At some time he lived at Crannon in Thessaly at the court of the
Scopads, and when their palace collapsed
in an earthquake *c.*515 he wrote a lament
for the family. He also wrote a lament on
Antiochus, son of Echecratidas. A beauti-
ful fragment, which depicts the plight of
Danaë and Perseus cast out on the sea in a
chest, may be part of a hymn. He wrote
an encomium for Scopas, of which a
section on virtue is extant. In 514 after
Hipparchus' murder he left Athens but
returned in the more democratic 490s.
The epitaph he wrote for the Athenian
dead at the battle of Marathon was
chosen rather than that by AESCHYLUS.
The Persian War (480/79) brought him
great fame: he commemorated the battle
of Thermopylae with a hymn (addressed
to the Homeric hero Achilles) in memory
of the Spartans who fell there under the
leadership of LEONIDAS (1) I, and he
wrote a famous epitaph on the Spartan
dead and a more personal one on his
friend the prophet Megistias. In his book
of elegies he commemorated the battles of
Artemisium and Plataea. He was a friend
of THEMISTOCLES and of PAUSANIAS (1)
and defended the former against the
abusive attacks of TIMOCREON. He also
wrote victory odes, one in praise of
Glaucus of Carystus, one, composed before 489, for Eualcidas of Eretria, and one
for the victors of Plataea in 479. About
476 he went to the court of HIERON (1) I
of Syracuse whom he reconciled to
THERON tyrant of Acragas (Agrigento),
and was buried at Acragas. He lived to a
great age and was admired for the simplicity with which he expressed the pathos
of death, yet lampooned by ARISTO-
PHANES (1) in *Clouds* as old-fashioned. A
professional poet, he usually worked to
commission, which is perhaps why he
gained the reputation of a money-grub-
ber: thus Pindar's phrase 'Muse for hire'
was applied to Simonides. Some of the
poetry which goes under his name, which

was collected in the fourth century, was not his. He appears to have been noted for his witty sayings, many of which were cynical. He was later said to have discovered the third note of the lyre and to have recognised the long vowels and geminated consonants of Greek. See J.H. Molyneux (*c*.1992) *Simonides*, Wauconda, IL: Bolchazy-Carducci.

Simylus 1. (C3–1 BC) A poet of unknown date who composed didactic poetry in the iambic metre, a few fragments of whose work survive.

2. (C1? BC) The writer of an extant Greek elegy on the mythological Roman girl Tarpeia in which it is said that she betrayed the Capitol for love not of a Sabine but of a Gaul.

Sitalces (died 421 BC) A king of the Thracian nation of the Odrysae, the son of Teres, Sitalces expanded his kingdom so that it spread from the Danube to the north coast of the Aegean Sea, bordering the Black Sea on the east and the Macedonian kingdom on the west. He married an Athenian woman, the sister of Nymphodorus, the Athenian representative (*proxenos*) in Abdera, through whose agency the Athenians approached him at the outset of the Peloponnesian War in 431 to gain his assistance against PERDIC-CAS (1) II the king of Macedonia. He remained friendly to Athens during the siege of Potidaea despite Spartan blandishments. In 429 he waged a brief and fruitless campaign against Chalcidice and Bottiaea, failing to replace Perdiccas with his nephew Amyntas, son of Philip. Sitalces' nephew, Seuthes, subsequently married Stratonice, a daughter of Perdiccas. Sitalces was killed in a war against the Triballi who occupied land to the north-west of his kingdom. See B. Isaac (1986) *The Greek Settlements in Thrace*, Leiden: EJ Brill.

Socrates (469–399 BC) An Athenian philosopher of the deme of Alopece, the son of parents of means, Sophroniscus a sculptor and Phaenarete a midwife. He married (arguably his second marriage) a woman named XANTHIPPE by whom he had two sons. He was himself rich enough to have served as a hoplite in the Peloponnesian War at the siege of Potidaea (431 BC) and the battles of Delium (424 BC) and Amphipolis (422 BC), and was well known for the courage and physical toughness he had displayed. Though he avoided normal political activity, he fulfilled his duties as a citizen, and was president of the Council of State and consequently chairman of the Assembly on the day when the victorious generals at Arginusae in 406 came up for trial; the generals were accused of failing to pick up the shipwrecked survivors and the corpses of dead Athenian sailors after the seabattle. Despite popular clamour he refused to put to the vote an illegal motion to try them *en masse*. In 404/3 he defied an order from the oligarchic government (the 'THIRTY TYRANTS') to arrest a man, Leon of Salamis, they wished to execute illegally. Despite his earlier wealth, he claimed later in life, e.g. at his trial, to be poverty-stricken, and it is hard to see how he could have earned a living during his fifties and sixties when he was constantly engaged in public discussion. He must instead have been supported by his rich friends. In early 399 he was accused of impiety, for introducing alien gods that the state did not recognise and for corrupting young men; found guilty and condemned to death by a majority of sixty out of a jury of 501 citizens; and after an interval of a month caused by a religious festival on Delos, was executed in spring of that year by drinking the poison hemlock. He could have escaped from prison (his friends were ready to bribe the jailer) but refused to do so on moral grounds. The background to the prosecution was probably a desire for vengeance by some democrats on one they held responsible for the political views of the oligarchs, many of whom, such as ALCIBIADES and CRITIAS, had once been among Socrates' associates. His fellow citizens, the jurymen who tried him, could accept religious non-conformity, but it was Socrates' assertion that he did not teach that they did not believe. However, in the eyes of many younger Greeks who had been sympathetic to and excited by his discussions, his death was a martyrdom in the cause of the liberty of the individual and the right to be guided by one's own intellect. Many of Socrates' followers left Athens after the trial in disgust or fear. There soon sprang up an 'industry' of writings to justify his work, mostly in the form of philosophical dialogues.

Though he wrote nothing, his influence was huge on the philosophical thought of his own time and thereafter, and on the life of Athens: he engaged in discussion all who were interested in his ideas and pursued topics of debate to their logical conclusion, often antagonising his interlocutors, whose most basic assumptions he would often demolish in argument. He started from the ironical premise that, whereas he himself knew that he knew nothing, other people were deluded into thinking that they had knowledge, which in fact was worthless and not knowledge at all. His dialectic method, known as the *elenchus*, involved a process of question and answer, often accompanied by a teasing irony, until his adversary was convinced of the rightness of Socrates' case, or desisted from the argument in frustration. Socrates believed that he had a divine mission to prove to his fellow men, by examining systematically the fundamental assumptions from which notions of conduct and morality arose, that they were in ignorance of the answers to profound questions, and he insisted on a precise definition of terms, a method of

procedure which may be regarded as a forerunner of formal logic.

We know of his life and his ideas from three main sources. The first, ARISTOPHANES (1) the writer of comedies, made him a character in his play *Clouds* (423), where he is presented, with mockery and a degree of hostility, as a typical sophist or professor of rhetoric and natural philosophy at the head of a school, who is willing to teach all comers for a fee, and claims to be able to pervert rational argument by making 'the weaker argument the stronger'. This appears to be a pastiche of the truth, namely that in his middle years Socrates became interested in the teachings of ANAXAGORAS and his successor ARCHELAUS (1), to the latter of whom he attached himself for a while, but was later disillusioned with such a standpoint and came to prefer Pythagorean teachings (see PYTHAGORAS 1). This account is borne out by what Socrates is made to say of himself in the early works of PLATO (1), the *Phaedo* and the *Apology of Socrates*.

The other two sources, deriving from men of a different generation, are favourable to Socrates, though they present somewhat different pictures of the man and his ideas, reflecting doubtless the personalities of the observers. The youthful Plato knew him as a constant associate for several years towards the end of Socrates' life, and wrote many dialogues in which he figures as the principal character. The most revealing of his works, the *Apology of Socrates*, a plausible version of the defence speeches he made at his trial, and the discussions of his last days in prison, the *Crito* and *Phaedo*, present a clear and informative portrait of the man: he comes across as cool-headed, serious, ironic and complex. He claims no knowledge and so does not teach, though he asserts that ultimately knowledge and virtue are the same thing and one cannot do wrong except through ignorance: a Socratic paradox that is hard to refute though apparently inconsistent with human experience. His very ignorance made him wiser than other men: his friend Chaerophon, he declares in the *Apology*, asked the Oracle of Delphi whether anybody was wiser than he; the response that nobody was wiser was claimed by Socrates to be a reference to their unawareness of their ignorance. Socrates also claimed to hear occasionally an inner voice that warned him against certain acts: it was this that prevented him from taking part in politics. He condemned much in traditional myth and religion, including the immorality of HOMER's gods. He was above all interested in ethics, and pursued the questions 'What is virtue?' and 'What is justice?' rather than the questions about the nature of the universe with which his predecessors had been concerned. Other early works which portray the Socrates of history are *Euthyphro* and Book 1 of the *Republic*.

We get a rather different picture of Socrates from XENOPHON (1), who was not so closely acquainted with him as Plato and was not a philosopher. Four of his works give information about Socrates: the *Defence Speech of Socrates*, *The Education of Cyrus*, *The Drinking-Party* and *Memoirs of Socrates*. Though Xenophon's Socrates conducts the same dialectical arguments and drawing of distinctions, the morality that he upholds is more conventional and traditional. The character that Xenophon presents us with is simpler and warmer; nor does Xenophon know anything of Socrates' earlier interest in natural philosophy. There has been much disagreement over the centuries as to which of the two authors represents the historical figure more accurately, and though the question is ultimately unanswerable, Plato has a richer, subtler and more credible Socrates to offer.

Other sources of information about Socrates also existed: followers such as AESCHINES (1) of Sphettus, PHAEDO of Elis, and ANTISTHENES wrote dialogues in which he figured, but only a few fragments of these survive. Nothing at all survives of the works of CEBES and ARISTIPPUS (1). A more important source is ARISTOTLE, who, though he was born long after Socrates' death, had a wealth of information about him, knowing as he did many of those who had frequented Socrates' circle. He makes it quite clear that Socrates played no part in the metaphysical speculation such as the Theory of 'Ideas' that is central to the works of Plato's middle period of writing. See G. Vlastos (1991) *Socrates, Ironist and Moral Philosopher*, Cambridge: CUP; G. Vlastos (1994) *Socratic Studies*, edited by M. Burnyeat, Cambridge: CUP; T.H. Irwin (1979) *Plato's Moral Theory*, Oxford: Clarendon Press; A.-H. Chroust (1947) *Socrates: Man or Myth*, London: Routledge & Kegan Paul; W.K.C. Guthrie (1971) *Socrates*, Cambridge: CUP.

Solon (*c*.639–*c*.559 BC) An Athenian statesman and poet, the son of Execestides, who claimed descent from the mythical King Codrus; his mother was related to PISISTRATUS. Solon was a nobleman (*eupatrid*) with the right to sit on the Areopagus or Council of State and to serve, if elected by his peers, as an archon for one year. He was reputed to be poorer than most of his class and perhaps engaged in trade to repair his fortunes: consequently he is reported to have travelled widely as a merchant. Nevertheless, he was talented in rhetoric and poetic composition and *c*.600 agitated successfully for the Athenians not to drop their claim to Salamis, an island which their neighbours the Megarians (see THEAGENES 1) had recently taken from Athens and which the Athenians despaired of repossessing, and he led the army which recaptured Salamis. The respective claims of Athens and Megara were submitted to Spartan arbitration which vindicated the claim of Athens, and Solon acquired land on the island. He was elected chief archon for the Athenian year 594/3 during which he promoted a war (the First Sacred War) in alliance with CLEISTHENES (1) of Sicyon on behalf of Delphi which had been occupied by Crissa. At some stage in his career, whether during his archonship or more probably about twenty years later, when he was by now a respected elder statesman, he was asked by the Areopagus, supported by the Assembly of citizens, to revise the law-code and solve the urgent crisis caused by widespread indebtedness and even enslavement of the peasants to their richer fellow citizens. Solon is said to have repealed all the laws of DRACO except for his mild homicide law and to have established a new law-code, probably more wide-ranging than Draco's, which the public could read inscribed on tablets, though in the later fifth and fourth centuries politicians tended to ascribe all the basic laws of Athens to Solon.

Solon's measures to allay the problem of debt were named the *seisachtheia*, 'shaking off burdens', and consisted of a ban on Athenian citizens offering themselves as collateral for debt which had led to the enslavement of many peasants in hard times when crops had failed or markets fallen. Most of these people were *hektemeroi*, that is 'sixth-part men', because in an almost feudal relationship the tenant farmer owed his landlord a sixth of his produce. Solon cancelled the arrangement and gave these citizens outright ownership of the land they worked; he also set free those who were already enslaved for debt, even repurchasing those who had been sold abroad. He forbade the export of all agricultural produce except olive oil and thus encouraged the production of olives and foreign trade in other goods; as a result food became cheaper and famine less of a threat. Weights and measures were standardised, and craftsmen from abroad were offered citizenship.

His constitutional changes weakened aristocratic privilege and gave rich traders and manufacturers as much power as the nobles. He created four new classes based on property, or rather the income derived from it: membership of these classes determined the right of citizens to hold office and participate in state activities. The richest men, those who earned 500 bushels-worth a year (*pentakosiomedimnoi*), were alone eligible to hold the treasurerships: they and the men who could afford to ride a horse into battle (*hippeis*, 'cavalry') were eligible for all other offices of state including the archonships. The 'teamsters' (*zeugitai*, men who owned a team of oxen) were eligible to serve in minor offices and on Solon's new Council of State; the lowest class, landless men who lived by selling their labour, the *thetes*, could attend the Assembly. The right to express wealth in terms other than agricultural produce probably followed the introduction of coinage to Attica just after the end of Solon's life. The new Council, consisting of four hundred members, a hundred from each tribe (Athenians were still divided into the four Ionic tribes), superseded the Areopagus in its political functions and prepared business for the Assembly, which now had the role of electing the archons. Solon also established a court of final appeal from all lower courts (the *Eliaia*), manned by a jury drawn by lot or otherwise from all citizens (or perhaps the whole Assembly sitting as a court), which broke the monopoly of the nobles in judicial matters. He allowed all citizens the right to prosecute wrongdoers in a new category of public lawsuits.

Solon's reforms, coupled with the humane and outward-looking dictatorship of PISISTRATUS, undoubtedly set Athens on the road to prosperity and power. Later Athenians saw him as the father of their democratic institutions and the bringer of social justice. Yet at the time his compatriots failed to appreciate his achievements, and most remained disgruntled. To avoid pressure to change his reforms in any way, he is said to have exiled himself from Athens for ten years, during which faction persisted, leading to the eventual seizure of power by Pisistratus. The latter appears to have tried to conciliate Solon, who warned the Athenians against Pisistratus' ambitions, by consulting him on matters of policy. During his absence (c.570–560) there were quarrels over the appointment of archons, and embitterment over loss of power (the nobles) or non-fulfilment of aspirations for land distribution (the poorer citizens). Solon was, however, his own propagandist and in his elegiac poems, which are extant, he shows that his aim was a compromise between the interests of the powerful and those of the weak. His achievement was great, however, and paved the way for the radical reforms of CLEISTHENES (2). He is said to have died in Cyprus and his ashes to have been buried in Salamis. The story of HERODOTUS that he met CROESUS, king of Lydia, is chronologically impossible. He was accounted one of the 'SEVEN SAGES'. See P.B. Brook (c.1990) *The Origins of Citizenship in Ancient Athens*, Princeton, NJ: Princeton University Press; W.G. Forrest (1966) *The Emergence of Greek Democracy*, London: Weidenfeld & Nicolson; O. Murray (1980) *Early Greece*, London: Fontana.

Sopater (C4/3 BC) An Alexandrian writer of farces, born at Paphos in Cyprus, of whose work some fragments survive. We have the titles of fourteen of his plays, from which it appears that some (e.g. *Hippolytus*, *Ghosts* and *Orestes*) took off myths or tragedies. A fragment from a play named *The Galatians* contains mockery of the Stoics, and three plays with titles based on the name *Bacchis* may be a triad.

Sophaenetus (C5/4 BC) A mercenary captain and writer from Stymphalus in Arcadia. In 401/0 he was one of the leaders of the Greek contingent in the army of CYRUS (2) which made its way northwards under XENOPHON (1) from Mesopotamia

to the Black Sea after the death of Cyrus at the battle of Cunaxa, as is described in Xenophon's *March Inland* (*Anabasis*). According to Stephanus of Byzantium he wrote his own *Anabasis*, now lost, which was perhaps used as a source by CRATIPPUS (1) and, through his work, by DIODORUS (3).

Sophocles 1. (c.496–406 BC) An Athenian writer of tragedies, the son of a rich manufacturer named Sophilus, Sophocles was born at Colonus a kilometre north of the city walls. His talent for music and gymnastics was soon recognised: he learnt music from Lamprus and played his lyre to accompany the victory hymn at a formal celebration of the triumph at Salamis in 480. We do not know when he began to write plays, but by 468 he was proficient enough to win first prize, beating AESCHYLUS in a dramatic contest with three plays probably including his lost *Triptolemus*. In his younger days he was an actor or chorus member, though he gave up fairly quickly because his voice lacked strength. He wrote many parts specifically for the actor Tlepolemus whose talents he understood and exploited. He wrote 123 plays and won at least twenty first prizes at the two Athenian dramatic festivals, the City Dionysia and the Lenaea. This means that the large majority of his plays were judged to be worthy of first prize by his contemporaries, as contestants presented at each festival three tragedies and a lighter 'satyr' play, which were judged as a single unit; the rest of his entries gained second prize. Of this enormous production, only seven tragedies (no two from any one entry) and one satyr play survive, of which only two can be dated: *Philoctetes* and *Oedipus at Colonus*. We know that *Antigone* won first prize; a play of his won second prize in 459; he was second to Aeschylus' son, EUPHORION, in 431, and to Aeschylus' nephew PHILOCLES at an unknown date, when his *King Oedipus* came second. ARISTOTLE tells us that he added a third actor to the traditional two of tragedy, introduced scene-painting, and increased the members of the chorus from twelve to fifteen. Unlike Aeschylus, he did not make the three tragedies of his trilogies enact a single continuous story.

His style is said by PLUTARCH to have firstly gone through a bombastic period and then through a harsh, artificial style before settling down to the maturity of his extant plays. Nevertheless his mature manner was not always graceful or easy, and he displayed a greater spread of styles than his contemporaries, ranging from striking naturalism of language (such as the guard's part in the *Antigone*) to formal symmetry. He was a master of the dramatically realised metaphor such as the blindnesses of Oedipus: his figurative blindness while his eyes were whole, but after his self-blinding his truer ability to 'see'. He was able to shock and to scare, as in the supernatural effects of his *Ajax*. In the *Philoctetes* he used a range of ambiguity in the oft-postponed departure of Philoctetes from Lemnos. His sense of the dramatic was acute, as the *King Oedipus* shows throughout, and is particularly powerful in the final scene of *Antigone*, where Creon's step-by-step destruction is complete. The recognition of facts and people previously unknown or misunderstood plays a fundamental part in Sophocles' dramas, but it invariably leads not to enlightenment and peace but to pain and disaster, as in the case of Oedipus in *King Oedipus*, Creon and Antigone, Ajax, and Deianira and Heracles.

He wrote at different times three tragedies based on the Oedipus myth: *King Oedipus*, the story of the downfall of a confident, humane monarch whose life is blighted as a result of his unknown origin in Thebes, the city he rules by virtue of solving the Sphinx's riddle: unwittingly he has killed his father, the previous king, and proceeded, without realising it, to marry his mother, the queen Jocasta, and had children by her, happy until the curse of Apollo, issued before his birth, is brought to fulfilment. In *Oedipus at Colonus* (the last of his plays, produced after his death by his grandson SOPHOCLES (2) in 401) Oedipus, accompanied in his exile from Thebes by his faithful daughter, Antigone, comes to Colonus in Attica where he is destined to find death and to bring a blessing to the place of his repose; but Creon, his successor at Thebes, having learnt that his tomb will bring divine favour to the land it lies in, tries to force him back to Thebes: Antigone appeals to Theseus to protect him from Creon's troops, and he then walks to his death in radiance, leaving his daughter to return home alone. In *Antigone*, written years earlier, she has returned home, but her two brothers, fighting for the right to rule Thebes, have killed each other in mortal combat, and the king, Creon, has buried his favourite, Eteocles, but ordered the hated Polynices to lie unburied outside the walls. Antigone refuses on religious and moral grounds to accept this order and buries the body; she is then condemned to death for her insolence. Walled up in a cave, she hangs herself in despair; her betrothed, Haemon, the king's son, comes to rescue her but finds only her corpse, at which he kills himself. Creon repents too late of his defiance of the gods, and loses his wife as well.

The other plays have no common story, though many common themes. *Electra* tells of Orestes' secret homecoming, reconciliation with his sister Electra, who believed he was dead, and their murder of their mother Clytaemestra and her lover. *Ajax* (*Aias*) is about the madness, humiliation and suicide of the Greek hero at Troy, who claimed the armour of the dead Achilles but was out-bidden by Odysseus. *Philoctetes* (produced in 409) presents the Greek archer Philoctetes, marooned by his comrades on the deserted island of Lemnos with his unerring bow by which he sustains himself, and tells of the mission of a Greek embassy who try to trick him into returning with them to Troy where his presence is indispensable for the Greek victory. In *The Women of Trachis*, the women of the title are the chorus of onlookers at the drama of the last days of the hero Heracles who is finally tormented and killed in posthumous vengeance by the centaur Nessus, whom he had killed for raping his wife, Deianira. We have part of one satyr play, the *Trackers*, and hundreds of fragments of Sophocles' other works.

Besides his theatrical career, Sophocles had a distinguished public life. In 443/2 he held the important post of Treasurer of the Delian League; he was twice on the board of ten generals, in 441/0 when Athens suppressed a revolt by Samos, and later with NICIAS (1); he was appointed a member of a board of ten advisers in 413 when news of the disaster that had befallen the Sicilian expedition reached Athens. He was a priest of the healing deity Halon and gave shelter to the snake-god Asclepius before his shrine was completed at Athens, and composed a hymn for that god. He was a friend of the statesman CIMON, of Cephalus the father of the orator LYSIAS, and of the writer ION of Chios. He wrote an elegiac poem for the philosopher ARCHELAUS (1), and had his portrait painted by the artist POLYGNOTUS. He wrote a poem for HERODOTUS. Unlike the other tragedians, he resisted the temptation to leave Athens to enjoy royal patronage elsewhere. At the festival of Dionysus in 406, when he competed for the last time, he dressed the chorus and actors in black in memory of EURIPIDES who had just died. Before his death his sons, IOPHON and Ariston, took him to court on the grounds that he was senile and unable to manage his affairs. He is said to have recited part of his new play, *Oedipus at Colonus*, which convinced the jury of his sanity. After his death Sophocles was honoured with a hero-cult under the name Dexion.

His plays remained popular and those which were regularly studied at school survived. They were often revived in Greece and elsewhere, and Aristotle regarded his *King Oedipus* as the perfect tragedy. See R.P. Winnington-Ingram (1980) *Sophocles*, Cambridge: CUP; C.M. Bowra, *Sophoclean Tragedy*, Oxford: Clarendon Press; B.M.W. Knox (1964) *The Heroic Temper*, Berkeley, CA: University of California Press; O. Taplin (1978) *Greek Tragedy in Action*, London: Methuen; C. Segal (1986) *Interpreting Greek Tragedy*, Ithaca, NY: Cornell University Press; H. Lloyd-Jones and N.G. Wilson (1990) *Sophoclea*, Oxford: Clarendon.

2. (C5/4 BC) The grandson of Sophocles (1), the son of Ariston. A playwright himself (nothing extant), he produced his grandfather's last play, *Oedipus at Colonus*, five years after the latter's death in 401.

Sophron (C5 BC) A writer of prose mimes from Syracuse. He wrote in .the Doric dialect and it is mainly for that reason that he was quoted some 170 times in later authors. One substantial fragment survives on papyrus. His work, which was divided between mimes about men and those about women, was admired by PLATO (1) and DURIS (2) of Samos: he strongly influenced his fellow Sicilian THEOCRITUS in his *Idylls* 2 and 15 and probably also HERODAS.

Sosibius (C3 BC) A historian from Sparta who worked at Alexandria, writing a lost account of the history and institutions of his native city.

Sosicrates (C2 BC) A local historian and biographer of philosophers; his lost works were used by ATHENAEUS and DIOGENES (5) Laërtius. He drew on the works of HERMIPPUS (2), SATYRUS and perhaps his contemporary APOLLODORUS (6). He seems also to have drawn on Apollodorus for his *History of Crete*.

Sosipater (C3 BC) A poet of the New Comedy of whose work a fragment survives in which a cook delivers a boastful speech.

Sosiphanes (later C4 BC) A Syracusan writer of tragedies who according to the *Suda* composed 73 plays and won first prize at Athenian festivals seven times. There is a fragment on the brevity of human happiness.

Sositheus (C3 BC) A writer of satyr plays from the Troad in Asia Minor who worked in Athens, Syracuse and Alexandria, where he was a member of the group named the 'Pleiad'. A 21-line fragment of his play *Daphnis or Lityerses* survives, containing a spiteful comment on the Stoic philosopher CLEANTHES. DIOSCORIDES wrote an epigram in praise of his revival of the satyr play.

Sosylus (C3/2 BC) A historian from Sparta who accompanied the expedition of Hannibal across the Alps into Italy and wrote a history of the campaign (*Hannibal's Achievements*) in seven books which were heavily drawn upon by POLYBIUS, despite his particular criticism of Sosylus in Book 3. 20,5. A papyrus fragment of Sosylus' fourth book has been found which disproves Polybius' harsh opinion.

Sotades 1. (C4 BC) An Athenian poet of the Middle Comedy of whose works we know three titles and have three fragments, including a long one about the cooking of fish.

2. (C3 BC) A satirical poet from Maronea in Thrace who lived and worked in Alexandria under PTOLEMY (2) II Philadelphus. He invented the obscene 'cinaedic' verse which he composed in the Ionic dialect in a metre of his own, the sotadean. He strongly disapproved of Ptolemy's marriage with his sister ARSINOË (2) II and wrote a rude verse upon it for which he was imprisoned or even put to death. He often wrote riddles in verse to satirise the great. He also wrote a sotadean version of HOMER's *Iliad* and a *Descent into the Underworld*. Some fragments of his work survive.

Sotion (C2 BC) A Peripatetic philosopher and writer from Alexandria who composed a work *The Succession of Philosophers* in thirteen books to show that every philosopher is the intellectual heir of a previous one, and a single book on the lampoons of TIMON (2) of Phlius. He postulated only two lines of succession: Ionic and Italian. His work was indirectly an important source for DIOGENES (5) Laërtius.

Speusippus (*c*.407–339 BC) An Athenian philosopher, the son of Eurymedon and Potone and thus a nephew of PLATO (1). Having attended the school of ISOCRATES, he joined Plato's school, the Academy, at its inception, went to Sicily with his uncle in 361 on his disastrous last visit there, and succeeded him as head of the Academy in 347, remaining in the post until his death. He had a powerful effect on the development of the work of the Academy, wrote extensively, and earned the respect of ARISTOTLE, who, however, felt unable to stay at the Academy once Plato was no longer its leader: he had little sympathy with the philosophical methods of Speusippus, though in all probability he took over those parts of Speusippus' thought, and especially the biological observations, that he found relevant to his own work.

Speusippus was not much interested in metaphysics but mainly in biology. The chief theme of his writings (of which only some fragments remain) was the need for definition. He published *Similarities* (*Homoia*) in ten books, in which he analysed the similarities between objects, including animals and plants. He extended his research into language, studying ambiguity of expression and finding distinctions similar to those of Aristotelian logic. He also wrote on Pythagorean mathematics, pursuing the study of the elements of number but rejecting both the equation of Plato's 'ideas' with numbers, and the claim that the elements of number are also the elements of all other things, holding that different kinds of reality need different kinds of elements. He also made two contributions to Academic ethics: he denied that pleasure was a good or an evil in itself, and he asserted that the good exists only in the final stages of development and not at the outset. He was succeeded at the Academy by XENO-CRATES. See H. Cherniss (1944) *Aristotle's Criticism of Plato and the Academy*, vol. 1, Baltimore, MD: Johns Hopkins Press.

Sphaerus (*c*.285–*c*.221 BC) A Stoic writer from Borysthenes on the Black Sea, he studied at Athens under ZENO (2) and CLEANTHES and was consulted by the Spartan king CLEOMENES (2) III about constitutional reform. He spent some time at Alexandria. He wrote extensively about every branch of philosophy, showing particular interest in ethics and politics and in the works of HERACLITUS. The Stoics valued his definitions highly. His works have not survived.

Staphylus (C3 or 2 BC) A historian from Naucratis in Egypt who worked at Alexandria. Considered important in ancient times, he wrote histories of certain Greek states and districts: Athens, Aetolia, Thessaly and Arcadia. Some fragments of his work survive, all relating to prehistory.

Stesichorus (*c*.600–550 BC) A poet from southern Italy or Sicily who spent his adult life in Sicily at Himera where a reference in ARISTOTLE's *Rhetoric* connects him with the tyrant PHALARIS, who conquered Himera. The *Suda* states that his real name was Teisias (so perhaps *Stesichorus* was a title) and that he composed twenty-six books of verse. His subject matter was the ancient myths, which he told at length and in detail in poems written in a metre with both choral

and lyric characteristics, with a large dactylic element such as to recall epic metre, and including frequent lengthy speeches. His work is distinguished from that of PINDAR and ALCMAN, who also recounted mythical stories, in the scope and length of his poems. The language is often Homeric, though the dialect is Doric. We know Stesichorus' work only through quotations by other authors and from fragmentary papyri. His poems are referred to in our sources by title rather than by number, which suggests that they were substantial, often longer than a thousand lines. Such were the *Story of Orestes*, *Helen*, *The Wooden Horse*, *The Sack of Troy*, *The Homecomings of the Heroes*, which all relate to the cycle of myths concerned with Troy; the *Story of Geryon*, *Cycnus*, and *Cerberus* relating to the myths of Heracles; concerned with the Theban cycle of myths were *Eriphyle* and *The Tale of Europa*; with the cycle concerning Meleager and the Calydonian boar-hunt, *Boar-hunters*; and with the Argonauts, *Pelias' Funeral-games*. He may also have written of the sufferings of the bucolic hero Daphnis, in which case he was an early pastoral poet.

Stesichorus was the first literary figure of the Greek West, and was unique in this style of composition, having no known successors, though his work indirectly led the way to the birth of tragedy. His themes were often taken up by artists, and are found in vase-painting (e.g. the AMASIS (2) painter) and sculpture. The *Phaedrus* of PLATO (1) relates that he was blinded for telling the traditional story of the rape of Helen by Paris in his *Helen*, but was cured by composing a *palinode* or recantation, denying that Helen ever went to Troy, but was replaced by a substitute, provided by Hera, to protect her virtue. He seems to have outraged the popular feeling which viewed Helen as a goddess.

Stesimbrotus (late C5 BC) A writer of biographies from Thasos who worked in

Athens, Stesimbrotus wrote lost biographies of THEMISTOCLES, THUCYDIDES (1) and PERICLES; there are some quotations of his work in PLUTARCH. He was critical of Themistocles and Pericles, incidentally praising CIMON; no information on his attitude to Thucydides has survived. He also wrote on HOMER and on the mysteries of Samothrace.

Sthenelus (C5 BC) An Athenian writer of tragedies, none of whose work has survived: his style is described by ARISTOTLE (*Poetics* 22) as prosaic. ARISTOPHANES (1) ridicules his insipid quality and in *Wasps* suggests that he used stage properties rather than words for effect, and PLATO (2) accused him of plagiarism.

Stilpon (C4/3 BC) A philosopher from Megara, probably a student of EUCLIDES (1). He became the third head of the Megarian school when it was the most popular school in Greece: there he taught the founder of Stoicism, ZENO (2), and MENEDEMUS (1) of Eretria; he was also a popular visitor to Athens. He wrote a score of lost philosophical dialogues. His approach to philosophy was Socratic and he was most interested in ethics, maintaining that people are responsible for their own conduct; there is evidence, however, of the influence of Cynic thought, which probably derived from contact with ANTISTHENES, in his recommending as a virtue the avoidance of pleasure and pain. He adhered to the monism of the Megarian school and rejected the Theory of Ideas of PLATO (1). He influenced Stoic logic, and rejected as false all statements of identity, unless tautologous.

Strabo (c.64 BC–AD 24) A geographer from Amisea in Pontus on the Black Sea, he was educated in Rome where he studied under teachers of the Peripatetic school though his philosophical views were Stoic. He may have derived his approach to the study of geography,

which he closely associated with the study of history, from POSIDONIUS whom he knew while a child and whose work he used. His first work, which is lost, was *Notes on History* (*Hypomnemata*) in forty-seven books, continuing the work of POLYBIUS. He travelled widely: to Egypt, where he stayed for several months while his patron, Aelius Gallus, acted as prefect, to Ethiopia and the Yemen, and he made many visits to Rome. He wrote an extant treatise, *Geography*, in seventeen books, using much material from authors whose work is otherwise lost, and producing what is for us an irreplaceable source of information not only about ancient geography but also about history and the life of his times. However he seldom claims to have seen at first hand the places he describes, and used much material from the library at Alexandria.

His approach to geographical writing was generally practical rather than theoretical, in comparison with that of his predecessor ERATOSTHENES, of whose work and ideas he was quite critical, though his own technical and mathematical powers are not above criticism. He did however include a wealth of information on a variety of topics which are strictly extraneous to geography, but which enrich his work greatly. He made a point of trying to enlighten Greeks and Romans about each other: he almost certainly held Roman citizenship. He understood the need of the rulers and military commanders of the Roman empire to have accurate geographical information at their disposal. He returned to his native Amisea in 7 BC and remained there until his death.

Stratocles (c.355–c.290 BC) An Athenian politician of the deme of Diomeia, the son of Euthydemus, he was the state prosecutor in the trial of HARPALUS in 324 when he accused DEMOSTHENES (2) of profiting from Harpalus' loot. In 307 he became the agent and supporter of ANTIGONUS (1) I the One-eyed and his son, DEMETRIUS

(3) I the Besieger, who restored democracy to Athens: he proposed lavish honours for Demetrius and won the hostility of the Athenians for his slavish sycophancy. After the defeat of Antigonus and Demetrius at Ipsus in 301, Stratocles lost his influence, but regained it in 294 when Demetrius gained the throne of Macedonia and control over Athens. A decree he passed in the Assembly in 292 to honour LYSIMACHUS' friend PHILIPPIDES is extant.

Straton 1. (died 269 BC) A Peripatetic (Aristotelian) scholar and writer from Lampsacus who studied at Athens at the Lyceum under THEOPHRASTUS: he went c.292 to Alexandria to the court of PTOLEMY (1) I to educate his son, the future PTOLEMY (2) II. He was probably involved in the founding of the Museum of Alexandria, the most important offshoot and true heir of the Lyceum. On the death of Theophrastus c.287 he returned to Athens to head the Lyceum, and remained in the post until his death. He was the last head of the Lyceum to do important original research.

DIOGENES (5) Laërtius gives a list of about forty of his works including ethics, logic, physics, cosmology, psychology and zoology. Only fragments of his writings survive, however. His preference was for natural science rather than ethics or politics, whence he was nicknamed *Physicus* 'The Physicist' as a result of his work on physics and cosmology. His main contribution to the study of nature was a readiness to use systematic experimentation as a tool of research. A proof of the existence of void (denied by ARISTOTLE) which was taken from a work by Straton and included by HERON in the introduction to his *Pneumatics* illustrates well Straton's methodology, which involved the construction of special apparatus to conduct the experiment. His findings fitted the atomic theory of DEMOCRITUS, but it seems likely that Straton conceived of the void as being tiny interstices between pieces of matter, and rejected the

atomists' theory of the external void. He reinforced his theory of the void from the ability of light to penetrate water, and formulated the basis of a correct theory of sound. One of his disciples was ERASISTRATUS, who experimentally weighed a bird with its droppings to prove weight change in the animal body. Straton preferred the theory of Democritus that all elements have gravity to the view of Aristotle, founder of the Lyceum, that fire and air have negative gravity, namely lightness rather than weight. According to Cicero, Straton attributed divinity to nature alone, and considered that all causes required to explain generation, growth and decay could be found in nature. This contradicted Aristotle's postulation of celestial divine movers, but was mainly directed against the Stoics. He was, however, true to Aristotle in accepting that the universe is geocentric, unique and uncreated. Straton also made progress in psychology, discovering the relation between the senses and the mind: he taught that every creature that has perception has a mind and, perhaps under the influence of his contemporary EPICURUS, saw man as a superior animal rather than considering animals as degenerate men. See B. Farrington (1967) *Greek Science*, London: Weidenfeld & Nicolson; D.J. Furley (1989) in *Cosmic Problems*, Cambridge: CUP.

2. (c.300 BC) A poet of the New Comedy, we have one fragment from a play of his in which a cook is described as fond of using Homeric and other obsolete words and phrases: it is therefore jokingly said that he must be a rhapsode's slave.

3. (C2 AD) A writer of epigrams from Sardis, whose works, mostly explicit and pederastic, were included in the *Greek Anthology* Books 11 and 12.

Stratonice (C3 BC) A daughter of DEMETRIUS (3) I the Besieger and of Phila the daughter of ANTIPATER (1): in 298 she was married to SELEUCUS (1) I and bore him a child; in 292, however, she was passed to his eldest son, ANTIOCHUS (1) I, the son of his first wife Apama, who took her east to the huge tract of land he was now appointed to rule as his father's partner in government and with the style of king. An almost certainly fictitious romantic love story was built around this unusual development, involving the name of the physician ERASISTRATUS, who was credited with diagnosing a life-threatening illness on the part of Antiochus as caused by a secret passion for his stepmother. However, by this time Demetrius was dead and Seleucus doubtless wished to enhance his son's position by uniting him with a woman of proved fertility. She bore her new husband three children, ANTIOCHUS (2) II, Seleucus and Apame, who was married to MAGAS of Cyrene.

Stratonicus (C4 BC) An Athenian musician and wit. He was a citharist who improved the instrument by increasing the number of strings to eleven. ATHENAEUS (350 d.) quotes a number of his witticisms.

Strattis (late C5 BC) An Athenian writer of comedies, many of which appear to have been parodies of tragedies. Nineteen titles of his plays are known, and several recall classical tragedies such as *Medea*, *The Phoenician Women* and *Philoctetes*. In his *Callippides*, the portrayal of Heracles as a glutton accorded with long-standing practice. No play survives, but seventy quotations from them are extant.

T

Tauriscus (C1 BC) A sculptor from Tralles in Asia Minor, the son of Artemidorus. He made some Hermerotes (combined statues of Eros and Hermes) which the Roman noble C. Asinius Pollio acquired. He also made, in collaboration with his brother Apollonius, a marble group at Rhodes of the Theban heroes Zethus, Amphion and Dirce, with the bull. This group was copied in the Farnese group found in the Baths of Caracalla at Rome.

Taxiles (C4 BC) An Indian king of a territory between the rivers Indus and Jhelum of which Takshashila (Taxila) was the capital. His real name was Ambhi (Greek: 'Omphis'). Being an enemy of PORUS, when he heard of the approach of the forces of ALEXANDER (3) III the Great in 327, he sent an envoy to the king to make his peace. In spring the following year, when Alexander crossed the Indus, he kept his kingdom, which Alexander used as his base. A Macedonian governor, Philippus, was appointed as Taxiles' superior, but the death of Alexander brought equality with the governor and then, after Philippus' murder, relief from foreign rule. Soon afterwards, however, his kingdom was absorbed by the Maurya empire of Chandragupta (SANDRACOTTUS).

Teleclides (C5 BC) An Athenian writer of Old Comedy who won several first prizes for his plays: three at the City Dionysia festival and five at the Lenaea. Eight titles are known, including *The Furies, Amphictions* and *Hesiods* (a type of plural subject common in CRATINUS' *oeuvre*). Seventy quotations from his works are extant, showing among other things hostility to PERICLES and a link between EURIPIDES and SOCRATES.

Teles (C3 BC) A Cynic philosopher from Megara who was the first such philosopher to write diatribes (brief discourses about morals, which were frequent compositions of the Cynic and Stoic schools) of which some quotations have survived. His interest lies in references in his work to earlier writers, such as BION (1), STILPON and CRATES (2) the Cynic.

Telesilla (C5 BC) A poet from Argos. Nine fragments of her poems survive showing that she wrote choral lyrics, often touching Argive affairs, for a choir of girls to sing. Her lyrics appear to have consisted of poetic versions of the stories of myths, with several references to the gods, Apollo and Artemis. She gave her name to a line of verse, the telesillean, a 'headless' glyconic, i.e. with the first syllable omitted. A statue at Argos depicted her putting a helmet on her head, and she was credited by PAUSANIAS (3), perhaps wrongly, with the plan to arm the women after Argos had been defeated by the Spartan king, CLEOMENES (1) I in 494.

Telestes (C5/4 BC) A poet from Selinus in Sicily who composed dithyrambs and won a first prize at Athens in 401. Four fragments of his poems survive from works entitled *The Argo*, *Asclepius* and *Hymenaeus*. His poetry was read by ALEXANDER (3) III the Great, and he was honoured with a statue at Sicyon.

Teleutias (early C4 BC) A Spartan admiral, a younger brother of King AGESILAUS II. He was appointed to command a fleet in the Corinthian Gulf in 392, when he swept the sea of the Corinthian fleet. The following year he operated in the Aegean, where he won Samos over to Sparta, cut off the democrats in Rhodes, and captured ten Athenian ships that were sailing to Cyprus to reinforce EVAGORAS. In 389 and 388 he led Spartan operations from Aegina against the Piraeus, on which he conducted a successful raid.

Terpander (early C7 BC) A musician and poet from Antissa in Lesbos where he was the leader of a guild of citharodes (singers who accompanied themselves on the cithara). He migrated *c.*680 to Sparta, then a great centre of culture, where he established a citharodic competition at the festival of Carnea in 676, which he won that year. He was said to have prevented the outbreak of a civil war in Sparta with his music. He won first prizes in four successive Pythian Games at Delphi. He was later credited with being an innovator in composition and the technology of instruments, composing a canon of seven 'nomes' (regulated styles for solo pieces for the cithara), following which he set his own songs and some lines from HOMER to the lyre, making up 'preludes' and drinking-songs for the cithara, and inventing an improved cithara with seven strings. A few fragments of text are ascribed to him, including a libation-song and a piece

resembling an ode of PINDAR. It is practically certain that these are not his work.

Thales (*c.*625–547 BC) A natural philosopher from Miletus in Asia Minor, the son of Examyes. ARISTOTLE considered him to be the first natural philosopher and cosmologist, and states that Thales held water to be the first principle of all things. HERODOTUS (1. 74) reports that Thales predicted the year of a solar eclipse, assumed, if true, to be that of 28 May, 585. He also states that Thales urged the Greeks of Ionia to combine in a political union with its capital at Teos. Thales was believed by later generations to have been an innovator in geometry, astronomy and engineering, but he left no written material, except perhaps for a verse handbook on navigation, *Astronomy for Sailors*, which has been attributed to him. He was credited by the ancients with some remarkable feats of measurement, such as a calculation of the height of the pyramids by their shadows, and the reckoning of the solstices and astronomic seasons. It is said that he considered the earth to be floating on water and that there were gods in every object, for example: he believed that a lodestone had a spirit that made it move. He owed a debt to his oriental and Egyptian predecessors in cosmology. He was accounted one of the SEVEN SAGES. See J. Barnes (1982) *The Presocratic Philosophers*, London: Kegan & Paul; and G.S. Kirk, J.E. Raven and M. Schofield (1982) *The Presocratic Philosophers*, Cambridge: CUP.

Thaletas (C7 BC) An early lyric poet from Gortyn in Crete who founded the *Gymnopaedia* '(games of) naked children', at Sparta. Thaletas is also said to have used his songs to prevent civil war or to drive off a plague. His compositions, which have not survived, encouraged obedience to law and included paeans (songs addressed to gods for various purposes) and songs for dancing. He invented new metres for poetry, the cretic and the paeonic.

Theaetetus (*c*.415–369 BC) A mathematician from Athens who was portrayed by his friend and teacher, PLATO (1), in the dialogue named after him. He learnt mathematics from Theodorus of Cyrene and elaborated the theories on which the tenth and thirteenth books of EUCLID's *Elements* are based. He formed the theory and definitions of irrational lines and devised methods to construct theoretically the five regular solids and worked out how to fit them into spheres.

Theagenes 1. (mid-C7 BC) A tyrant of Megara who attacked his rich enemies by destroying their cattle, and won popular support and an armed guard. He encouraged his Athenian son-in-law, CYLON, to seize power in Athens. He built a water conduit and fountain-house in Megara which have been excavated. He may have been responsible for the seizure of Salamis from Athens, but was eventually expelled from Megara.

2. (early C6 BC) A Homeric scholar from Rhegium (Reggio in Calabria). In his lost critical work, *Homer*, he interpreted the gods allegorically, claiming that they were in reality powerful natural phenomena and that their quarrels were the raging of the elements.

Theages (C5 BC) The son of Demodocus and a member of the circle of SOCRATES whose bad health PLATO (1) refers to in the *Republic*, calling it 'the bridle of Theages' as it prevented him from a political career and steered him into philosophy. Though mentioned in Plato's *Apology*, he was dead by 399. *Theages*, a pseudonymous work foisted on Plato, probably from the circle of XENOCRATES in the later fourth century, is mainly concerned with Socrates' 'divine sign'.

Theano (C6 BC) The name, according to tradition, of the wife of PYTHAGORAS (1) and the mother of Myia and Arignote. However, she may have been otherwise related to Pythagoras (perhaps a disciple) as she was the wife of Brontinus. DIO-GENES (5) Laërtius attributes writings to her, but seven letters and a fragment of a work *On Piety* ascribed to her must be dated later than Pythagoras' time.

Themistocles (*c*.524–459 BC) An Athenian statesman of the deme of the Phrearrhii who was the leader of Athens in the Persian wars of 480/79. He was a member of an ancient clan, the Lycomidae, but his mother was not of Athenian blood. He was elected eponymous archon for the year 493/2, five years before election to the archonship was suppressed in favour of sortition, a reform he may have supported and which had the effect of reducing the authority of the archons in favour of that of the elected generals. Themistocles was a product of the reforms of CLEISTHENES (2), elected by the extended franchise enacted thereby; he had the foresight to anticipate a Persian attack and organised the building of Piraeus as a harbour in place of the exposed roadstead at Phaleron. Whether he played any part in the trial of MILTIADES in 493, we do not know. In 490, the year of the battle of Marathon, he was elected general of his tribe. Though ostracism, the procedure of voting once a year for the exile of a citizen whose presence in Attica was considered undesirable, was invented *c*.487 to prevent the re-establishment of the tyranny, its use in the years leading up to the Persian invasion of 480 effectively eliminated all opposition to Themistocles, leaving him the uncontested leader of Athens during a crisis. In 483 he persuaded the people to spend Athens' greatly increased wealth, which was derived from the silver mines at Laurium, on improving the navy rather than on a hand-out to the citizens. That year XERXES, the Persian king, ordered a ship canal to be dug through the peninsula of Athos to facilitate his attack on Greece, though Themistocles based his argument to the people on the threat from Aegina, an island close to Athens with which she was constantly at war, and which he suggested might join the Persians. So the fleet was increased from seventy to two hundred fighting ships, and Athenian naval power was established.

The ostracised rivals of Themistocles, including ARISTIDES (1), were allowed to return in time for the struggle with Persia. In 480 Themistocles was an elected general and his influence exceeded that of his colleagues. He led an Athenian naval force into Thessaly under the supreme command of the Spartan, EURYBIADES, to a position at Artemisium in Euboea where an indecisive battle was fought over three days. During the retreat down the Euripus channel, Themistocles left messages that were designed to win the support of the Greeks manning the ships of Xerxes. He played a decisive part in the victory at Salamis, though he did so to some extent in spite of his allies, the Spartans, the natural leaders of Greek resistance. HER-ODOTUS reports the warnings that were received from the oracular shrine at Delphi, which seems to have tried to maintain a neutral stance in the war. One oracle, however, Themistocles interpreted as predicting the possibility of a victory at the island of Salamis. After the loss of Thermopylae, the Spartans and the other Peloponnesians wished to withdraw all Greek forces to the Peloponnese and take cover behind a defence work on the Isthmus of Corinth. Themistocles persuaded the Athenians to abandon their city and had them transported to Salamis, Aegina and the Peloponnese. He persuaded Eurybiades to revoke a hasty decision to withdraw the fleet from the bay of Salamis. However, as time went by and the Peloponnesian Greeks feared that a land attack and, consequently, a retreat, were imminent, he secretly warned the Persians that they could trap the Greek

fleet and destroy it, and offered to change sides. Xerxes, perhaps concerned by the approach of autumn, seized the opportunity that Themistocles' message seemed to offer and decided to attack. His ships sailed into the bay (probably at night). Warned by a deserting Tenian ship, the Greeks attacked at dawn and defeated the Persian fleet in the narrow waters so decisively that its remnant retired to Asia. During the winter that followed, Themistocles was honoured at Sparta as no non-Spartan had ever been before.

He was not involved in the military actions of 479, but the following winter, after the Persian menace was removed, he went to Sparta ahead of an embassy to negotiate a Spartan request that Athens should not rebuild her city walls. He instructed his countrymen to hasten the rebuilding, meanwhile denying at Sparta that they were working on the walls. When reports came that he was lying, he urged the Spartans to send an embassy to find out the truth, but the embassy were detained as hostages on their arrival in Athens to ensure the safety of the Athenian embassy. Thus, when the walls had reached a reasonable height, he was able to admit the truth and return home with impunity. He also ensured that the Piraeus was strongly fortified, claiming that it would make an excellent base against any future Persian naval attack. The aftermath of the Persian War saw a pro-Spartan conservative revival at Athens under the leadership of CIMON, and Themistocles' influence waned. In 476 he was the chorus-leader in a tragedy by PHRYNI-CHUS (1), which won first prize, but by 470 he suffered ostracism and moved to Argos, intriguing with people in the Peloponnese who opposed Sparta. The Spartan government got wind of these intrigues and c.468 accused Themistocles of having plotted with PAUSANIAS (1). At Athens he was tried in his absence and condemned to death. He escaped to the west, Corcyra and Epirus, then to Macedonia, whence he crossed the sea to Asia, where the new Persian king, ARTAXERXES (1) I, after his accession in 465, granted him the governorship of Magnesia on the Maeander in Phrygia. He died there (a story that he killed himself was known to the historian, THUCYDIDES 2). His family was allowed to return to Athens. A hostile attitude to him is evident in all ancient sources except Thucydides who admired him. See R.J. Lenardon (1978) *The Saga of Themistocles*, London: Thames & Hudson; and A.J. Podlecki (1975) *The Life of Themistocles*, Montreal; London: McGill-Queen's University Press.

Theocritus (c.300–c.260 BC) A pastoral poet from Syracuse who was the son of Praxagoras and Philinna. He appears to have left Syracuse early in life, perhaps for political reasons connected with the anarchy following the death of AGATHOCLES (1), and then to have lived in southern Italy and Cos, where he met PHILETAS and may have studied under him. He may also have studied medicine there, perhaps at the school of his father's namesake. He also knew and perhaps studied under the epigrammatist, ASCLEPIADES (1) of Samos. He did not, however, know the poet ARATUS (1), and the person of that name mentioned in his poetry is another. It was probably on Cos that he met Nicias of Miletus, a poet and doctor whom he mentions in three of his poems. He remained attached to his homeland and tried c.275 to persuade HIERON (2) II, the tyrant of Syracuse, to become his patron (cf. *Idyll* 16). After failing in this request, he appealed instead c.274 to PTOLEMY (2) II Philadelphus, king of Egypt. The connection with Cos, the king's birthplace, may have helped him, and about that time he composed an encomium, *Idyll* 17, on the king and his deified parents. While in Alexandria he must have known CALLIMACHUS (3), with whose novel views about poetry he clearly sympathised. His own poems, designated by posterity as *eidyllia* ('miniature

pictures'), accord closely with Callimachus' preference for the well-crafted, single-theme poem of limited length and a defined moment of time. His poems were probably all composed in Cos or Alexandria, though the inspiration of Sicily and southern Italy remained with him. Research on the botanical material in his poems has shown a Coan rather than a Sicilian location for the composition of the pastoral *Idylls*. Nearly all our information about his life rests on inferences from his works.

His chief works, the *Idylls* (a deceptive term, for his poems are much more robust and energetic than the word 'idyll' suggests), are mostly composed in hexameter verse in a literary form of the Doric dialect, the speech of his native Syracuse, and mark the beginning of a new genre of poetry, the rustic or bucolic (less than a third of the idylls are on bucolic subjects, however), which was later imitated by the Roman poet Virgil in his *Eclogues*, and to some extent by the Greeks, MOSCHUS and BION (2). However, Theocritus used different metres and the Aeolic dialect in the last three idylls and the Ionic dialect in 22. Of the works attributed to Theocritus, there survive thirty longer poems (the *Idylls*), twenty-four epigrams and a few fragments. Some of these poems, however, are manifestly not his work (*Idylls*, 19, 20, 21, 23 and the last three epigrams), and some are of dubious authorship (*Idylls*, 25, 27) as it was a common practice to ascribe imitations to the master.

The order in which they have come down to us cannot be the chronological order of composition (the early poem to Hieron, for example, is number 16), but relates to the subject matter and dialect, and the evidence from papyri for the original order is conflicting. The first part of the collection consists of the bucolic poems, his most characteristic work, which present in the dramatic form of dialogues or contests between country folk, with charming freshness and vigour, the country life of Sicily. We may assume these to be his earliest work and the work on which his fame was built. His seventh idyll, *Harvest Home* (*Thalysia*), gives the clearest indication of his literary tastes, as it includes a discussion of current poetry and a song competition. There are also poems of action based on myth where a critical moment or scene is enacted and explored. Two poems, 13 and 22, retell episodes from the myth of the Argonauts, seeming perhaps to reprove APOLLONIUS (1), the contemporary epic writer, for the enormity of his epic *Argonautica*. Theocritus' poems show great talent for conveying dramatic action and humour. Contrasting with his earlier rustic poems, which both charm and tease, and with the scenes drawn from myth, there are two urban mimes (2 and 15) in the style of SOPHRON, which also recall the works of the contemporary HERODAS. Related to them is 14 which shows features of the New Comedy. Theocritus had a lively visual imagination and was a brilliant writer of descriptions of objects and scenes, such as the cup in *Idyll* 1. His *oeuvre* contains some powerful and original poems, and expanded, with permanent effect, the range of subjects considered fit for poetic treatment. Love and art are particularly important in his work. See A.F.S. Gow (ed.) (1950) *Theocritus*, Cambridge: CUP (text, translation and commentary); R. Hunter (1996) *Theocritus and the Archaeology of Greek Poetry*, Cambridge: CUP; and G.O. Hutchinson (1990) *Hellenistic Poetry*, Oxford: Clarendon Press.

Theodectes (*c*.375–334 BC) A writer of tragedies and an orator from Phaselis in Lycia who lived and worked in Athens, where he successfully competed in the dramatic festivals. He was a pupil of PLATO (1), ISOCRATES and possibly ARISTOTLE, though the latter was his junior. Between 372 and his death he competed in thirteen festivals and won seven first prizes at the City Dionysia festivals and one at the Lenaea festival. Some frag-

ments of his fifty plays survive which show him to have followed in the footsteps of EURIPIDES. We have a number of titles of his works: *Lynceus*, praised by Aristotle for its structure, *Mausolus*, written to honour his late patron, MAUSOLUS, satrap of Caria, *Philoctetes*, in which the hero is wounded in his hand, not his foot, *Aias, Alcmaeon, Helen, Oedipus, Orestes* and *Tydeus*.

He took part in a competition in oratory at Halicarnassus to deliver an encomium in honour of Mausolus. Cicero in his *Orator* (172) comments on the polished quality of his prose. Theodectes also wrote a book on rhetoric, in which he analysed the virtues of the different sections of a speech, and which was admired by Aristotle, who published a lost summary of it entitled *Theodectea*. He died aged 41 while travelling to Eleusis. ALEXANDER (3) III the Great, who knew him through his acquaintance with Aristotle, honoured his memorial at Phaselis.

Theodoridas (C3 BC) A Syracusan poet who wrote dithyrambs and hexameters as well as epigrams against his enemies in the form of epitaphs, including one aimed at MNASICLES. He also wrote genuine epitaphs, a poem dedicated to the god of Love, a dithyramb entitled *The Centaur*, and lewd songs. Much of his work survives in the *Palatine Anthology*.

Theodorus 1. (*c*.550–*c*.520 BC) A versatile artist and technologist from Samos. Though none of his work survives intact, we have much information on his achievements from later authors. He worked for CROESUS, for whom he made two large silver bowls for dedication at Delphi, and for POLYCRATES (1), for whom he made the famous gold signet ring with an engraved emerald seal which he threw in the sea, and he made a golden vine which DARIUS (1) I acquired. He is said to have invented a number of tools used by builders, including the line, rule, lathe and lever, and to have made great strides in clay modelling and the casting of bronze statues (a realistic self-portrait in bronze by Theodorus was known in Roman times). He collaborated with Telecles in making a statue of Apollo for Samos, and they are said by DIODORUS (3) to have gone to Egypt to find the correct proportions for modelling the human body.

As an architect, he designed an assembly hall, the Scias, for Sparta, and was involved in the design of the temple of Artemis at Ephesus, where he seems to have suggested the inclusion of a dampproof course in the foundations, and that of Hera at Samos (built by Rhoecus), about which he wrote a book, not extant.

2. (late C5 BC) A mathematician from Cyrene who taught PLATO (1) and THEAETETUS. He had been an associate of SOCRATES and had studied under the philosopher PROTAGORAS. According to Plato he proved that the square roots of the non-square numbers up to seventeen are irrational.

Theodosius (*c*.100 BC) An astronomer and mathematician from Bithynia who wrote on the properties of the sphere. He wrote *Spherics* in three books, in which he treated circles on the surface of the sphere; *Habitations*, on the variations in astronomical phenomena in different parts of the Earth; and *Days and Nights*, a treatise in two books on the lengths of day and night throughout the year (all these works are extant). He also wrote a commentary on ARCHIMEDES' *Method*. STRABO credited him with the invention of a sundial that could be used anywhere.

Theognis 1. (C6? BC) An elegiac poet from Megara. A collection of nearly 1,400 extant lines of verse is attributed to him in manuscripts, but only a fraction of this number is likely to be his genuine work. The collection seems to be a compilation from Hellenistic anthologies of

extracts from the works of several poets: there is material attested elsewhere as the work of MIMNERMUS, SOLON, TYRTAEUS and Evenus of Paros. Some scholars believe that the genuine poems of Theognis can be distinguished by a 'seal', which is mentioned near the start of the collection and is thought to be a reference to his addressing a friend named Cyrnus or Polypaides. The poems that contain this address are markedly individual and very frank. On the basis of this evidence, some 300 lines are now attributed with confidence to Theognis, namely the poems addressed to Cyrnus and a few quotations by early sources that name Theognis. The man who emerges expresses the traditional aristocratic morality, is a person of strong feelings, is bitter towards his enemies, complains of the treachery of friends; robbed of his lands, he is compelled by political turmoil to go into an unwelcome exile, desirous of revenge for the wrongs he feels he has suffered. There are some references to historical events, though they cover such a great length of time that it is even disputed which century he lived in.

Other poems in the collection, *Theognidia*, were composed for performance at drinking parties (*symposia*) and reflect the life and preoccupations of Greeks in general of the period up to the Peloponnesian War (431–404). This wider collection contains many poems about the pleasure of society and parties. 'Book 2', the final section of all, derives from a separate manuscript consisting of erotic poems that are often banal and usually on pederastic themes, and may well have been composed at Athens in the fifth century. The collection as a whole offers a valuable insight into the thoughts and feelings of Greek men in the sixth and fifth centuries BC and also contains some gems. See M.L. West (1974) *Studies in Greek Elegy and Iambus*, Berlin; New York: de Gruyter; and T.J. Figueira and G. Nagy (eds) (1997) *Theognis of*

Megara, Ann Arbor, MI: Books on Demand.

2. (C5 BC) An Athenian writer of tragedies who was stated by a scholiast to be the same as the Theognis who was one of the THIRTY TYRANTS of Athens in 404/3. ARISTOPHANES (1) mocked him in two of his comedies for his boring work.

Theon 1. of Alexandria (C1 BC) A literary commentator and head of the school of Alexandria, the son of Artemidorus of Tarsus, who was himself author of a commentary on the bucolic poets. He wrote extensive commentaries on the Alexandrian poets and a lexicon of the vocabulary of drama. He also wrote a handbook of syntax. Fragments of his work survive. Theon was succeeded by APION as head of the school.

2. of Smyrna (C1 AD) A mathematician and Platonist who wrote a lost commentary on the *Republic* of PLATO (1), and an extant elementary work on arithmetic, *Aspects of Mathematics Useful for Reading Plato*, which includes material on musical harmony and astronomy. A work of his on the order in which to study Plato's works has recently been discovered in an Arabic translation.

Theophilus (C4 BC) An Athenian writer of comedies of whose works twelve extracts survive. We know the titles of eight plays and that he won first prize in 329.

Theophrastus (*c*.370–*c*.287 BC) A philosopher and scientist from Eresus in Lesbos who was the pupil, friend and collaborator of ARISTOTLE, and his successor as head of the Peripatetic school. Theophrastus joined Aristotle after the latter had left the Academy on the death of PLATO (1), migrated to Assos in the Troad near Lesbos and stayed with him there and at Athens from 335 until in 322 Aristotle was forced to leave Athens and he became head of the school that Aristotle had founded there. Theophrastus was the teacher, associate and friend of the Athenian ruler DEMETRIUS (2) of Phaleron, a general and later the governor of Athens under CASSANDER, through whose influence he was permitted, though a foreigner, to own property at Athens. From 317–315 he advised Demetrius on constitutional law and was highly influential in his revision of Athenian law, but, after the fall of Demetrius in 307, he was forced to leave Athens temporarily by a law of Sophocles prohibiting philosophical schools unless they were sanctioned by the Assembly. However, the law was quickly repealed. Through Demetrius' influence, Theophrastus developed friendly contacts with Cassander and PTOLEMY (1) I, and also taught DINARCHUS. He was succeeded on his death by STRATON (1).

Theophrastus was a tireless researcher and writer. He continued to explore the fields of knowledge that had interested his predecessor, though he made some departures from Aristotle's doctrine in the direction of greater reliance on empirical observation and a more naturalistic approach in ethics, and questioned Aristotle's heavy reliance on teleological arguments in discussing natural processes. The vast majority of his copious output is lost to us, though it was known to Cicero, Seneca, PLUTARCH, PORPHYRY and other ancient scholars. We learn much from DIOGENES (5) Laërtius who wrote his biography, including lists of his works. Fragments of his work, *The Doctrines of the Natural Philosophers* (including the extant work, *On the Senses*) in eighteen books, show that he developed and criticised Aristotle's work on the systems of his predecessors. It is the first doxography or treatise setting out the teachings of earlier philosophical writers in a systematic way, with an arrangement by topics. His *Laws*, also in eighteen books, was a comparative study of the laws and customs of the Greek cities. He collaborated with EUDEMUS in modifying Aristotle's modal logic, and advanced the study of propositional logic. He believed the universe to be eternal and the heavens to be divine, but rejected the existence of 'ether' as a fifth element. The philosopher EPICURUS adopted his doctrine of meteorology.

His extant works, the text of which is notoriously faulty, are mainly concerned with biology, a passion he shared with Aristotle, and a subject in which he laid the foundations for future research. His two surviving botanical works are *Researches into Plants*, in nine books, concerned with the descriptions and classification of plants, and *The Aetiology of Plants*, in six books, about their physiology. In his *Metaphysics*, named after Aristotle's work of the same title, he criticises some of his predecessor's weaker arguments, but otherwise offers no progress. We also have several short treatises of which the first three, *Fire*, *Winds* and *Stones*, may have been parts of a larger work entitled *Physics*. His *Meteorology* was preserved in Arabic. We also have *Sweat*, *Paralysis*, *Swooning*, *Odours* and *Tiredness*. His best-known work is, however, the *Characters*, which contains thirty sketches describing types of people who in some way deviate from normal behaviour. Besides illustrating Aristotle's analysis of human virtues and vices in the *Ethics*, the work was a practical handbook for teachers of rhetoric and comic writers. Chaucer's wife of Bath complained of his hostile views on marriage, which she derived, perhaps inaccurately, from a compilation made by Jerome. See also DIOCLES.

Theopompus 1. (reigned *c.*720–*c.*670 BC) A king of Sparta of the Eurypontid house. TYRTAEUS declares him, together with his colleague, Polydorus, responsible for the original Spartan conquest of Messenia in 710, and a reform of the Spartan constitution by which the powers and procedures of the Spartiate assembly were regulated and curtailed. The assembly (*Apella*) would no longer have the right to propose or amend legislation, but could only vote on proposals put to it by the kings and council. This reform, laid down in the Great *Rhetra*, was in later times attributed to the legendary LYCURGUS (2).

2. (active *c.*410–*c.*370 BC) An Athenian writer of comedies, of whose works we know the titles of twenty, including *Odysseus*, *Penelope* and *The Sirens*, which are on Odyssean themes.

3. (*c.*378–*c.*320 BC) A historian from Chios, the son of Damasistratus. He studied under ISOCRATES (who had lived in Chios) at Athens and worked as a speech-writer. He and his father were exiled from Chios *c.*334 for their pro-Spartan sympathies. In 332, however, ALEXANDER (3) III the Great had him restored to oppose the pro-Persian leaders of Chios. However, when Alexander died in 323, he was forced to flee again and wandered about, everywhere an outcast, until he found momentary refuge at the court of PTOLEMY (1) I at Alexandria. However, Ptolemy decided to eliminate him as a troublemaker, and Theopompus barely escaped with his life. Though he received help from friends, he died soon afterwards.

He was greatly influenced by Isocrates and wrote political pamphlets on subjects similar to those of his teacher. Known titles are: *Letters from Chios*, *A Panegyric on Philip II* and *Advice to Alexander*. He also wrote an attack on PLATO (1) and his followers. He travelled widely in Greece in pursuit of material for his historical works, conducted careful research and stayed for some time at the court of PHILIP (1) II. His works of history were: an *Epitome of Herodotus* in two books; a *History of Greece*, continuing the work of THUCYDIDES (2) down to 394, the battle of Cnidus, in twelve books, to be compared with XENOPHON'S (1) work of the same name, but evidently much fuller; and *The History of Philip*, his most ambitious work, published after 324 and running to fifty-eight books of which many fragments and quotations survive. This last work was far more than a biography of the Macedonian king or even an account of his reign: he is the central focus of a work that ranged widely over Greek and non-Greek events during that time. Theopompus' standpoint was aristocratic and pro-Spartan, his style was self-conscious and rhetorical, and his interests were extremely wide, including geography, religion, 'miracles' and myths, so that there were frequent digressions in the work. He was also inclined to moralise and to condemn the objects of his study, but one man stood out from this constant vilification, his ideal statesman, Philip. See W.R. Connor (1968) *Theopompus and Fifth-Century Athens*, Washington, DC: Center for Hellenic Studies, distributed by Harvard University Press, Cambridge, MA.

Theramenes (died 404 BC) An Athenian statesman, the son of Hagnon who had led the colonisation of Amphipolis. Theramenes was a moderate conservative whose wish to restrain the excesses of the radical democracy led ultimately to his downfall at the hands of radical oligarchs. He came to the fore in 411 when he played a leading part in setting up the rule of the narrowly oligarchic Four Hundred at Athens. Then, four months later, as the plans of the oligarchs misfired and opposition came from the army and fleet at Samos, he sought to open up the government to a much larger body, an assembly of 'Five Thousand', already promised by the Four Hundred, and now proposed as representing the element needed to complete the revival of the 'ancestral constitution'. He played an important part in the constitution-making. He also led the force that destroyed the fort established by the oligarchs at Eëtionea in the Piraeus. After the fall of the Five Thousand, he was given a naval command in 410 and sailed his squadron into Hellespontine waters to assert Athenian supremacy at sea and

expel supporters of the radical oligarchs. He also helped ARCHELAUS (2), king of Macedonia, to capture Pydna. Theramenes had been instrumental in persuading the Five Thousand to recall ALCIBIADES from exile and co-operated with his leadership of the Aegean fleet. His involvement in the victory at Arginusae near Lesbos in 406 and the subsequent failure of the Athenians, owing to a storm, to pick up the survivors and the dead from the sea, is controversial. Then only a ship's captain, he along with THRASYBULUS (2) was put in command of the mission. Bad weather impeded the rescue attempt, but he was later put on trial at Athens for negligence. In the upshot, however, the generals who had commanded the fleet were found guilty of negligence in illegal proceedings and executed. XENOPHON (1) criticised Theramenes for shifting the blame due to him on to the generals, but the usually critical ARISTOPHANES (1) did not reproach him when he mentioned him the following year in *Frogs*. In 404 he was appointed by the people, now starving as a result of the naval blockade, as envoy to negotiate peace with Sparta. He deliberately stayed there for three months to ensure Athenian compliance with whatever terms could be obtained. On his return, he was made a member of a board of ten to arrange the surrender, and attended the Peloponnesian League's congress to receive the final humiliating terms.

In summer 404 Theramenes played a major role in the establishment of the THIRTY TYRANTS, the oligarchic government that LYSANDER favoured. He was entrusted personally with the choice of ten of this board of thirty, whose ostensible task was to draw up a constitution, and initially he collaborated with his radical friend CRITIAS, who returned from exile. In early autumn he pressed for the creation of a list of 3,000 citizens who would be entitled to take part in government. A split soon developed, however, and when he protested at the growing number of executions Critias impeached him before the council and accused him of living up to his nickname 'Buskin' (*Kothurnos*), a boot that fits either foot. Theramenes defended himself so powerfully, however, that he appeared likely to convince the councillors, so Critias brought in an armed band, struck Theramenes' name off the list of the Three Thousand and pronounced the death sentence. He was torn from the altar and led off to drink hemlock, after which he sarcastically toasted 'the handsome Critias'. He was seen by writers of the fourth century, such as ARISTOTLE, as a genuine moderate. He must, however, take much of the blame for the disastrous events of 404/3. See D. Kagan (1987) *The Fall of the Athenian Empire*, Ithaca, NY; London: Cornell University Press.

Theron (ruled *c*.489–473 BC) A tyrant of Acragas (Agrigento) on the south coast of Sicily who beautified his city and ruled mildly and benevolently. He formed an alliance with Syracuse by marrying his daughter, Demarete, to GELON. He may have fought alongside Gelon against the Carthaginians *c*.486, from whose ally, Tertillus, he took Himera on the north coast in 483. In 480 the Carthaginians under HAMILCAR came in force to recover Himera, but were defeated soundly by Theron and Gelon. Theron, a patron of the arts and literature, used the spoils taken from the Carthaginians to improve his city. He was honoured by his countrymen as a hero after his death, but his son Thrasydaeus, who succeeded him, was quickly overthrown.

Thespis (C6 BC) The supposed first writer of tragedies, from the Attic deme of Icaria. An almost mythical figure, he is credited by the *Suda* with the invention of the mask always worn by actors in ancient Greek productions and with the first production of a tragedy at the Athenian March festival of the City Dionysia. He is mentioned on the Parian Marble

inscription as being active in the decade following 538. He may have received encouragement from the tyrant PISISTRATUS. Aristotle is reported by Themistius as stating that Thespis' innovation consisted of adding speaking parts to the already flourishing choric performances at the festival. Evidence for him is, however, very thin.

Thibron 1. (died 391 BC) A Spartan general who in autumn 400 led a large force of Sparta's Peloponnesian allies and Helots to Ionia with the aim of defending Greek cities from the Persian satrap TISSAPHERNES, a task previously undertaken by the Athenian navy. He took Magnesia, but failed to take Tralles, and the following spring reinforced his army with 6,000 men from the mercenary Greek army that had fought for CYRUS (2). That year he had further successes, taking most of Aeolis, but failing to capture Larissa. He was then ordered by the ephors to direct his attack at Caria to the south, but, while he was at Ephesus preparing for the offensive, he was replaced by DERCYLIDAS. He returned to Sparta where he was charged with having permitted the looting of allied Greek cities, was tried and exiled. He was recalled by 391 when he was again sent to Asia Minor against the Persians. With an army of 8,000 men based at Ephesus he attacked Struthas, a newly appointed satrap in charge of Ionia and the coast. However, he behaved recklessly and allowed himself to be caught off-guard by a Persian cavalry force as he led a disorganised raiding party, and was killed along with much of his force. An author named Thibron, who may be the same man, is recorded by ARISTOTLE (*Politics*, 1333) as having written a book praising LYCURGUS (2) and his militaristic constitution.

2. (died 322 BC) A Spartan mercenary leader who in 324 murdered his commander, HARPALUS, in Crete, and replaced him at the head of his troops. He sailed with the troops to Africa, where he seized the territory of Cyrene and expelled the oligarchic rulers. OPHELLAS, the Macedonian general sent by PTOLEMY (1) I, ended his short-lived barony there and captured him.

Thirty Tyrants The oligarchic government at Athens in 404/3 BC set up by CRITIAS and THERAMENES under the direction of the Spartan general LYSANDER. It behaved extremely harshly and during its brief rule executed some 1,500 people, including Theramenes himself. Most of the thirty were dead within a year of their fall from power in September 403.

Thrasybulus 1. (early C6 BC) A tyrant of Miletus, friendly with the Corinthian tyrant PERIANDER, who HERODOTUS (5. 92) asserts was corrupted by him. During his reign Miletus was constantly at war with the Lydians until ALYATTES made terms with them, granting Miletus the status of a friend and ally.

2. (died 388 BC) An Athenian general and statesman, the son of Lycus of the deme of Steiria. While serving as a ship's captain in the fleet based at Samos in 411, he was caught up in events caused by the revolution of the Four Hundred at Athens and, with THRASYLLUS, he supported the Samian democrats whom the oligarchs, led by PISANDER, had tried to overthrow. The army and fleet at Samos, angered by reports of atrocities at Athens, elected Thrasybulus and Thrasyllus as generals and on Thrasybulus' proposal recalled ALCIBIADES from exile. In September 411 he was one of the commanders of the fleet that won the battle of Cynossema and had further successes leading up to Alcibiades' victory of Cyzicus in 410. At Arginusae in 406 he was again a ship's captain, and, like Theramenes, was charged with failing to rescue the survivors and pick up the dead bodies after the victory.

In 404, when the rule of the THIRTY TYRANTS was set up, Thrasybulus was banished and made his escape to Thebes, where he proved to be a focus for the democratic opposition. With seventy fellow exiles and the help of ISMENIAS, he seized the border-fort of Phyle from which he launched an attack on the occupying forces. In May 403 he led 1,000 supporters in a night attack on the Piraeus, which he took by storm, killing Critias, and when the Spartans declared an amnesty, he supported the reconciliation of the moderates and democrats in the city and the Piraeus. He became, with Anytus, a leader of the restored democratic state and attempted to enact a grant of citizenship to the metics and slaves who had supported his cause in the civil war, but was defeated by Archinus.

In the period following the restoration of democracy, and during the Corinthian War (395–386), Thrasybulus did much to enhance the influence of Athens and to restore her lost empire. He commanded the Athenian troops in the serious defeat at Nemea in 394. In 390 he led a fleet of forty ships, with a roving commission, which won back many Athenian allies in the Aegean Sea, but which lacked financial support from Athens which was spending revenue on state pay once more. After taking Byzantium with the help of the local democrats, therefore, he resorted to imposing a duty of 10 per cent on goods passing out of the Black Sea. He then sailed southwards, spending 389 in the area of Lesbos, and the following year turned his attention to the south of Asia Minor. At Aspendos on the River Eurymedon his troops pillaged the inhabitants' possessions and in revenge they killed Thrasybulus in his tent. He was one of the few bright lights of Athenian leadership during her darkest days, but had faults, including his failure to finish off DERCYLIDAS in the Hellespont in 390 and his policy of trying to restore the imperial pretensions that Athens could no longer afford. See Thucydides, *History*, Book 8;

Xenophon, *Hellenica*, Books 1–4; and D. Kagan (1987) *The Fall of the Athenian Empire*, Ithaca, NY; London: Cornell University Press.

Thrasyllus (died 405 BC) An Athenian politician and general who came to the fore in 411 when he was serving with the fleet at Samos. He organised resistance with THRASYBULUS (2) to the blandishments of the envoys whom the oligarchs sent from Athens, and joined the Samian democrats in their stand. He was elected general and assisted Thrasybulus in winning the naval victory of Cynossema. He was involved in naval campaigns in 410 and 409, operating in Ionia. He was elected general for the year 406/5 and was in command at the naval victory at Arginusae. However, along with his colleagues, he was illegally tried and executed for the failure of the fleet to rescue the shipwrecked survivors and retrieve the dead bodies of the Athenian sailors lost in the battle, which was caused by bad weather. For bibliography, see THRASYBULUS (2).

Thrasymachus (later C5 BC) A sophist and teacher of rhetoric from Chalcedon who is a major participant in the dialogue of Book 1 of PLATO (1)'s *Republic*, where he asserts the argument that 'justice' is what suits the strongest in society. The dramatic date of the book is *c*.420 and many argue that it represents a real memoir of SOCRATES, though Plato was a small child at the time. A part of an extant work Thrasymachus wrote *The Constitution*, refers to the 'ancestral constitution' beloved of the oligarchs of the time. His work shows a well-developed style including periodic structure and carefully controlled speech rhythm.

Thucydides 1. (*c*.500–*c*.423 BC) An Athenian conservative politician, an aristocrat, the son of Milesias, and related by marriage to the leading statesman CIMON. He succeeded Cimon as the leader of the traditionalist party and became the chief critic of PERICLES in the Assembly, being particularly hostile to Pericles' use of the Delian League's funds to build the temples on the Acropolis at Athens. He is said to have organised his party in the Assembly as a block. His outspoken attacks on Pericles led to his banishment for ten years through the process of ostracism *c*.443, which marked the end of his political career. He was prosecuted *c*.426 by Cephisodemus. He was related to THUCYDIDES (2). See D. Kagan (1969) *The Outbreak of the Peloponnesian War*, Ithaca, NY; London: Cornell University Press.

2. (*c*.455–*c*.400 BC) The historian of the first twenty years of the Peloponnesian War (431–404), he was an Athenian, born at Halimus, the son of Olorus and Hegesipyle, as well as a kinsman of both CIMON and THUCYDIDES (1), the politician. His father, an Athenian named after a Thracian king, had estates and a gold mine in the part of Thrace facing Thasos, which Thucydides inherited. In his youth he became a strong admirer of Pericles, the imperialist leader of the radical democratic party, despite his family connections with the conservatives. He was a victim of the plague at Athens *c*.430, but recovered and was a general in 424 when he was in command of a force at Thasos and was called upon to save Amphipolis from the Spartan general BRASIDAS. He hastened there with seven ships, but the city had surrendered before he could reach it. However, he secured the nearby port of Eion. Because he had not prevented the fall of Amphipolis, he was banished for twenty years. He went to live on his estates in Thrace and was able to travel widely, even to the Peloponnese, to collect material for his *History*, which he says he began to work on from the start of the war. There is a tradition that he was assassinated. He was buried in the family tomb of Cimon.

He did not complete his grand design of writing the history of the whole war, and the eight books (his own division) that have come down to us show varied levels of revision. The work falls into five distinct parts. Book 1 is an introductory section, including a great deal of material on the previous history of Greece, beginning from the point where HERODOTUS left off at the end of the Persian War in 479. Thucydides begins Book 1 with a long preface setting out his own philosophy on the writing of history and emphasising the importance of the war that is his subject in comparison with the events of earlier times. He is anxious to provide posterity with a warning of the way men will behave, human nature being what it is. He also gives a detailed account of the events and negotiations that led up to the outbreak of the war. Though he disapproved of Herodotus' all-encompassing approach to the writing of history, he accepted the desirability of filling in the gap between the two great wars of the fifth century and gives in some detail an account of the final years of THEMISTOCLES and PAUSANIAS (1) (the latter is of dubious accuracy). His longest digression is a summary history of the fifty years of more or less peaceful Greek history between 479–431 in which he traces the rise of Athens' imperial power. There are still, however, some inadequacies and gaps in his account of this period.

The second section, from the beginning of Book 2 to Book 5. 24, is a continuous account of the Archidamian War, and shows a high degree of finish, including speeches put in the mouths of the political and military leaders. It contains incidental references, added subsequently, to events much later in the war, such as the fall of Athens. The third section, the rest of Book 5, is short and deals with the period of unstable peace before the Sicilian expedition of 415. It contains no speeches except for the 'Melian Dialogue', but sets out documental evidence. The fourth section, Books 6 and 7, the most highly revised of the five sections, is an account of the expedition sent by the Athenians to

Sicily, ostensibly to win redress for wrongs done by Selinus to the people of Segesta, but in reality to attack Syracuse, the strongest power on the island and one tied by blood and affection to the Peloponnesians. Thucydides, fascinated by the progress of the expedition and the blunders and weaknesses that caused its failure, is at his best in this taut and dramatic account which bears comparison with tragedy or epic. The last section is the rest of his work, Book 8, which is unrevised, long, and covers only two years of the Decelean War, and stops abruptly in mid-sentence. There are no speeches in this section, but again there is a citing of documental evidence (compare the third section): perhaps these are signs of its relatively unfinished state. It is uncertain which elements in the various sections of the work were composed near the time of each event, and which were inserted much later: Thucydides appears to have been a consummate reviser and to have spent much time in a constant process of updating his narrative as his ideas developed or new information came to light. There are several references to the collapse of Athens in 404, but none to events of the fourth century. There is some evidence for the hand of an editor in the version of his work that has come down to us – an editor with great respect for his author, who was perhaps his continuator, XENOPHON (1). However, the work that has come down is of such high quality that the impression of a unified whole is inescapable, fulfilling Thucydides' expressed aim to produce something of permanent value to be cherished for ever (see Book 1. 22, 4).

His style is extremely personal and cannot easily be rendered in another language. The speed of his narration, the poetic and often antiquated language, and the contortions of word order to lend emphasis to a word or phrase are highly characteristic of him. He often casts his thoughts in antithetical modes, but shuns the use of formally balanced phrases and sentences. He is a sparing user of meta-phor and uses assonance only to bring out contrasts. He experimented with ways of expressing abstractions and employed a rich mixture of diction and structures in his often long and loosely organised periodic sentences.

Thucydides' speeches have been much debated. The style in which they are written is complex and sometimes almost impenetrable. It is highly doubtful that he had access to the actual speeches of political or military figures, apart from sketchy notes, even when he was present himself. He himself admits that he wrote simply what he thought his speakers were most likely to have said. There is evidence that some of the speeches were added very late in the process of composition, such as Pericles' *Funeral Speech* (2. 35ff.) and PERICLES' speech justifying the war (2. 60ff.), though others may have been inserted soon after delivery from notes taken at the time. Thucydides relied on a powerful historical imagination in supply-ing speeches that were intended to convey accurately the aspirations, reasonings and fears of the major protagonists in the events he describes.

Thucydides did not hide his prejudices, likes or dislikes, but wrote with great candour. His admiration for Pericles is not sufficiently tempered by criticism of his defective strategy for defeating the Peloponnesians, which fell apart right at the outset of the war. He disapproved unfairly of CLEON and other 'demago-gues', who were in fact the heirs of Pericles. He also fails to explain the purpose of the Athenian decree forbidding Megaran goods from the ports of the Athenian empire. A serious defect is the omission of any account of the relations between Athens and Persia. However, he was a writer with a strong sense of responsibility who set his own standards of 'scientific' accuracy to which he made great efforts to adhere: he did not write the first story he came across and even avoided following his own general

impressions, but constructed his account of events from the most reliable primary evidence he could lay his hands on. In this respect, he was adopted as a model by a few other ancient historians, such as Ephorus and Polybius. He is, indeed, a far superior historian to the entertainers and moralisers who so often passed for historians in later centuries. See *Thucy-dides' History of the Peloponnesian War*, trans. by Rex Warner (1954) Harmonds-worth: Penguin Books; F.E. Adcock (1973) *Thucydides and His History*, Ham-den, Conn.: Archon Books; W.R. Connor (1984) *Thucydides*, Princeton, NJ: Prince-ton University; L. Edmunds (1975) *Chance and Intelligence in Thucydides*, Cambridge, MA: Harvard University Press; S. Hornblower (1988) *Thucydides*, London: Duckworth; L. Hunter, *Thucy-dides*, Toronto: Hakkert; G.E.M. de Ste Croix (1972) *The Origins of the Pelopon-nesian War*, London: Duckworth; H.D. Westlake (1935) *Studies in Thucydides and Greek History*, London: Methuen; and A.G. Woodhead (1970) *Thucydides on the Nature of Power*, Cambridge, MA: Harvard University Press.

Timachidas (C2/1 BC) A Rhodian writer on drama (see ARISTOPHANES (1), EURI-PIDES, MENANDER 1), epic poet and anti-quarian, fragments of whose works survive. He wrote a lost epic entitled *Dinner*, in more than eleven books, and an extant list of dedications in the temple of Athena at Lindus.

Timaeus 1. If a real person, he was contemporary with SOCRATES and a fol-lower of PYTHAGORAS (1), from Locri in southern Italy. He was the main character in the *Timaeus* of PLATO (1). A much later work in Doric Greek, passed off as the work of Timaeus, is a paraphrase of Plato's dialogue.

2. (*c*.356–*c*.260 BC) A historian of Sicily, southern Italy and Libya (the 'Greek West') from Tauromenium (Taormina) in

Sicily, the son of Andromachus who was the second founder of the city and its ruler from 358. He left his native city *c*.315 to escape the rule of AGATHOCLES (1), tyrant of Syracuse, who had taken the city and who ruled most of Sicily for the next twenty-five years. He settled in Athens, where he spent the next fifty years working on his historical writings, and it is uncertain whether he returned to Sicily in old age. While at Athens he studied rhetoric under PHILISCUS (1).

His works included an accurate list, combining the Olympiads with the names of each year's victors, the names of kings and ephors of Sparta, of eponymous archons at Athens and of the priestesses of Hera at Argos, to produce a reliable system of comparative dating. His *History* in thirty-eight books, up to the death of Agathocles in 289, was supplemented by an account of the wars between Pyrrhus and the Romans. Some 164 fragments of his work survive and his work is known indirectly from the great use that DIODORUS (3) made of it as a source. POLYBIUS was highly critical of Timaeus' work, but began his own history from the end of that of Timaeus. Timaeus started with a geographical and ethnographical introduction (1–5), including information about colonisation and the relationships of the various cities. The accession of DIONYSIUS (1) I marks the end of Book 15, and the tyrannies of Dionysius I and DIONYSIUS (2) II take up Books 16–33. The last five books concern the period of Agathocles. His great hero was TIMOLEON.

Timaeus was criticised by Polybius for his failure to verify his material or to do historical research. He spent his working life in the background, did not travel, used second-hand evidence, mostly from earlier writers, and had no military or political experience. On the other hand, he must have learnt much from his greatly experienced father. He was extremely critical of other historians, and was nicknamed 'Slanderer' by his detractors. He had a considerable impact on the writing of history, and was the first Greek historian to concern himself with the Romans. See T.S. Brown (1958) *Timaeus of Tauromenium*, Berkeley, CA: University of California Press; and L. Pearson (1987) *The Greek Historians of the West*, Atlanta, GA: published for the American Philological Association by Scholars Press.

Timanthes (late C5 BC) A painter from Cythnus who worked in Sicyon. He was best known for a painting of the sacrifice of Iphigenia, showing the grief of the bystanders and the figure of Agamemnon with his head covered in his cloak.

Timocharis (early C3 BC) An Alexandrian astronomer who was the first we know of to make systematic observations. His recorded observations of the planet Venus, the Moon, and the declinations of stars were used by the later astronomers, HIPPARCHUS (2) and PTOLEMY (17).

Timocles (C4 BC) A late writer of the Middle Comedy, reminiscent of the Old Comedy for his satirical attacks on politicians, of whose plays we have fragments and know the titles of twenty-seven, four of which appear to have been burlesques based on myth. He won a first prize at a Lenaea festival *c*.325. Fragments reveal attacks on DEMOSTHENES (2) (whom he accuses of never uttering an antithesis), HYPERIDES, and other politicians. He lived until the time of DEMETRIUS (1) of Phaleron and refers to the Supervisors of Women that he instituted.

Timocreon (C6/5 BC) A lyric and elegiac poet from Ialysus in Rhodes of whose work many substantial fragments survive, showing variety of tone and range and a vigorous talent for abuse and parody. He supported the Persians in the war of 480/79, and was probably taken to Susa, the capital of Persia, as a guest of the king. He mocked THEMISTOCLES for failing to be re-elected general and to be given a prize for excellence after the battle of Plataea because he was bitter that Themistocles had not fulfilled an agreement to restore him to Ialysus after the war. He also quarrelled with his fellow poet SIMONIDES, who had attacked his character and style. He was an athlete and won a pentathlon, but had the reputation of a glutton.

Timoleon (*c*.390–*c*.334 BC) A Corinthian aristocrat who liberated Sicily of tyrants. He assassinated his own brother, the Corinthian tyrant Timophanes, *c*.365. Some twenty years later he led a small expedition of seven ships (which he manned with 700 mercenaries) from the mother city to suppress the tyranny of DIONYSIUS (2) II at Syracuse. He landed at Tauromenium (Taormina) in 344 where he received the support of its ruler, Andromachus. He defeated the Syracusan tyrant of Leontini, Hicetas, at Adranum and received strong reinforcements from sympathetic states in Greece, including Corinth and Corcyra. He took Syracuse without bloodshed with Dionysius' co-operation (their common interest being to oppose Hicetas) and, after collaborating with him for a few months, sent Dionysius into exile at Corinth.

The Carthaginians, who wished to expel the Greeks from Sicily, had already received appeals for help against the liberators from Dionysius and Hicetas, and sent a strong naval force under Mago to seize Syracuse, which they blockaded with the co-operation of Hicetas. After Timoleon had established a base at Catana, he received reinforcements from Greece, and gained possession of Messana. Mago, realising that Syracuse was now beyond his grasp, retired to western Sicily where he committed suicide. Timoleon occupied Syracuse where he destroyed the citadel, recalled well-disposed exiles and, with the help of Corinthian experts, revised the constitution to eliminate tyranny and extreme democracy. As Carthage was still preparing for a decisive

blow at the Greeks in Sicily and had gathered a large army in the west of the island, in spring 341 he made a daring incursion into Carthaginian territory with a much smaller force. He enticed the enemy inland and caught them off their guard while they were crossing the River Crimisus, and won a devastating victory. Carthage continued to support the tyrants in Sicily, but in 339 he made a treaty with them, limiting their sphere of influence on the island to the west beyond the River Halycus. Over the following years until his death he put an end to most of the remaining tyrannies in Greek Sicily.

His achievement in reviving Greek Sicily was remarkable, and was lauded by his enthusiastic supporter, the historian TIMAEUS (2). After a decline of fifty years, Sicily was reinvigorated by thousands of new settlers from Greece, whom he invited, and began once again to prosper. Timoleon reserved to himself the office of a general with over-riding power, but resigned *c*.335 possibly because he had become blind. He is difficult to assess because our sources, mainly dependent on Timaeus, are biased in his favour. He was buried in the market-place of Syracuse. See R.J.A. Talbert (1974) *Timoleon and the Revival of Greek Sicily*, Cambridge: CUP; and H.D. Westlake (1952) *Timoleon and His Relations with Tyrants*, Manchester: Manchester University Press.

Timon 1. (C5 BC) A rich Athenian who, believing himself to be the victim of ingratitude from those he had helped, shut himself off from all his fellow citizens, except his friend ALCIBIADES. He is mentioned by ARISTOPHANES (1), is the subject of a dialogue by LUCIAN, and crops up in PLUTARCH's *Life of Antonius*. Shakespeare drew material for his tragedy, *Timon of Athens*, from the latter two.

2. (*c*.320–*c*.230 BC) A philosophical writer and poet from Phlius who, as a young man in poverty, worked as a dancer. He studied Sceptic philosophy under STILPON at Megara and PYRRHON at Elis, and moved to Chalcedon where he made money by teaching. He later moved to Athens. He was a prolific writer, though what remains of his work is very fragmentary. He left much information on the philosophical system of Pyrrhon, who wrote nothing himself. His dialogue *Python* is set on a journey that he and Pyrrhon made to Delphi and is concerned to show how Pyrrhon achieved his famous peace of mind. He wrote a hexameter poem in three books containing lampoons of philosophers who were not of the school of Pyrrhon, entitled *Silloi* ('Squints') (cf. XENOPHANES); he also parodied HOMER. Nothing has survived of his dramatic works.

Timotheus 1. (*c*.450–*c*.360 BC) A dithyrambic poet and musician from Miletus whom EURIPIDES encouraged. Though at first unpopular because of his innovations, he won a victory in a competition for vocal accompaniment to the cithara *c*.420, and composed a dithyrambic nome entitled *The Persians*, in which he changed the rules established by TERPANDER by adding an eleventh string to the instrument. More than 200 lines of this work are preserved on a papyrus, which offers a dramatic account of the battle of Salamis mainly from the point of view of the defeated Persian sailors. The metre of the verse is free and irregular, but the text is written out as prose in the papyrus. Timotheus was regarded by PHERECRATES as the most successful musical innovator of his generation – something Timotheus himself advertises in the final lines of *The Persians*. Euripides wrote the prologue for it, and is said to have been influenced by Timotheus' work.

2. (*c*.415–354 BC) An Athenian general, the son of CONON (1) and a friend of PLATO (1) and JASON of Pherae. A rich man and an aristocrat, he was a pupil of ISOCRATES who later praised his economy in public office. He was prominent in the creation of the Second Athenian Confederacy of 378, using diplomacy rather than military force to extend the league, and won an important naval victory over Sparta off Alyzia in Acarnania in 375, leading to Athenian control of the seas both east and west of the mainland and a short-lived treaty of peace in July 374. He helped the democrats at Corcyra without changing the constitution of the island, and landed some democratic exiles in Zacynthus, which led to the collapse of the peace. In 373 Timotheus won the help of Jason, ruler of Thessaly, but could not pay his men. He was unsuccessfully prosecuted by CALLISTRATUS and IPHICRATES, but had to give up his naval command to Iphicrates, and went to Egypt where he served King ARTAXERXES (2) II as a mercenary.

In 366 he was reinstated at Athens and given a new command with a fleet of thirty ships and a force of 8,000 mercenaries. He was to support Ariobarzanes, a Persian satrap in revolt against Artaxerxes. He limited his campaign to a siege of Samos, however, which lasted ten months, before he moved on to the Hellespont, where he took Sestos, and then in 364 he allied himself with Perdiccas, king of Macedonia, and captured Potidaea, Torone and the Macedonian towns of Pydna and Methone. Athens sent settlers to the places he had conquered, showing her contempt for the treaty known as the Peace of PELOPIDAS. He failed twice in trying to take Amphipolis, burning his fleet at the second attempt in 360. In the Social War of 357–355, Timotheus, with CHARES and Iphicrates, commanded a fleet that was heavily defeated in 356 at Embata off Chios, and Chares, the only commander who had taken part in the battle, denounced him for cowardice. He was fined 100 talents and left Athens. He died in Chalcis. At his best he was an outstandingly able general and his decline coincided with that of his native city.

3. (C4 BC) A sculptor who is known to have worked on two monuments from which sculptural remains survive, the Mausoleum of Halicarnassus where, according to Pliny the Elder, he shared the carving of the friezes with Scopas, LEO-CHARES and Bryaxis, and the temple of Asclepius at Epidaurus, where the building inscription names him as a contractor. It is not possible, however, to distinguish his work from that of others.

Tisias (C5 BC) A Syracusan teacher of rhetoric who studied under CORAX, and is attested by PLATO (1) in the *Phaedrus* as teaching that probability is an important tool in argument and that we can re-evaluate things by the use of speech.

Tissaphernes (late C5 BC) A Persian sa-trap of Sardis in Asia Minor, the son of Hydarnes. He came to power *c*.413 through his suppression of the revolt of the previous satrap, Pissuthnes. From then until 408 he exercised supreme power in western Asia Minor. He exacted tribute from the Greek cities of the coast and, for a time, appeared to support Sparta in the Peloponnesian War, making a treaty with her in 412, while in fact he refrained from giving active help and aimed at the exhaustion of both sides. In 408 he was sent to govern Caria, and CYRUS (2), the son of King DARIUS (2) II, replaced him the next year in his role as supreme commander, with instructions to support Sparta. In 404 Tissaphernes accused Cy-rus of disloyalty to the new king, ARTAX-ERXES (2) II, but Cyrus cleared his name. In 401 Tissaphernes saved the king by travelling rapidly to Susa to warn him of Cyrus' mobilisation, and led the king's cavalry at the battle of Cunaxa, where his bold action saved the day. He negotiated with the 10,000 Greek mercenaries, whom the death of Cyrus had marooned in Mesopotamia, and offered to lead them to safety, but he treacherously killed their leaders at a meeting. He once again took charge of western Asia Minor. His harsh-ness in taxing them caused the Greeks to appeal to Sparta and, in the war that followed, he avoided meeting the enemy, leaving it to PHARNABAZUS to face their attacks until he was defeated by AGESI-LAUS II in 395 near Sardis. This led to his removal from power, and he was sum-moned by Ariaeus to Colossae in Phrygia, where he was arrested in his bath, and executed at Celaenae.

Tolmides (mid-C5 BC) An Athenian gen-eral who in 456 ravaged the Spartan coast and Cythera and burnt the Spartan fleet at Gytheum. He proceeded to the Corin-thian colony of Chalcis and settled the Messenians in his force at Naupactus, becoming a thorn in the flesh of Corin-thian trade and naval power. He also defeated the army of Sicyon, a Peloponne-sian ally. In spring 446 he captured Chaeronea in Boeotia, but was killed in a counter-attack at Coronea by oligarchic exiles from the neighbouring states. A treaty was made by which Athens re-nounced her gains in Boeotia.

Tryphon (C1 BC) A Greek grammarian from Alexandria whose works are lost, though they were used by DIDYMUS, APOLLONIUS (7) Dyscolus and HERODIAN. He wrote on orthography, parts of speech, accentuation and dialects. He also pub-lished material on music, botany and zoology.

Tyrtaeus (mid-C7 BC) An elegiac poet from Sparta who, by his verses, inspired the Spartans in their newly adopted mili-taristic way of life. Five books of his poems were collected in Alexandrian times. According to the *Suda*, they con-tained three distinct genres of poetry: exhortations to fight to the death in Sparta's wars; political poetry, of which one poem, later entitled *Good Govern-ment* (*Eunomia*) or *The Constitution*, is partly known to us; and perhaps war songs, not in elegiac couplets, but in the simpler metres of such poems, though the language of the martial and professional songs we possess does not seem early enough to be his. The *Suda* makes the improbable statement that he served as a general in the Second Messenian War and led the capture of the Messenian stronghold at Ithome.

About 250 lines of his verse have survived, most of it elegiac in metre, epic in style and Ionic in dialect. His *Eunomia* is concerned with the political unrest of the time and the fear that the Spartans were forgetting the loyalty due to their kings and elders. In it he quotes an oracle that regulates with divine sanction the various roles of the kings, elders and the mass of Spartiate men – it shows some similarity to the Great *Rhetra* (see LYCUR-GUS 3). His poetry was obligatory fare for generations of Spartan soldiers on campaign for as long as the city maintained its warlike independence. PLATO (1) and PAU-SANIAS (3) tell a preposterous story that Tyrtaeus was a lame schoolmaster from Athens who was ordered by an oracle to go to Sparta and help the Spartans in their difficulties. This may have arisen from the fact that Tyrtaeus was born at Aphidna in Laconia, whereas there is another Aphidna in Attica. See C. Prato, *Tyrtaeus* and M.L. West (1974) *Studies in Greek Elegy and Iambus*, Berlin; New York: de Gruyter.

X

Xanthippe (C5 BC) The wife of SOCRATES. XENOPHON (1) reports that ANTISTHENES criticised her for her shrewish behaviour to her husband.

Xanthippus 1. (C6/5 BC) An Athenian politician, the father of PERICLES and, being married to Agariste, a niece of CLEISTHENES (2), an ally of the ALCMAEONIDS. In 489 he successfully prosecuted MILTIADES for deceiving the people in his expedition to Paros, but was exiled in 484 as a result of a vote of ostracism. He was recalled in 480 with the other exiles to join the Athenian opposition to the invasion of Xerxes. He was elected general for 479 and commanded the Athenian fleet and marines at the victory of Mycale. Later in the same year he led the Athenian contingent and some Ionian Greeks to Sestos, which they besieged for six months into the winter and captured along with much booty. He killed the Persian commander and his son, and ransomed many prisoners. He was eponymous archon the following year. After his death, the youthful Pericles used some of this wealth to fund the chorus of the *Persians* of AESCHYLUS in 472.

2. (C3 BC) A Spartan mercenary commander who was hired by Carthage to fight in the First Punic War. After reforming the Carthaginian army, he led it to a brilliant victory in 255 against the Roman general Regulus, taking advantage of the elephants and cavalry that were at his disposal. He may have gone from Carthage to Alexandria, for PTOLEMY (3) III used a man of the same name in controlling the lands beyond the Euphrates.

Xanthus 1. (C7 BC) A poet from Greek Italy or Sicily, some of whose works STESICHORUS is said by the fourth century Homeric scholar Megaclides to have adapted, notably a poem about Orestes. He says that the Greek army changed Electra's name from Laodice because she was unmarried (*alektros*).

2. (C5 BC) A historian of Lydia from Sardis, the capital of Lydia, the son of Candaules. He wrote a lost *History of Lydia* in four books from the earliest times probably to the fall of Sardis to the Persians in 546. A contemporary of HERODOTUS, he lived until the time of THUCYDIDES (2). The fragments of his work that survive suggest that while he was willing to include traditional mythical material in his text, he tried to validate it with scientific and rational arguments. Nicolaus of Damascus used his work as a source, but how accurately he did so is contentious (the transmission may not have been direct). EPHORUS says that Herodotus used his work, but we are unable to test the assertion.

Xenagoras (C2 BC) A compiler of chronologies of Greek history and the author of a work on *Islands* of which fragments survive.

Xenarchus (C4 BC) A writer of the Middle Comedy of whose work we have eight titles and some fragments which show a lively and outspoken approach, including a parody of tragic style and a speech by a young man showing his rejection of prostitutes in favour of married women.

Xenocles (late C5 BC) An Athenian tragedian, the son of CARCINUS (1), who was frequently the butt of the humour of ARISTOPHANES (1). He had a reputation for using the latest technology in staging his plays. He beat EURIPIDES in the contest of 415 with his *Oedipus, Lycaon* and *Bacchants* followed by his satyr play, *Athamas*.

Xenocrates (*c*.395–314 BC) A philosopher from Chalcedon, the son of Agathenor. He studied under PLATO (1), accompanying him on one of his visits to Sicily. After Plato's death he spent some time with ARISTOTLE at Assos. He succeeded SPEUSIPPUS as head of the Academy in 339. The Athenians held him in great respect and appointed him as their ambassador to ANTIPATER (1) in 322. Except for some fragments, his copious works have not survived, and our understanding of his contribution to the thought of the Academy is limited. He appears to have foreshadowed some of the ideas of Neoplatonism (see PLOTINUS) in his work on the relationship between the stars and the gods. He wrote on ethics from a strictly practical point of view. SEXTUS EMPIRICUS says that he was the first to divide philosophy into three distinct parts, logic, ethics and physics.

Xenophanes (*c*.570–*c*.478 BC) A poet and philosopher from Colophon in Ionia who left his native city aged 25, almost certainly to escape from Persian rule, and for his remaining sixty-seven years lived the life of a wandering exile in Sicily. Fragments of his works survive, including two long elegiac poems, one on the right manner to arrange a drinking party (*symposium*), the other defending his works and setting them in the context of political life. He rejected the traditional view of virtue as athletic or military ability in favour of intellectual strength of the sort he possessed. These fragments may be part of a satirical poem entitled *Silloi* (Squints) (cf. TIMON 2), said to be in iambic and hexameter verse and also containing philosophical material. He is thus claimed as the first poet to write satire. He is also said to have written an epic poem on the foundation of the Greek colony at Elea in Italy. His work may be compared with that of his near contemporaries TYRTAEUS and SOLON.

He took his tenets of natural philosophy from the school of Miletus in Ionia, though he was himself a keen observer of nature, and held that the universe grew from a mingling of earth and water, and that moisture will gradually dissolve it and it will again be renewed. The heavenly bodies he explained as being derived from clouds that rise from the sea. He was not, however, a dogmatist and claimed no more than probability for his views. He opposed the traditional Greek religious teachings found in HOMER and HESIOD, being critical of the behaviour of the gods in Homer's poems, and instead postulated a supreme cosmic deity whose control of the universe is achieved by effortless thought. He may have accepted the existence of subordinate gods co-operating with the supreme god, but he rejected supernatural explanations of natural phenomena. He is thus at the origin of a theological tradition that included PLATO (1), ARISTOTLE and the Stoics. See J.H. Lesher (1992) *Xenophanes of Colophon*, Toronto: University of Toronto Press; J. Barnes (1982) *The Presocratic Philosophers*, vol. 1, London: Kegan & Paul; and G.S. Kirk, J.E. Raven and

M. Schofield (1982) *The Presocratic Philosophers*, Cambridge: CUP.

Xenophon 1. (*c*.428–354 BC) An Athenian writer and military man who was the son of Gryllus of the deme of Erchia. His family was relatively rich, but the period of his youth was a time of political discord and danger for most Athenians, especially the rich. He was an associate of SOCRATES and was therefore implicated in the circle of oligarchs, who twice caused revolution against the democratic constitution, and was a member of the Athenian cavalry corps for which his wealth qualified him. In 404 he gave limited support to the THIRTY TYRANTS, and opposed the democrats in the civil war that brought the Thirty down, but was saved from punishment by the amnesty of 403/2. However, in 401, finding life uncomfortable in Athens under the restored democracy, he enrolled, at the suggestion of his Boeotian friend Proxenus, but against the advice of Socrates, in the mercenary army of CYRUS (2), which the latter was raising to win the throne of Persia from his elder brother, ARTAXERXES (2) II. Xenophon fought at the battle of Cunaxa in Mesopotamia in which Cyrus was killed. After TISSAPHERNES had murdered the generals commanding the Ten Thousand, the Greek army elected Xenophon their leader and he successfully led them out of danger on a hazardous march during the winter of 401/400, taking a route northwest from the region of Bagdad along the River Tigris to the land of the Carduchi (Kurds) near Lake Van, then over several mountain ranges to the Black Sea at Trapezus (Trebzon), where the army hailed the sea as their guarantee of a safe homecoming. At Byzantium he took service with Seuthes, a Thracian king, who unsuccessfully tried to persuade him to stay there permanently with the offer of a marriage alliance and estate. He might have returned to Athens in 399, but instead, along with the majority of the Ten Thousand, he joined the Spartan army led by THIBRON (1) that was sent to Asia Minor to recover the Greek cities under Persian rule. Later in the year Thibron was replaced by DERCYLIDAS, with whom Xenophon appears to have been on closer terms, and in 396 the Spartan king, AGESILAUS II, with whom Xenophon developed a close friendship, took command. He marched back to Sparta in 394 with the king and on the way fought on the Spartan side at the battle of Coronea in Boeotia when Agesilaus' force defeated a mixed army of Boeotians, Athenians and others. Xenophon was thus precluded from returning to Athens and was formally exiled. However, Agesilaus obtained an estate at Scillus near Olympia for him, and he became the Spartan representative (*proxenos*) at Olympia. He married and had children, including a son named Gryllus. There he lived a peaceful life for twenty years until 371 when Sparta was weakened by the defeat of Leuctra, and Elis took Scillus. He found refuge in Corinth, where he lived until 366 when Athenians were expelled from Corinth. However, his exile had been rescinded *c*.368, and there is evidence that he returned to Athens, but perhaps died on a visit to Corinth. His son was killed serving in the Athenian cavalry at the battle of Mantinea in 362.

Xenophon was a productive writer, and, as far as we know, all he published has survived. His works are very diverse in subject matter and hard to date. Most of his work would have been written while he had the leisure to do so at Scillus and Corinth. He often returned to a work he had written and added further material. He was interested in history, and sought to complete the unfinished account of the Peloponnesian War by THUCYDIDES (2), naming his work *A History of Greece* (*Hellenica*). This work, in seven books, was composed in two parts at widely different times. The first part, from 411 to the surrender of Samos in 404, may have been written *c*.380; the rest, extending to the battle of Mantinea in 362, is likely to have been written in the last years of his life. In many ways it is an unsatisfactory work, lacking the great qualities of Thucydides' history, and, with notable omissions, perhaps reflecting Xenophon's long absences from the central stage of Greek affairs. The work shows ignorance of Athenian affairs and the chief focus of attention is Sparta, though there is evidence of a growing disillusion with that city. The work is more of a memoir than a history. The *March Inland* (*Anabasis*) is a first-hand account of the rebellion of Cyrus and the march of his Greek mercenaries under Xenophon's leadership back to Greek-speaking territory on the coast of the Black Sea, as well as subsequent events. It is readable and often exciting, written in such a way as to distance Xenophon the protagonist in the events from Xenophon the author. There is an underlying panhellenic agenda in the work, suggesting that if the Greeks combined they might overthrow Persian hegemony in Asia Minor. The *Education of Cyrus* (*Cyropaedia*) in eight books is a romanticised and partly fictional life of the Persian king CYRUS (1) the Great, with emphasis on his youth and showing great interest in the question of leadership both in the civil and military spheres. It has been suggested that Xenophon was responding to the ideas of PLATO (1) on the training of statesmen. At a later date he added a further section in which he is much harsher on Persian failings.

He wrote several works around his acquaintance with Socrates. The short *Defence Speech* (*Apology*) is markedly different from that of Plato's: it purports to show that Socrates was deliberately provocative in his speech and was ready to face death for his opinions. Xenophon was not in Athens at the time of the trial and probably obtained information about it from Hermogenes and CALLIAS (2). The *Drinking-Party* (*Symposium*) is an account of the conversations at an imaginary reunion set at the house of Callias at Athens *c*.422, which is capped by a speech by Socrates on the subject of love, perhaps in imitation of Plato's work of the same name. Xenophon may have written it *c*.371 to win the approval of Callias who was working for peace between Athens and Sparta. The *Memoirs of Socrates* (*Memorabilia*), a group of varied conversations in four books, is Xenophon's attempt to present his friend as a man of traditional religion and morality in his own mould. He presents the case for acquitting Socrates of the charges he had to face at his trial, and discusses matters of religion, education, family and friendship. The work is a lively picture of a Socrates who is as much concerned with daily life and its problems as with philosophy. Socrates is also the major speaker in the dialogue, *Estate Management* (*Oeconomicus*), which is in two parts, a conversation with Critobulus about agriculture and the life of the countryman and another with Ischomachus about the management of the household. The latter contains a reported conversation between Ischomachus and his wife, and is interesting for the stereotyped attitude it reveals to the role of women in the family.

Agesilaus, written on the Spartan king's death in 359, is less a biography than an encomium of a man of action whom Xenophon greatly admired, and repeats many passages from the *Hellenica*. It parades the many virtues of its subject, but offers little independent historical material. *Hieron* is an imaginary dialogue between the tyrant of Syracuse, HIERON (1) I, and the poet SIMONIDES, who visited Syracuse in 476, in which the latter asserts that it is pleasant to be a tyrant – a claim that Hieron refutes. *Horsemanship*, a subject in which Xenophon shows real expertise, is a basic manual, perhaps written for his sons, about the buying, maintaining and riding of horses, and is well informed and thorough. It includes exercises and instruction in cavalry fighting. It is the oldest such work extant. *The Cavalry Commander* (*Hipparchicus*) was probably written late in his life and seeks to improve the cavalry of Athens. It discusses in a haphazard way the duties and powers of the commander and the tactics to be employed in the field. *Hunting (Cynegeticus)* is a highly technical work explaining the manner of ancient hunting (the prey being hares or occasionally deer or boar, but not foxes). Hunting was done on foot with nets and hounds. *Ways and Means* is his advice to the Athenian politicians on how to overcome the city's lack of funds, and argues for a new imperialism based on consensus and the admission of resident aliens to increase industry and trade – it may have influenced EUBULUS (1). His *Constitution of Sparta* was written *c*.388 when he was grateful to the Spartans for his home at Scillus and presents an explanation of a system that differed radically from those in other Greek states. He attributed the founding of the constitution to LYCURGUS (2). He added a final, critical chapter at a later date.

As a writer Xenophon, for all his experience of life, had the limitations of his conventional background and education. His style is clear and fluent, even charming, without strongly individual features. His subject matter ranges more widely than any other Greek author whose work has survived. For the *Constitution of Athens* see XENOPHON (2). See J.K. Anderson (1974) *Xenophon*, London: Duckworth; W.E. Higgins (1977) *Xenophon the Athenian*, Albany, NY: State University of New York Press; and Penguin translation of *Anabasis* by R. Warner with an introduction by G.L. Cawkwell.

'Xenophon' 2. (C5? BC) The writer of a short treatise in three chapters on the Athenian constitution, *The Constitution of Athens (Athenaion Politeia)*, which was preserved among the works of XENOPHON (1). The standpoint from which the work was written was that of opposition to the democratic government of the later fifth century, though the author feels compelled to express admiration for the achievements of the democracy, pointing to the close connection between sea power and the emancipation of the poor, who provided the oarsmen. It has been suggested that the work may originally have been part of a 'symposium dialogue', and its use as historical evidence is contested. See W.R. Connor (1992) *New Politicians of Fifth-century Athens*, Indianapolis, IN: Hackett Pub. Co.; J.T. Roberts (1994) *Athens on Trial*, Princeton, NJ: Princeton University Press; and G. de Ste Croix (1972) *The Origins of the Peloponnesian War*, London: Duckworth.

3. of Ephesus (C2 AD) A novelist, the author of *The Ephesian Story of Anthia and Habrocomes*. Nothing is known of his life or place of origin, though the *Suda* assigns him to Ephesus and says that he was a historian who wrote a history of Ephesus. The name may have been adopted as a pen name from the fourth century BC writer. The novel, in five books, is melodramatic and simplistic, and owes a debt to folk-tale. It may be an abridgement of a longer original version in ten books. See Translation by G. Anderson in B.P. Reardon (ed.) (*c*.1989) *Collected Ancient Greek Novels*, Berkeley, CA; London: University of California Press.

Xerxes (reigned 486–465 BC) A king of Persia, the son of DARIUS (1) I and Atossa. His father selected him for the succession and bequeathed to him his project to bring the independent Greek states to heel after the Ionian revolt. At the outset of his reign he had to put down a rebellion in Egypt, and rebellions in Babylon followed. HERODOTUS is our main authority for the great expedition against Greece for which Xerxes made extensive preparations. He won the support of Carthage and several cities of the Greek mainland, assembled a huge army of widely differing contingents, and led the expedition in person. He achieved two outstanding feats of technology: he had a pontoon bridge of boats built across the Hellespont and a ship canal dug through the neck of the Athos peninsula in Chalcidice. He reached Sardis in autumn 481 and launched the expedition in the spring of 480, marching it through territory under his control as far as Thessaly. He won a considerable advantage at Thermopylae, where he annihilated a force of Greeks under the Spartan king LEONIDAS (1) I, and at Artemisium, where he drove off a combined Greek fleet. He then proceeded through central Greece, laid Attica waste and sacked Athens, which had been evacuated of all but a few who insisted on remaining. In late September, influenced by a deceitful message from THEMISTOCLES, Xerxes sent the Persian fleet into the narrow sea between Salamis and the mainland to remove the Greek navy, which was proving an obstacle to further progress, and his navy was soundly defeated.

After this setback Xerxes returned to Asia, and his kinsman and general Mardonius continued the war until the Persians were forced back by the victorious Greeks in 479 at the battles of Plataea and Mycale. Xerxes consequently lost control of many cities on the coast of Asia Minor. The war with the Greeks may have been a pinprick to the mighty empire. It is not mentioned in any Persian document and his power and reputation in Persia were unaffected by it. The remainder of his reign is rather obscure. He built on a magnificent scale at Persepolis and Ecbatana, and commissioned a series of relief carvings at Persepolis showing the extent and structure of his empire, including images of the diverse ethnic types to be found therein. He was murdered by ARTABANUS (2) in a palace intrigue. He was succeeded by his youngest son, ARTAXERXES (1) I. See J.M. Cook (1983) *The Persian Empire*, New York: Schocken Books; and A.R. Burn (1962) *Persia and the Greeks*, London: Arnold.

Z

Zaleucus (C7 BC) The law-maker of Locri in southern Italy. The code of laws which he established *c.*650, and which remained in force at Locri for more than two centuries, was notorious for its harshness, but suited the conservative, aristocratic society of the colony. It is said to have observed the principle of 'an eye for an eye' and to have prescribed specific penalties for each crime. He strove to discourage extravagance, and is said to have restricted the alienability of land. He was the first of a series of Greek lawgivers that included DRACO and SOLON at Athens.

Zeno 1. of Elea (*c.*490–454 BC) A philosopher from Elea (Velia) in southern Italy who was a pupil and close friend of PARMENIDES. In PLATO (1)'s dialogue *Parmenides* he is represented as reading from a book, probably the one in which he supported Parmenides' monism by citing his famous set of four paradoxes, known to us from ARISTOTLE's *Physics*, namely Achilles and the Tortoise, the Arrow, the Dichotomy, and the Stadium, which purported to prove that motion and spatial division are impossible. His method, according to Plato, was to reduce the arguments of his opponents to absurdity by deriving contradictory consequences from them. According to fragments cited by Simplicius, he denied the reality of plurality, i.e. of physical objects, arguing that if there are many things they must be both finite and infinite in number and size. Plato saw such assertions as attacks on common sense in defence of the monist theory of Parmenides with its apparent reckless disregard of generally accepted ideas. Aristotle attempted to refute them, although it is possible that Zeno's underlying purpose was to challenge the basis of our understanding of the world we perceive. Aristotle regarded Zeno as the founder of dialectical argument. He had an influence on education and the development of mathematics and physics. We know his writings only through quotations in other authors' works. See H.D.P. Lee (1936) *Zeno of Elea*, Cambridge: CUP; W.C. Salmon (ed.) (1970) *Zeno's Paradoxes*, Indianapolis, IN: Bobbs-Merrill; J. Barnes (1982) *The Presocratic Philosophers*, London: Routledge & Kegan Paul; and G.S. Kirk, J.E. Raven and M. Schofield (1982) *The Presocratic Philosophers*, Cambridge: CUP.

2. of Citium (335–263 BC) The founder of Stoic philosophy, from Citium in Cyprus, the son of Mnaseas. He came to Athens in 313 where he attended the lectures of POLEMON (1), head of the Academy, from whom he adopted a doctrine of nature, and the Megarian philosopher DIODORUS (1) Cronus. He was, however, converted to the Cynic school of philosophy by CRATES (2), influenced by which he wrote the lost *Republic*

(*Politeia*). Later, he was deeply influenced by the writings of Socrates' disciple ANTI-STHENES. He then developed his own system of philosophy, and *c*.300 he opened a school in a hall in the Painted Colonnade (*Stoa Poikile*) in the Athenian market-place (agora), from which his system took its name, Stoicism. He tried to confine his audience to serious students of philosophy and excluded the general public. He nevertheless won respect among the Athenians and the friendship of ANTIGONUS (2) II Gonatas, king of Macedonia, who invited him to his court. However, he sent two of his students instead.

None of his considerable output of writings survives, though his philosophy became very widespread and its tenets are well known. He divided his teachings into three areas that were independent of each other; logic and theory of knowledge, ethics, and physics including metaphysics. His successors developed the system in various ways until CHRYSIPPUS finally perfected the system, especially in the technical aspects of logic, and laid down a version that came to be regarded as orthodox. Zeno's physics, a materialistic determinist system, included elements taken from HERACLITUS and were strongly influenced by the ideas of ARISTOTLE, and his logic owed a debt to Antisthenes and Diodorus, but was later developed with great originality. He was probably most interested in ethics, which is usually considered the most characteristic element of the Stoic system. He taught that virtue is the only real good, though other advantages may reasonably be sought, such as health and wealth, but the attainment of virtue on its own is enough to produce happiness, which is the ultimate purpose of life. Zeno, unlike some of his successors, admitted that there could be exceptions to moral rules. See A.A. Long (1974) *Hellenistic Philosophy*, London: Duckworth; J. Rist (1969) *Stoic Philosophy*, Cambridge: CUP; and B. Inwood (1985) *Ethics and Human Action in Early Stoicism*, Oxford: Oxford University Press.

3. of Tarsus (C3/2 BC) He succeeded CHRYSIPPUS as head of the Stoa in 204, but wrote little.

4. of Rhodes (C2 BC) A historian and politician of Rhodes whose work was used as a source by POLYBIUS, despite the excessive patriotism he found in it.

5. of Sidon (born *c*.150 BC) An Epicurean philosopher who was head of the school before PHAEDRUS (3). He upset Cicero who heard him lecture during his stay in Athens in 79 and 78 by his quarrelsome behaviour and insulting references to SOCRATES and CHRYSIPPUS. However, PHILODEMUS was his friend and pupil and is known to have admired him greatly. His *Free Speech* offers a selection of Zeno's teachings and his *Signs* reports his lectures and disputes with opponents.

6. (C2 BC) A medical writer and physician who followed the tradition of HEROPHILUS.

Zenodorus (*c*.200 BC) A mathematician whose work, *Figures with Equal Perimeters*, was preserved in the works of PAPPUS and the mathematician Theon of Alexandria.

Zenodotus (born *c*.325 BC) A scholar from Ephesus who studied under PHILETAS of Cos and *c*.284 was called to Alexandria by PTOLEMY (2) II to tutor his children and organise the newly established library as its first head. He began the collection and classification of books for the library, especially the Greek epic and lyric poets, and compiled an alphabetical glossary of HOMER and the first critical editions of Homer, HESIOD, PINDAR and ANACREON. He is believed to be the first to divide Homer's poems into books, and to have invented the obelus to mark lines he considered spurious. See

R. Pfeiffer (1968) *History of Classical Scholarship*, Oxford: Clarendon Press.

Zeuxis (C5/4 BC) A painter from Heraclea in southern Italy who moved to Athens, perhaps around 430, and is mentioned as a young man in the *Protagoras* of PLATO (1). ARISTOPHANES (1) in *Acharnians* refers to his painting of Eros crowned with roses. He painted a picture of Alcmena for Acragas and decorated the palace of ARCHELAUS (2), king of Macedonia. Quintilian said that he discovered how to add highlights to the technique of shading. He painted a bunch of grapes that is said to have deceived the birds, and said that he should have added the figure of a boy to scare the birds off. LUCIAN praised his painting of Centaurs. He also painted an idealised Helen of Troy from more than one model, a Menelaus weeping, and a Penelope who seemed the soul of chastity. Pliny the Elder said that he 'entered the door which APOLLODORUS (1) opened and stole his art'. He was, however, arrogant and gave away paintings that he said were beyond price. See C.M. Robertson (1975) *A History of Greek Art*, Cambridge: CUP.

Zoilus (C4 BC) A Cynic philosopher and teacher of rhetoric from Amphipolis who was a bitter critic of ISOCRATES, PLATO (1) and HOMER, to such an extent that he came to be known as 'Homer's scourge'. Some fragments of his writings survive: works of criticism of the aforementioned writers, a speech in praise of the people of Tenedos, a work on *Figures of Speech*, a *History of Greece*, from mythical times to the death of PHILIP (1) II, and a work on Amphipolis.

Zonas (C1 BC) An orator and epigrammatic poet from Sardis, nine of whose poems are in the *Greek Anthology*. His subject matter was rustic and about everyday life, and his work has much charm.

Glossary

Academy   The school founded by Plato (1) in a public gymnasium just outside the walls of Athens (to the north-west of the Dipylon Gate) in an area sacred to the hero Academus. The school continued the philosophical work of Plato and survived until the first century BC. The heads of the Academy were: Plato (1); Speusippus; Xenocrates; Polemon (1); Crates (3); Arcesilaus, founder of the 'New Academy' who introduced a sceptical doctrine into Platonism; Carneades, a profound critic of previous doctrines; Clitomachus; Metrodorus of Stratonicaea; and Philon (4) of Larissa, the last head of the school, whose pupil, Antiochus (15) of Ascalon, returned to the doctrines of the fourth century.

Acroterion   Acroteria were decorative figures of stone or terracotta placed at the three corners of the pediments of Greek buildings.

Agora   The market-place at Athens, as well as in other Greek cities. It was the focal point of commercial activity and contained some buildings of political importance, such as the Council Chamber and the Tholos, a circular building where the councillors were fed.

Amphiction   Literally 'one who dwells nearby'. The term refers to the states of Central Greece that were neighbours of the small state of Delphi, which contained the Delphic Oracle. The states formed a league to protect the sanctuary and ensure the autonomy of Delphi.

Anthology   A collection of epigrams (see p. 153). The *Greek Anthology* is a huge collection, based on earlier collections, of such poems. The first anthology was the *Garland* of Meleager of Gadara. It originally contained the works of forty-six poets, including Sappho, which was subsequently enlarged and re-edited – the final version being the *Palatine Anthology*. Straton (3) published a collection of his own pederastic poems, and Agathias collected the poems of his contemporaries in a '*Cycle*'. A second *Garland*, arranged alphabetically and thematically, was made by Philippus of Thessalonica in the first century AD. The edition made by Cephalas in the tenth century was rediscovered in 1606 by Salmasius in Heidelberg, whence its name 'Palatine'. Another shortened and inferior version of the Anthology, which circulated as the *Greek Anthology* until the *Palatine Anthology* came into its own in the nineteenth century, was made in the fourteenth century by Planudes. For further information, see A. Cameron, *The Greek Anthology*, Oxford; Clarendon Press: 1993.

Archon An Athenian magistrate, elected annually. There were nine archons in office at any one time in Athens. The term is normally used to refer to the eponymous archon – so called because the year was known by his name. The other two important achonships were the 'king' archon (his functions were priestly) and the polemarch, which was a military post. The archons, who were originally elected, were chosen by lot after 487 BC.

Bucolic Rustic, of the countryside, especially concerned with cowherds and shepherds. It was usually applied to the bucolic poets, Theocritus, Moschus and Bion (2).

Chiliarch A Macedonian military title meaning 'Commander of a Thousand' which was given to the second-in-command in the army of Alexander (3) the Great. The post was held by a succession of generals during his invasion of Asia and had the connotation of the Vizier in oriental courts.

Council At Athens the Council prepared business for the Assembly. In the classical period the members of the Council, five hundred in number, were selected by lot in equal proportion from the ten tribes established by Cleisthenes (2). See Solon.

Cynic The name given to the philosophy established by Diogenes (2) of Sinope, so called because of his allegedly shameless behaviour. We have virtually no writings of the Cynics, and the nature of their beliefs is controversial and difficult to retrieve. More a way of life than a school of philosophy, Cynicism seems to have consisted of living according to nature in a primitive way.

Deme A political division of territory in Attica corresponding roughly with the English parish in its administrative sense. As Athenian citizens had no surnames, they were identified by their personal name, their patronymic, and the name of their deme. See entry on Cleisthenes (2).

Diatribe (see Teles) A short speech expressing arguments of an ethical nature.

Dithyramb A choric song associated with the cult of Dionysus. At Athens there were established competitions in the composition and choral singing of dithyrambs at the great city festivals.

Doric, Dorian A branch of the Greek peoples of antiquity distinguished by their dialect. They were a proud and warlike people who despised the easy living of the Ionic and Aeolic peoples of the eastern mainland and the coastlands of Asia Minor. The principal Dorian states were Sparta, Argos, Corinth and the Cretan cities. Dorians also colonised the southern islands of the Aegean and the southern coastline of Asia Minor. There were also Doric colonies overseas such as Cyrene, Taras and Syracuse. The term was also bestowed on a style of architecture notable for its simplicity and robustness.

Eclectic An approach to philosophy wherein aspects of different systems are combined at the discretion of the thinker.

Elegiac A poetic metre that makes use of alternate hexameter and pentameter lines. Originally a sung lament, it came to be used for epitaphs and other inscriptions, as well as for poems of a variety of subject matter, including the erotic.

Eleusinian Mysteries   At Eleusis on the coast of Attica the cult of the goddess Demeter and her daughter Persephone, wife of Hades and hence goddess of the Underworld, was practised with secret rites. It was necessary to undergo strict and secret initiation ceremonies to participate in the ritual, which was believed by adherents to enable them to gain knowledge of the Underworld and special privileges after death.

Ephebe   A juvenile male. At Athens in the late fourth century the ephebes were young men of 18–20 who were enrolled into a programme of military and civic training which lasted for two years prior to their being admitted to full citizenship.

Ephor   At Sparta the ephors ('overseers') were a board of five magistrates, elected annually, of which the senior ephor was eponymous and gave his name to the year in which he held office. They were very powerful in civil and foreign affairs, though they had no active military function. They made most of the decisions affecting state policy, negotiated with ambassadors from abroad, presided over the Council (*Gerusia*) and Assembly (*Apella*) and acted as judges.

Epigram   A short poem on a single theme. The literary epigram developed from the writing of inscriptions, including epitaphs. It was greatly extended in Hellenistic times when a variety of metres was used.

Epyllion   A modern term for a miniature epic poem that, instead of relating the whole of a story, concentrates on a single episode or scene from a myth and often dwells on the emotions of the characters concerned.

Harmost   A Spartan governor of a city under Spartan rule.

Helot   The Spartans enslaved the original population of Laconia which they settled and ruled from some time around 1000 BC. These serfs ('helots') were owned by the state and were allowed to live on the land and enjoy communal rights of a limited kind, but were subject to strictly applied rules about their employment and domicile and, because of their large numbers, were a source of fear to the Spartan state. The Messenians were reduced to the same status until they were freed by the Thebans after the battle of Leuctra. Other Greek states which relied on agriculture had such serfs, but we hear little of them.

Herm   A short, rectangular pillar that was surmounted by a male head and bore an erect phallus on its front. It represented the god Hermes, and was sacred to him. The pillars were to be found outside Athenian houses. There was a widespread mutilation of these statues on the eve of the Sicilian expedition in 415 BC.

Hoplite   An infantryman who was equipped with heavy body-armour, including a metal helmet, breastplate, and greaves on the lower legs, and was armed with a sword and a spear.

Ionic, Ionian   A branch of the Greek peoples in antiquity who were distinguished by their dialect which was spoken on the islands of the central Aegean and in Ionia, in the middle of the coastland of Asia Minor. The Attic dialect, spoken at Athens, was closely related to it and the Athenians considered themselves to be Ionians. The Ionians were the source of literature, philosophy and historical writing in Greece, though the Dorians looked down on them for their 'softness'. A style of architecture characterised by its grace and elaborate decoration is known as Ionic.

Lyceum A gymnasium and garden with covered walks in a sanctuary outside the walls of Athens that was dedicated to Apollo. Socrates frequented the place and held discussions there with his youthful friends, and Aristotle made it his headquarters while he lived as a metic (q.v.) at Athens, renting a building nearby. Theophrastus, an Athenian citizen, bought property at the Lyceum which was passed down. The members of Aristotle's school were called Peripatetic (q.v.).

Magus Among the Persians the magi were learned men, experts especially in religion and religious rituals and practice. They were regarded with great awe: we derive the word 'magic' from magus.

Medism Among the Greeks, the voluntary alliance of Greek cities or individuals with Persia.

Metic A resident foreigner in Athens and other cities whose rights were severely restricted, for instance they could not participate in political life, had to be represented in court by a patron, and were heavily taxed. They were very numerous at Athens in the fifth and fourth centuries.

Mysteries Religious rituals that were secret and esoteric because they were believed to grant special powers or favours to participants. In Greece there were mystery cults centred on Orpheus, Dionysus, and Persephone (see Eleusinian Mysteries).

Neoplatonism A modern term for the renewal in the third century AD by Plotinus of Platonic philosophy, which was very influential from the third to the sixth centuries.

Obol The smallest denomination of coinage at Athens and in many other Greek cities. The value of an obol is almost impossible to estimate in terms of modern money: it represented less than a workman's daily pay, but was enough for a family to subsist on. The word originally meant 'a spit', since metal spits were used in primitive times as a means of exchange. See Talent.

Pediment The triangular-shaped gable-end of the roof of a Greek temple that stood above the columns at the narrow end of the building and which was often decorated with statuary (see Acroterion).

Peripatetic The name given to the school of philosophy that was founded by Aristotle at the Lyceum (q.v), so called from its covered walks (*peripatoi*) in which the members of the school could stroll as they talked.

Polemarch Under the Athenian constitution, the polemarch ('war-leader') was the third in rank of the three great officers of state known as the archons. His function up to the time of the Battle of Marathon (490 BC) was to act as the commander-in-chief, but after 487, when the archons ceased to be elected but were appointed by lot, the office fell into obscurity and gave place to the board of ten elected generals.

Rhetorician A specialist in the art and theory of rhetoric or public speaking and, in particular, a teacher of rhetorical skills, which were considered supremely important in ancient cities, especially democratic ones.

Satrap The Greek rendering of a Persian term for the governor of a province of the Persian empire, usually a kinsman of the king, though its use was frequently imprecise. The term continued in use in the empire of Alexander (3) III the Great and the kingdoms of some of his successors.

Sceptic Literally: 'enquirer'. A school of philosophy characterised by a refusal to accept any doctrine, as well as by a suspension of judgement on everything. Its founder was Pyrrhon of Elis whose views were propagated by Timon (2) of Phlius. Another version of scepticism, based on the methods of Socrates as reported by Plato (1), was developed in the Academy in Hellenistic times by Arcesilaus and his successors.

Scoliast An ancient annotator of a text, who wrote his notes in the margins of the text. We know the identity of a couple of them, but most *scholia* are anonymous.

Sophist A teacher of professional skills, such as public speaking and the art of disputation. The term developed in meaning and, by the second half of the fifth century BC, a sophist was typically a travelling professor who taught such skills for a fee. Sophists varied greatly in their methods and the subjects they taught, and the main purpose of their teaching was to impart proficiency in making a good living. The word took on a derogatory meaning, especially under the influence of philosophers, who decried the selling of knowledge.

Stoa, Stoic The *Stoa Poikile* ('painted colonnade') on the edge of the market-place (agora) of Athens was an open colonnade that housed a collection of pictures that were painted on panels. It was the meeting place in the early third century of the followers of the philosopher Zeno (2) of Citium, who took their name, Stoics, from it.

Suda The name of a lexicon or encyclopaedia, less correctly known as *Suidas*, which dates from the tenth century AD. It was compiled from other encyclopaedic works and suffers from its remoteness from its original sources. It is also subject to interpolation. It is, however, an invaluable authority for much that would have otherwise been totally lost.

Sufet A magistrate or high state official at Carthage, analogous to the Athenian archon or the Roman consul.

Tagos The title given to the leading general of the Thessalian confederation of states in the fifth and fourth centuries BC.

Talent A measure of weight applied to precious metals. At Athens the Euboic system was in use in which the talent was 25.86 kilograms. At Athens a talent would refer to that weight of silver.

Tyrant The term is used in Greek history to refer to an absolute ruler whose power was based on force. It carries no implication as to the manner in which power was exercised, and many Greek tyrants were regarded as fair and just, as well as efficient rulers.

Appendix I

Chronological table of Greek and Hellenistic times BC

We acknowledge with thanks the kind permission granted us to use the chronological tables and lists of rulers that are based on tables and lists in *Chronology of the Ancient World* by Elias J. Bickerman, revised edition published in 1980 by Thames & Hudson.

776	The traditional date of the first Olympic Games.
754	The first ephors at Sparta.
c. 750	Cumae colonised by Chalcis. Greek trading post in Syria at Al Mina.
c. 733	Syracuse founded by Corinth.
c. 720	Sparta conquers Messenia.
c. 706	Sparta founds Taras (Tarentum) in Italy.
683	First recorded archon of Athens.
c. 669	Battle of Hysiae: Argives defeat Sparta.
c. 660	Byzantium colonised by Megara.
c. 650	Cypselus tyrant of Corinth.
648	Archilochus active.
c. 640	Tyranny of Theagenes at Megara begins. Coinage invented in Asia Minor.
c. 632	Cylon tries to seize power at Athens.
c. 630	Therans settle Cyrene in Libya. Messenians revolt from Sparta.
c. 625	Periander becomes tyrant of Corinth.
c. 621	The laws of Draco passed at Athens.
c. 610	Tyranny of Thrasybulus at Miletus. Foundation of Naucratis, a Greek trading post on the Nile.
c. 600	Cleisthenes becomes tyrant of Sicyon. Phocaeans found Massilia. Corinthians found Potidaea and Apollonia. Sappho, Alcaeus and Pittacus at Mytilene.
594	Solon's archonship at Athens.
582	Damasias' archonship at Athens. The first Pythian Games.
c. 582	The end of the tyranny at Corinth.
c. 575	Coinage is introduced to Athens.
c. 571–555	Tyranny of Phalaris at Acragas (Agrigento).

566	The first Panathenaea at Athens.
c. 561	The first tyranny of Pisistratus at Athens.
c. 560	Croesus becomes king of Lydia. Sparta makes war on Tegea.
c. 556	Pisistratus in exile.
546	Cyrus conquers Lydia and the Greek cities of Asia. Pisistratus tyrant at Athens.
c. 530	Pythagoras at Croton.
528/527	Death of Pisistratus. Hippias succeeds him.
525	Cambyses conquers Egypt.
c. 523	Death of Polycrates of Samos.
522	Accession of Darius I.
514	Assassination of Hipparchus by Harmodius and Aristogiton.
c. 512	Darius invades Scythia and conquers Thrace.
511	Spartan expedition against Athens.
510	Cleomenes leads second Spartan expedition, and drives out Hippias from Athens.
508/507	Cleisthenes' constitutional reforms at Athens.
499	Outbreak of the Ionian Revolt against Persia.
498	Pindar's first extant poem (*Pyth*. 10).
c. 498	The Ionians take and burn Sardis, capital of the Lydian satrapy.
c. 494	Persian victory over Ionians at the battle of Lade. Fall of Miletus. Sparta defeats Argos at Sepeia.
493	Archonship of Themistocles at Athens.
c. 492	Trial of Miltiades at Athens.
490	Darius' expedition against Eretria and Athens. Destruction of Eretria. Battle of Marathon.
489	Miltiades' expedition against Paros, his trial, fine and death.
487	First election of archons by lot at Athens. War between Athens and Aegina.
486	Death of Darius I. Megacles ostracised.
484	Xanthippus ostracised. Aeschylus' first victory.
c. 483	Discovery of a new deposit of silver at Laurium used to expand the Athenian navy.
482	Aristides ostracised. Hieron wins the horse-race at Delphi.
481	Xerxes in Sardis. Greek congress at the Isthmus.
480	Xerxes invades Greece. Battles of Artemisium, Thermopylae and Salamis. Carthage invades Sicily and is defeated at Himera. Anaxagoras in Athens.
479	Greeks defeat Mardonius the Persian general at Plataea, and win the sea battle of Mycale. The Ionians defect from Persia. Athenians take Sestos. Athens reoccupied.
478	Walls of Athens rebuilt. Pausanias' expedition to Cyprus and Byzantium. Hieron becomes tyrant of Syracuse. The Confederacy of Delos founded.

476/475	Cimon's campaign in Thrace.
474	Hieron defeats the Etruscans at sea off Cumae.
472	Aeschylus' *Persians*.
c. 471	Themistocles ostracised.
468	Sophocles' first victory.
c. 468	Revolt and fall of Naxos.
c. 467	Athenian forces defeat the Persians at the Eurymedon.
c. 465	Revolt of Thasos.
464	Earthquake at Sparta. Revolt of helots and Messenians. Siege of Mount Ithome.
c. 463	Thasos surrenders.
462	Spartan appeal to Athens for help. Cimon dismissed by Spartans from Ithome. Constitutional reform of Ephialtes (2) at Athens. Egypt revolts against Persia.
461	Cimon ostracised. Murder of Ephialtes.
460	Athenian expedition to Egypt. Capture of Memphis.
c. 459/458	War between Athens and Sparta. Megara changes sides and joins Athenian alliance. Athens defeated at Halieis. Battle of Cecryphaleia.
457	Long Walls built linking Athens with Piraeus. Athens defeated by Sparta at Tanagra, but wins battle of Oenophyta and conquers Boeotia. Accessibility to the archonship widened to include 'teamsters' (*zeugitae*). Athens conquers Aegina.
456	Death of Aeschylus.
455	Euripides' first production.
454	Athenians defeated in Egypt. Treasury of Delian Confederacy moved to Athens. Pericles' expedition to the Corinthian Gulf.
451	Truce of five years between Sparta and Athens. Thirty-year peace between Sparta and Argos. Citizenship law at Athens.
c. 450	Death of Themistocles.
450/449	Cimon in Cyprus. Death of Cimon.
449	Athens and Persia make peace.
448	Sparta sends expedition to Delphi.
447	Boeotians defeat Athenians at Coronea: Athens loses Boeotia. Parthenon begun.
446	Euboea revolts from Athens and is reduced. Athens loses Megara.
446/445	Athens makes thirty-year peace with the Peloponnesians. Pindar's last datable poem (*Pyth*. 8).
444/443	Panhellenic colony of Thurii founded in Italy. Thucydides (1) ostracised.
442/441	Euripides wins his first victory.
441/440	Samos revolts.
439	Surrender of Samos.
438	Phidias' statue of Athena Parthenos consecrated.

437	Amphipolis founded. Pericles' expedition to the Black Sea.
435	Corinth and Corcyra dispute over Epidamnus: defeat of Corinth at sea off Leucimme.
433/432	Athens allies with Corcyra: battle of Sybota. Athens renews treaties with Rhegium and Leontini.
432	Potidaea revolts and is besieged by Athens. Athenians pass a decree to outlaw Megaran goods from imperial ports.
431	Beginning of the Peloponnesian (Archidamian) War. Thebans attack Plataea. Spartans invade and ravage Attica nearly every year of the war.
430	Plague breaks out at Athens. Pericles' attack on Epidaurus fails: he is tried and fined. Potidaea falls. Phormio is sent to Naupactus.
429	Thebans besiege Plataea. Death of Pericles. Phormio's brilliant victories in north-west,
428	Revolt of Mytilene. Death of Anaxagoras. Birth of Plato.
427	Fall of Mytilene and Plataea. Corcyra's civil war. Gorgias of Leontini leads an embassy to Athens: Athenian expedition to Sicily under Laches.
426	Demosthenes (1) campaigns in north-west Greece, wins battle of Olpe.
425	Athenian fortification of Pylos and occupation of Sphacteria. Cleon active. He secures the rejection of peace terms, and raises the pay of juries. Tribute of dependencies is reassessed.
424	Athenians defeated at Delium. Brasidas takes Torone and Amphipolis. Thucydides (2) exiled.
423	Truce for one year between Athens and Sparta. Aristophanes' *Clouds*.
422	Cleon recaptures Torone. Cleon and Brasidas killed at Amphipolis. Aristophanes' *Wasps*.
421	Peace of Nicias. Athens and Sparta make alliance for fifty years. Spartan alliance with Boeotia.
420	Athens, Argos, Mantinea and Elis form an alliance.
418	Sparta defeats Argos at Mantinea: fifty-year alliance between them established.
417	Hyperbolus ostracised. Argos and Athens renew their alliance.
416	Athens forces Melos to submit.
415	Athenian expedition to Sicily. Mutilation of the herms. Alcibiades, recalled to face trial, escapes to Sparta. Euripides' *Troades*.
414	The Athenian expeditionary force invests Syracuse.
413	Beginning of Decelean War. Sparta invades Attica, and seizes and fortifies Decelea. Athenian disaster in Sicily.
412	Revolt of Athens' allies. Agreement between Persia and Sparta. Athens besieges Chios.

411	Revolution of the Four Hundred oligarchs at Athens. The government of the Five Thousand installed. The fleet and army at Samos stand by the democracy. Athenian victories at Cynossema and Abydos. Aristophanes' *Lysistrata* and *Thesmophoriazusae* performed.
410	Restoration of democracy at Athens. Athenian victory at Cyzicus. Athenians reject peace terms.
409	Carthaginians invade Sicily and destroy Selinus and Himera.
408	Athens regains Byzantium.
407	Alcibiades returns to Athens, and is restored to power as a general.
406	Athenians defeated at Notium. Alcibiades withdraws. Athenian naval victory of Arginusae. Trial of the generals. Peace offer rejected by Athens. Death of Euripides and Sophocles. Second Carthaginian invasion of Sicily.
405	Spartan admiral Lysander destroys the Athenian fleet at Aegospotami. Rise of Dionysius, tyrant of Syracuse, who makes peace with Carthage. Peloponnesians blockade Athens.
404	Surrender of Athens. Rule of the Thirty Tyrants. Destruction of the Long Walls. Death of Alcibiades. Democratic exiles seize Phyle and the Piraeus.
403	Fall of the Thirty. Restoration of Athenian democracy. Fall of Lysander. Cyrus' rebellion and battle of Cunaxa. Retreat of the Ten Thousand Greek mercenaries led by Xenophon.
400	Sparta makes war on Tissaphernes. Campaign of Thibron in Asia Minor.
399	Trial and death of Socrates. Andocides' speech *On the Mysteries*.
398	Agesilaus II becomes Eurypontid king of Sparta on the death of Agis I. Lysias' speech *Against Nicomachus*. Dercylidas' campaign in Asia Minor.
397	War between Carthage and Syracuse. Dionysius captures Motya.
396	Agesilaus campaigns in Asia Minor. Siege of Syracuse.
395	Corinthian War begins. Lysander killed after suffering defeat at Haliartus.
394	Recall of Agesilaus to Greece. Battle of Cnidus at which the Spartan navy is defeated by Conon and the Persians. Work begins on rebuilding the Long Walls at Athens.
393	Winter: embassy of Antalcidas to Tiribazus.
392	Death of Conon. Carthage and Syracuse make peace. Peace congress at Sparta (winter): Athens rejects the terms.
c. 391	Evagoras of Cyprus revolts from Persian rule with Athenian support.

390	Iphicrates defeats a Spartan force at Lechaeum. Spartan fleet captures Samos. Dionysius besieges Rhegium.
389	Dionysius takes Caulonia. Plato visits Italy and Sicily.
387	Antalcidas cuts off an Athenian fleet in the Hellespont. Fall of Rhegium to Dionysius.
386	The King's Peace (or the Peace of Antalcidas).
385	Sparta reduces Mantinea. Artaxerxes II tries to recover Egypt.
383	Dionysius' second war with Carthage.
381	Evagoras makes peace with Persia. Spartans besiege Phlius.
380	Isocrates' *Panegyricus*.
379	Phlius and Olynthus surrender to Sparta. Pelopidas liberates Thebes from pro-Spartans.
378	Thebes and Athens allied. Agesilaus invades Boeotia. Second Athenian confederacy founded.
376	Athenians defeat Spartan fleet off Naxos.
375	Timotheus defeats Peloponnesian fleet off Acarnania. Chabrias campaigns in north Aegean.
374	Peace between Athens and Sparta. Athens allied with Jason of Pherae. Death of Evagoras.
373	Jason of Pherae in alliance with Amyntas of Macedonia.
371	Peace of Callias between Athens and Sparta. Battle of Leuctra: Thebans defeat Sparta.
370	Assassination of Jason. Arcadian Confederacy formed in alliance with Thebes. Epaminondas' first campaign in the Peloponnese. Messene founded.
c. 369	Megalopolis founded.
c. 368	Third war between Dionysius and Carthage.
367	The Tearless Battle. Dionysius II succeeds his father. Plato visits Syracuse. Peace made between Syracuse and Carthage. Aristotle joins the Academy.
366	Epaminondas' third campaign in the Peloponnese. Failure of congress at Thebes. Dion exiled from Syracuse. Satraps' revolt.
365	Dionysius II helps Sparta against Thebes.
364	Thebes destroys Orchomenus. Battle of Cynoscephalae between Thebes and Pherae: Pelopidas killed. Epaminondas takes Byzantium from Athens.
362	Battle of Mantinea: Theban victory, but Epaminondas killed. Common Peace agreed, except by Sparta.
361	Alliance of Athens and Thessalian Confederacy against Alexander of Pherae. Agesilaus II in Egypt. Plato and Speusippus in Syracuse.
360	Persian rule re-established in Asia Minor. Death of Agesilaus.
359	Philip II becomes regent, then king, of Macedonia. Assassination of Alexander of Pherae.

358	Philip makes a formal treaty with Athens.
357	Athens recovers Euboea and the Chersonese. Philip takes Amphipolis. The Social War between Athens and her allies. Eubulus in power at Athens.
356	Philip founds Philippi, takes Pydna and Potidaea, and defeats the Illyrians and Paeonians. Birth of Alexander the Great. Athenians defeated at battle of Embata. Trial of Timotheus and Iphicrates. Dion besieges Ortygia.
355	Athens recognises independence of Chios, Cos, Byzantium and Rhodes. Delphi seized by Phocis: Amphictionic Council declares Sacred War on Philomelus of Phocis.
354	Battle of Neon. Death of Philomelus. Murder of Dion.
353	Onomarchus of Phocis takes Orchomenus. Athens allies with Cersobleptes of Thrace. Philip takes Methone, but suffers setbacks in Thessaly from Onomarchus. Death of Mausolus.
352	Chares retakes Sestos. Onomarchus killed. Philip takes Pherae and Pagasae, and advances to Thermopylae. Death of Phayllus.
351	Charidemus in the Hellespont. Demosthenes' *First Philippic*.
350	Artaxerxes aids Thebes.
349	Olynthus allied with Athens. Demosthenes' *Olynthiacs*.
348	Phocion in Euboea. Philip takes Olynthus.
347	Dionysius II recovers Syracuse. Death of Plato.
346	Peace of Philocrates between Athens and Philip. Demosthenes' *On the Peace*. Philip subdues Phocis, joins the Amphictions and presides at the Pythian Games.
344	Timoleon sails to Sicily and frees Syracuse from Dionysius II. Demosthenes' *Second Philippic*. Isocrates' *Letter to Philip*. Philip campaigns in Illyria.
343	Aeschines tried and acquitted. Aristotle becomes tutor of Alexander.
342	Persia reconquers Egypt. Philip campaigns in Thrace. Timoleon's unsuccessful campaign against Hicetas.
341	Demosthenes at Byzantium. Euboean Confederacy formed. Carthaginian campaign against Syracuse. Timoleon defeats them at Crimisus. Demosthenes' *Third Philippic*.
340	Philip besieges Perinthus and Byzantium. Athens declares war on him. Demosthenes' *Fourth Philippic*.
339	Philip raises siege of Byzantium. Philip's expedition to Thrace. Amphissan War begins. Philip seizes Elatea. Timoleon makes peace with Carthage.
338	Philip destroys Amphissa. Philip wins battle of Chaeronea and forms a confederacy of Greek states at Corinth. Lycurgus becomes treasurer of Athens. Death of Isocrates.
337	The Greek Confederacy under Philip declares war on Persia.

336	Philip assassinated. Alexander succeeds him and is elected general of the Greeks.
335	Alexander campaigns in Illyria and Thrace. He destroys Thebes. Aristotle settles in Athens.
334	Alexander invades the Persian empire, and wins the battle of Granicus. Democracies set up in Ionia. Sieges of Miletus and Halicarnassus. Alexander conquers Lycia and Pamphylia, and winters at Gordium.
333	Alexander conquers Cilicia and wins battle of Issus. Birth of Zeno.
332	Alexander takes Tyre by siege and conquers Egypt. Agis III of Sparta opposes Macedonia.
331	Alexandria founded. Battle of Gaugamela. Alexander occupies Babylon, Susa and Persepolis. Agis defeated at Megalopolis and killed.
330	Death of Darius III. Alexander kills Philotas and Parmenion. Aeschines' *Against Ctesiphon*. Demosthenes' *On the Crown*.
329	Alexander enters Bactria.
328	Conquest of Bactria and Sogdiana. Alexander marries Roxane. Alexander murders Cleitus. Pages' conspiracy: Callisthenes executed.
327	Alexander invades India.
326	Alexander defeats Porus. His army mutinies on the Beas. Nearchus' voyage down the Jhelum. Defeat of the Malli.
325	Alexander returns from India by way of Gedrosia.
324	Alexander and Nearchus re-unite and reach Susa. Restoration of Greek exiles. Macedonians mutiny at Opis. Death of Hephaestion. Harpalus at Athens. Demosthenes tried and exiled.
323	Alexander dies at Babylon. Perdiccas ('regent') takes power in Asia. The Lamian War in Greece. Athens and Aetolia in alliance. Demosthenes returns to Athens.
322	Perdiccas conquers Cappadocia for Eumenes. Ophellas conquers Cyrene for Ptolemy. Battle of Crannon ends Lamian War. Death of Aristotle, Demosthenes and Hyperides.
321	Eumenes defeats Craterus. Perdiccas murdered in Egypt: Antipater becomes 'regent'. Antigonus appointed commander against Eumenes, and defeats him. Menander's first play produced.
319	Death of Antipater. Polyperchon 'regent'. Ptolemy seizes Syria. Cassander executes Demades.
318	Eumenes captures Babylon. Polyperchon declares freedom of Greece. Phocion executed.
317	Cassander makes Demetrius of Phaleron ruler of Athens. Agathocles takes power in Syracuse.

316	Antigonus defeats and kills Eumenes. Cassander takes Pydna and kills Olympias and Alexander IV. Cassander, now ruler of Macedonia, rebuilds Thebes.
315	War of the satraps against Antigonus, who occupies Syria.
314	Antigonus proclaims freedom of the Greek cities.
312	Ptolemy's victory over Antigonus at Gaza. Seleucus regains Babylon. Carthaginians invade Sicily. Zeno in Athens.
310	Agathocles invades Africa.
308	Magas seizes Cyrene.
307	Demetrius the Besieger frees Athens.
306	Demetrius' naval victory over Ptolemy near Cyprus. Antigonus and Demetrius declare themselves kings. Syracuse and Carthage make peace. Epicurus opens his school at Athens.
305	Demetrius' unsuccessful siege of Rhodes. The satraps take royal titles.
304	Agathocles declares himself king. Demetrius re-forms the Confederacy of Corinth.
301	Battle of Ipsus: Antigonus defeated and killed by Seleucus and Lysimachus. Zeno founds the Stoa.
299	Seleucus and Demetrius in alliance.
297	Death of Cassander and his son. Lachares seizes power at Athens.
296	Coalition against Demetrius.
295	Ptolemy takes Cyprus, Seleucus Cilicia and Lysimachus Ionia. Lachares flees from Athens.
294	Demetrius takes Athens and becomes king of Macedonia.
292	Antiochus I becomes joint king of Seleucus' eastern territories.
291	Demetrius takes Thebes, and fights Aetolia and Pyrrhus of Epirus.
289	Death of Agathocles. Demetrius prepares to invade Asia.
287	Fall of Demetrius. Pyrrhus and Lysimachus partition Macedonia. Demetrius crosses to Asia.
286	Ptolemy seizes the Phoenician coast and islands.
285	Demetrius surrenders to Seleucus. Lysimachus king of all Macedonia.
283	Death of Demetrius: his son, Antigonus Gonatas, claims Macedonia. Ptolemy II succeeds his father.
281	Seleucus defeats and kills Lysimachus at Corupedium. Antigonus takes Athens. Murder of Seleucus by Ptolemy Ceraunus, who seizes the throne of Macedonia.
280	Achaean Confederacy founded. Antiochus I and Ptolemy II at war. Pyrrhus invades Italy.
279	Galatians invade Macedonia and Greece. Ceraunus killed. Galatians repelled at Delphi. Antigonus and Antiochus make a treaty.

278	Pyrrhus crosses into Sicily. The Galatians invade Asia Minor. Ptolemy II takes Miletus.
277	Anarchy in Macedonia. Antigonus defeats the Galatians at Lysimachia.
276	Antigonus Gonatas becomes king of Macedonia, and marries Antiochus' sister, Phila.
275	Pyrrhus defeated in Italy near Beneventum. Hieron II takes command of Syracusan forces. Antiochus defeats the Galatians.
274	Pyrrhus overruns Macedonia. First Syrian War. Antiochus defeats Ptolemy II in Syria.
272	Death of Pyrrhus at Argos. Hieron II seizes power at Syracuse.
271	End of the First Syrian War.
270	Fall of Rhegium. Death of Epicurus. Death of Arsinoe II. Theocritus' appeal to Ptolemy II.
c. 269	Hieron II defeats the Mamertines.
267	Coalition of Athens, Sparta and Egypt against Antigonus II Gonatas: the Chremonidian War.
265	Battle of Corinth. Death of Areus II, king of Sparta.
264	The First Punic War between Rome and Carthage begins.
263	Hieron of Syracuse becomes an ally of Rome. Eumenes I succeeds Philetaerus at Pergamon. Death of Zeno the Stoic, who is succeeded by Cleanthes.
262	Antigonus takes Athens. The Romans capture Acragas (Agrigento).
261	Accession of Antiochus II. Ptolemy II and Antigonus II make peace.
260	Second Syrian War begins: Ptolemy II fights Antigonus II and Antiochus II.
259	Antiochus II recovers Ephesus.
c. 255	Death of Magas of Cyrene. Demetrius the Fair becomes king of Cyrene. Peace between Ptolemy II and Antigonus II.
253	End of Second Syrian War.
252	Antiochus II marries Berenice II.
251	Aratus frees Sicyon.
250	Insurrection of the Parthians in Bactria.
248	Hieron renews his alliance with Rome.
246	Accession of Seleucus II and Ptolemy III, who begin the Third Syrian War.
245	Aratus' first generalship of the Achaean League.
244	Agis IV becomes king of Sparta.
243	Agis takes Corinth.
241	End of the First Punic War: Rome occupies Sicily. End of the Third Syrian War. Accession of Attalus I of Pergamon. Death of Agis.

239	Accession of Demetrius II of Macedonia. Seleucus II defeated at Ancyra and loses his possessions in Asia Minor.
238	Antiochus the Hawk defeated by Attalus I, who is proclaimed king of Pergamon. War of the Brothers begins.
237	Cleomenes III becomes king of Sparta.
231	Seleucus' expedition against the Parthians. Chrysippus head of the Stoa.
229	Accession of Antigonus III Doson of Macedonia. Aetolian and Achaean Confederacies expand. Athens recovers independence from Macedonia. Antiochus the Hawk defeated near Pergamon.
228	Demetrius is made ruler of Pharos. Sparta at war with the Achaean League.
227	Revolution at Sparta organised by Cleomenes. Antigonus III's expedition to Caria.
225	Argos and Corinth ally with Cleomenes. Aratus negotiates with Antigonus.
224	Dictatorship of Aratus of Sicyon who allies with Antigonus. Antigonus takes Argos and forms the Hellenic Confederacy.
223	Antigonus and Aratus destroy Mantinea. Cleomenes razes Megalopolis. Accession of Antiochus III.
222	Battle of Sellasia: Antigonus defeats Cleomenes and takes Sparta.
221	Accessions of Philip V of Macedonia and Ptolemy IV. The Social War begins in Greece. Revolt of Achaeus.
219	Demetrius of Pharos flees to Philip V. Fourth Syrian War between Ptolemy IV and Antiochus III begins. Rhodes declares war on Byzantium. Cleomenes dies in Egypt.
218	Philip V sacks Thermum.
217	Peace of Naupactus between Philip and Aetolia. Battle of Raphia: Ptolemy defeats Antiochus and makes peace.
216	Antiochus III and Attalus I attack Achaeus. Egyptian natives unsettled.
215	Philip operates in Peloponnese and allies with Hannibal. Achaeus blockaded in Sardis.
214	Philip attacks Messene.
213	Marcellus besieges Syracuse. Death of Aratus. Achaeus captured and killed. Philip captures Lissus in Illyria.
212	Antiochus III subdues the revolt of governor Molon of Media and recovers Armenia.
211	Syracuse falls to the Romans: Archimedes killed.
210	Antiochus campaigns in Media.
209	Antiochus campaigns in Parthyene. Arsaces III makes peace.
208	Philip wins victories over the Romans by land. Antiochus attacks Bactria.

207	Philopoemen defeats Sparta at Mantinea. Philip raids Aetolia.
206	Nabis becomes king of Sparta. Philip makes a separate peace with the Aetolians. Antiochus makes peace with Euthydemus of Bactria.
205	Rome makes Peace of Phoenice with Philip.
204	Accession of Ptolemy V.
203/202	Alliance of Philip and Antiochus against Ptolemy.
202	Antiochus invades southern Syria. Rhodes declares war on Philip. Rome rejects Aetolian appeal for help.
201	Attalus and Rhodes seek Roman help against Philip. War between Sparta and the Achaean Confederacy. Antiochus takes Gaza. Philip in Asia Minor. Battles of Chios and Lade. Philip blockaded at Bargylia.
200	After an ultimatum, the Romans declare war on Philip: the Second Macedonian War. Philip takes Abydos. Antiochus wins a victory at Panion and receives Roman embassy.
199	The Aetolians ally with Rome.
198	The Achaeans ally with Rome. Antiochus reduces southern Syria, including Palestine.
197	Romans defeat Philip at battle of Cynoscephalae. Peace made between Rome and Macedonia. Antiochus campaigns in Asia Minor and occupies Ephesus. Accession of Eumenes II of Pergamon.
196	Flamininus proclaims 'freedom of the Greeks' at the Isthmian Games. Romans settle Greek affairs. Antiochus advances into Thrace and meets Roman embassy at Lysimachia. Ptolemy V crowned at Memphis.
195	Nabis, defeated, submits to Rome. Antiochus makes peace with Egypt. Hannibal joins Antiochus at Ephesus. Death of Eratosthenes, who is succeeded by Aristophanes of Byzantium as head of the Library at Alexandria.
194	Roman troops evacuated from Greece. Antiochus in Thrace. Antiochus reopens negotiations with Rome.
193	Aetolians offer support to Antiochus. Nabis violates his treaty with Rome and attacks the Achaeans. Breach between Antiochus and Rome.
192	Nabis is defeated and dies. Antiochus declares war on Rome. Sparta forced into the Achaean League. Antiochus, at the instigation of the Aetolians, crosses to Greece.
191	Romans defeat Antiochus at Thermopylae. Antiochus flees to Ephesus. His fleet is defeated at Corcyrus.
190	Antiochus' fleets defeated at Side and Myonesus. Scipios land in Asia and defeat Antiochus at Magnesia.
189	Ambracia falls, and the Aetolians submit to Rome. Sparta secedes from the Achaean League.

188	Philopoemen and the Achaeans force Sparta to submit. Rome makes treaty of Apamea with Antiochus: affairs of Asia settled.
187	Accession of Seleucus IV.
186	Roman embassy to Philip. Prusias I of Bithynia attacks Pergamon.
184	Philip's son Demetrius is sent to Rome as a hostage.
183	Messenians revolt against the Achaeans: death of Philopoemen. Two-year war between Pontus and Pergamon.
181	Philip campaigns in the Balkans. Accession of Ptolemy VI.
180	Philip executes his son Demetrius. Aristarchus of Samothrace succeeds Aristophanes of Byzantium as head of the Library.
179	Perseus' accession as king of Macedonia.
175	Accession of Antiochus IV.
172	Roman mission to Greece, instigated by Eumenes' complaints against Perseus.
171	Third Macedonian War breaks out between Rome and Perseus.
170	Perseus wins a victory in Thessaly. Joint rule of Ptolemy VI, Cleopatra II and Ptolemy VII in Egypt.
169	Romans under Philippus attack Macedonia. Genthius of Illyria supports Perseus. War between Syria and Egypt.
168	Battle of Pydna: Aemilius Paullus defeats Perseus and ends Macedonian independence.
167	Romans plunder and enslave Epirus. They divide Macedonia into four and Illyria into three protectorates. Hostages of the Achaean league, including Polybius, deported to Italy. Perseus' library brought to Rome.
166	Maccabee risings in Palestine.
165	Antiochus campaigns in the east against the Parthians.
164	Roman mission to weaken Syria. Seleucid regent Lysias defeats the Hasmoneans in Palestine. Demetrius I Soter reaches Syria.
161	Expulsion of Greek philosophers and teachers from Rome.
160	Defeat and death of Judas Maccabaeus. Accession of Attalus II of Pergamon.
159	Prusias of Bithynia compelled to make peace with Pergamon.
157	Judaea becomes an independent state headed by the high priest.
156	Dispute between Oropus and Athens began.
155	Embassy of the philosophers (Carneades, Critolaus and Diogenes) to Rome.
152	Alexander Balas, rival of Demetrius, recognises Jonathan as high priest.
151	Return of Achaean prisoners from Italy to Greece.

150	Death of Demetrius Soter. Alexander Balas becomes king under the protection of Egypt.
149	Rising in Macedonia under Andriscus (Fourth Macedonian War). Sparta secedes from the Achaean League: Diaeus urges war.
146	War between Rome and the Achaean League: defeat of Diaeus by Mummius. Corinth sacked. Macedonia is turned into a Roman province.
145	Egypt intervenes in Syria and wins battle of Oenoparus. Death of Ptolemy and Balas. War between Antiochus VI, supported by Diodotus Tryphon, and Demetrius II.
142	Diodotus Tryphon claims the throne of Syria. The Jews gain independence.
141	Demetrius II makes concessions to the Jews under the high priest Simon. Mithridates I of Parthia annexes Babylonia.
139	Parthians defeat and capture Demetrius II. Antiochus VII of Side gains the throne. Accession of Attalus III of Pergamon.
138	Suicide of Diodotus Tryphon.
134	Death of high priest Simon. John Hyrcanus becomes high priest. Judaea once more under Seleucid power.
133	Attalus III wills his kingdom to Rome.
132	Revolt of Aristonicus in Pergamon after the death of Attalus.
131	Civil War in Egypt. Ptolemy VIII Physcon driven from Alexandria. Cleopatra II rules alone.
130	Antiochus of Side killed in a war with the Parthians.
129	Senate refuses to confirm gift of Phrygia to Mithridates V of Pontus. Ptolemy is restored to his throne, but civil war continues. Death of Carneades. Restoration of Demetrius II.
121	Assassination of Mithridates V of Pontus at Sinope.
118	Reconciliation of Ptolemy with his first wife, Cleopatra II: amnesty and restoration of order in Egypt.
116	Death of Ptolemy. Egypt loses Cyrene.
115	Mithridates VI seizes power in Pontus and inaugurates his policy of expansion.
109	Death of Panaetius.
103	Alexander Jannaeus becomes priest-king of Judaea.
101	Mithridates and Nicomedes II of Bithynia partition Paphlagonia and occupy Galatia.

Appendix II

List of rulers

Kings of Macedonia

Amyntas I	second half of C6 BC
Alexander I	*c*.495–*c*.450/440 BC
Perdiccas II	*c*.450/440–413 BC
Archelaus	413–399 BC
Orestes	399–396 BC
Aeropus	396–393 BC
Amyntas II	393–392 BC
Pausanias	393–392 BC
Amyntas III	393–370 BC
Alexander II	370–369/368 BC
Ptolemaeus	369/368–365 BC
Perdiccas III	365–359 BC
Philip II	359–336 BC
Alexander III the Great	336–323 BC
Philip III Arrhidaeus	323–316 BC (in name only)
Alexander IV	323–312 BC (in name only)
Antigonus I the One-eyed	312–301 BC (in name only)
Cassander	301–297 BC (official); from 319 BC de facto
Pyrrhus of Epirus	295–294 BC
Demetrius I the Besieger	294–287 BC
Ptolemy Ceraunus	281–279 BC
Antigonus Gonatas	276–239 BC
Demetrius II	239–229 BC
Antigonus Doson	227–221 BC
Philip V	221–179 BC
Perseus	179–168 BC

Kings of Sparta

Agiads

Anaxandridas	*c*.560–520 BC
Cleomenes I	*c*.520–490 BC
Leonidas I	490–480 BC

Pleistarchus	480–459 BC
Pleistoanax	459–409 BC
Pausanias	409–395 BC
Agesipolis I	395–380 BC
Cleombrotus I	380–371 BC
Agesipolis II	371–370 BC
Cleomenes II	370–309 BC
Areus I	309–265 BC
Acrotatus	265–262 BC
Areus II	262–254 BC
Leonidas II	254–235 BC
Cleomenes III	235–222 BC
Agesipolois III	219–215 BC

Eurypontids

Ariston	c.550–515 BC
Demaratus	c.515–491 BC
Leotychidas II	491–469 BC
Archidamus II	469–427 BC
Agis II	427–400 BC
Agesilaus II	399–360 BC
Archidamus III	360–338 BC
Agis III	338–331 BC
Eudamidas I	c.331–c.305 BC
Archidamus IV	c.305–275 BC
Eudamidas II	c.275–244 BC
Agis IV	c.244–241 BC
Eudamidas III	241–c.228 BC
Archidamus V	228–227 BC
Eucleidas	227–221 BC
Lycurgus	219–c.212 BC
Pelops	c.212–c.200 BC (under guardianship of Machanidas and, from c.206 BC on, of Nabis)
Nabis	before 195–192 BC

Kings of Persia

Cyrus (in Iran)	559–530 BC
Cyrus (in Babylonia)	539–530 BC
Cambyses	530–522 BC
Bardya (Smerdis, Gaumata)	522– killed by Darius on 29 September
(Nebuchadnezzar III)	522 BC
Darius I	522–521 BC
(Nebuchadnezzar IV)	521 BC
Darius I	521–486 BC
Xerxes	486–465 BC
Artaxerxes I	464–423 BC
Darius II	423–404 BC
Artaxerxes II	404–359 BC
Artaxerxes III	359–338 BC

| Arses | 338–336 BC |
| Darius III | 336–331 BC |

Both Nebuchadnezzars were Babylonian pretenders not recognised in Persia.

The Ptolemies

Ptolemy I Soter*	305–282 BC
Ptolemy II Philadelphus	282–29 Jan. 246 BC
Ptolemy III Euergetes I	246–222 BC
Ptolemy IV Philopator	222–205 BC
Ptolemy V Epiphanes	204–180 BC
Ptolemy VI Philometor	180–145 BC
Joint rule of Ptolemy VI, Ptolemy VIII and Cleopatra II	5 Oct. 170 BC (expulsion of Philometor 164–163 BC)
Ptolemy VII Neos Philopator	145–144 BC (associated on the throne)
Ptolemy VIII Euergetes (Physcon)	145–116 BC
Cleopatra III and Ptolemy IX Soter II (Lathyros)	116–107 BC
Cleopatra III and Ptolemy X Alexander	107–101 BC
Ptolemy X Alexander I and Cleopatra Berenice	101–88 BC
Ptolemy IX Soter II	88–81 BC
Cleopatra Berenice and Ptolemy XI Alexander II	80 BC
Ptolemy XII (Auletes)	80–58 BC
Berenice IV	58–55 BC
Ptolemy XII (Auletes)	55–51 BC
Cleopatra VII and Ptolemy XIII	51–47 BC
Cleopatra VII and Ptolemy XIV	47–44 BC
Cleopatra VII and Ptolemy XV (Caesarion)	44–30 Aug. 31 BC

*Ptolemy I counted his regnal years from the death of Alexander the Great

The Seleucids and their successors

Seleucus I Nicator	311–281 BC
Antiochus I Soter	281–2 June 261 BC
Antiochus II Theos	261–(summer) 246 BC
Seleucus II Callinicus	246–225 BC
Seleucus III Soter	225–223 BC
Antiochus III (the Great)	223–187 BC (early summer)
Seleucus IV Philopator	187–175 BC (3 Sept.)
Antiochus IV Epiphanes	175–174 BC (?)
Antiochus V Eupator	163–162 BC

Demetrius I Soter	162–150 BC
Alexander Balas	150–145 BC
Demetrius II Nicator	145–140 BC
Antiochus VI Epiphanes	145–142 BC
Antiochus VII (Sidetes)	138–129 BC
Demetrius II Nicator (restored)	129–125 BC
Cleopatra Thea	126 BC
Seleucus V	125 BC
Antiochus VIII (Grypus)	125–96 BC
Antiochus IX (Cyzicenus)	122–95 BC
Seleucus VI Epiphanes Nicanor	96–95 BC
Demetrius II Philopator	95–88 BC
Antiochus X Eusebes	95–83 BC
Antiochus XI Philadelphus	94 BC
Philip I Philadelphus	94–83 BC
Antiochus XII Dionysus	87–84 BC
(simultaneously Tigranes of	
Armenia)	(83–69) BC
Antiochus XIII (Asiaticus)	69–64 BC
Philip II	65–64 BC

The Attalids of Pergamum

Philetaerus	283–263 BC
Eumenes I	263–241 BC
Attalus I Soter	241–197 BC
Eumenes II Soter	197–160 BC
Attalus II	160–139 BC
Attalus III	139–133 BC
(Eumenes III = Aristonicus)	(133–129) BC

Appendix III
Maps

We acknowledge with thanks the kind permission granted us to use maps from *Atlas of Classical History*, edited by Richard J.A. Talbert, first published in 1985 by Croom Helm Ltd.

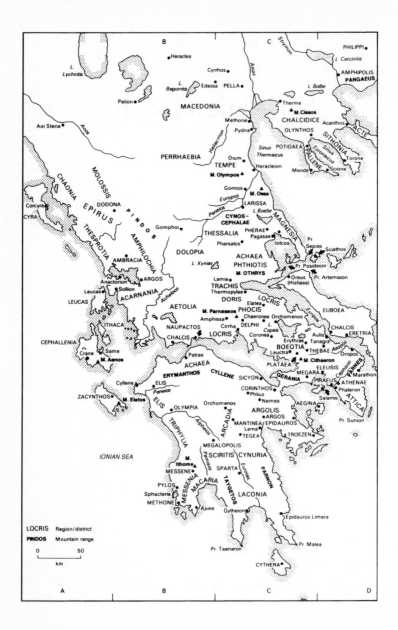

Map 1 The Greek Lands

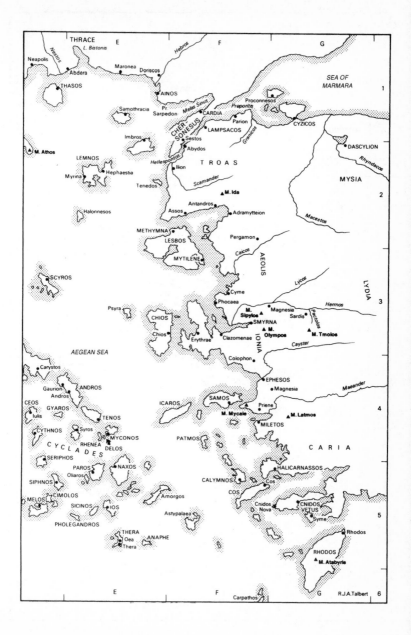

THRACE E   F   G

Neapolis   Nestos   SEA OF
      Abdera   Maronea Doriscos   MARMARA
  THASOS   L. Bistonis
                                                                        1
            Samothracia   AINOS   Proconnesos
                     Pr   Melas Sinus   Propontis
                     Sarpedon CARDIA   Parion
                 Imbros   CHER- LAMPSACOS   Granicos CYZICOS
                        SONESUS Sestos   DASCYLION
  M. Athos   Abydos   Rhyndacos
      LEMNOS   Hellespontos Ilion   TROAS   MYSIA
   Myrina   Hephaestia   Scamander   Macestos
           Tenedos   M. Ida   2
                         Antandros
       Halonnesos   Adramytteion
                        Assos
                     METHYMNA   Pergamon
                        LESBOS   Caicos
                                                            AEOLIS   LYDIA
                        MYTILENE   Lycos
                                        Cyme   Magnesia   Hermos
                                        Phocaea   M.   Sardis Pactolus   3
   SCYROS   Psyra   Sipylos
                     CHIOS   Erythrae SMYRNA M.
                                      Clazomenae Olympos M. Tmolos
              Chios   IONIA
   AEGEAN SEA   Colophon   Cayster

      Carystos   EPHESOS   Maeander
    Gaurion ANDROS   Magnesia
      Andros   SAMOS   Priene   4
  CEOS   GYAROS   ICAROS   M. Mycale   M. Latmos
   Iulis   MILETOS
  CYTHNOS   Syros TENOS
         RHENEA MYCONOS   PATMOS   CARIA
  SERIPHOS   DELOS
       PAROS   NAXOS   HALICARNASSOS
  SIPHNOS Oliaros   CALYMNOS Cos
  MELOS CIMOLOS   COS   CNIDOS
      SICINOS IOS   Amorgos   Cnidos VETUS   5
  PHOLEGANDROS   Astypalaea   Nova   Syme
                                              Rhodos
            THERA ANAPHE
            Oea   RHODOS
            Thera   M. Atabyris

      E   F   Carpathos G   R.J.A.Talbert 6

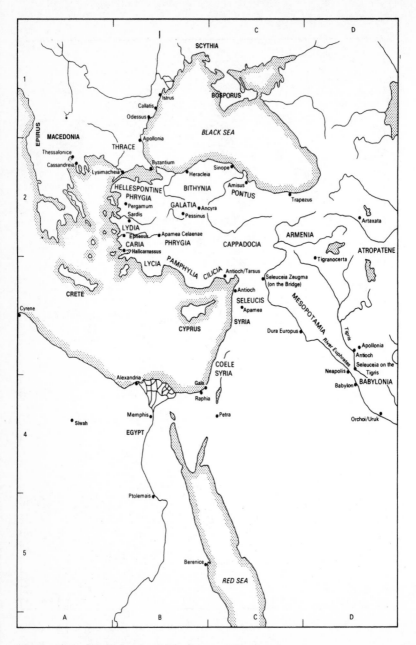

Map 2 Alexander's Conquests and the Successor Kingdoms

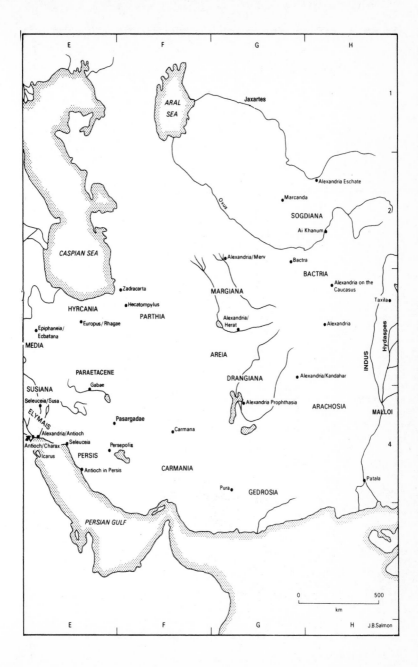

E   F   G   H

ARAL SEA

Jaxartes

1

• Alexandria Eschate

• Marcanda

Oxus

SOGDIANA

2

Ai Khanum •

CASPIAN SEA

• Alexandria/Merv   • Bactra

BACTRIA

• Zadracarta   MARGIANA   • Alexandria on the Caucasus

HYRCANIA   • Hecatompylus   Taxila •

PARTHIA   Alexandria/

• Europus/Rhagae   Herat   • Alexandria

• Epiphaneia/
Ecbatana

MEDIA   AREIA

PARAETACENE   DRANGIANA   • Alexandria/Kandahar

SUSIANA   • Gabae   ARACHOSIA

Seleuceia/Susa   • Alexandria Prophthasia   MALLOI

ELYMAIS   • Pasargadae

• Alexandria/Antioch   • Carmana

Antioch/Charax   Seleuceia   4

Icarus   • Persepolis

PERSIS   CARMANIA

• Antioch in Persis

              Pura •   GEDROSIA   • Patala

PERSIAN GULF

                           0   500

                              km

E   F   G   H   J.B.Salmon

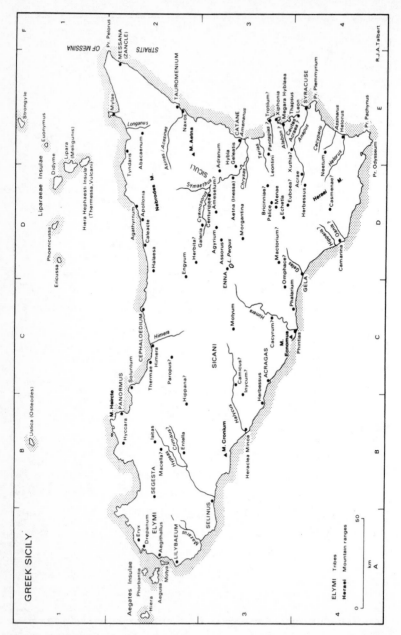

Map 3 Greek Sicily